LIBRARY OF SECOND TEMPLE STUDIES

64

formerly the Journal for the Study of the Pseudepigrapha Supplement Series

T&T CLARK • LIBRARY OF BIBLICAL STUDIES

THE ARAMAIC AND EGYPTIAN LEGAL TRADITIONS AT ELEPHANTINE

An Egyptological Approach

ALEJANDRO F. BOTTA

t&t clark

Published by T&T Clark International
A Continuum imprint
The Tower Building, 11 York Road, London SE1 7NX
180 Maiden Lane, Suite 704, New York, NY 10038

www.continuumbooks.com

British Library Cataloguing-in-Publication Data
A catalogue record for this book is available from the British Library

ISBN: 978-0-5671-2036-6 (paperback)

Typeset by Data Standards Ltd, Frome, Somerset, UK
Printed and bound in Great Britain by the MPG Books Group

Contents

List of Tables

Acknowledgments

'Everything is vague to a degree you do not realize till you have tried to make it precise.'

Bertrand Russell, *The Philosophy of Logical Atomism*, p. 5.

This work is a modified, revised, and updated version of my 2001 Hebrew University of Jerusalem's dissertation written under the supervision of Prof Bezalel Porten.

First and foremost I want to express my deep appreciation and gratitude to Prof Porten who guided the dissertation from its inception and always gave so generously of his time and knowledge ever since I first stepped into his office in Mount Scopus. His unparalleled knowledge of the Elephantine material has helped me to avoid several pitfalls over the years. Thanks also to my dissertation committee: Professors Sarah Groll, Israel Eph'al, and Shemuel Ahituv, who provided several valuable suggestions for pursuing this research. Special thanks to Janet Johnson and Shemuel Ahituv for offering critical comments to the dissertation and for their continuous support.

During my doctoral studies I received financial support from the Deutscher Akademischer Austausch Dienst, the World Council of Churches, the Memorial Foundation for Jewish Culture, the Israel Foreign Ministry, and the Institute for Jewish Studies of the Hebrew University of Jerusalem.

This book could not have been written without the mentorship and encouragement of many teachers, colleagues, and friends over the years. Prof Steven Voth first awakened my interest in the field of Ancient Near Eastern studies at the Instituto Bíblico Buenos Aires. Steve had just finished his PhD at HUC-JIR in Cincinnati and in his classes he showed a passion for both, the Hebrew Bible and the Ancient Near East, especially Assyriology. My 'wrong turn' into Egyptology happened during my studies at the University of Buenos Aires under the supervision of Prof Alicia Daneri de Rodrigo. Alicia suggested the Jewish Colony of Elephantine as my research topic when I joined the Programa de Estudios de Egiptología (PREDE-CONICET) in Buenos Aires, which led to my first contact with Prof Porten and the later completion of my Ph.D. under his supervision.

Thanks to my teachers during my first year in Jerusalem at the Rothberg International School (Hebrew University), Prof Ann Killebrew (now at Pennsylvania State University, Prof Avi Hurvitz, and Prof Michael Stone. I had the privilege of studying with Prof Sarah Groll during 1995–1997 and worked on her project, 'A Grammar of El-Amarna Texts.' For the following ten years Sarah welcomed me at her home to discuss Egyptological matters, share stories, or just to talk about life. She is deeply missed. May her memory be for a blessing.

Prof Karl-Theodor Zauzich and Prof Gernot Wilhelm welcomed me at Die Julius-Maximilians-Universität Würzburg (kein anderer Wein will mir schmecken!) where I had the opportunity to study, thanks to a DAAD fellowship. My gratitude to my teachers in Würzburg, Prof Dr Karl-Theodor Zauzich, Prof Dr Horst Beinlich, Prof Dr Hans-Werner Fischer-Elfert (now in Leipzig); PD Dr Friedhelm Hoffmann (now in Heidelberg), Prof Dr Gernot Wilhelm, Prof Dr Josef Bauer, PD Dr Thomas Richter (now in Frankfurt), PD Dr Jeanette Fincke (now in Heidelberg). Special thanks to Prof Dr Günther Vittmann for many courtesies.

After the topic of my dissertation was suggested by Bezalel Porten, I was very fortunate to be able to discuss it with Prof Yochanan Muffs during one of his visits to Jerusalem in 1997, before submitting the dissertation proposal. Prof Muffs wrote what has become an almost canonical text in the study of Ancient Near Eastern legal formulae. His kind words of encouragement and reaffirmation of the need of an Egyptological approach to the Aramaic legal formula gave me additional motivation to pursue this path of research.

Prof Janet Johnson welcomed me at the Oriental Institute in Chicago and extended me the privilege of working at the Demotic Dictionary Project. Her scholarship and kindness are a model to imitate. Thanks also to Prof Martha Roth (now Dean of the Faculty of the Humanities) for so graciously providing me access to the card files of the Chicago Assyrian Dictionary (now completed). Prof Robert Ritner and Prof Dennis Pardee (Oriental Institute) have offered comments and encouragement at various stages of my research.

Special thanks to Prof Reuven Yaron who has always welcomed me at his home to discuss issues related to the Aramaic papyri, the transmission of legal formula in the Ancient Near East, 'Das syrisch-römische Rechtsbuch' (לא עליך מלאכה לגמור ולא אתה בן חורים ליבטל), or suggest ideas for further research. It has been an honor.

The Aramaic Studies Section of the Society of Biblical Literature has provided a forum where I was able to present some of the material discussed here and benefit from comments, criticism, and suggestions from the best scholars in the discipline. Especial thanks to Stephen Kaufman, Meir Lubetzki, Douglas Gropp, Andrew Gross, and Annalisa Azzoni for their reactions to my presentations and encouragement.

My friends in Israel have always provided love, support, and a home away from home, thanks to Itamar Singer and Graciela Gestoso-Singer, Irene Shiron-Grumach, Deborah Swenney, Arlette David, Dan'el Kahn, Edgar Nof, Netta Bar-Yosef, Adrian Kramer, Yitzhak Mendelson, Iris Avivi, Sergio Eial Bluer and Graciela Bluer, Aldina Quintana, Graciela Cerra (now in Bielefeld) Amir Fink and Yossi. My life in Jerusalem was greatly affected by a terrorist attack in 1995. I want to especially express my deep gratitude to Mr Israel Roi, then leading the Rothberg International School, Mr Jacob Reimer, Head of Security of the Hebrew University, Sergio Bluer, Dr Yitzhak Mendelson, to Bituach Leumi, Magen David Adom, and to the doctors of Hadassah Hospital Ein Kerem, Intensive Care Unit, General Surgery Unit, Plastic Surgery, and Ear, Nose and Throat Surgery for their care and support during those hard times and subsequent recovery. Rivka Cohen, Hannah Naeh, Joan Davenney, Noam Eisenman, and Yona Peter Malina, were not as fortunate. May their memory be for a blessing.

My gratitude to my friends at the École biblique et archéologique française in Jerusalem, specially Cecilia and Alejandro Duarte (now in Ceuta), Kevin McCaffrey (now who knows where), José Loza Vera (now back in Mexico), Krzysztof Modras, Emmile Puech, Marcel Sigrist, Krzysztof Sonek, François Langlamet (your kindness will be remembered always), Pawel Trzopek, Francolino Gonçalves, Paolo Garutti, Etienne Nodet, and Christian Eeckhout who have always welcomed me as family at the École.

Thanks are due to the following libraries for many courtesies: Hebrew University Library; École biblique et archéologique française in Jerusalem; Oriental Institute (University of Chicago); Ludwig-Maximilians-Universität München; Bridwell Library (Southern Methodist University); Widener Library and Andover-Harvard Theological Library (Harvard University); Jewish National Library; Instituts für Ägyptologie and Institut für Altertumswissenschaften Lehrstuhl für Altorientalistik (Uni Würzburg); and Boston University.

The previous work of K. Sethe and J. Partsch, E. Seidl, K-Th. Zauzich, P. W. Pestman, S. P. Vleeming, B. Menu, M. Malinine, S. Allam on Egyptian law and legal formulae; that of R. Yaron, Y. Muffs, B. Porten, and H. Z. Szubin on Aramaic law and legal formulae; and the unsurpassed epigraphic work of A. Yardeni is what has made this study possible. 'Due to their wisdom we grow wise and are able to say all that we say' (Isaiah di Trani ben Mali). Of course I take full responsibility for mistakes, omissions, or the inevitable shortcomings of a work of this kind.

I thank the editor of the Library of Second Temple Studies series, Lester L. Grabbe, for accepting the manuscript for publication and the staff at T & T Clark for patiently dealing with so many font and format problems. Rachel Vogelzang, my research assistant at Boston University, read through the manuscript and offered valuable comments and corrections.

Finally, I am immensely grateful to my family for their love, care, and support during all these years. I dedicate this book to my mother, Inés Farfalla, and to the memory of my father, Angel Félix Botta, who always encouraged me and my sisters to pursue our education.

Alejandro F. Botta
JPLicks - City of Brookline
May 12, 2009

Abbreviations

ÄAT	Ägypten und Altes Testament
AHDO	*Archives d'Histoire du Droit Oriental*
AHW	Wolfram von Soden, *Akkadische Handwörterbuch*, 3 vols. (Wiesbaden: Harrassowitz, 1965–81)
ALASP	*Abhandlungen zur Literatur Alt-Syren-Palästinas und Mesopotamiens*
AJSL	*American Journal of Semitic Languages*
AJT	*American Journal of Theology*
AncSoc	*Ancient Society*
AOAT	Alter Orient und Altes Testament
AOF	*Altorientalische Forschungen*
APF	*Archiv fur Papyrusforschung und verwandte Gebiete*
ARM	*Archives Royales de Mari* (Paris: P. Geuthner, 1946–)
ASAE	*Annales du Service des antiquités de l'Égypte*
AuOr	*Aula orientalis*
BASOR	*Bulletin of the American Schools of Oriental Research*
BdE	Bibliothèque d'Étude
BGU	Königliche Museen Berlin, Ägyptische Urkunden, Griechische Urkurden (Berlin)
Bib	*Biblica*
BIE	*Bulletin de l'Institut d'Égypte*
BIFAO	*Bulletin de l'Institut français d'archéologie orientale*
BM	British Museum
BO	*Bibliotheca orientalis*
BZAW	Beihefte zur Zeitschrift für die alttestamentliche Wissenschaft
CAD	*Chicago Assyrian Dictionary*, 27 vols. (Chicago: Oriental Institute, 1956–2007)
CAH	J. Boardman and N. G. L. Hammond (eds.), *The Cambridge Ancient History*, 2nd edn. (Cambridge: Cambridge University Press, 1982)
CdE	*Chronique d'Égypte*
DE	*Discussions in Egyptology*

DG	W. Erichsen, *Demotisches Glossar* (Copenhagen: E. Munksgaard, 1954)
DJD	Discoveries in the Judaean Desert
DMOA	Documenta et Monumenta Orientis Antiqui
DNWSI	J. Hoftijzer and K. Jongeling, *Dictionary of the North-West Semitic Inscriptions*, 2 vols., Handbuch der Orientalistik, part 1: Nahe und der Mittlere Osten, 21.1-2 (Leiden, New York, and Cologne: E. J. Brill, 1995)
ErIsr	*Eretz Israel*
EVO	*Egitto e Vicino Oriente*
GM	*Göttinger Miszellen*
HSS	*Harvard Semitic Studies*
HUCA	*Hebrew Union College Annual*
HWB	R. Hannig, *Grosses Handwörterbuch Ägyptisch–Deutsch (2800–950 v. Chr.): die Sprache der Pharaonen.* Kulturgeschichte der antiken Welt; Bd. 64, 4th Edn. (Mainz: P. von Zabern, 2006)
IEJ	*Israel Exploration Journal*
ILR	*Israel Law Review*
JACiv	*Journal of Ancient Civilizations*
JAOS	*Journal of the American Oriental Society*
JARCE	*Journal of the American Research Center in Egypt*
JBL	*Journal of Biblical Literature*
JEA	*Journal of Egyptian Archaeology*
JEN	*Joint Expedition with the Iraq Museum at Nuzi* (New Haven: American Schools of Oriental Research, 1927–)
JESHO	*Journal of the Economic and Social History of the Orient*
JJP	*Journal of Juristic Papyrology*
JNES	*Journal of Near Eastern Studies*
JRAS	*Journal of the Royal Asiatic Society*
JSJ	*Journal for the Study of Judaism*
JSOTSS	Journal for the Study of the Old Testament, Supplement Series
JSS	*Journal of Semitic Studies*
JSSEA	*Journal of the Society for the Study of Egyptian Antiquities*
KAI	*H. Donner and W. Röllig, Kanaanäische und aramäische Inschriften*, 2nd. edn. (Wiesbaden: Harrassowitz, 1966–69)
LÄ	*Lexicon der Ägyptologie*
Liddell-Scott	H. G. Liddell and R. Scott, *A Greek–English Lexicon*, 9th edn. (Oxford: Clarendon, 1996)

MDAIK	*Mitteilungen des Deutschen archäologischen Instituts Kairo*
Mitteis, *Chrestomathie*	*L. Mitteis and U. Wilcken Grundzüge und Chrestomathie der Papyruskunde* (Hildesheim: Olms, 1963, reprint of 1912 edn. Published by B. G. Teubner)
MUSJ	*Mélanges de l'Université Saint-Joseph*
OA	*Oriens antiquus*
OLA	Orientalia Lovaniensia Analecta
OLZ	*Orientalische Literaturzeitung*
Or	*Orientalia*
P.BM	Greek Papyri in the British Museum
P.Giss.	Griechische Papyri im Museum des oberhessischen Geschichtsvereins zu Giessen
P.Leid.	*Papyri Graeci Musei Antiquarii Lugduni-Batavi*, ed. C. Leemans (Leiden: Brill, 1843–85)
P.Tebt.	Tebtunis Papyri
PAT	D. R. Hillers and E. Cussini, *Palmyrene Aramaic Texts* (Baltimore: Johns Hopkins University Press, 1996)
PRU	*Le Palais Royal d'Ugarit* (Paris: Imprimerie Nationale, 1955–)
PSBA	*Proceedings of the Society of Biblical Archaeology*
RAAO	*Revue d'assyriologie et d'archéologie orientale*
RB	*Revue Biblique*
RdE	*Revue d'Égyptologie*
RHDFE	*Revue Historique de Droit Français et Étranger*
RIDA	*Revue Internationale des Droits de l'Antiquité*
RSO	*Rivista degli Studi Orientali*
SAAS	State Archives of Assyria Studies
SAK	*Studien zur altägyptische Kultur*
SAOC	Studies in Ancient Oriental Civilization
SB	*Sammelbuch griechischer Urkunden aus Aegypten*
TAD	B. Porten and A. Yardeni, *Textbook of Aramaic Documents from Ancient Egypt* (Jerusalem: Hebrew University of Jerusalem, 1989–99)
TSSI	J. C. L. Gibson, *Textbook of Syrian Semitic Inscriptions*, 3 vols. (Oxford: Clarendon, 1971–82)
TynBul	*Tyndale Bulletin*
UF	*Ugarit-Forschungen*
VT	*Vetus Testamentum*
Wb	*A. Erman und H. Grapow, Wörterbuch der aegyptischen Sprache* (Leipzig: J. C. Hinrichs, 1926–63)
WDSP	Wadi Daliyeh Samaria Papyri
WZKM	Wiener Zeitschrift für die Kunde des Morgenlandes

YOS	*Yale Oriental Series*
ZA	*Zeitschrift für Assyriologie*
ZÄS	*Zeitschrift für Ägyptische Sprache und Altertumskunde*
ZAW	*Zeitschrift für die alttestamentliche Wissenschaft*
ZDMG	*Zeitschrift der Deutschen Morgenländischen Gesellschaft*
ZSSRA	*Zeitschrift der Savigny-Stiftung, romanistische Abteilung*
ZVRW	*Zeitschrift für vergleichende Rechtswissenschaft*

1

Introduction: The Egyptological Approach to the Study of Aramaic Legal Formulae

Since the dawn of history and through the millennia, the Near East has been a crossroads of different peoples, civilizations, and empires, in a continuous and complex process of cultural interchange. During the fifth century BCE, the Jewish colony of Elephantine at the border of the Persian empire was a vivid example of such a cross-cultural environment. At Elephantine, language, religious customs, and legal practices were a synthesis of inherited traditions and new influences in a dynamic and fluid process of assimilation and differentiation.

The result of such a situation provides a rich context for comparative studies for the linguist, and for the historian of religion and legal systems. Given a corpus of legal documents originating in the Jewish colony of Elephantine, a corpus which has many similarities to that of their contemporary Egyptian counterparts, one of the main questions which arises is the origin of the legal formulary that they employed, i.e., to what extent the formulary belongs to the Semitic legal tradition and to what extent it was influenced by the local Egyptian legal formulary. The general subject of this monograph, therefore, will be the study of the interrelationships between the legal formulary traditions of the inhabitants of the Jewish colony of Elephantine and the legal formulary traditions of the Egyptians as reflected in their legal documents.

In his *Introduction to the Law of the Aramaic Papyri*, R. Yaron stated that 'the documents will gain in interest and importance if it is possible to establish, at least to some extent, their relationship to other systems of ancient law, earlier and later, within Egypt and outside it'.[1] This attempt to understand the connections between the law and legal formulae of the Aramaic papyri and the law and legal formulae of the ancient Near East and Egypt was carried out mostly by Assyriologists and Semitists,

1 R. Yaron, *Introduction to the Law of the Aramaic Papyri* (Oxford: Clarendon Press, 1961), 99.

sometimes with opposite conclusions from the few studies undertaken from the Egyptological perspective.[2]

In 1912 Revillout reminded us that 'Locus regit actum'[3] complaining about the abundant use of Babylonian and Persian materials to illuminate the law of the Aramaic papyri in contrast to the scant references to Egyptian legal history,[4] even though these papyri were found in Egypt. Revillout provided the first attempt to understand the Aramaic papyri in light of their Egyptian context. In his brief treatment, he dealt with the monetary units used in the papyri, the different jurisdictions presented in them, and some aspects of the marriage contracts. He concluded that 'en ce qui touche le fond même du droit de nos contrats égypto-araméens, il est absolument égyptien'.[5]

The striking similarities between the Aramaic and Demotic deeds were not only noticed by Egyptologists such as Revillout[6] and Spiegelberg,[7] but were also discussed by Talmudists such as L. Blau.[8] These scholars already had pointed out the similar structure and legal formulae that are found in both Egyptian and Aramaic legal documents. At that time, their consensus was that the Aramaic legal formulae were borrowed from Egyptian legal practices, although the necessary historic-philological ground for such assertion was very often lacking. In his review of Sayce and Cowley, Nöldeke published a personal communication by Spiegelberg which affirmed that רחק and שנא in their technical legal meaning were a

2 See the bibliography listed in B. Porten, *Archives from Elephantine: The Life of an Ancient Jewish Military Colony* (Berkeley and Los Angeles: University of California Press, 1968), 334 n. 1. R. Ritner's recent contribution to the discussion offers an excellent example of the rich possibilities of the Egyptological approach, R. Ritner, 'Third Intermediate Period Antecedents of Demotic Legal Termonology', in K. Ryholt, ed., *Acts of the Seventh International Conference of Demotic Studies, Copenhagen, 23–27 August 1999* (Copenhagen: Carsten Niebuhr Institute of Near Eastern Studies, Museum Tusculanum Press, 2002), 343–59.

3 'The location determines the act', a traditional (and still accepted) legal proposition originating in Roman law. See, R. Genin-Meric, *La maxime 'locus regit actum,' nature et fondement* (Paris: Librairie générale de droit et de jurisprudence, 1976).

4 E. Revillout, 'Supplément sur les contrats égypto-araméens d'Elephantine', in *Les origines égyptiennes du droit civil romain; nouvelle étude faite d'après les textes juridiques hiéroglyphiques, hiératiques et démotiques, rapprochés de ceux des Assyro-Chaldéens et des Hébreux, avec un premier supplément sur les contrats égypto-araméens d'Eléphantine, un index alphabétique des questions juridiques, économiques et historiques, un index alphabétique des noms propres et des addenda* (Paris: P. Geuthner, 1912), 52.

5 Revillout 'Supplément', 55.

6 Revillout 'Supplément', 52–60.

7 See his personal communications in T. Nöldeke, 'Die aramäischen papyri von Assuan', *ZA* 20 (1907): 145.

8 L. Blau, 'Zur demotischen und griechischen Papyrusurkunde', in *Judaica: Festschrift zu Herman Cohens siebzigsten Geburtstage* (Berlin: B. Cassirer, 1912), 207–26.

'Nachahmung einer ägyptischen Ausdruckweise',[9] but without adducing any evidence in support. Egyptian loan words and personal names in the Aramaic papyri were pointed out by W. Spiegelberg, B. Courouyer, and K.-Th. Zauzich,[10] and some aspects of linguistic interference between the Aramaic and Demotic legal documents were traced by G. K. Tepstad.[11]

E. Seidl devoted a steadily increasing amount of attention to the Aramaic papyri from the perspective of Egyptian legal history. In his first publications, he recognized the similarity in their formulae and legal conceptions. Based on this fact, and on the chronological precedence of some of the Demotic papyri, he concluded that the Aramaic legal formulary was dependent on its Egyptian counterpart.[12] He stated that:

> Up to the present it has been impossible to prove that during the Persian period any part of the law of the Near East was adopted by the Egyptians. We find on the contrary that certain Aramaic documents drawn up by Jewish soldier colonists at Aswan where they formed the Persian garrison were literal translations into Aramaic of clauses taken from Egyptian forms of contract.[13]

In a later monograph, Seidl dealt more extensively with the relationships of the Egyptian law to the law of the ancient Near East.[14] He summarized the differences and similarities between the Aramaic and Saite legal documents, giving a more balanced picture. Seidl contrasted the schemata of the Egyptian and Babylonian legal documents but found similarities in formulary and procedure. He was inclined to accept a Near Eastern origin for the satisfaction clause (טיב לבבי), but proposed an Egyptian origin for the 'document of withdrawal', the practice of transferring the old documents with the property to the new owner, and the legal status of the woman. Nevertheless, the Aramaic papyri would exhibit neither a

9 T. Nöldeke, 'Die aramäischen Papyri von Assuan', *ZA* 20 (1907): 145.

10 W. Spiegelberg, 'Ägyptisches Sprachgut in der aus Ägypten stammenden aramäischen Urkunden der Perserzeit', in *Orientalischen Studien Theodor Nöldeke zum 70 Geburstag gewindet* (Giessen: Töpelmann, 1906), 1093–1115; B. Couroyer, 'Termes égyptiens dans les papyri araméens du Musée de Brooklyn', *RB* 61 (1954): 554–59; K.-T. Zauzich, 'Ägyptologische Bemerkungen zu den neuen aramäischen papyri aus Saqqara', *Enchoria* 13 (1995): 115–18. For a complete list of Egyptian, Old Persian, Akkadian and Greek loan-words in the Aramaic papyri, see T. Muraoka and B. Porten, *A Grammar of Egyptian Aramaic* (Leiden: Brill, 1998), Appendix III, 370–82.

11 G. K. Tepstad, 'Contributions to the Study of the Aramaic Legal Papyri of Elephantine' (Ph.D. diss., University. of California, Los Angeles, 1989).

12 E. Seidl, 'Rechtgeschichte. Sammelbericht, Übersetzungen und Abhandlungen zum vorptolomäischen Rechte Ägyptens (1903–1929)', *Kritische Vierteljahre Schrift* 2 (1931): 53–54.

13 E. Seidl, 'Law', in S. R. K. Glanville, ed., *The Legacy of Egypt* (Oxford: Clarendon Press, 1942), 210.

14 E. Seidl, *Ägyptische Rechtgeschichte der Saiten- und Perserzeit*, 2nd edn. (Glückstadt: J. J. Agustin, 1968), 85–88.

complete assimilation of Egyptian law and formulary, nor a fully independent development, but a middle way between these extremes.[15] Seidl still denied, however, the possibility that Near Eastern legal practices could have come to Egypt through the Aramaic documents and even suggested a possible Egyptian influence on the Aramaic formulary before the Aramaic papyri were produced in Egypt.[16]

E. Y. Kutscher[17] and Y. Muffs[18] saw the Aramaic tradition as the origin or the medium in which West Semitic legal traditions influenced the Egyptian documents. However, in the 'Addenda et Corrigenda' to his book, Muffs corrected his previous position and suggested that earlier contacts between Mesopotamia and Egypt could explain the similarity of Egyptian and Akkadian legal formulae.[19]

In 1968, B. Porten[20] compared the schemata of Demotic and Aramaic conveyances, loans, and marriage documents, listing many similarities in the way the Jews of Elephantine, the Aramaeans of Syene, and the Egyptians conducted certain activities. In a recent article (1992), Porten noted 35 expressions in Egyptian documents that have Aramaic equivalents.[21] He offered four possible explanations for these equivalents: (1) the Aramaic borrowed from the Demotic, (2) the Demotic borrowed from the Aramaic, (3) both borrowed from a third source, (4) both evolved independently if coincidentally. The problem still remained to determine which was the original legal tradition of each of the listed terms, 'ideally, we should be able to probe the Semitic background of every Aramaic term as Muffs did for *ṭyb lbby* (Demotic *ḥꜣt=y mtr.w*) and see if the Demotic equivalent has roots in earlier Egyptian'.[22] In this way, it would be possible to assess which legal tradition is the borrower and which is the lender.

Aramaists, however, have approached the legal documents of Elephantine only in three ways thus far:[23] first, comparing them to the later Aramaic legal tradition;[24] second, as part of a self-contained

15 Seidl, *Ägyptische Rechtgeschichte*, 86.

16 Seidl, *Ägyptische Rechtgeschichte*, 87.

17 E. Y. Kutscher 'New Aramaic Texts', *JAOS* 74 (1954): 233–48.

18 Y. Muffs, *Studies in the Aramaic Legal Papyri from Elephantine* (Leiden: Brill, 1969), 190–92.

19 Muffs, *Studies*, 205.

20 Porten, *Archives from Elephantine*, 334–43.

21 B. Porten, 'Aramaic-Demotic Equivalents: Who is the Borrower and Who the Lender?' in J. Johnson, ed., *Life in a Multi-Cultural Society: Egypt from Cambyses to Constantine and Beyond*, SAOC 51 (Chicago: Oriental Institute, 1992), 259–64.

22 Porten, 'Aramaic-Demotic Equivalents', 264.

23 Summarized by Muffs, *Studies*, 12.

24 See Kutscher, 'New Aramaic Texts' and also A. D. Gross, *Continuity and Innovation in the Aramaic Legal Tradition*, SJSJ 128 (Leiden: Brill, 2008).

system;[25] and more recently from the point of view of the Assyriological legal tradition.[26] However, there is still a fourth possible approach, which has long been neglected by Aramaists, and that is to study the Elephantine legal documents from an Egyptological perspective.[27] As Kutscher pointed out, 'these papyri, when put in the focus of these studies, will assume a kind of pivotal interest for this entire field and may well change the entire conception of legal evolution in the areas concerned'.[28]

In this direction, E. Cruz-Uribe suggested an Egyptian origin of the withdrawal clause, but based only on the occurrence of the verb *wꜣy* in previous literary – non-legal – texts.[29] A more significant contribution was more recently offered by R. Ritner,[30] who presented 24 Egyptian antecedents of the 35 Aramaic-Demotic parallels listed by Porten.[31] Ritner's work has demonstrated the urgent need to deepen the study of the Egyptian roots of Aramaic-Demotic legal formulae previously considered to be of foreign origin.

The aim of this research is, therefore, to compensate for the lack of attention to the relationship between Egyptian and Aramaic legal traditions, with the intention of completing the picture that we have of the Elephantine documents and of the legal traditions reflected in them. According to B. Levine, their legal formulae 'could be analyzed as composites, containing several originally unconnected components, each of which bears close affinities to a different stratum of the legal tradition of the ancient Near East',[32] but more recently he limited those strata to: (1) Terms and formulae that most likely entered Aramaic from Akkadian in the Neo-Assyrian period; (2) Terms and formulae that entered Elephantine Aramaic from Akkadian in the Neo-Babylonian period; and (3) Terms and formulae native to West Semitic/Aramaic and not take from Akkadian.[33]

An Egyptological approach, that at the same time will provide the ancient Egyptian roots of some of West Semitic legal terminology, might confirm the influence of foreign legal practices on other Aramaic formulae

25 Yaron, *Introduction*.

26 Muffs, *Studies*, and E. Cussini, 'The Aramaic Law of Sale and the Cuneiform Legal Tradition' (Ph.D. diss., Johns Hopkins University Press, 1993).

27 See the remarks by E. Cussini, '[S]ince the richest portion of the early Aramaic legal corpus is from Egypt, it would be appropriate to inquire into the relations to Egyptian legal tradition', Cussini, 'Aramaic Law of Sale', 7.

28 Kutscher, 'New Aramaic Texts', 233–48.

29 E. Cruz-Uribe, *Saite and Persian Demotic Cattle Documents, A Study in Legal Forms and Principles in Ancient Egypt* (Chico, Calif.: Scholars Press, 1985), 63.

30 Ritner, 'Third Intermediate Period Antecedents', 343–59.

31 Porten, 'Aramaic-Demotic Equivalents', 259–64.

32 Levine, 'On the Origins', 46.

33 B. Levine, 'Prolegomenon', to Y. Muffs, *Studies in the Aramaic Legal Papyri from Elephantine* (Leiden: Brill, 2003), xxxviii–xxxix.

which do not have their roots in Egypt and it could allow us to point to those formulae which are indigenously Aramaic, without any known roots in either the Mesopotamian or Egyptian tradition. In seeking the Egyptian parallels and antecedents to the Aramaic formulary, we hope to balance the current scholarly perspective, based mostly upon Aramaic and Assyriological comparative studies.

More specifically, we want to probe the legal purpose, meaning, and origins of two legal formulae that appear in the Demotic and Aramaic instruments.[34] The first one is the so-called שליט formula and is used to establish a party certain rights in a transaction. The second one is based on the verb 'to be far', Demotic *wy*, Aramaic רחק, and is called 'the withdrawal formula'. In Demotic, its constitutive element is the expression '*tw=y wy.k r-r=k n X Property*': 'I am far from you regarding the X Property.' This formula is one of the essential features of the Demotic *sẖ n wy* ('Abstandsschrift', or 'document of withdrawal')[35] and is also attested in a variety of other documents.[36] It is expressed in Aramaic by *rḥqt mnkm mn X property*, 'I withdrew from you from X property' and its variations,[37] which is also a central formula in the *spr mrḥq*.[38]

In close connection with the Demotic withdrawal clause, we shall also analyse the Demotic formula *iw=y r dy.t wy=f r-r=k* ('I will cause him to be far from you') based on the same verb. This second formula is one of the clauses in the *sẖ ḏbꜣ ḥḏ* ('Geldbezahlungsschrift', or 'document concerning money')[39] and can be defined as a defension clause.[40] It functions as a warranty against third party claims on the sold property and is one of the various kinds of warranties that a seller offers a buyer.

Focusing on the Egyptian perspective, we intend to demonstrate the Egyptian origin of the withdrawal clause, and to locate the Aramaic legal formulary in the context of the Egyptian legal tradition. We begin our

34 A distinction should be made between a contract and the legal instrument that registers the transaction. The instrument was concerned with obtaining enforcement of the contract in the case of eventual litigation. See R. H. Pierce, *Three Demotic Papyri in the Brooklyn Museum* (Oslo: Universitetsforlaget, 1972), 83.

35 See M. Depauw, *A Companion to Demotic Studies* (Brussels: Fondation egyptologique Reine Elisabeth, 1997), 143.

36 See below 6.2, 'The Uses of *wy* in the Saite and Persian Periods (664–332 BCE)'.

37 See B. Porten and A. Yardeni, *Textbook of Aramaic Documents from Ancient Egypt* (hereafter *TAD*) (Jerusalem: Hebrew University, Department of the Jewish People, Texts and Studies for Students, 1989), vol. 2, *Contracts*, B2.7:7, 16; B2.8:6; B2.9:9; B2.10:4; B3.2:7; B3.4:11, 13; B5.2:8; B5.5:5, 8. For רחיק in a legal sense: B2.2:15; B2.8:11; B2.9:15.

38 *TAD* B2.2:15; B2.8:5-6; B2.9:15; B2.10:4; B3.6 is a document of withdrawal, but does not include a withdrawal formula.

39 See Depauw, *Companion*, 140–2.

40 See R. Yaron, 'On Defension Clauses of Some Oriental Deeds of Sale and Lease from Mesopotamia and Egypt', *BO* 15 (1958): 15–22; idem, *Introduction to the Law of the Aramaic Papyri* (Oxford: Clarendon Press, 1961), 89.

study with a survey of previous works on the legal documents and a brief description of the legal practices attested in Elephantine: 2. 'The Elephantine Community and Aramaic Law'. In the following chapter we set the stage for our Egyptological approach to the Aramaic documents by examining relevant aspects of the Egyptian legal history: 3. 'The Egyptian Formulary Tradition'. Our study of the function and origins of the שליט clause (4. 'Challenging the Consensus: The שליט Clause') opens the door for considering the possibility of an Egyptian origin for an Aramaic legal formula and its Mesopotamian counterpart. The following three chapters (5. 'The "Withdrawal" and Related Formulae in the Aramaic Legal Tradition', 6. 'The use of *wꜣy* in the Egyptian Legal Tradition', and 7. 'A Comparison of the Aramaic and Egyptian Uses of Withdrawal Formulae') constitute the core of this monograph and are dedicated to demonstrating the Egyptian roots of the legal formulae associated with the metaphor of 'withdrawal'. Chapter 8 summarizes the achieved results and offers some suggestions for redefining the way we approach the study of Aramaic and Demotic legal formulae.

The main sources for this study are the Aramaic legal documents from Elephantine and their counterparts in the Egyptian legal tradition. The rest of the corpus of Aramaic documents, the Mesopotamian deeds, and the Greek and Coptic papyri will also be used for comparisons.

2

The Elephantine Community and Aramaic Law

Movement of people was a common phenomenon in the ancient Near East and this is especially true for the first millennium BCE. Originating in voluntary migration in the search for better resources, in forced emigration, or deportation, a variety of ethnic groups settled in new territories. Most of the relevant studies on ethnicity focus on classification and typology in an attempt to provide a universal definition. For example, W. W. Isajiw lists more than ten cultural attributes as the basis for ethnic group classification.[1] Any kind of objective criteria used to define an ethnic group usually overlap with the fact that an essential characteristic of ethnic identity is its subjective and relational character. In the following paragraphs we regard an ethnic group as having, generally speaking, four characteristics: (1) being biologically self-perpetuating; (2) sharing fundamental cultural values; (3) making up a field of communication and interaction; and (4) having a membership which identifies itself, and is identified by others, as constituting a category distinguishable from other categories of the same order. These various groups became part of military colonies or garrisons and/or civilian settlements established primarily for economic reasons. The eighth through the sixth centuries BCE witnessed the establishment of an increasing amount of Phoenician and Greek colonies in the coasts of the Mediterranean and Black Seas.[2] The Assyrian expansion which included the conquest of the Aramaean

1 W. W. Isajiw, 'Definitions of Ethnicity', *Ethnicity* 1 (1974): 2. See also F. Barth, 'Introduction', in *Ethnic Groups and Boundaries: The Social Organization of Cultural Differences*, ed. F. Barth (Bergen: Universitetsforlaget; London: Allen & Unwin, 1969), 11; S. Jones, *The Archaeology of Ethnicity: Constructing Identities in the Past and Present* (London and New York: Routledge, 1997), esp. chs. 4 and 5. And also the useful discussion for the historian of the various approaches to ethnicity as a category for the historical analysis in J. M. Hall, *Ethnic Identity in Greek Antiquity* (Cambridge: Cambridge University Press, 1997), 17–33.

2 For a general view of Greek colonization see A. J. Graham, 'The Colonial Expansion of Greece', in *CAH*, vol. 3, pt. 3, 83–162; idem, 'The Western Greeks', in *CAH*, vol. 3, pt. 3, 163–95; J. M. Cook, 'The Eastern Greeks,' in *CAH*, vol. 3, pt. 3, 196–221. For a general view of Phoenician colonization see W. Cullican, 'Phoenicia and Phoenician Colonization', in *CAH*, vol. 3, pt. 2, 461–546; H. G. Niemeyer, 'Expansion et Colonisation', in *La Civilisation*

states and Israel entailed one- or two-way deportations. During this process, people originating in Babylonia, Cuthah, Avva and Sepharvaim settled in North Israel (2 Kgs 17.24).[3] The fall of the Assyrian empire at the hands of the Medes and Babylonians,[4] and the subsequent fall of Babylon at the hands of Cyrus,[5] greatly increased the migrational process in the Near East. During the seventh through the fifth centuries BCE, there were numerous cosmopolitan enclaves, which sheltered several groups of people in active interaction with each other. The presence of foreign colonies in Egypt is well documented, the best known being the Ionian community.[6] The establishment of Greek and Carian colonies in Egypt dates from the times of Psammetichus I (664–610 BCE), who established garrisons at Marea, Daphnae, and Elephantine. Gyges, king of Lydia (ca. 680–650 BCE), supplied him with Carian and Ionian troops to help him in his struggle for supremacy in the Delta. Carians are also seen in the service of Judaean kings (2 Kgs 11.4, 19).[7] The cosmopolitan character of Elephantine and Syene is exemplified by the presence there of Babylonians (*TAD* B2.2:19 – witness), Caspians (*TAD* B2.7:18, 19; B3.4:23, 24 – witnesses; B3.4:2 – parties of the document; B3.5:11; B3.12:4, 12; B3.12:4-5 – owners of the property); Khwarezmians (*TAD* B2.2:2 and B2.3:23 – parties of documents); Bactrians (party in *TAD* D2.12:2); Medes (*TAD* B3.6:17 – witness); Magians (*TAD* B3.5:24 – witnesses); Persians, Jews, and Aramaeans alongside the Egyptian

Phénicienne et Punique, Handbuch der Orientalistik 20, ed. V. Krings (Leiden: Brill, 1995), 247–67. For the Phoenicians in Egypt, see G. Scandone and P. Xella, 'Égypte', also in *La Civilisation Phénicienne et Punique*, 632–39.

3 For a study of the Assyrian deportation policy see B. Oded, *Mass Deportations and Deportees in the Neo-Assyrian Empire* (Wiesbaden: Harrassowitz, 1979); and more specifically for Israel, N. Na'aman, 'Population Changes in Palestine following Assyrian Deportations', *Tel Aviv* 20 (1993). 104–12, K. L. Younger Jr., 'The Deportation of the Israelites', *JBL* 117 (1998): 201–27. For the deportation of Arameans, see P. Dion, *Les Araméens à l'âge du fer: histoire politique et structures sociales* (Paris: J. Gabalda, 1997), 217 ff.

4 See J. Oates, 'The Fall of Assyria (635–609 B.C.)', in *CAH*, vol. 3, pt. 2, 162–93.

5 See T. C. Young Jr., 'The Early History of the Medes and the Persians and the Achaemenid Empire to the Death of Cambyses', in *CAH*, vol. 3, pt. 2, 24–46.

6 See M. M. Austin, *Greece and Egypt in the Archaic Age* (Cambridge: Cambridge Philosophical Society, 1970).

7 See F. K. Kienitz, *Die politische Geschichte Ägyptens vom 7. bis zum 4. Jahrhundert vor der Zeitwende* (Berlin: Akademie-Verlag, 1953), 35–47; T. F. R. G. Braun, 'The Greeks in Egypt', in *CAH*, vol. 3, pt. 3, 32–56; C. A. La'da, *Foreign Ethnics in Hellenistic Egypt*, Prosopographia Ptolemaica 10 (Leuven, Paris, and Dudley, Mass.: Peeters, 2002). Another very active group in Egypt during the Late Period were the Phoenicians, for which see J. Leclant, 'Les Phéniciens et l'Egypte', in *Atti del II Congresso Internazionale di Studi Fenici e Punici* (Rome: CNR – Istituto per la Civiltà Fenicia e Punica, 1991), 6–17.

population, who were serving in the various detachments.[8] For example, in the legal documents, there is a mention of a wall built by the Egyptians in *TAD* B3.10:9 and B3.11:4, and in *TAD* D2.25:7 an Egyptian signed as witness in Demotic script. The garrison (חילא)[9] was divided into detachments (דגל) and subdivided into centuries (מאה).[10] The 'hundred' unit was also used in Israel for both military and civil service.[11]

Cultural contacts between Egyptians and Semites occurred not only on Egyptian soil but in Mesopotamia as well.[12] These cosmopolitan situations, where bilinguism was often present,[13] might naturally have resulted in legal transplants and blending of legal traditions. At the very beginning of the process of establishing themselves in a foreign setting, a group of immigrants would tend to live according to its customary law. The increasing necessity of social intercourse, however, compels the formulation of a sort of basic code of socio-legal behaviour that will facilitate the newcomers' interaction with the already established new neighbours. A certain degree of compatibility in their legal customs must have existed among the various ethnic groups present in Elephantine-Syene allowing them to achieve a common legal basis for their economic and social interactions as evidenced by the Aramaic contracts.[14] The

8 See Porten, *Archives from Elephantine*, 28–42. During the Egyptian New Kingdom, the title 'standard-bearer' was also used for the commander of ethnic groups, 'the standard-bearer of the Sherden', 'the standard-bearer of the Tjuk'. A. R. Schulman, *Military Rank, Title and Organization in the Egyptian New Kingdom* (Berlin: B. Hessling, 1964), 23. For the uses of standards (*tȝy sryt)* in the Egyptian army see Schulman, *Military Rank*, 69–71.

9 *TAD* B2.9:5; B8.10:6.

10 *TAD* A5.5:7; B4.4:8; B4.3:11; B4.4:6; B4.4:10; C3.15:19-20, 31, 54.

11 See Exod. 18.21; Num. 31.48; 2 Kgs 11.14, 19 and *passim*. See A. Temerev, 'Social Organization in Egyptian Military Settlements of the Sixth–Fourth Centuries BCE', in *The Word of the Lord Shall Go Forth*, ed. C. L. Meyers and M. V. O'Connor (Winona Lake: Eisenbrauns, 1983), 523–24, who suggests that the 'hundred' might have been a term for civilians recruited to perform various types of service.

12 For Egyptians in Babylon, see D. J. Wiseman, 'Some Egyptians in Babylon', *Iraq* 28 (1966): 154–58; I. Eph'al, 'The Western Minorities in Babylon in the 6th–5th Centuries BC: Maintenance and Cohesion', *Or* 47 (1978): 74–90; R. Zadok, 'On Some Egyptians in First-Millennium Mesopotamia', *GM* 26 (1977): 63–68; idem, 'On Some Egyptians in Babylonian Documents', *GM* 64 (1983): 73–75; for Egyptians living in Assur in the mid-7th century, see O. Pedersén, *Archives and Libraries in the City of Assur: A Survey of the Material from the German Excavations* (Uppsala: Uppsala University; Stockholm: Almqvist & Wiksell, 1985–86), 125–29; V. Donbaz and S. Parpola, *Neo-Assyrian Legal Texts in Istanbul* (Saarbrücken: In Kommission bei DSV Saarbrücker Druckerei und Verlag, 2001). I would like to thank Prof. Janet Johnson for pointing me to these two works.

13 See A. Lemaire and H. Lozachmeur, 'Remarques sur le Plurilinguism en Asia Mineur à L'Époque Perse', in *Antiquités Semitiques I. Mosaïques de langues, mosaïque culturelle. Le bilinguisme dans le Proche Orient ancien. Actes de la table ronde du 18 novembre 1995 organisé par l'URA 1062, 'Etudes Sémitiques'*, F. Briquel-Chatonnet, ed. (Paris: Adrien Maisonneuve, 1996), 91–123.

14 See above for people from the various ethnic groups mentioned in the contracts.

relationship between trade and cultural diffusion has been studied from both the archaeological and the theoretical perspectives.[15] The emergence of regional and international trade since the third millennium probably caused business law to be one of the first realms where various groups had to find a common ground for economic interaction. Although the study of trade has been focused on the professional merchant, the resultant cultural interaction can be extrapolated to the buying and selling activities of private individuals and groups.[16]

The importation of a community's customary laws into a foreign context represents one of the ways legal transplants[17] are produced. Alan Watson classifies major legal transplants into three categories: (a) when a people moves with its laws into a different country with a comparable culture, (b) when the territory into which the people moves has no comparable culture, and (c) when one community of people accepts a large part of the legal system of another people.[18] In the case of the Aramaeans and Jewish groups, we assume that the move to Egypt was to a country of a comparable culture (case (a)).[19]

In Saqqara, we find a similar case to that of Elephantine. The Saqqara papyri bear witness to the life of a cosmopolitan community, which included Babylonians, Aramaeans, Sidonians, Jews, Moabites, Ionians, Carians, and Hyrcanians.[20] However, the extent of the legal compatibility and mutual acceptance among those groups is hard to determine with certainty. Making such a determination could be important when deciding the degree of legal interaction that the aforementioned groups had with one another.[21]

15 See the pertinent chapters in J. A. Sabloff and C. C. Lamberg-Karlovsky, *Ancient Civilization and Trade* (Albuquerque: University of New Mexico Press, 1975).

16 See K. R. Venhof, 'Some Social Effects of Old Assyrian Trade', XXIII Reencontre Assyriologique Internationale, July 1976, *Iraq* 39 (1977): 109–18. See also W. F. Leemans, 'The Importance of Trade', XXIII Reencontre Assyriologique Internationale, July 1976, *Iraq* 39 (1977): 1–10; G. Steiner, 'Kaufmanns- und Handelsprachen im Alten Orient', *Iraq* 39 (1977): 11–18.

17 I.e. 'the moving of a rule or a system of law from one country to another', Watson, *Legal Transplants*, 21.

18 Idem., 29–30. These situations, which provide a favourable context for legal transplants, would necessarily provide the same favourable context for the borrowing of legal formulae.

19 The 'otherness' of Egypt in relation to the rest of the ancient Near East is reflected only in Egyptian sources and is completely absent in the other countries' view of Egypt.

20 N. Aimé.-Giron, *Textes araméens d'Égypte* (Cairo: Imprimerie de l'Institut Français d'Archéologie Orientale, 1931), 58; and Segal, *Aramaic Texts*, 8–9.

21 In addition to the Elephantine intermarriage cases (Mibtahiah & Esḥor and Ananiah & Tamet), a documented case of intermarriage in Saqqara is provided by the stele published in I. Mathieson *et al.*, 'A Stela of the Persian Period from Saqqara', *JEA* 81 (1995): 23–41. Further evidence will be necessary to assess the degree of interaction among other groups.

When various groups of immigrants need to interact in a context that was potentially foreign to all, there is a strong necessity for establishing a common legal ground for business, which can include a significant component of the native legal tradition. To understand the possibilities of interaction between the Jewish and Egyptian systems of law, it is crucial to determine how compatible, or how closely related, the patterns of culture and civilization of the Jewish immigrants were to the culture and civilization of their Egyptian neighbours. The political and cultural connections between Egypt and Canaan have been a subject of extensive study,[22] as has the influence of Egyptian wisdom and wisdom-motifs in the Hebrew Bible.[23] The West Asiatic presence in Egypt is well documented by epigraphic and archaeological material as well as by the presence of loan words.[24] By the time of the New Kingdom, foreigners and foreign communities were a prominent characteristic of Egyptian society. The testimony of the Hebrew Bible regarding the sojourn of the Hebrews in Egypt suggests a living memory of the connections between Egypt and the people of Israel.[25] Egypt was always an important presence for the elites of Israel and Judah,[26] and by the time of Jeremiah there were Jews living in Lower Egypt (in Migdol, Tahpanhes, and Memphis) and in Upper Egypt (Jer. 44.1).[27]

Knowing with certainty the place of origin of the Jewish colonists of Elephantine and the date of their arrival in Egypt would also play an

22 See W. Helck, *Die Beziehungen Ägyptens zu Vorderasien im 3. un 2. Jahrtausend v. Chr.*, 2nd edn. (Wiesbaden: Harrassowitz, 1971); D. R. Redford, *Egypt, Canaan and Israel in Ancient Times* (Princeton: Princeton University Press, 1992) and the bibliography cited there.

23 See N. Shupak, *Where can Wisdom be found?: The Sage's Language in the Bible and in Ancient Egyptian Literature* (Fribourg, Switzerland: University Press; Göttingen: Vandenhoeck & Ruprecht, 1993); and most recently J. D. Currid, *Ancient Egypt and the Old Testament* (Grand Rapids: Baker Books, 1997) and the bibliography cited there.

24 Helck, *Die Beziehungen*, 515–76; Hoch, *Semitic Words*; P. Saretta, 'Egyptian Perceptions of West Semites in Art and Literature During the Middle Kingdom (An Archaeological, Art Historical and Textual Survey)' (Ph.D. diss., New York University, 1997).

25 The historical background of the Exodus narratives is still a matter of controversy. See J. K. Hoffmeier, *Israel in Egypt: The Evidence for the Authenticity of the Exodus Tradition* (Oxford: Oxford University Press, 1997); N. P. Lemche, *The Israelites in History and Tradition* (Louisville: Westminster John Knox Press, 1998); K. A. Kitchen, *On the Reliability of the Old Testament* (Grand Rapids: Eerdmans, 2003), 241–312 and the bibliography discussed there.

26 See P. S. Ash, *David, Solomon and Egypt: A Reassessment* (Sheffield: Sheffield Academic Press, 1999); and M. Görg, *Die Beziehungen zwischen dem alten Israel und Ägypten. Von den Anfängen bis zum Exil* (Darmstadt: Wissenschaftliche Buchgesellschaft, 1997); C. R. Higginbotham, *Egyptianization and Elite Emulation in Ramesside Palestine: Governance and Accommodation on the Imperial Periphery* (Leiden: Brill, 2000).

27 The story of Esther presents a wide Diaspora of Jews in the 127 Persian provinces (Est. 8.9).

important role in determining the relationships among them, as well as with the other foreign groups and with the local Egyptians. Although the ultimate origin of the Jewish group should undoubtedly be looked for in Judah, it is also possible that the group did not come directly from Judah to Elephantine but had already settled previously elsewhere in the Diaspora. In such a case, the question is for how long or for how many generations they had been abroad, and where they had settled before coming to Elephantine. While the Aramaic papyri from Elephantine provide rich information about the social and economic life of this Jewish community in the Diaspora, they provide very limited clues for determining when the colony was established and the origin of its inhabitants. The papyri only tell us that the temple of YHW was already built when Cambysses marched into Egypt (*TAD* A4.7-8.13-14), providing 527–525 BCE[28] as terminus *ante quem* for the building of the temple. To elucidate this matter would contribute to determining the colonists' legal tradition. R. C. Steiner, following Vleeming and Wesselius, has suggested recently that the origins of the Aramaeans from Syene should be looked for in Bethel where they settled after being deported from Rashu. But this conclusion is only possible assuming that *P. Amherst* 63 comes from Elephantine, for which there is no certain evidence.[29]

A. E. Cowley[30] suggested that the Jewish mercenaries who were established in Elephantine were part of the forces led by Psammetichus II against Ethiopia,[31] left there to protect the southern border against Ethiopia in the first quarter of the sixth century BCE. E. Kraeling, after discussing previous theories, proposed that the Aramaic community was established as a replacement of the previous garrison that defected to the Nubians, and that Jewish elements settled in Elephantine into an already existing Aramaic community, perhaps under Amasis (570–526 BCE).[32] Bezalel Porten, after a most exhaustive discussion of the matter,[33] considered three different periods when Jews from the land of Israel might have settled in Elephantine: (1) the period from the Syro-Ephraimite War until the siege of Jerusalem, 735 to 701 BCE; (2) the period when

28 See L. Depuydt, 'Egyptian Regnal Dating under Cambysses and the Date of the Persian Conquest', in *Studies in Honor of William Kelly Simpson*, ed. P. Der Manuelian (Boston: Dept. of Ancient Egyptian, Nubian and Near Eastern Art, Museum of Fine Arts, 1990), 179–90, and D. Devauchelle, 'Un problème de chronologie sous Cambyse', *Transeuphratène* 15 (1998): 9–17.

29 R. C. Steiner, 'Papyrus Amherst 63: A New Source for the Language, Literature, Religion and History of the Arameans', in *Studia Aramaica*, JSS Supplement 4, eds. M. J. Geller, J. C. Greenfield, and M. P. Weitzman (Oxford: Oxford University Press, 1997), 204.

30 Cowley, *Aramaic Papyri*, xvi.

31 The letter of Aristeas (§13) is the source for this information.

32 Kraeling, *Brooklyn*, 41–48, esp. 48.

33 Porten, *Archives from Elephantine*, 1–28.

Manasseh supported Egypt in her rebellion against Assyria, middle of the seventh century; and (3) the period between the accession of Jehoiakin, 609 BCE, and the flight to Egypt led by Johanan b. Kareah.[34] For Porten, 'there is little doubt that the Elephantine "Jews" came from Judah'.[35] In a recent paper he provided additional support for the theory that 'sees the establishment of the Jewish garrison with Temple at Elephantine ca. 650 BCE as very similar to the establishment of the Jewish garrison with Temple in the land of Onias – disaffected priests with prophetic support entering into service of the king and building a Temple like the one in Jerusalem'.[36]

Edda Bresciani presented an alternative hypothesis regarding the origins of the Elephantine colony. According to her, the foundation of the colony should be dated not long after the end of the Babylonian exile. The existence of a temple in Elephantine, following her argument, would be very hard to imagine before the destruction of the Jerusalem temple by the Babylonians in 586 BCE. Bresciani supports her argument with the fact that the prophet Jeremiah does not include among his accusations against the Jews of Egypt the fact of having another temple in opposition to the Jerusalem theological tradition (Jer. 44.1). The resulting situation is that, according to Bresciani, the foundation of the colony and the temple should be dated not long before the arrival of Cambysses in Egypt. The Jewish colonists of Elephantine could have belonged to the Jewish group exiled to Babylon who, after the decree of Cyrus, intended to return to Jerusalem, but possibly because of disagreements with the leaders of Jerusalem, or for other reasons, they decided not to settle down in Judah, but to continue on to Egypt, taking refuge in Elephantine under the auspices of the Pharaoh Amasis.[37]

Accepting the Mesopotamian origin of the colonists, and, therefore, a date for the foundation of the colony in the last third of the sixth century, according to Bresciani, resolves the problems of the Aramaic-speaking character of the colony and of the presence in Elephantine of a temple of YHW, which would have been in contradiction with the Deuteronomistic doctrine of only one sanctuary in Jerusalem.[38] However, these two

34 Porten, *Archives from Elephantine*, 13.

35 Porten, *Archives from Elephantine*, 18 n. 66.

36 B. Porten, 'Settlement of the Jews at Elephantine and the Arameans at Syene', in *Judah and Judeans in the neo-Babylonian Period*, O. Lipschits and J. Blenkinsopp, eds. (Winona Lake: Eisenbrauns, 2003), 458. I want to thank Prof. B. Porten for providing me a copy of his article before publication.

37 E. Bresciani, 'The Diaspora: Egypt, Persian Satrapy', in *The Cambridge History of Judaism*, vol. 1, eds. W. D. Davies and L. Finkelstein (Cambridge: Cambridge University Press, 1984), 368.

38 The lack of Hebraisms in the language of the Jews of Elephantine has made Bresciani discard the hypothesis of the origin of the colonists in Israel-Judaea. 'The Diaspora', 368.

factors, the use of Aramaic as business and day-to-day language and the presence of a temple of YHW,[39] can be explained by other circumstances. The official use of Aramaic through the Assyrian empire[40] and its widespread use already long before the Persians gained the dominance of the Near East would provide an adequate context for a Jewish community either in the Diaspora or in their own homeland[41] to become more than acquainted with the Aramaic language and to be able to speak and write it without any traces of Hebraisms.[42] Therefore, any of the dates listed by Porten[43] could also provide the historical context for explaining the use of Aramaic instead of Hebrew. The existence of a Jewish Colony in Elephantine already in exilic times might be suggested by Isa. 49.12, according to the better reading of 1QIsa[a] where the prophet declares the return of the exiles 'from the land of the Syenians (מארץ סוניים)'.[44] The building of a temple in Elephantine could have been an attempt to provide an alternative place of worship as a reaction to Manasseh's paganization of the Jerusalem temple, as Porten suggests,[45] or to cover the religious needs of the Jewish community, as would have been the case of

39 The traditional opinion that the book of Deuteronomy excludes the possibility of other sanctuaries has been criticized already by A. C. Welch, *The Code of Deuteronomy* (London: J. Clarke & Co., 1924), 195; idem, 'When was the Worship of Israel Centralized at the Temple?' *ZAW* 43 (1925): 250–55; and more recently by J. N. M. Wijngaards, *The Dramatization of Salvific History in the Deuteronomic School* (Leiden: Brill, 1969), 23ff; and B. Halpern, 'The Centralization Formula in Deuteronomy', *VT* 31 (1981): 20–38. See also G. J. Wenham, 'Deuteronomy and the Central Sanctuary', *TynBul* 22 (1971): 103–18. On the other hand, it has been reaffirmed by B. M. Levinson, *Deuteronomy and the Hermeneutics of Legal Innovation* (Oxford: Oxford University Press, 1997), 23ff. See also R. Albertz, *A History of Israelite Religion in the Old Testament Period* (Louisville: Westminster John Knox Press, 1994), 195–231; and the recent discussion by M. D. Knowles, *Centrality Practiced: Jerusalem in the Religious Practices of Yehud and the Diaspora in the Persian Period*, Archaeology and Biblical Studies 16 (Atlanta: Society of Biblical Literature, 2006).

40 Cf. the Ashur ostracon (ca. 652 BCE) sent from Uruk, *KAI* 233 = *TSSI* II, 20, 15. Cf. Lipiński, *The Aramaeans*, 420.

41 Isa. 36.11 and 2 Kgs 18.26 witness to the fact that the Judahite officials were conversant in Aramaic already at the end of the 8th century BCE. Cf. Porten, *Archives from Elephantine*, 16.

42 For the widespread use of Aramaic in the Assyrian empire see H. Tadmor, 'The Aramaization of Assyria: Aspects of Western Impact', in *Mesopotamien und seine Nachbarn: politische und kulturelle Wechselbeziehungen im alten Vorderasien vom 4. bis 1. Jahrtausend v. Chr. XXV. Rencontre assyriologique internationale Berlin, 3. bis 7. Juli 1978*, H.-J. Nissen and J. Renger, eds. (Berlin: D. Reimer, 1982), vol. 2, 449–69; Dion, *Les Araméens*, 217–20.

43 See above, p. 22; Porten, *Archives from Elephantine*, 13.

44 D. W. Parry and E. Qimron, *The Great Isaiah Scroll (1QIsa[a]): A New Edition* (Leiden: Brill, 1999), 83. The MT has מארץ סינים. On the other hand, the LXX translated 'from the land of the Persians' (δὲ ἐκ γῆς Περσῶν).

45 Porten, 'Settlement of the Jews at Elephantine', 458.

the Jewish sanctuaries in Hellenistic times.[46] Even in the second century BCE there were several Jewish communities with sanctuaries in Egypt.[47] This would exclude Babylon as the only place of origin that would make possible these two characteristics of the Elephantine Jewish community. In addition, the Jewish neighbourhood at Elephantine has recently been excavated,[48] and the architectural study of the layout of the temple has led S. Rosenberg to suggest that, 'the Jewish mercenaries originated in the former northern kingdom of Israel and not in Judah'.[49]

If the main wave of Jewish mercenaries/colonists arrived in Egypt sometime during the period 735–609 BCE, the subsequent process of adaptation to the new context would also explain why there is no clear trace in the Jewish documents from Elephantine of the tradition reflected in the few examples that the Hebrew Bible provides regarding sale documents.[50] The foundation of the Jewish colony in Elephantine could have happened years after the first arrival of Jewish soldiers and their families to Egypt, thus providing a period of interaction with other groups before the Jewish colonists became established in Elephantine. An early date for the foundation of the colony does not necessarily imply that the permission for the construction of a temple was immediately granted. The date of the arrival of the colonists in Elephantine and the date of the foundation of the temple need not necessarily correlate.[51] The temple could have been founded many years after the arrival of the Jewish colonists. Moreover, it is possible that not all the colonists came from the same place.

Regardless of the place of origin of the Jewish colonists, two things are certain: first, that they would have brought with them certain laws and legal formulae and, second, that a process of interaction began when they

46 Cf. A. Kasher, *Jews in Hellenistic and Roman Egypt: the Struggle for Equal Rights* (Tübingen: J. C. B. Mohr, 1985), 106–67. Conflict with the Jerusalem elite could have been the cause for the erection of two other temples in Leontopolis and Samaria. See Porten, *Archives from Elephantine*, 116–18. But see E. S. Gruen, 'The Origins and Objectives of Onias' Temple', *Scripta Classica Israelica* 26 (1997), 47–70, who proposed that the Onias temple was not built in defiance of the temple in Jerusalem but 'to provide a center of worship for pious Jews in Egypt for whom the fate of their homeland must have seemed to be in grave jeopardy'. 'Origins and Objectives', 69.

47 Josephus, *Ant.* 13.66. Cited by Gruen, 'Origins and Objectives', 60.

48 C. von Pilgrim, 'Der Temple des Jawveh', in *Stadt und Tempel von Elephantine*, W. Kaiser *et al.*, eds. *MDAIK* 55 (Cairo: German Archaeological Institute, 1999), 142–45; idem, 'Das Aramaische Quartier im Stadtgebiet der 27. Dynastie', in *Stadt und Tempel von Elephantine*, G. von Dreyer *et al.*, eds., *MDAIK* 58 (Cairo: German Archaeological Institute, 2002), 192–97.

49 S. G. Rosenberg, 'The Jewish Temple at Elephantine', *NEA* 67 (2004): 12.

50 Yaron, 'Schema', 59–60; idem, *Introduction*, 15.

51 But see Porten, 'Settlement of the Jews of Elephantine', who proposed a unique event leading to the foundation of both the temple and the Jewish community.

reached Egypt and, either immediately or after a time, settled down in Elephantine. To define the extent to which these new immigrants felt at home in the legal realm is one basis for determining the degree of interaction. In accordance with the 'personal' rather than territorial character of law in the ancient Near East,[52] it is possible that these new immigrants were granted the right to live according to their own laws and customs. There are other examples of ethnic minorities in the ancient Near East who were allowed to live according to their laws. The Egyptian settlement in Babylon[53] included 'an assembly of the elders of the Egyptians', which was allowed to pass a verdict in a case involving Egyptians.[54]

It is beyond of the scope of this monograph to determine the amount of Egyptian influence on the legal practice of the Jewish colonists. However, the presence of Babylonians, Caspians, Khwarezmians, Bactrians, Medes, Magians, Persians, Aramaeans, and Egyptians within the legal documents of the Jewish community, suggests that the business law which governed the transactions of the Jewish soldiers was not different from that which governed the transactions of the rest of the ethnic groups represented in Elephantine-Syene. Although we do not have legal documents originating from such groups, a certain agreement in business practices should be inferred from the high degree of social intercourse among the different groups reflected in the documents of the Jewish group. Two of the scribes, Nabutukulti bar Nabuzeribni (*TAD* B2.11) and Raukhshana bar Nergal (u)shezib (*TAD* B3.9),[55] have non-Hebrew-Aramaic names and patronymics, and another two, Attarshuri bar Nabuzeribni[56] (*TAD* B2.3 and B2.4) and Bunni bar Mannuki (B3.2), have a non-Hebrew-Aramaic

52 A personal system of law applies different laws to the various sections of the population according to their racial origin. See E. Vitta, 'The Conflicts of Personal Laws' Part I, *ILR* 5 (1970): 171–202; idem, 'The Conflicts of Personal Laws' Part II, *ILR* 5 (1970): 337–51.

53 *Bit al misiraya* 'The Egyptian Settlement'. See E. Unger, *Babylon. Die heilige Stadt nach der Beschreibung der Babylonie*, 2nd edn. (Berlin: De Gruyter, 1970), 81–82.

54 J. N. Strassmaier, *Inschriften von Cambyses, König von Babylon* (Leipzig: Eduard Pfeiffer, 1890), no. 85.

55 Nabutukulti is an Akkadian name, and also Akkadian is the patronymic Nabuzeribni (M. H. Silverman, *Religious Values in the Jewish Proper Names at Elephantine* (Kevelaer: Verlag Butzon & Bercker; Neukirchen-Vluyn: Neukirchener Verlag, 1985), 61–62; Porten, *Elephantine Papyri*, 201 n. 32); Raukhshana is a Persian name (Grelot, *Documents araméens*, 489; Porten, *Elephantine Papyri*, 235 n. 20) while the patronymic Nergal(u)shezib is Akkadian (Silverman, *Religious Values*, 62); Grelot, *Documents araméens*, 483; and Porten, *Elephantine Papyri*, 235 n. 20 consider it Akkadian or Aramaean.

56 The grandfather of Nabutukulti bar Nabuzeribni.

element in their names.[57] The progressive assimilation that we find in the onomasticon both in Elephantine-Syene and in Saqqara points to the cultural compatibility of the various groups attested in both places. Assimilation in the onomasticon, however, does not necessarily imply the absolute assimilation of the ethnic group. There are examples from Saqqara where a father bears a Semitic name while his son bears an Egyptian name (*TAD* C3.6:10),[58] and vice versa, fathers with Egyptian names and sons with Semitic names (*TAD* C3.6:11; C4.3:18). There is also one example of a brother with a Semitic and a sister with an Egyptian name (*TAD* B8.4:15). A similar situation is found in Elephantine-Syene.[59] This kind of interaction must have had consequences in the legal realm. As Porten pointed out, 'non-Jewish scribes were eligible to draw up deeds of conveyance since the pertinent law was common to all foreign settlers in Elephantine'.[60] Moreover, the lack of any evidence of an autonomous Jewish court suggests that, 'the disputes arising out of Aramaic and out of Demotic contracts were adjudicated upon by the same forum'.[61] This situation would naturally promote the establishment of a common business law shared by all the ethnic groups. In the matter of legal documents, the scribes of the various groups would have kept at the beginning a formulary related to their place of training. As they began to interact with other people, however, their customs would have been increasingly permeable to foreign influences. The degree of foreign influence on their original legal formulary tradition would vary according to their contact with the local people and other foreigners and, also, according to the degree of acceptance of standard local legal formulae for procedures that involved official authorities. It is possible to assume that the formulary of the various legal instruments would receive varying amounts of local influence. For instance, agreement/contracts made by the colonists with the locals or with other foreign residents, such as claims and sales, would be more exposed to influences than documents drawn privately among the colonists, such as those related to marriage, where a

57 The name Bunni is West Semitic and is attested in Nehemiah 9.4; 10.16; 11.15; Porten, *Elephantine Papyri*, 206 n. 19. Mannuki is Akkadian (Grelot, *Documents araméens*, 478; Porten, *Elephantine Papyri*, 206 n. 19).

58 Cf. the recent treatment by B. Porten, in consultation with G. Vittmann, 'Egyptian Names in Aramaic Texts' in K. Ryholt, ed., *Acts of the Seventh International Conference of Demotic Studies. Copenhagen, 23–27 August 1999* (Copenhagen: Carsten Niebuhr Institute of Near Eastern Studies, Museum Tusculanum Press, 2002), 283–328.

59 See Porten, *Elephantine Papyri*, 84–88. This situation was also attested in Babylon where we find Egyptians bearing Babylonian names but still being listed as Egyptians. See E. Unger, *Babylon*, 81–82.

60 Porten, *Archives from Elephantine*, 194; and again, 'deeds of conveyance and loan bear great similarity, indicating like practices in economic matters', 299.

61 Yaron, 'Schema', 49.

more conservative tradition would prevail. This assumption is confirmed by Porten's comparison of the schemata of the Aramaic and Demotic documents regarding deeds of conveyance, loan contracts and marriage contracts.[62] Finally, it is possible to also assume that the amount of local Egyptian influence on the Jewish and Aramaic documents would increase over time.

2.1. *The Study of the Aramaic Legal Documents: State of the Question*

More than a century has passed since the first Aramaic legal papyrus was brought to light.[63] In 1903, A. E. Cowley[64] published the first legal document – a loan contract – and a few years later in 1906, Sayce and Cowley[65] offered to the academic community eleven papyri, all of them legal documents, plus three ostraca.

The cuneiform counterparts of some of the Aramaic legal phrases were noted primarily by Lidzbarski, Ungnad, and San Nicolò;[66] the latter tried to understand the law of the Aramaic papyri as an integral part of the Near Eastern legal tradition. According to San Nicolò, the Jewish colonists lived according to Western Asian laws that they had brought with them to Egypt.[67] An additional attempt to interpret the legal formulae and practices reflected in the Aramaic papyri in light of the cuneiform legal tradition had been made by F. E. Peiser.[68]

In 1908, F. Buhl presented a balanced picture of the linguistic, religious, and legal aspects of the papyri. He estimated that the legal formulary of the Aramaic papyri was influenced by the Babylonian and Egyptian

62 Porten, *Archives from Elephantine*, 334–43.

63 The first legal document to be discovered, *TAD* B8.5 (1842–45), consisted of several fragments. See *TAD* B, *Introduction*, p. v. For a list of the whole corpus of published Aramaic texts from Egypt, see B. Porten, 'Egyptian Aramaic Texts', in E. M. Meyers, ed., *The Oxford Encyclopedia of Archaeology in the Near East* (Oxford: Oxford University Press, 1997), 2: 213–19, and Appendix 1: 'Egyptian Aramaic Texts', 393–410.

64 A. E. Cowley, 'Some Egyptian Aramaic Documents', *PSBA* 25 (1903): 202ff., 264, 311ff. (*TAD* B4.2).

65 A. H. Sayce and A. E. Cowley, *Aramaic Papyri Discovered at Assuan* (London: A. Moring, 1906).

66 M. Lidzbarski, *Ephemeris für semitische Epigraphik*, vol. 2 (Giessen: J. Ricker, 1908), 210–50; vol. 3 (Giessen: J. Ricker, 1915), 70–84, 238–60; A. Ungnad, *Aramäische Papyrus aus Elephantine. Kleine Ausgabe unter Zugrundlegung von Eduard Sachau's Erstausgabe* (Leipzig: J. C. Hinrichs, 1911), esp. 42–52; M. San Nicolò, 'Vorderasiatisches Rechtsgut in den ägyptischen Eheverträgen der Perserzeit', *OLZ* 30.4 (1927): 217–21.

67 M. San Nicolò, 'Die Stellung der Keilschrifturkunden in der voderasiatischen Rechstentwicklung', *ZSSRA* 48 (1928): 42.

68 F. E. Peiser, 'Review of *Die jüdisch-aramäischen Papyri von Assuan sprachlich und sachlich erklärt*, by W. Stacrk', *OLZ* 10 (1907): 622–27, and 11 (1908), 24–26, 73–79.

civilizations in equal measure.[69] E. Pritsch[70] offered a more systematic study of the law and the legal formulae of the Aramaic papyri in 1912, discussing the schemata, style, and terminology of the documents. He also provided a German translation and a brief systematic presentation of the law of the documents recognizing different traditions (Hebrew, Persian, Egyptian and Mesopotamian) in the formulary of the documents.[71]

The importance of the Elephantine papyri for the study of ancient Judaism, the Bible, and the history of the legal institutions of the Persian period was widely recognized very soon. In 1918, M. Sprengling offered an English translation of the papyri which had been published up to that point;[72] in 1923, A. Cowley[73] re-edited all the papyri which had been discovered. Despite the pioneering efforts of Pritsch, the legal aspect of the papyri was not the first to come to the attention of scholars. Rather, at the beginning of the century most of the articles dealing with the papyri were concerned essentially with matters of language and religion. More than half of Cowley's introduction was devoted to clarifying problems regarding the religion of the Jews of Elephantine, a topic that he considered 'the most important arising from a study of these papyri'.[74] Nevertheless, Cowley noted previous studies which had demonstrated some similarities between the Aramaic and Old Babylonian legal formulae. In his Introduction, he mentioned the enumeration of relatives of the parties, the fine for breaking the contract, the definition of the boundaries of the property, plus certain legal phrases, such as דין ודבב, טיב לבבי, באבני מלכא, and גרי as taken by the Persians from the Babylonians or based on the Babylonian legal system,[75] thus suggesting that the 'connection with Babylonian Law is well worthy of a thorough study'.[76]

In 1953, E. Kraeling[77] published seventeen additional Aramaic documents with an extensive introduction gathering all the known facts about the Jewish colony at Elephantine. In his introduction, Kraeling addressed the issue of the origins of the law reflected in the papyri. Since the Persians

69 F. Buhl, 'Remarques sur les papyrus juifs d'Elephantine', *Oversigt over det Kongelige Danske Videnskabernes Selskabs, Forhandlinger* 2 (1908): 37–64.

70 E. Pritsch, 'Jüdische Rechtsurkunden aus Aegypten', *ZVRW* 27 (1912): 7–70.

71 Pritsch, 'Jüdische Rechtsurkunden', 14–15.

72 M. Sprengling, 'The Aramaic Papyri of Elephantine in English', *AJT* 21 (1917): 411–52 and 22 (1918): 349–75.

73 A. E. Cowley, *Aramaic Papyri of the Fifth Century B.C.* (Oxford: Clarendon Press, 1923).

74 Cowley, *Aramaic Papyri*, xxviii.

75 Cowley, *Aramaic Papyri*, xxix, referring to B. Meissner, *Beiträge zum altbabylonischen Privatsrecht* (Leipzig: J.C. Hinrichs, 1893).

76 Cowley, *Aramaic Papyri*, xxx.

77 E. Kraeling, *The Brooklyn Museum Aramaic Papyri* (New Haven: Yale University Press, 1953). Paradoxically, these papyri were the first to be discovered (1893).

conquered the Neo-Babylonian empire, they permitted its laws and customs to continue:

> It is not surprising, therefore, to find the people of Elephantine producing legal and business documents in which the Babylonian influence is as obvious as is that of the English common law in contemporary American legal documents.[78]

The Babylonian influence also extended, according to Kraeling, to the Demotic legal documents, but the closer similarities between the Aramaic and Demotic texts, compared to the similarities of either set to legal texts originating in the Mesopotamian realm, caused Kraeling to believe that the Aramaic documents 'were not unaffected by their Egyptian environment'.[79] In his review of Kraeling's publication, Y. Kutscher[80] provided commentaries about various legal clauses and their possible connection with the Mesopotamian legal realm. He argued against the view that sees the Aramaic documents as merely borrowing either from the Mesopotamian or from the Egyptian legal documents. He defended the case in favour of the innovative character of the Aramaic legal tradition, proposing that the Aramaic documents were the bridge between the Mesopotamian and Egyptian legal worlds.[81]

In 1954 and 1966, respectively, G. R. Driver,[82] and E. Bresciani and M. Kamil[83] added more Aramaic letters to the corpus. Although the letters did not deal with legal matters, they provided more information about the social life of the Aramaeans in Egypt and about their relationships with the Persian administration and their Egyptian neighbours.

More recently, in 1983, J. B. Segal[84] published 202 fragments of papyri and 26 ostraca found in Saqqara. Of particular interest in this collection are the legal and judicial texts containing fragmentary court records.[85] From outside Egypt, the Samaria papyri are a valuable source for comparison. Dated to the fourth century, the corpus comprised eighteen fragmentary documents. In 1985, F. M. Cross published a slave-convey-

78 Kraeling, *Brooklyn*, 50.

79 Kraeling, *Brooklyn*, 52.

80 Y. Kutscher, '"New Aramaic Texts", Review of *The Brooklyn Museum Aramaic Papyri*, by E. Kraeling', *JAOS* 74 (1954): 233–48.

81 Kutscher, 'New Aramaic Texts', 244.

82 G. R. Driver, *Aramaic Documents of the Fifth Century B.C.* (Oxford: Clarendon Press, 1954).

83 E. Bresciani and M. Kamil, 'Le lettere aramaiche di Hermopoli', in *Atti dell'Accademia Nazionale dei Lincei, Memoire*, 8th series, 12.5 (1966), 356–428.

84 J. B. Segal, *Aramaic Texts from North Saqqâra. With some fragments in Phoenician* (London: Egypt Exploration Society, 1983).

85 Thirteen of the Saqqara papyri were included in *TAD* B. See below, Table I, p. 28.

ance, the best-preserved document of the corpus.[86] D. M Gropp edited nine of them in his dissertation, and published the whole corpus recently.[87]

The similarities between the legal formulae of the Aramaic papyri and other legal traditions continued to provide the incentive for more detailed comparative studies. In two books and several articles, Rabinowitz[88] attempted to relate many of the Aramaic legal formulae to the Egyptian and Mesopotamian deeds and to trace the origins of some of the formulae. Considering the Aramaic papyri as a sample of extra-biblical Jewish law, he sought to demonstrate their influence on Demotic, Greek, and Byzantine documents, and Roman law. However, because he referred mostly to later Demotic documents, he was unable to trace any Egyptian influence on the Aramaic deeds and considered them to be borrowers from the Jewish Aramaic legal tradition.[89]

The study of the law of the Aramaic papyri gained in precision and systematism with the work of R. Yaron. Beginning with his analysis of the schemata of the legal documents (1957), and following with his study of the marriage documents (1958) and conveyances (1960),[90] Yaron set the standard for the legal studies of the corpus. A year later (1961) in his *Introduction to the Law of the Aramaic Papyri*, he offered the most comprehensive study of the law of the Elephantine documents.[91] He discussed the schemata of the documents, the system of courts and procedures, slavery, adoption, marriage and divorce, succession, and the law of property and obligations. Yaron's last two chapters were dedicated to methodological issues regarding the comparison of the law and formulae of the Aramaic papyri with other legal traditions and to

86 F. M. Cross, 'Samaria Papyrus I: An Aramaic Slave Conveyance of 335 BCE Found in Wadi ed Daliyeh', *ErIsr* 18 (1985): 7–17.

87 D. M. Gropp, 'The Samaria Papyri from Wadi ed-Daliyeh. The Slave Sales' (Ph. D. diss., Harvard University, 1986); idem, *Wadi Daliyeh II: The Samaria Papyri from Wadi Daliyeh*, DJD 28 (Oxford: Clarendon Press, 2001), 1–116.

88 J. J. Rabinowitz, *Jewish Law: Its influence on the Development of Legal Institutions* (New York: Bloch, 1956); idem, *Studies in Legal History* (Jerusalem: s.n, 1958); idem, 'A Legal Formula in the Susa Tablets, in an Egyptian Document of the Twelfth Dynasty, in the Aramaic Papyri and in the Book of Daniel', *Bib* 36 (1955): 74–77; idem, 'A Legal Formula in the Egyptian-Aramaic, and Murabba'at Documents', *BASOR* 145 (1957): 33–34; idem, 'Some Notes on an Aramaic Contract from the Dead Sea Region', *BASOR* 136 (1954): 15–16; idem, 'Neo-Babylonian Legal Documents and Jewish Law', *JJP* 13 (1961): 131–75; idem, 'Demotic Papyri of the Ptolemaic Period and Jewish Sources', *VT* 7 (1957): 398–400.

89 See the criticism in R. Yaron, 'Jewish Law and other Legal Systems of Antiquity', *JSS* 4 (1959): 308–31.

90 R. Yaron, 'The Schema of the Aramaic Legal Documents', *JSS* 2 (1957): 33–61; idem, 'Aramaic Marriage Contracts from Elephantine', *JSS* 3 (1958): 1–39; idem, 'Aramaic Marriage Contracts: Corrigenda and Addenda', *JSS* 5 (1960): 66–70; idem, 'Aramaic Deeds of Conveyance,' *Bib* 41 (1960): 248–74 and 379–94.

91 Yaron, *Introduction*, 99–128.

discussing the points of contact between the Akkadian and Demotic legal traditions related to the papyri. He listed the similarities of phraseology and schemata, suggesting the possible original tradition of several kinds of clauses.[92] He proposed that the origin of the Aramaic legal formulary could be found prior to the Neo-Babylonian and Neo-Assyrian period.

E. Volterra also dedicated his efforts to clarifying some legal aspects of the papyri,[93] sometimes in open polemic with Yaron. The differences between Volterra and Yaron were mostly based on their different interpretations of the terms 'Aramaean of Syene' and 'Jews of Elephantine'. Volterra interpreted these denominations as designating different groups and adduced many cases of homonymy in the colony.[94] In 1965, A. Verger, a student of Volterra, published his study *Ricerche Giuridiche sui Papiri Aramaici di Elefantina*,[95] dealing with the schemata of the documents, marriage and divorce, slavery, legal process and conveyances. As mentioned by Yaron in his review,[96] Verger's best contribution is in the realm of litigation and procedure.

In 1968, B. Porten published the most comprehensive study to date on the life of the Jewish colony of Elephantine.[97] Although Porten does not concentrate on the legal documents, one finds pertinent commentaries concerning this aspect throughout his study.[98] An appendix compares the similarities between the schemata of the Aramaic and the Demotic legal documents.

92 Yaron, *Introduction*, 99. See the methodological discussion below 2.3, 'Legal Traditions in Contact: Methodological Considerations'.

93 E. Volterra, 'Osservazione sul divorzio nei documenti aramaici', in *Studi orientalistici in onore di Giorgio Levi della Vida*, vol. 2 (Rome: Istituto per l'Oriente, 1956), 586–600; idem, 'Le affrancazioni di schiavi nei documenti aramaici del V secolo a.C.', *RSO* 32 (1957): 675–96 (= *Scritti in onore di Giuseppe Furlani*).

94 See E. Volterra, 'Review of *The Brooklyn Museum Aramaic Papyri*, by E. Kraeling', *Iura* 6 (1955): 349–60; idem, 'YHDW e 'RMY nei Papiri Aramaici del V Secolo Provenienti dall'Egitto', in *Rendiconti dell'Accademia Nazionale dei Lincei, Classe di Scienze morali, storiche e filologiche*, 8th series, 18, 3–4 (1963), 131–73. His arguments, however, were clearly refuted by Yaron. See R. Yaron, 'Identities in the Brooklyn Museum Aramaic Papyri', *Bib* 39 (1958): 344–54; idem, 'Who is Who in Elephantine?', *Iura* 15 (1964): 167–72 and the response by E. Volterra, 'Osservazioni alla Nota del Prof. R. Yaron', *Iura* 15 (1964): 173–80.

95 A. Verger, *Ricerche giuridiche sui papiri aramaici di Elefantina* (Rome: Centro di studi semitici, Istituto di studi del Vicino Oriente, Università, 1965) and also his previous articles; idem, 'Note sul diritto dei papiri aramaici', *OA* 3 (1964): 47–89; idem, 'L'amministrazione della giustizia nei papiri aramaici di Elefantina', *Rendiconti della Academia Nazionale dei Lincei*, 8th series, 19 (1964), 75–94; idem, 'Intorno a P. Brooklyn 8', 294–315. Verger sometimes adopts a polemical tone against the views of Yaron, but his arguments do not stand close scrutiny.

96 R. Yaron, 'Review of *Ricerche giuridiche sui papiri aramaici di Elefantina*, by A. Verger', *JSS* 12 (1967): 311.

97 B. Porten, *Archives from Elephantine: The Life of an Ancient Jewish Military Colony* (Berkeley and Los Angeles: University of California Press, 1968).

98 *Archives from Elephantine*, 'Purchase of a House', 213–16; 'Marriage of Jehoishma', 221–25; etc.

In 1969, Y. Muffs provided a thorough study of the Aramaic טיב לבבי clause, literally 'my heart is satisfied', as a term of quittance.[99] He sought to demonstrate the Neo-Assyrian influence on the Aramaic legal terminology and practice as found in Elephantine,[100] and presented twelve close correspondences between the Neo-Assyrian and Aramaic legal expressions.[101] For Muffs, 'the Aramaic formulary is the recipient of over two millennia of cuneiform legal experience; it is the culmination of many developments and inner-Assyriological trends, thus an amalgamation of various cuneiform traditions'.[102] In a very detailed philological and legal analysis, Muffs argued for the ultimate Mesopotamian origins of the Aramaic טיב לבבי and although his approach was mainly Assyriological, he also analysed some of the Egyptian analogues. At first, Muffs proposed the Aramaic formulary as the historic medium by which the legal elements of the Western cuneiform tradition were introduced into Egypt. Later, evidence of earlier contacts between the Egyptian and cuneiform legal traditions led him to reconsider his proposal and to suggest a much earlier period for such transferences.[103]

Certain aspects of the law of the papyri (for example, the law of marriage[104] and of slavery)[105] have been discussed by scholars in more detail than others. The Mesopotamian influence on the formulae of the

99 Y. Muffs, *Studies in the Aramaic Legal Papyri from Elephantine* (Leiden: Brill, 1969).

100 In this direction, see also F. M. Fales, 'La tradition assyrienne à Élephantine d'Égypte: nouvelles donnés et perspectives', *Transeuphratène* 9 (1995): 119–30.

101 Muffs, *Studies*, 180–87, but see the commentaries by R. Yaron, 'Review of *Studies in the Aramaic Legal Papyri from Elephantine*, by Y. Muffs', *RB* 77 (1970): 413–15.

102 Muffs, *Studies*, 14.

103 Muffs, *Studies*, 'Addenda et Corrigenda', 205. For Egyptian antecedents of the satisfaction clause see, Ritner, 'Third Intermediate Period Antecedents', 347; A. F. Botta, 'Looking for Some Satisfaction: Egyptian Antecedents of טיב לבבי', forthcoming.

104 Yaron, 'Aramaic Marriage Contracts'; S. Greengus, 'The Aramaic Marriage Contracts in the Light of the Ancient Near East and Later Jewish Materials' (MA thesis, University of Chicago, 1959); Yaron, 'Aramaic Marriage Contracts: Corrigenda and Addenda'; idem, *Introduction*, 44–64; A. M. Mann, 'The Jewish Marriage Contracts from Elephantine: A Study of Text and Marriage' (Ph.D. diss., New York University, 1985); Volterra, 'Osservazione sul divorzio'; J. A. Fitzmyer, 'A Re-Study of an Elephantine Marriage Contract (AP 15)', in *Near Eastern Studies in Honor of William Foxwell Albright*, ed. H. Goedicke (Baltimore: Johns Hopkins University Press, 1971), 137–68; M. J. Geller, 'The Elephantine Papyri and Hosea 2.3: Evidence for the Form of Early Jewish Divorce Writ', *JSJ* 8 (1977): 139–48; idem, 'New Sources for the Origin of the Rabbinic Ketubah', *HUCA* 49 (1978): 227–45; A. Azzoni, 'The Private Life of Women in Persian Egypt' (Ph.D. diss., Johns Hopkins University, 2000). Azzoni devotes five chapters to study the legal position on women in the Elephantine documents of wifehood, 'Private Life of Women', pp. 21–128. She is also preparing a chrestomaty of Aramaic legal documents; idem, *Aramaic Legal Texts from the Neo-Assyrian to the Roman Empire*, forthcoming.

105 Verger, *Ricerche Giuridiche*, 105–30; E. Volterra, 'Le affrancazioni di schiavi'; Yaron, *Introduction*, 36–40.

Aramaic deeds of sale was the subject of a dissertation by E. Cussini.[106] By studying the entire formulary of the sale documents, and by supporting her treatment of the Elephantine documents with the Samaria corpus, the Dura Europos slave sale, and the Palmyrean cession texts, Cussini was able to advance beyond previous studies, pointing to the fragmentation and the different lines of development of the Aramaic legal tradition.[107] A recent work by A. D. Gross, on the other hand, highlights the evidence that points to both continuity and diversity within the Aramaic formulaic tradition. Gross offered a very valuable study of some of the legal formulae used in the Neo-Assyrian Aramaic conveyances, the Elephantine documents, the Wadi ed-Daliyeh texts, the Jewish-Aramaic and Nabataean materials from the Judaean desert, and the Syriac deeds.[108]

The study of the Elephantine legal papyri has also been enriched in recent years due mainly to the collaborative work of B. Porten and H. Z. Szubin. In a series of articles, they deal with many legal aspects of the documents clarifying obscure points and adding new meaning to the texts.[109]

Some of the legal formulae utilized in the Aramaic papyri also received special attention. The function of the טיב לבבי clause was reexamined by

106 E. Cussini, 'The Aramaic Law of Sale and the Cuneiform Legal Tradition' (Ph.D. diss., Johns Hopkins University, 1993).

107 'Aramaic Law of Sale', 213–23.

108 A. D. Gross, *Continuity and Innovation in the Aramaic Legal Tradition*, SJSJ 128 (Leiden: Brill, 2008). Gross discusses the acknowledgement of receipt clause (pp. 47–101), the investiture clause (102–67), and the warranty clause (168–219).

109 B. Porten and H. Z. Szubin, '"Abandoned Property" in Elephantine: A New Interpretation of Kraeling 3', *JNES* 41 (1982): 123–31; idem, '"Ancestral Estates" in Aramaic Contracts. The Legal Significance of the Term *mhḥsn*', *JRAS* (1982): 3–9, idem, 'Exchange of Inherited Property at Elephantine (Cowley 1)', *JAOS* 102 (1982): 651–54; idem, 'Litigation concerning Abandoned Property at Elephantine (Kraeling 1)', *JNES* 42 (1983): 279–84; idem, 'Testamentary Succession at Elephantine', *BASOR* 252 (1983): 35–46; idem, 'Hereditary Leases in Aramaic Letters', *BO* 42 (1985): 283–88; idem, 'Litigants in the Elephantine Contracts: The Development of Legal Terminology', *Maarav* 4 (1987): 45–67; idem, 'A Dowry Addendum: Kraeling 10', *JAOS* 107 (1987): 231–38; idem, 'Royal Grants in Egypt: A New Interpretation of Driver 2', *JNES* 46 (1987): 39–48; idem, 'An Aramaic Deed of Bequest (Kraeling 9)', in *Community and Culture: Essays in Jewish Studies in Honor of the Ninetieth Anniversary of the Founding of Gratz College*, N. Waldmam, ed. (Philadelphia: The College; Ardmore, Pa.: Seth Press, 1987), 179–92; idem, 'A Life Estate of Usufruct: A New Interpretation of Kraeling 6', *BASOR* 269 (1988): 29–45; idem, 'An Aramaic Joint Venture Agreement: A New Interpretation of the Bauer-Meissner Papyrus', *BASOR* 288 (1992): 67–84; idem, 'The Status of the Handmaiden Tamet: A New Interpretation of Kraeling 2 (*TAD* B3.3)', *ILR* 29 (1995): 43–64; idem, 'The Status of a Repudiated Spouse: A New Interpretation of Kraeling 7 (*TAD* B3.8)', *ILR* 35 (2001): 46–78.

Yaron and Westbrook.[110] Although the withdrawal formula was not the central topic of Muffs's monograph, he offered some relevant comments on it. In his analysis of semantic equivalents of *libbašu ṭab*, Muffs also argued in favour of a Mesopotamian origin of רחק, comparing the Aramaic term with the Elamite *duppur* and the Akkadian *rêqu* and *nêsu* as terms for quittance.[111] In the most recent treatment of רחק, F. M. Cross thought he detected a similar legal meaning in the biblical book of Ezekiel.[112] The clause referring to the boundary description of the property in the conveyances was also analysed by B. Levine and by B. Porten.[113] The שליט clause was the subject of an article by D. M. Gropp,[114] who also compared the formulary of the Wadi Daliyeh documents with the Elephantine documents.[115] In the most recent treatment of Aramaic legal formulae, A. D. Gross studied the receipt, investiture (i.e. the שליט clause), and the warranty clauses.[116] His conclusion that the שליט clause stems from West Semitic legal traditions, however, should be revised in the light of Egyptian antecedents predating the West Semitic occurrences.[117]

The great interest that the Aramaic papyri created in the scholarly world has been demonstrated by the new editions that have appeared following the aforementioned *editio princeps*. In 1972, P. Grelot[118]

110 In his review of Muffs, Yaron disagrees with Muffs's interpretation of טיב לבבי as quittance formula and regards it as a volitional statement. R. Yaron, 'Review of *Studies in the Aramaic Legal Papyri from Elephantine*, by Y. Muffs', *RB* 77 (1970): 408–16; B. Levine, 'On the Origins of the Aramaic Legal Formulary at Elephantine', in J. Neusner, ed., *Christianity, Judaism and other Greco-Roman Cults. For Morton Smith at Sixty* (Leiden: Brill, 1975), defended Muffs's views. R. Westbrook, on the other side, regarded it as a receipt clause, R. Westbrook, 'The Phrase "His Heart is Satisfied" on Ancient Near Eastern Legal Sources', *JAOS* 111 (1991): 219–24.

111 Muffs, *Studies*, 117–20.

112 F. M. Cross, 'A Papyrus Recording a Divine Legal Decision and the Root *rḥq* in Biblical and Near Eastern Legal Use', in *Texts, Temples and Traditions: A Tribute to Menahem Haran*, ed. M. V. Fox *et al.* (Winona Lake: Eisenbrauns, 1996), 311–20. See our discussion of Cross's article in 'רחק in the Bible, a Reevaluation', *Bib* 87 (2006): 418–20.

113 Levine, 'Aramaic Legal Formulary', 48–53; B. Porten, 'Boundary Descriptions in the Bible and in Conveyances from Egypt and the Judean Desert', in L. H. Schiffman, E. Tov, and J. C. VanderKam, *The Dead Sea Scrolls: Fifty Years After Their Discovery. Proceeding of the Jerusalem Congress, July 20–25, 1997* (Jerusalem: Israel Exploration Society, 2000), 852–61 with 6 figures.

114 D. M. Gropp, 'The Origin and Development of the *šalliṭ* Clause', *JNES* 52 (1993): 31–36.

115 D. M. Gropp, 'The Wady Daliyeh Documents Compared to the Elephantine Documents', in L. H. Schiffman, E. Tov, and J. C. VanderKam, eds., *The Dead Sea Scrolls, Fifty Years after their Discovery: Major Issues and New Approaches, Jerusalem 20–25 July 1997* (Jerusalem: Israel Exploration Society, 2000), 826–35.

116 Gross, *Continuity and Innovation in the Aramaic Legal Tradition*, receipt, 46–91, investiture, 92–150, warranty, 151–93.

117 See below Chapter 4, 'Challenging the Consensus: The שליט Clause'.

118 P. Grelot, *Documents araméens d'Ègypte* (Paris: Éditions du Cerf, 1972).

published a French translation of the documents previously published by Cowley and Kraeling and a selection of the letters published by G. R. Driver and Bresciani-Kamil. In 1974, B. Porten and J. Greenfield[119] translated a selection of the previously published Aramaic documents into English and Hebrew. But the most significant, complete revision and up-to-date edition of the whole corpus of the Aramaic documents from Egypt was begun in 1986 and concluded in 1999, by B. Porten and A. Yardeni.[120] The four volumes cover almost the whole *corpus* of Aramaic texts from Egypt, improving upon previous editions by providing hand copies as well as new readings and reconstructions; the *Textbook of Aramaic Documents from Ancient Egypt* should be considered the final textual source for the study of the Aramaic corpus from Egypt.

A volume containing all the Aramaic papyri from Elephantine and many others in Hieratic, Coptic, Greek, Latin, and Arabic with very detailed commentaries, including commentaries on the legal formulae, was also recently published by B. Porten *et al.*[121] Dating from the 6th Egyptian Dynasty (ca. 2200–2150 BCE) to 948 CE, this collection clearly displays the continuity of some of the legal formulae through the millennia. A section of the introduction dedicated to the 'Blending of Legal Traditions' briefly analyses the similarities between the Aramaic, Demotic, Coptic and Greek schemata and formulae.[122]

Reinforced by Muffs's monograph on the clause טיב לבבי, a remarkable consensus regarding the Mesopotamian origin of the legal tradition of the Aramaic legal documents from Elephantine has emerged among scholars.[123] In spite of this apparent consensus, however, it would be a serious mistake to suppose that major historical problems regarding the development and spread of the cuneiform legal tradition and its influence on the Aramaic documents from Elephantine had finally been resolved.[124] By concentrating solely on the cuneiform legal traditions, the

119 B. Porten and J. Greenfield, *Jews of Elephantine and Arameans of Syene (Fifth Century BCE), Fifty Aramaic Texts with Hebrew and English Translations* (Jerusalem: Hebrew University, 1974).

120 B. Porten and A. Yardeni, *Textbook of Aramaic Documents from Ancient Egypt*, vol. 1: *Letters* (Jerusalem: Hebrew University, 1986); vol. 2: *Contracts*; vol. 3: *Literature, Accounts and Lists* (Jerusalem: Hebrew University, 1993); vol. 4: *Ostraca and Assorted Inscriptions* (Jerusalem: Hebrew University, 1999).

121 B. Porten *The Elephantine Papyri in English: Three Millennia of Cross-Cultural Continuity and Change* (Leiden: Brill, 1996).

122 Porten, *Elephantine Papyri* 18–22.

123 See Fales, 'La tradition assyrienne'; E. Cussini, 'The Aramaic Law of Sale and the Cuneiform Legal Tradition' (Ph.D. diss. Johns Hopkins University); Levine, 'On the Origins', 46; Gropp, 'Wadi Daliyeh Documents', 826–35; idem, *Wadi Daliyeh II*, 32; E. Lipiński, *The Aramaeans: Their Ancient History, Culture, Religion* (Leuven: Peeters, 2000), 574.

124 See the commentaries by Levine, 'On the Origins', 44.

Assyriological approach to the Aramaic documents has proved itself unable to determine the degree of Egyptian influence. From the Egyptological side, such a study of the Aramaic papyri is lacking. As J. C. Greenfield stated not long ago about the Elephantine texts, 'we are not at all sure as to what may be local in origin and what may come from the Arameo-Assyrian background'.[125]

A crucial methodological issue turns on whether or not one can rightly encompass such a variety of different traditions at work in the formation of Aramaic legal formulary at Elephantine. An understanding of the nature of the process that shaped the legal formulary is as important as the recognition of the deep historical roots of the Aramaic legal formulary within the ancient Near Eastern legal traditions. Although it would be unrealistic to claim that an Egyptological approach can resolve all these questions, such an approach will move the discussion in a direction which will throw new light on the debate.

Table I: Aramaic Legal Documents from Egypt[126]

No.	*TAD*	Editions	Document	Date BCE	Archive	Place[127]
1	B1.1	Bauer-Meissner	Land lease	515	Unknown	Korobis
2	B2.1	Sayce-Cowley A, Cowley 5	Grant of a built wall	471	Mibtahiah	Elephantine (F)
3	B2.2	Sayce-Cowley B, Cowley 6	Withdrawal from land	464	Mibtahiah	Syene[128]
4	B2.3	Sayce-Cowley D, Cowley 8	Bequest of house	459	Mibtahiah	Syene
5	B2.4	Sayce-Cowley C, Cowley 9	Grant of usufruct	460 or 459	Mibtahiah	Syene
6	B2.5	Sachau Plate 35, Cowley 48	Fragment from betrothal contract	Middle of 5th century	Mibtahiah	Elephantine (F)
7	B2.6	Sayce-Cowley G, Cowley 15	Document of wifehood	449	Mibtahiah	Elephantine (F)
8	B2.7	Sayce-Cowley E, Cowley 13	Grant of house	446	Mibtahiah	Elephantine (F)
9	B2.8	Sayce-Cowley F, Cowley 14	Withdrawal from goods	440	Mibtahiah	Syene

125 J. C. Greenfield, 'The Aramaic Legal Texts of the Achaemenian Period', *Transeuphratène* 3 (1990): 87.

126 Based on *TAD*, vol. 2: *Contracts*. Thirty-five fragments from contracts were published by Porten and Yardeni in *TAD* 4, D2: 1–35.

127 The place listed below is the place of production of the document when it is known. When the place of production is not known, we added an (F) for the place where the document was found.

128 Both parties were from Elephantine, but the document was written in Syene by Itu b. Abah.

No.	*TAD*	Editions	Document	Date BCE	Archive	Place
10	B2.9	Sayce-Cowley H, Cowley 20	Withdrawal from goods	420	Mibtahiah	Elephantine (F)
11	B2.10	Sayce-Cowley J, Cowley 25	Withdrawal from house	416	Mibtahiah	Elephantine (F)
12	B2.11	Sayce-Cowley K, Cowley 28	Apportionment of slaves	410	Mibtahiah	Elephantine
13	B3.1	Sachau Plates 28, 29, Cowley 10	Loan of silver	456 (?)	Ananiah	Elephantine
14	B3.2	Kraeling 1 + 18/4	Withdrawal from *hyr*	451	Ananiah	Syene?[129]
15	B3.3	Kraeling 2	Document of wifehood	449	Ananiah	Elephantine
16	B3.4	Kraeling 3	Sale of abandoned property	437	Ananiah	Elephantine
17	B3.5	Kraeling 4	Bequest of apartment to wife	434	Ananiah	Elephantine
18	B3.6	Kraeling 5	Testamentary manumission	427	Ananiah	Elephantine
19	B3.7	Kraeling 6	Life estate of usufruct	420 (?)	Ananiah	Elephantine
20	B3.8	Kraeling 7 + 15 + 18/1, 3, 8, 13, 18, 19, 22, 26, 30	Document of wifehood	420	Ananiah	Elephantine
21	B3.9	Kraeling 8	Adoption	416	Ananiah	Syene
22	B3.10	Kraeling 9	Bequest in contemplation of death	404	Ananiah	Elephantine
23	B3.11	Kraeling 10	Dowry addendum	402	Ananiah	Elephantine
24	B3.12	Kraeling 12	Sale of apartment to son-in-law	402	Ananiah	Elephantine
25	B3.13	Kraeling 11	Loan of grain	402	Ananiah	Syene

129 In the case of *TAD* B3.2, the place of production was not mentioned in the document. Considering the Aramaean character of the name Bunni bar Mannuki, we assume that the document was produced in Syene, the usual place of activity of the Aramaean scribes.

No.	*TAD*	Editions	Document	Date BCE	Archive	Place
26	B4.1	Sachau Plate 38, Cowley 49 + P. Berlin 23104	Fragmentary receipt or cancellation of debt	Beginning 5th century	Unknown	Elephantine
27	B4.2	Sayce-Cowley L, Cowley 11	Loan of silver	Ca. 487	Unknown	Elephantine
28	B4.3	Sachau Plate 27, Cowley 3	Fragmentary obligation to deliver grain	483	Unknown	Elephantine
29	B4.4	Sachau Plate 25, 26 Cowley 2	Idem, second copy	483	Unknown	Elephantine
30	B4.5	Sachau Plate 15, Cowley 29	Fragmentary deed of obligation	407	Unknown	Elephantine
31	B4.6	Sachau Plate 34, Cowley 35 + No. 69 of 96 Frags. 35	Deed of obligation	400	Unknown	Elephantine
32	B4.7	Segal 35	Fragmentary deed of obligation	?	Unknown	Saqqara
33	B5.1	Sachau Plate 30, Cowley 1	Exchange of inherited shares	495	Unknown	Elephantine
34	B5.2	Sachau Plate 58,3, Cowley 65,3	Fragment of document of withdrawal	Last quarter of 5th century	Unknown	Elephantine
35	B5.3	P. Berlin 13607	Fragment from end of conveyance	First half of 5th century	Unknown	Elephantine
36	B5.4	Sachau Plate 35, Cowley 47	Fragment from gift of house contract	Middle of 5th century	Unknown	Elephantine
37	B5.5	Sachau Plate 33, Cowley 43 + Sachau Plate 61,4, Cowley 68,4 + 43	Mutual quitclaim	400[130]	Unknown	Elephantine

130 Porten proposed the date 420–400 BCE, *Elephantine Papyri*, 259. M. Folmer preferred the later date – 400 BCE – based on linguistic analysis. See M. L. Folmer, *The Aramaic Language in the Achaemenid Period: A Study in Linguistic Variation* (Leuven: Peeters, 1995), 780.

No.	*TAD*	Editions	Document	Date BCE	Archive	Place
38	B5.6	Segal 8	Fragmentary conveyances of slaves	4th century	Unknown	Saqqara
39	B6.1	Kraeling 14	Beginning from document of wifehood	446	Unknown	Elephantine
40	B6.2	Sachau Plate 10, Cowley 36	Dowry fragment from document of wifehood	Second half of 5th century	Unknown	Elephantine
41	B6.3	Sachau Plate 31, Cowley 46	End of document of wifehood	Ca. third quarter of 5th century	Unknown	Elephantine
42	B6.4	Sachau Plate 33, Cowley 18 and Nos. 71 + 79 pf 96 Frags.	End of document of wifehood	Last third of 5th century	Unknown	Elephantine
43	B7.1	Sachau Plate 32, Cowley 45	Obligation to take judicial oath	413	Unknown	Elephantine
44	B7.2	Sachau Plate 26, Cowley 7	Obligation to make judicial declaration	401	Unknown	Elephantine
45	B7.3	Sachau Plate 32, Cowley 44	Oath text	Late 5th century	Unknown	Elephantine
46	B7.4	Sachau Plate 39, Cowley 59	Endorsement of oath document	?	Unknown	Elephantine
47	B8.1	Segal 29	Report of court record	After 467/6 or 446/5	Unknown	Saqqara
48	B8.2	Segal 10 + 44	Court record: slaves	Ca. 440	Unknown	Saqqara
49	B8.3	Segal 5	Court record: slaves	Ca. 440 (?)	Unknown	Saqqara
50	B8.4	Segal 28 + 30 + 61	Court record: assault and battery	431	Unknown	Saqqara
51	B8.5	Cowley 69	Court record: rent, imprison-ment, payment	?	Unknown	Saqqara
52	B8.6	Segal 9	Court decision: slaves, reclaiming valuables, assault	?	Unknown	Saqqara

No.	*TAD*	Editions	Document	Date BCE	Archive	Place
53	B8.7	Segal 4	Record of interrogation: slaves	?	Unknown	Saqqara
54	B8.8	Segal 1	Record of interrogation	?	Unknown	Saqqara
55	B8.9	Segal 2	Court record: slave, suit, oath	?	Unknown	Saqqara
56	B8.10	Segal 3 + 16	Court record: document, fields	?	Unknown	Saqqara
57	B8.11	Segal 21	Court record: rent, a blind man	?	Unknown	Saqqara
58	B8.12	Segal 6	Court record	?	Unknown	Saqqara

2.2 *Legal Practices at Elephantine*

The purpose of this section is to introduce the reader into the legal *Sitz im Leben* of our discussion of Aramaic and Egyptian legal terminology, drawing a general picture of the legal life of the colony as it can be inferred from the documents and comparative material.[131]

2.2.1. *Personal Status*

The documents tend to reflect the personal status of one of the parties *vis-à-vis* the other. In letters among equals, the term 'to my brother' is used (אל אחי *TAD* A3.6:1, 5) while someone would address his superior as his 'lord' (מראי) or 'lady' (מראתי) and describe himself as his 'slave' (עבדיך) or 'servant' (*TAD* A4.7:1; A4.2:1, 17; A3.7:1). This is also valid for family relationships where a father is addressed as 'my lord' (מראי) and the sender describes himself as 'his servant' (עבדך).[132]

131 For detailed studies about the social life of the Elephantine community see Porten, *Archives from Elephantine*, 187–301, and G. Vittmann, *Ägypten und die Fremden im ersten vorchristlichen Jahrtausend* (Mainz am Rhein: Philip von Zabern, 2003), 84–119. For a recent treatment of the colony legal practices see B. Porten, 'Elephantine', in *A History of Ancient Near Eastern Law*, R. Westbrook, ed., vol. 2 (Leiden: Brill, 2003), 863–81.

132 See, Porten, *Elephantine Papyri*, B4 n. 2. Cf. Gen. 45.8.

2.2.1.1. *Citizens*

With the exception of the Neo-Assyrian empire, where every person in their controlled territory was considered an Assyrian (*mār Aššūr, aššūrāyu*),[133] the concept of 'citizenship' appears in the ancient Near East closely associated with the social status of 'free person' and 'private owner'. In first-millennium Babylonia *mār banî*, literally 'son of a good person', denoted 'free man' and *mār banûtu* the 'status of a free man'.[134] During the New Kingdom and Third Intermediate period Egyptians used the word *nmḥ* to refer to a 'free person, citizen' having also in some cases the connotation of 'private owner'[135] and the designation *ʿnḫ-n-ni.wt* for 'citizeness',[136] but in legal documents the dominant trend is to identify the parties by their occupation and/or geographical connection. In Elephantine the parties of contracts were identified by their ethnic association (Jewish and/or Aramaean etc.),[137] and detachment (דגל). According to Porten[138] the expression 'citizens of Elephantine' (בעלי יב) is used by the leaders of the Jewish community (Jedaniah and his colleages) to refer to the whole Jewish colony.[139] The semantic field of the word בעל suggests, however, that it might refer only to the leadership, landowners, or heads of families.[140] The expression (city name + בעל) is used in the Bible in that sense (Josh. 24.11; Judg. 9.6; 20.5; 1 Sam. 23.11).

2.2.1.2. *Slaves*

Slavery as a dominant form of production appears very late in ancient societies and perhaps only Ancient Greece and Rome can be considered

133 Radner, 'Neo-Assyrian Period', 892.

134 See Oelsner, Wells, and Wunsch, 'Neo-Babylonian Period', 926. Cf. M. Dandamaev, 'The Neo-Babylonian Citizens', *Klio* 63 (1981), 45–49, idem, 'The Composition of the Citizens in First Millenium Babylonia', *AOF* 24 (1997): 135–47; M. Roth, 'A Case of Contested Status', in *DUMU-E2-DUB-BA-A: Studies in Honor of Åke W. Sjöberg*, ed. H. Behrens *et al.* (Philadelphia: University Museum, 1989), 486–87.

135 *Wb* II, 268.

136 Jasnow, 'Third Intermediate Period', 795–6. Cf. A. Gardiner, 'The Dakhlel Stela', *JEA* 19 (1933): 21; and the Inscription of Maatkare in A. Gardiner, 'The Gods of Thebes as Guarantors of Personal Property', *JEA* 48 (1962): 66; R. Parker, *A Saite Oracle Papyrus from Thebes in the Brooklyn Museum [Papyrus Brooklyn 47.218.3]*. Brown Egyptological Studies 4 (Providence, R.I.: Brown University Press, 1962), 50; B. Menu, 'Women and Business Life in the First Millenium B.C.' in *Women's Earliest Records From Ancient Egypt and Western Asia* ed. B. Lesko (Atlanta, Ga.: Scholars Press, 1989), 197.

137 See the discusssion on the ethnic designation below 2.2.3.3, 'Parties'.

138 See, Porten, 'Elephantine,' 871.

139 See also, Porten, *Elephantine Papyri*, B19.22 n.71.

140 Cf. *DNWSI* I, 184, s.v. *bʿl*, esp. (2), (4) and (5).

lave societies.[141] Slaves, however, have a ubiquitous presence in the ancient Near East. The presence, function, and status of slaves and servants in Ancient Egypt is a continuous object of debate.[142] As A. B. Lloyd states, 'the question of serfdom and slavery in Ancient Egypt has given rise to considerable debate, and some commentators have gone so far as to doubt the very existence of slavery in the Late Period'.[143] The mention of servants/slaves (*b3k*) in official documents and private contracts, however, points to the existence of such an institution.[144] Evidence from the Middle Kingdom attests to West Semites receiving an Egyptian name given by their master in addition to their original Semitic name. During the New Kingdom Asiatic slaves received an Egyptian name and their children received Egyptian names. All the slaves mentioned in the Elephantine documents had Egyptian names, like the brothers Petosiri and Bela, sons of Tabi, slaves of Mibtahiah (*TAD* B2.11) and Ta(p)met (*TAD* B3.6) a handmaiden of Meshullam b. Zaccur later married to Ananiah b. Azariah and manumitted after his death (*TAD* B3.6); with the exception of Jedaniah b. Takhoi (*TAD* B3.9), a houseborn slave born of a Egyptian mother adopted later by Uriah b. Mahseiah.[145]

In his description of a hired labour force in the Aramaean states, E. Lipinski states, 'In the Aramaean mentality, a man's labour is distinct from his person: it is a salable and marketable commodity that can be sold to others without this implying a change in his social condition or personal subjection to an employer.'[146] Similar words have been used to describe the Hebrew servant, 'Ein eigentlicher Sklave is der Hebräer nie; sein Körper (*gufo*) wie man sagte, wird nicht Eigentum des Herrn, sondern nur seine Arbeitskraft, so das er also personliche Recht behalt.'[147] Slavery

141 N. Maezawa, 'Slave Societies in the Greco-Roman Antiquity', in T. Yuge and M. Doir, eds. *Forms of Control and Subordination in Antiquity* (Leiden: Brill, 1988), 16.

142 For a collection of texts see A. M. Bakir, *Slavery in Pharaonic Egypt* (Cairo: Institut Français d'Archéologie Orientale, 1952).

143 A. B. Lloyd, 'The Late Period', in B. G. Trigger, B. J. Kemp, D. O'Connor, and A. B. Lloyd, *Ancient Egypt: A Social History* (Cambridge, London, New York, New Rochelle, Melbourne, and Sydney: Cambridge University Press, 1983), 314.

144 W. C. Hayes, *A Papyrus of the Late Middle Kingdom in the Brooklyn Museum* (New York: Brooklyn Museum, 1955), 92ss.

145 Yaron, *Introduction*, 36–40; Verger, *Ricerche Giuridice*, 141–78; Porten, *Archives from Elephantine*, 203–05.

146 Lipiński, *The Aramaeans*, 552.

147 S. Krauss, *Talmudische Archäologie* (Leipzig: Gustav Fock, 1912), 42, cited by I. H. Weinfeld, *Labor Legislation in the Bible and the Talmud* (New York: Yeshiva University Press, 1974), 18. For a comparative study of slaves in the Hebrew Bible and the ancient Near East see I. Cardellini, *Die biblischen 'Sklaven'-Gesetze im Lichte des keilschriften Sklaven rechts: Ein Beitrag zur Tradition, Überlieferung und Redaktion der alttestamentlichen Rechtstexte* (Bonn: Peter Hanstein, 1981). See also C. Hezser, *Jewish Slavery in Antiquity* (Oxford: Oxford University Press, 2005), 44–68.

was not necessarily a permanent status in Elephantine and, perhaps, serfdom or servanthood would be a better word to describe it.[148] Ta(p)met, the servant mentioned in the document of wifehood *TAD* B3.3:7 when she married Ananiah b. Azariah was probably born free and seems to have become a free person later on (*TAD* B3.5; B3.6).[149] Servants bore a brand in their right hands with the name of their master as stated in *TAD* B2.11:4-5: 'PN, a slave (...) branded on his right hand (with) a brand reading (in) Aramaic like this (belonging) to Mibtahiah.' Contemporary Demotic texts attest to the practice of self-sales (*sẖ bȝk*) where the person sells himself as servant for a limited period.[150] Slaves in Elephantine were considered as any other movable property and, as such, were seizable as security in case of unpaid debts (*TAD* B3.1:10; *TAD* B3.13:11).

2.2.2. *Jewish and Aramaean Scribes at Work*

'Be a scribe!' (*ir sš*) encourages Nebmare-nakht, the 'scribe of the army and commander of the cattle of the house of Amun', to the scribe Wenemdiamun,[151] following with a list of the advantages that come with the profession. According to Ben Sira, the scribe's profession not only increases wisdom but also gives to its bearers the privileges of being sought out for the council of the people, being prominent in the assembly, sitting on the judge's bench, and understanding law and justice (Ben Sira 38.24-34). The office of the 'scribe' was widespread in the ancient Near East, yet the various Near Eastern words we translate as 'scribe' (Egyptian *sš*, Aramaic and Hebrew ספר, etc.) can denote persons involved in quite a number of different activities. In addition to his legal and literary activities, the Egyptian scribe was the essential element in the bureaucratic

148 See I. J. Gelb, 'Definition and Discussion of Slavery and Serfdom', *UF* 11 (1980), 283–98.

149 See Porten, *Archives from Elephantine*, 205; and also R. Westbrook, 'The Female Slave', in *Gender and Law in the Hebrew Bible and the Ancient Near East*, ed. V. Matthews *et al.* (Sheffield: Sheffield Academic Press, 1998), 214–38.

150 Manning, 'Demotic Law', 834; B. Menu, 'Les rapports de dépendance en Egypte à l'époque saïte et perse', *RHDFE* 55 (1977), 396; B. Menu, *Recherches sur l'histoire juridique economique et sociale de l'ancienne Egypte II* (Cairo: Institut Français d'Archéologie Orientale, 1998), 382.

151 P. Lansing 7.7 from the 20th Dynasty. A. Gardiner, *Late-Egyptian Miscellanies* (Brussels: Édition de la Fondation égyptologique Reine Élisabeth, 1937), 106; R. A. Caminos, *Late-Egyptian Miscellanies* (London: Oxford University Press, 1954), 396.

organization of the state as demonstrated by the extensive list of activities associated with the title.[152]

In ancient Israel,[153] scribes are attested as royal officials in pre-exilic times, as is the case with the 'scribe of the king' (סֹפֵר הַמֶּלֶךְ 2 Kgs 12.11); and, also, with the הַסֹּפֵר שַׂר הַצָּבָא הַמַּצְבִּא אֶת־עַם הָאָרֶץ 'scribe as army commander in charge of the conscription' (2 Kgs 25.19).[154] On the other hand, there are examples from Egypt of a 'scribe in command of the army', in P. Anastasi I 6.8 and 13.5, one of his responsibilities being the registering of recruits (12.1). In New Kingdom Egypt, there were also the following scribes' titles attested in the service of the military, *sš sḥw n p3 mšʿ* 'scribe of the assembly of the army', *sš n t3 tj-nt-ḥtry* 'scribe of the chariotry', *sš n p3 s3* 'scribe of the company', *sš dnj n p3 mšʿ* 'scribe of the distribution of the army', *sš nfrw* 'scribe of elite troops', *sš ḫtm* 'scribe of the fort', *sš jwʿyt* 'scribes of the garrison', *sš ssmwt* 'scribe of horses', *sš*

152 See W. Schenkel, 'Schreiber', in *LÄ* V, 698–700. The autobiography of Udjahorresnet presents the case of an Egyptian scribe at the service of Darius. See E. Otto, *Die biographischen Inschriften der ägyptische Spätzeit*, Probleme der Ägyptologie 2 (Leiden: Brill, 1954), 169–73.

153 See D. W. Jamienson-Drake, *Scribes and Schools in Monarchic Judah: A Socio-Archaeological Approach*, The Social World of Biblical Antiquity Series 9, JSOTSS 109 (Sheffield: Sheffield University Press, 1991), 152–54; C. A Rollston, 'Scribal Education in Ancient Israel: The Old Hebrew Epigraphic Evidence', *BASOR* 344 (2006), 47–74; R. Byrne, 'The Refuge of Scribalism in Iron Age I Palestine', *BASOR* 345 (2007), 1–31. For Mesopotamia, see B. Landsberger, 'Scribal Concepts of Education', in *City Invincible*, eds. C. H. Kraeling and R. M. Adams (Chicago: University of Chicago Press, 1960), 94–102; W. Hallo, 'New Viewpoints on Cuneiform Literature', *IEJ* 12 (1962): 13–26; W. Yuhong, 'High-Ranking "Scribes" and Intellectual Governors During the Akkadian and Ur III Periods', *JACiv* 10 (1995): 127–45. K. Radner, *Die Neuassyrischen Privatrechtsurkunden als Quellen für Mensch und Umwelt*, SAAS 6 (Helsinki: Neo-Assyrian Text Corpus Project, 1997), 83–88 = 'Zur sozialen Stellung der Schreiber'. For Ugarit, see W. H. van Soldt, 'Babylonian Lexical, Religious and Literary Texts and Scribal Education at Ugarit and Its Implications for the Alphabetic Literary Texts', in Manfried Dietrich and Oswald Loretz, eds., *Ugarit. Ein ostmediterranes Kulturzentrum im Alten Orient. Ergebnisse und Perspektiven der Forschung. I. Ugarit und seine altorientalische Umwelt*, ALASP 7 (Münster: Ugarit-Verlag, 1995), 171–212; and I. Márquez-Rowe, *The Royal Deeds of Ugarit: A Study of Ancient Near Eastern Diplomatics* (Münster: Ugaritic-Verlag, 2006), 99–138. For Egypt, see R. J. Williams, 'Scribal Training in Ancient Egypt', *JAOS* 92 (1972): 214–21; S. P. Vleeming, 'Some Notes on Demotic Scribal Training in the Ptolemaic Period', in *Proceedings of the 20th International Congress of Papyrology, Copenhagen, 23–29 August, 1992* (Copenhagen: Museum Tusculanum Press, University of Copenhagen, 1994), 185–87; W. J. Tait, 'Some Notes on Demotic Scribal Training in the Ptolemaic Period', in the same volume, 188–92.

154 According to Jer. 52.25, where ספר appears without the definite article, and to the LXX translation of 2 Kgs 25 'τὸν γραμματέα τοῦ ἄρχοντος', it might be possible to emend the text. See C. Schams, *Jewish Scribes in the Second-Temple Period*, JSOTSS 291 (Sheffield: Sheffield Academic Press, 1998), 77; and also T. Mettinger, *Solomonic State Officials: A Study of the Civil Government Officials of the Israelite Monarchy* (Lund: Gleerup, 1971), 20.

mnfꜣt 'scribe of the infantry', *sš ḫnrt n pꜣ mšꜥ* 'scribe of the prison of the army', *sš n jḥw* 'scribe of the stable'.[155]

Twelve other individuals receive the title of סופר 'scribe' in the Hebrew Bible.[156] The presence of scribes as administrative officials is also attested in the Achaemenid administration (Est. 8.9). Ezra is referred to as סֹפֵר מָהִיר בְּתוֹרַת מֹשֶׁה (Ezra 7.6)[157] and סָפַר דָּתָא דִּי־אֱלָהּ שְׁמַיָּא 'scribe of the law of the God of heaven' (Ezra 7.12)[158] besides two other 'scribes' Shimshai (Ezra 4.18, 17, 23) and Zadok (Neh. 13.13). Ezra's title could be associated with his function within the Persian administration, as well as with his leadership position in the Jewish community.[159] Jews and Egyptian scribes were also to be found associated with their respective temples and sacred institutions.[160] The Aramaic papyri from Egypt mention the ספרי מדינתא 'scribes of the province' (*TAD* A6.1:6) = Egyptian *sḫ n tš*,[161] and the ספרי אוצרא 'scribe of the treasury' (*TAD* B4.4:12, 14) = Egyptian *sḫ n pr-ḥḏ*. Unknown individuals are called ספרא in *TAD* C3.8IIIB: 37 and *TAD* C3.19: 32. Ahiqar is called a ספר חכים ומהיר ('wise and skilful scribe' *TAD* C1.1:1, 35). None of the scribes responsible for writing the Aramaic documents, however, receives such a title. The title of scribe was given later to an individual called Hanniah (חניה ספרא) in an account of the third century BCE (*TAD* D8.6:3) and to another named Joseph (יוסף ספרא) in another account also from the third century BCE (*TAD* D8.13:3). The Aramaic documents also mention a 'Scribe of the Book of the God' (*TAD* B8.12:4: פסחמצנוחי = Demotic: *pꜣ sḫ mḏꜣ.t nṯr*).[162]

Aramaean scribes were active as functionaries, as is documented in *TAD* A3.3:5 where a complaint should be addressed to the scribe. Were the Jewish and Aramaean scribes who wrote the Aramaic documents from Elephantine also functionaries of or associated with the Persian administration? Regrettably, there is no evidence of their activities more than the

155 See Schulman, *Military Rank*, 62–65.

156 Seraiah (2 Sam. 8.17), Sheva (2 Sam. 20.25); Elihoreph and Ahijah sons of Shisha (1 Kgs 4.3); Shebna (2 Kgs 18.18, 37; 2 Kgs 19.2); Shaphan, son of Azaliah son of Meshullam, (2 Kgs 22.3, 8, 12 = 2 Chron. 34.15, 18, 20); Shavsha (1 Chron. 18.16); the Levite Shemaiah, son of Nethanel (1 Chron. 24.6); Jonathan (1 Chron. 27.32; Jeiel (2 Chron. 26.11); Elishama (Jer. 36.12, 20–21); Baruch, son of Neriah (Jer. 36.26, 32); Jonathan (Jer. 37.15, 20).

157 ספר מהיר is the equivalent of Egyptian *pꜣ sḫ spd* 'the sharp scribe'. See A. Rainey, 'The Soldier-Scribe in *Papyrus Anastasi* I', *JNES* 24 (1965): 24.

158 Cf. H. H. Schaeder, *Esra der Schreiber* (Tübingen: Mohr, 1930).

159 See Y. Avishur and M. Heltzer, 'The Scribe and Priest Ezra: A Leader under Achaemenian Rule', *Transeuphratène* 29 (2005): 17–36.

160 See J. Quaegebeur, 'Sur la "Loi Sacréen" dans l'Égypte Gréco-Romaine', *AncSoc* 11–12 (1980–81): 236–38.

161 P. Rylands 9 7.1; 16.2; 17.13.

162 K.-Th. Zauzich, 'Ägyptologische Bemerkungen zu den neuen aramäischen Papyri aus Saqqara', *Enchoria* 13 (1985): 116.

documents they wrote, the mention of some of them in lists, and as witnesses of legal transactions. Nathan son of Ananiah signed as witness in *TAD* B2.3:32 and B2.4:20; Mauziah son of Nathan was correspondent in *TAD* A3.5:9; A4.3:12; and A4.10:2, and is mentioned in a list dated in the middle of the fifth century BCE (*TAD* D3.17:1); Haggai son of Shemaiah signed as witness in *TAD* B2.7:19 and is mentioned in the disbursement of barley to the Syenian garrison (*TAD* C3.14:3). Gemariah son of Ahio is mentioned in a letter (*TAD* D7.9:2). However, it is not a coincidence that the scribes Mauziah and Shemaiah, father of the scribe Haggai, were two of the five Jewish communal leaders during the conflict related to the destruction of the temple and the subsequent attempt to rebuild it, a communal position where it is not strange to find scribes.

Despite their expert command of the Aramaic language and legal formulae, the professional status of some of the Elephantine and Syenian scribes has been denied on palaeographic grounds by Joseph Naveh. He classified the cursive Aramaic script of the fifth century BCE as formal-cursive, extreme-cursive, and vulgar-cursive.[163] Assuming a one-to-one correlation between the scribe's script and his professional legal skills, he stated that the formal cursive would be that produced by scribes in government offices, the extreme cursive would be that of an educated person and the vulgar cursive that of the people not accustomed to writing frequently. He characterized the script of the writer of the Arsames letters as formal cursive and the script of the Elephantine documents written by Mauziah son of Nathan, Nathan son of Anani, and of Haggai son of Shemaiah, as semi-formal cursive,[164] all of them being professional scribes according to Naveh.[165] The other scribes who would qualify as professional scribes according to their semi-formal cursive script are Gemariah son of Ahio and Hosea son of Hodaviah (all of them were Jews from Elephantine). The situation is different in Syene, where the only Aramaic scribe with a semi-formal script would be Peṭeese b. Nabunathan (*TAD* B2.8). The rest of the scribes produced their documents either in semi-extreme cursive (Itu b. Abah; Attarshuri b. Nabuzeribni; Nabutukulti b. Nabuzeribni; Raukhshana b. Nergal(u)shezib; Shaweram b. Eshemram) or in extreme cursive (Bunni b. Mannuki).[166]

Naveh has described Bunni as an 'unprofessional scribe', for his 'extreme cursive hand, almost without shading'.[167] Bunni son of

163 J. Naveh, *The Development of Aramaic Script* (Jerusalem: Israel Academy of Sciences and Humanities, 1970), 24.

164 Naveh, *Aramaic Script*, 36.

165 Naveh, *Aramaic Script*, 22; followed by Porten, *Archives from Elephantine*, 192–93 and Folmer, *Aramaic Language*, 31.

166 Naveh, *Aramaic Script*, 31–32, 36.

167 Naveh, *Aramaic Script*, 36. Porten considers the script of Shaweram b. Eshemram also as extreme cursive. Porten, *Archives from Elephantine*, 193.

Mannuki, therefore, was considered a non-professional scribe based solely on palaeographic grounds. The question that arises immediately is: Is it possible to assess the professional office of a scribe based solely on his script? It is necessary to be cautious when relating the development of the script with the social position (professional, semi-professional, unprofessional) of the scribe. The script of Ḥor of Sebennytos, a Demotic scribe of the first half of the second century BCE, has been described as 'atrocious',[168] but his 'professional' character is not in doubt. In Roman Judaea, as suggested by rabbinic texts, scribes were available in village markets.[169] These scribes displayed possibly a different degree of formalization in their script, but they were professionals, that is, they made a living off their skill and legal knowledge. Mediaeval copyists, all of them 'professionals', also displayed various types of scripts. Therefore, a less formal script in the Aramaic legal documents from Elephantine should not be associated with a lack of professionalism of the scribe. The Elephantine scribes, who wrote in 'semi-formal' script, were not necessarily semi-professional. It would not be unusual if the professional script from a scribe of the Persian administration in the centre of the empire would be more 'formal' than the script of a professional scribe in the extreme periphery of the Persian empire. In consequence, while it seems that the script of the Jewish scribes was more formal than the script of the Aramaean scribes, we assume that all of the scribes producing legal documents in Elephantine-Syene were professional scribes who were able to handle the language with precision and style.[170]

When analysing the legal formulary of Aramaic papyri from Egypt, one of the most significant methodological issues is deciding whether all the papyri belong to the same or to different evolving scribal and legal traditions.[171] The fact that the papyri were written in the same language is not determinative when deciding whether they belong to the same or to a different scribal or legal tradition. We face the same problem as the linguist who must determine the extent of the corpus to analyse, based on which he will be able to describe the characteristics of the dialect he is dealing with. Stanislav Segert's grammar, for example, has been criticized

168 J. Ray, 'Literacy in the Late and Persian Periods', in *Literacy and Power in the Ancient World*, eds. A. K. Bowman and G. Woolf (Cambridge: Cambridge University Press, 1994), 62.

169 M. D. Goodman, *State and Society in Roman Galilee, A.D. 132–212* (Totawa, N. J.: Rowman & Allanheld, 1983), 57–59; idem, 'Texts, Scribes and Power in Roman Judaea', in *Literacy and Power in the Ancient World*, 102–03.

170 Cf. B. Porten, 'The Letter of Jedaniah to Bagavahya', in M. Lubetski, Claire Gottlieb, and Sharon Keller, eds., *Boundaries of the Ancient Near Eastern World* (Sheffield: Sheffield Academic Press, 1998), 241.

171 For a definition of 'scribal tradition' and 'legal tradition', see below 2.3.3, 'Levels of Analysis'.

on the grounds that he did not consider the linguistic variation among the different dialects of Aramaic and therefore extrapolated characteristics of one dialect to another.[172] Studies in Aramaic dialectology have shown evidence of morphological and syntactical variations within the Aramaic texts from Egypt.[173] In addition, we have examples of Aramaic documents originating in Samaria, which display variations in their formulary from that of the Aramaic documents from Egypt. It is clear, then, that there were different formulary traditions within the Aramaic documents. We know other cases in the ancient Near East where several scribal traditions were present in the same city, and, even if they belonged to the same legal tradition, their legal formularies included some variations.[174]

The differences in style between two of the Elephantine scribes, Mauziah b. Nathan, and Haggai b. Shemaiah, were noted by Porten.[175] His remarks are very important for showing that documents produced by two contemporary scribes, even working in close proximity, could display substantial variations in style. Table II is based on Porten's remarks.

172 Joüon, 'Notes grammaticales, lexicographiques et philologiques sur les papyrus araméens d'Égypte', *Mélanges de l'Université Saint Joseph* 18 (1934), and Folmer, *Aramaic Language*, are the only linguistic studies that took into account the various scribal traditions attested in the Aramaic documents. The implications of the different origin of the scribes from Elephantine-Syene for the legal formulary, however, did not pass unnoticed in Yaron, *Introduction*, 12–13.

173 The narrative story and the proverbs in the Ahiqar story are written in different dialects as noted in E. Y. Kutscher, 'Aramaic', in T. A. Seebok, ed., *Current Trends in Linguistics*, vol. 6: *Linguistics in South West Asia and North Africa* (The Hague: Mouton, 1970), 347–412. The dialect of the proverbs of Ahiqar has been described as an independent dialect, different from the Imperial Aramaic and dated ca. 750–650 BCE. See I. Kottsieper, *Die Sprache der Ahiqarsprüche*, BZAW 194 (Berlin: De Gruyter, 1990), 181. For Aramaic dialectology see J. Greenfield, 'The Dialects of Early Aramaic', *JNES* 37 (1978): 93–99; H. L. Ginsberg, 'Aramaic Dialect Problems', *AJSL* 50 (1933): 1–9, and 52 (1936): 95–103; E. Y. Kutscher, 'Biblical Aramaic: Eastern Aramaic or Western Aramaic?' in *Proceedings of the First World Congress of Jewish Studies* (Jerusalem: Magnes Press, 1952), 123–27; S. A. Kaufman, *The Akkadian Influence on Aramaic* (Chicago: University of Chicago Press, 1974), 152–60. The Hermopolis Letters also show pecularities in syntax and morphology as against the Elephantine material. For an analysis of the phonological, morphological, and morphosyntactic variations of Imperial Aramaic, see Folmer, *Aramaic Language*, 705–12. Dialect variations were also present among the Greek population of Egypt during Hellenistic times. See W. Clarysse, 'Ethnic Diversity and Dialect among the Greeks of Hellenistic Egypt', in *The Two Faces of Graeco-Roman Egypt: Greek and Demotic and Greek-Demotic Texts and Studies Presented to P. W. Pestman*, P. L. Bat. 30, eds. A. M. F. W. Verhoogt and S. P. Vleeming (Leiden: Brill, 1998), 1–14.

174 Nuzi is one of the best documented cases, see A. H. Friedman, 'Economic Geography and Administration at Nuzi' (Ph.D. diss., Hebrew Union College, Jewish Institute of Religion, Ohio, 1982), ch. 5, 'Notes on Scribal Activity at Nuzi', pp. 199–211.

175 B. Porten, 'The Jews in Egypt', in *The Cambridge History of Judaism*, vol. 1, eds. W. D. Davies and L. Finkelstein (Cambridge: Cambridge University Press, 1984), 396.

Table II: Haggai and Mauziah

Haggai son of Shemaiah	Mauziah son of Nathan
אם 'Moreover'[176]	אפם 'Moreover'[177]
אדרנג 'Guarantor'[178]	Not used when expected.[181]
הנבג 'Partner'[179]	"
הנגית 'Associate'[180]	"
קבל על ... ל 'Complain against ... to.'[182]	Not used when possible.[183]
כסף צריף 'Pure silver'[184]	Never used by Mauziah.
Spelling of foreign names:	Spelling of foreign names:
תפמת[185]	תמת[188]
בגזשת[186]	בגזושת[189]
שתבר[187]	שתיבר[190]
Simple construct or apposition:	Expanded genitive with זי:
אבגרן כסף 'penalty silver'[191]	אבינרנא זי כסף 'penalty of silver'[192]

176 *TAD* B3.4:16, 19 (437 BCE); B3.10:21 (404 BCE); B3.11:14 (402 BCE).

177 *TAD* B2.9:15 (420 BCE); B2.10:16 (416 BCE); B3.5:16 (434 BCE).

178 *TAD* B3.10:18 (404 BCE); B3.11:12 (402 BCE); B3.12:27 (402 BCE); [B4.6:10]. Used also by Shaweram b. Ehemram b. Eshemshezib, *TAD* B3.13:9 twice (402 BCE).

179 *TAD* B3.6:5 (427 BCE); B3.10:18 (404 BCE); B3.11:12 (402 BCE); B3.12:27 (402 BCE). Unknown scribe, *TAD* B5.5:9 (last quarter 5th century BCE).

180 *TAD* B3.6:5 (427 BCE); B3.10:18 (404 BCE); B3.11:12 (402 BCE); B3.12:27 (402 BCE); B5.5:9 (last quarter 5th century BCE).

181 *TAD* B2.9:10-11 (420 BCE); B2.10:9-10 (416 BCE).

182 *TAD* B3.10:19f. (404 BCE); B3.11:12f. (402 BCE); B3.12:28 (402 BCE). Used also by Attarshuri b. Nabuzeribni B2.3:13 (460 or 459 BCE); Nathan b. Ananiah B3.1:12, 18 (456 BCE); Unknown Scribe B5.4:7 (mid-5th century BCE). Bunni b. Mannuki B3.2:5f. (451 BCE).

183 *TAD* B3.5:12ff. (434 BCE); B2.9:10ff. (420 BCE); B2.10:9ff. (416 BCE).

184 *TAD* B3.6:9 (427 BCE); B3.10:20 (404 BCE); B3.11:11 (402 BCE); B3.12:30 (402 BCE). Used also by Pelatiah b. Ahio *TAD* B2.1:7, 28 (471 BCE); and by Shaweram b. Eshemram b. Eshemshezib B3.13:6 (402 BCE).

185 *TAD* B3.6:2, 11, 18; B3.12:1, 3, 11, 24, 35 (427 BCE).

186 *TAD* B3.4:2, 10, 23, 25 (437 BCE); B3.12:4, 12, 31 (402 BCE).

187 *TAD* B3.4:2, 8 (437 BCE).

188 *TAD* B3.5:2, 6 (434 BCE).

189 *TAD* B3.5:3 (434 BCE).

190 *TAD* B3.5:11 (434 BCE).

191 B3.6:8, 14 (427 BCE) by Haggai b. Shemaiah; B3.7:17 (420 BCE) by Unknown Scribe; B3.9:7 (last quarter of 5th century BCE) by Unknown Scribe; B3.10:20 (402 BCE) by Haggai b. Shemaiah; B3.11:10, 14 (402 BCE) by Haggai b. Shemaiah; B3.12:30 (402 BCE) by Haggai b. Shemaiah or כסף אבינרן 'silver penalty' *TAD* B3.13:6 (402 BCE) by Shaweram b. Eshemram b. Eshemshezib.

192 *TAD* B2.9:14f. (420 BCE); B2.10:15 (416 BCE); B3.8:31 (420 BCE); also 'cash of silver' תכונה זי כסף *TAD* B3.8:5f. (420 BCE) instead of 'silver cash' כסף תכונה *TAD* B2.6:6 (458 or 445 BCE) by his father Nathan b. Ananiah.

Haggai son of Shemaiah	Mauziah son of Nathan
מן יומא זנה ועד עלמן 'From this day and forever'[193]	מן יומא זנה עד עלם 'From this day forever'[194]

Although it would be no surprise to find variations in style between two different scribes, it is more surprising to find variations in the expression of the same clause by the same scribe in different documents. Porten also points out that[195] Haggai son of Shemaiah wrote the clause for introducing the boundaries of the property in five different ways, and a similar inconsistency is shown by Mauziah son of Nathan, who wrote the same clause in three different ways. The variations in their use of this clause are displayed in Table III.

Table III: Boundaries

Mauziah b. Nathan	Haggai b. Shemaiah
אף הא אלה תחומי ביתא זך Moreover, behold these are the boundaries of that house.[196] (B2.7.13 446 BCE)	והא אלה תחמי ביתא זך And behold these are the boundaries of that house. (B3.4.7 437 BCE)
והא זנה תחומי ביתא זך And behold this [*sic*] are the boundaries of that house. (B3.5.8 434 BCE)	והא תחומי ביתא And behold the boundaries of the house. (B3.10.8 404 BCE)
הא תחומוהי Behold its boundaries. (B2.10 416 BCE)	ודנה תחומוהי And this [*sic!*] are its boundaries. (B3.11.3 402 BCE)

193 'From this day and forevers' [*sic*] *TAD* B3.4:11 (437 BCE) and B3.12:23 (402 BCE) by Haggai b. Shemaiah. Haggai has once a dittography and no conjunction in B3.11:8 (402 BCE) מן יומא זנה זנה עד עלם 'from this this [*sic!*] day forever'.

194 'From this day forever', *TAD* B2.9:10 (420 BCE); B3.5:5 (434 BCE); B3.8:4 (420 BCE); B6.1:4 (446 BCE) rather than מן יומא זנה ועד עלם 'from this day and forever', *TAD* B2.3:9 (460 or 459 BCE) by Attarshuri b. Nabuzeribni; B2.8:7 (440 BCE) by Peteesi b. Nabunathan; B2.6:4 (458 or 445) by his father Nathan b. Ananiah; B2.11:7 (410 BCE) by Nabutukulti b. Nabuzeribni; B5.5:4 [8] (last quarter of 5th century BCE) by Unknown Scribe; B3.3:4 (449 BCE) by his father Nathan b. Ananiah.

195 Porten, 'The Jews in Egypt', 396–97.

196 Cf. the same expression by Itu b. Abah: אף הא אלה תחומי ארקא זך *TAD* B2.2:7 (464 BCE).

Mauziah b. Nathan	Haggai b. Shemaiah
	והא זנה תחומי ביתא And behold this [*sic!*] are the boundaries of the house. (B3.12.8-9 402 BCE)
	זנה תחומוהי ביתא This [*sic!*] are its boundaries (of) the house. (B3.12.16-17 402 BCE)

These variations present in the formulae of the same scribe make it difficult to decide how much consistency we can expect from the rest of the scribal traditions. This situation undermines the conclusion of M. L. Folmer that the considerable variation between the spelling of Nathan son of Ananiah and his son Mauziah son of Nathan indicates that the latter did not receive his scribal education from his father.[197] However, this situation can at the same time jeopardize the whole model of scribal traditions if no consistencies at all are to be found. It is however expected that the scribes exercised more flexibility in non-constitutive matters and kept a more rigid standard in constitutive matters, where legal formulae were used. We will see, however, that certain particular features do emerge as scribal characteristic use of legal formulae. Furthermore, a division between Elephantine and Syenian scribes is supported by linguistic features present only in the documents by scribes with Akkadian-Aramaic patronymics.[198]

The study of the patronymics of the scribes shows that the majority of scribes with Hebrew-Aramaic patronymics were active in Elephantine and that the majority of scribes with Aramaic or Akkadian patronymics were active in Syene. The consequences of the various origins of the scribes' patronymics for the legal formulary were noticed early by Yaron, who stated that:

> The nationality of the scribes is of obvious importance, since it was their task to supply the proper formulas for the documents, to find the proper legal expression for the wishes of the parties. In doing so, a scribe would naturally draw on his own legal system, with which he was familiar. [199]

Yaron's statement supports the assumption that the Aramaic documents written in Egypt did not belong to one and only one legal and/or scribal

197 Folmer, *Aramaic Language*, 715.

198 See Folmer, *Aramaic Language*, 718–22.

199 Yaron, *Introduction*, 12–13.

tradition. However, because of the characteristics of the Jewish colony of Elephantine (geographical confinement and high degree of socio-economic interaction), it is possible at least to assume a common legal tradition for the Jewish group with regard to the Elephantine documents, although the particular scribal tradition to which the documents belong needs to be proven in each case. Several scribal traditions can coexist inside a common legal tradition and, in such a case, variations in the legal formulary do not imply a variation in the law to which the documents refer.[200] Moreover, in Elephantine-Syene we are not dealing with the original legal and formulary tradition of each of the ethnic groups which are represented in the documents, but with the resultant legal and formulary status quo achieved through decades of adaptation and assimilation to the new context.

This legal and formulary common ground would have permitted the various types of economic and social interchanges among the members of the different groups. Persians, Bactrians, Caspians, Khwarezmians, Babylonians, Egyptians,[201] and other ethnic groups are represented in the legal documents, and since all these groups were participating in the same kind of socio-military organization, it is likely that documents drawn up by these groups would not display great differences regarding legal practices and formulae.

2.2.3. *The Framework of the Documents*

The Aramaic legal documents from Elephantine are regularly composed according to a general objective framework (Date, Parties, Scribe, Witnesses, Endorsement) into which the operative section is inserted.[202] The documents are drawn up in the first person by the party undertaking obligations without any dialogue reflecting the offer and acceptance of the terms described in the contract. Instead, there is usually a certificate of performance and a declaration of satisfaction with the quality of the performance. The operative section is characterized by its subjective and personal quality; it constitutes the core of the legal function of the document, describing the legal changes that have taken place. For every type of transaction, there is a corresponding set of legal formulae constituting the operative section. In this chapter, we deal with the framework of the documents, while the operative section of documents including Withdrawal Clauses, will be dealt with separately in Chapter 3.

R. Yaron arranged the schemata of the Aramaic documents in two

200 There are several well-attested scribal schools at Nuzi belonging to a common legal context. For an examination of the relevant Nuzi material see Friedman, 'Economic Geography'.

201 See the references above at footnotes 7–13.

202 Cf. Yaron, 'Schema'; Porten, *Elephantine Papyri*, 74.

groups according to differences in their formulation of the date, place, parties, and scribe-witnesses sequence.[203] According to this division, group A comprises *TAD* B1.1; B5.1; B4.4; B4.3 and B4.2. Group B would comprise the rest of the documents.[204] No attempts have been made to re-classify the schemata of the Aramaic legal documents on the basis of different criteria.[205] The variations in the formulary could be explained by the evolution of a unique formulary over time, as proposed by Yaron, or by the existence of different and parallel scribal traditions, as suggested by E. Newman-Pochne.[206] Considering the plurality of scribal traditions present in Egypt and the Near East, it is risky to propose *a priori* a unique formulary tradition for the Egyptian Aramaic documents. Most likely, as the study of other Near Eastern cases has shown, there were several scribal and formulaic traditions in the Aramaic-speaking community in Egypt; however, this approach does not disregard the possibility of some kind of common diachronic evolution of the Aramaic legal formulary. In the following discussion, we analyse the schemata of the documents based mostly on the scribal-traditions model.

We will have, therefore, not only one legal formulary in force in Elephantine but several competing scribal traditions producing slightly different legal formularies. Although we can assume the conservative character of each of these scribal traditions, the passing of the legal formulary from father (or teacher) to son (or student)[207] was not unaffected by updates or stylistic variations, and the study of the Aramaic legal documents from Egypt demonstrates that their formulaic tradition was neither rigid nor uniform. We now proceed to analyse the framework of the documents.

2.2.3.1. *Date*

All the Aramaic legal documents from Egypt begin with the date, following standard Egyptian practice.[208] The oldest documents, which belong to the period of Darius I (522–486 BCE) and the beginning of the

203 Yaron, 'Schema', 33; and idem, *Introduction*, 7–8.

204 Yaron, 'Schema', 33.

205 See also the remarks by Porten to Yaron's classification, *Archives from Elephantine*, 196–99.

206 I had the opportunity to discuss with Dr Newman-Pochne his approach to the development of the legal formulary of the Elephantine documents during the academic year 1992–93. See also E. Newman-Pochne. ביב - דמותם וכתבם של שלושה סופרים יהודיים מן המה ה־5 לפנה'ס', הסופרים (MA thesis, Hebrew University of Jerusalem, 1989).

207 In the case of Nuzi, G. Wilhelm has proposed that the scribal patronymic should be better understood as a sign of teacher–student relationship rather than a father–son relationship. G. Wilhelm, *Untersuchungen zum Ḫurro Akkadischen von Nuzi*, AOAT 9 (Kevelaer, Neukirchen-Vluyn: Butzon &. Bercker, 1970), 9.

208 The letters, on the other hand, when dated, were dated at the end, *TAD* A3.8; A3.9; A4.7; A4.8.

reign of Xerxes (486–465 BCE), have only Egyptian dates.[209] It seems that after Cambyses marched into Egypt, in about 527–525 BCE,[210] it took some years for the Babylonian calendar, used by the Persians, to be imposed upon the Jewish colony of Elephantine, probably by the end of Darius' reign. *TAD* B3.3-4 (483 BCE) still has only an Egyptian date. The Persian defeat at Marathon in 490 BCE and the subsequent rebellion in Egypt in 486 BCE (Herodotus VII.1, 3) certainly had their effect, and perhaps the Persian domination was seen at the beginning of the fifth century BCE as something that was not going to last for long.[211] The first document double-dated with both Babylonian[212] and Egyptian dating in Elephantine-Syene is *TAD* B2.1 (Year 15 of Xerxes = 471 BCE), written by Pelatiah b. Ahio. From this date until 431 BCE, all of our documents are double-dated with the inclusion of the Babylonian date. It is possible, as Kraeling suggests, that at some point during the Persian domination the scribes from Elephantine-Syene, now in the service of the Persian empire, were required to give the date according to both the Egyptian and the Babylonian calendars.[213] This measure would not necessarily have been taken at the very beginning of the Persian period. It must have taken a certain amount of time to introduce Persian reforms in the Egyptian practices.

The next document that has reached us with only the Egyptian date is *TAD* B8.4 (431 BCE). At the last third of the fifth century BCE, the tendency was to return to the use of an exclusively Egyptian date,[214] possibly a consequence of the progressive integration of the Persian officials into Egyptian life.[215] Exceptions to this tendency are *TAD* B2.11 (410 BCE), written by Nabutukulti b. Nabuzeribni; *TAD* B3.10 (404 BCE); and B3.11 (402 BCE), written by Haggai b. Shemaiah. This last mentioned scribe, Haggai b. Shemaiah, is a good example for the shift back to the practice of dating the documents exclusively with Egyptian dates. He wrote *TAD* B3.10 (404 BCE) and B3.11 (March 402 BCE) with

209 *TAD* B1.1, 515 BCE; B5.1, 495 BCE; D2.1, 484 BCE; D2.1, 484 BCE; B4.3, 483 BCE; B4.4, 483 BCE; and D2.2, 483 BCE.

210 See Depuydt, 'Egyptian', 179–90; E. Cruz-Uribe, 'The Invasion of Egypt by Cambyses', *Transeuphratène* 25 (2003): 9–60.

211 See Kienitz, *Die politische Geschichte*, 67–75, and J. D. Ray, 'Egypt 525–402 B.C.', *CAH*, vol. 4, 264.

212 For the calendar used in Elephantine see R. A. Parker, 'Some Considerations on the Nature of the Fifth-Century Jewish Calendar at Elephantine', *JNES* 14 (1955): 271–74, and B. Porten, 'The Calendar of the Aramaic Texts from Achaemenid and Ptolemaic Egypt', *Irano-Judaica* 2, eds. S. Shaked and A. Netzer (1990): 13–32.

213 Kraeling, *Brooklyn*, 51.

214 *TAD* D2.11; B4.5, 407 BCE; D2.12, 403 BCE; B3.12, 402 BCE; B5.5, 420–400 BCE; B3.13, 402 BCE; B7.2, 401 BCE; and B4.6, 400 BCE.

215 N. Grimal, *A History of Ancient Egypt* (Oxford; Cambridge, Mass.: Blackwell, 1992), 371.

both Egyptian and Babylonian dates and B3.12 (December 402 BCE) and B4.6 (400 BCE) with Egyptian dates only. The latter examples from the documents of Haggai b. Shemaiah imply that the shift in the dating practices is not to be attributed to differences among the different scribal traditions but to other factors, which include changes in the political situation in Egypt.[216]

That the changes in the dating practices are not dependent on the Elephantine-Syene scribes' preferences is also suggested by the fact that a coherent picture of the dating practices attested in Elephantine-Syene arises from documents originating elsewhere in Egypt. The Memphite shipyard journal *TAD* C3.8 (473–471 BCE)[217] includes Babylonian and Egyptian dates (in that order);[218] the fragment of disbursement of wine *TAD* C3.12:29 (420 or 411 BCE)[219] includes Egyptian and Babylonian date (in that order).[220] The disbursement of barley to the Syenian garrison *TAD* C3.14 (401–400 BCE) is double-dated with the Babylonian and Egyptian calendar (in that order). Papyri with only Egyptian dates reappear after 413 BCE. These are the fragmentary account of silver from Saqqara *TAD* C3.11 (ca. 416 BCE), which is dated according to the Egyptian calendar (by year only); the fragmentary record of memoranda *TAD* C3.13 (417–411 BCE), which is dated according to the Egyptian calendar only;[221] and the collection account for YHW, *TAD* C3.15 (400 BCE), which is dated according to the Egyptian calendar (day, month, and year). The fragmentary account of grain *TAD* C3.16 (ca. 400 BCE) is dated by year only (possibly the Egyptian date exclusively).

The evidence of the dating practices attested in the Aramaic documents from Egypt shows that they were dated following the Egyptian calendar before the Persian conquest. This is also true for the Aramaic letters from this period.[222] For most of the Persian period (second half of the reign of

216 Amyrtaeus II initiated a new period of Egyptian independence in 404 BCE, which would last until 343 BCE.

217 Dated on the basis of chronological synchronism Years 13–15 of Xerxes. Porten-Yardeni, *TAD* 3, 73.

218 Lines I.1; I.7; I.9; I.12; II.3; IIIA.1; IIIB.8; IIIB.15; IIIB.23; IIIB.29; IV.4. Discordant with this is the customs account of import and export duties *TAD* C3.7 (475 BCE), dated on the basis of calendrical, historical and palaeographical considerations (Porten-Yardeni, *TAD* 3, Excursus 3, xx-xxi), which is dated following the Egyptian calendar only, by month and year, and subsequently by day and month.

219 Dated, also according to chronological synchronism Porten-Yardeni, *TAD* 3, 73.

220 This is, however, due to the fact that the Babylonian date is New Year's.

221 Lines I. 12, year x of Darius.

222 The four letters with exclusively Egyptian dates also follow the same pattern. They are dated either at the very beginning of the Persian period (*TAD* A3.3 ca. 475 BCE), at the end of it (*TAD* A3.8 and A4.2 dated palaeographically in Naveh, *Aramaic Script*, 33 and 36, to the last quarter of the fifth century, and the late fifth century BCE respectively), or at the very beginning of the 29th Dynasty (*TAD* A3.9, 399 BCE). See Porten, 'Calendar', 16–17.

Xerxes, the reign of Artaxerxes I and the first half of Darius II) however, the tendency of including both dates predominates.[223] Yet, with the death of Darius II in 404 BCE, the Egyptian rebellion that followed, and the recovery of independence by the Egyptian 28th Dynasty with Amyrtaeus of Sais, the tendency reverses, and the inclusion of the Babylonian date begins to disappear.[224]

As for the sequence, almost all of the Aramaic documents produced in Egypt express the date in the order as day–month–year,[225] which is in harmony with the Samaria papyri,[226] the Aramaic ostraca from Beer-Sheba and Idumea,[227] the Neo-Babylonian tradition,[228] and the post-exilic biblical usage.[229] In this aspect, there is no noticeable Egyptian influence on the Aramaic documents from Egypt.

The dating of the Aramaic documents is fairly consistent and the evidence available does not show any difference among the practices of the various scribes. As stated above, the determining factor in the variations of the dating practices of the Aramaic papyri from Egypt

223 Porten, 'Calendar', 16.

224 The first Aramaic document dated in the reign of Amyrtaeus is *TAD* B4.6 (year 5). For the chronology of the 28th Dynasty see Kienitz, *Die politische Geschichte*, 166–67, and A. B. Lloyd, 'Egypt, 404–332 B.C.', *CAH*, vol. 4, 337–40.

225 The only exception is *TAD* B1.1 (P. Bauer-Meisner from Korobis), which uses the sequence year–month–day following the traditional Egyptian way of expressing the date in legal documents. See for example, *P. Berlin* 9784 and 9785 (Thebes, fourteenth century BCE). This situation will change in the Demotic documents by no longer noting the day and reducing the date to the sequence year–month. The mention of the day in the dating practices of the Demotic scribes will appear again after 186 BCE. See P. W. Pestman, J. Quagebeur, and R. L. Vos, *Recueil de textes démotiques et bilingues* (Leiden: Brill, 1977), vol. 2, pp. 12–13 n. b.

226 Gropp, *Wadi Daliyeh II*, 5.

227 J. Naveh, 'The Aramaic Ostraca', in *Beer-Sheba* I, Y. Aharoni ed. (Tel Aviv: Tel Aviv University, 1973), 79–82; Gropp, 'Samaria Papyri', 5. See also A. Lemaire, 'Les Formules de Datation en Palestine au premier Millénaire avant J.-C.', in *Proche-Orient Ancien Temps Vécu, Temps Pensé*, ed. F. Beiquel-Chatonet and H. Lozachmeur (Paris: Jean Maisonneuve, 1998), 53–82.

228 Cf. H. Petschow, *Die neubabylonischen Kaufformulare* (Leipzig: T. Weicher, 1939), 44. The earlier Mesopotamian tradition, on the other hand, expresses the date in the sequence month–day–year.

229 Yaron, 'Schema', 61. Zech. 1.7; 7.1; Est. 2.16; 3.7; Hag. 1.15; 2.10. This is not, however, completely consistent; Est. 8.9 and 9.2 uses month–day and Hag. 1.1 follows the old sequence year–day–month. The standard form for pre-exilic events in Kings is to mention only the year and the king (for example, 1 Kgs 15.9, 25, 28; 22.41 and *passim*). At the end of the book, beginning with the attack of Nebuchadnezzar on Jerusalem, the sequence is year–day–month (2 Kgs 25.1) when referring to Zedekiah king of Judah, but day–month–year when referring to the king Nebuchadnezzar (2 Kgs 25.8), and then, again, year–day–month when relating the release of Jehoiachim (2 Kgs 25.27). The book of Ezekiel uses mostly the sequence year–month–day.

should be understood in terms of the changes in the political situation of the country.

2.2.3.2. *Place of Execution*

Some of the scribes included the place of execution of the document, either at the beginning of the document after the date (*TAD* B3.9; D2.9; B5.5; B2.10; B3.8; B3.7; and B2.9), at the end of the document following the name of the scribe (*TAD* B2.8; B2.4; B2.3; B2.2; B1.1; B3.11; B3.10 and B3.12), or in both places (*TAD* B3.12; B7.1; B2.11). Looking first at the evidence from Syene arranged according to the scribal tradition (Table IV), all of the scribes included the place of execution of the document.

Table IV: Syene: Mention of the Place of Production of the Document

Date BCE	Abah's Tradition	Nabuzeribni's Tradition	Nabunathan's Tradition	Nergarl(u)shezib's Tradition	Eshemshezib's Tradition
464	B2.2 B				
460/459		B2.3 B			
460/459		B2.4 B			
451					
440			B2.8 B		
416				B3.9 T	
410		B2.11 (Elephantine) T + B			
402					B3.13 T + B

For the better part of the fifth century, the tendency in Syene was to write the place at the bottom (**B**) after the name of the scribe (*TAD* B2.2, 464 BCE; B2.3 and B2.4, 460–459 BCE; B2.8, 440 BCE). During the last quarter of the fifth century, we have the first document with the place of execution at the top (**T**) (*TAD* B3.9, 416 BCE) and documents with the mention of the place both at the top and the bottom (*TAD* B2.11, 410 BCE; B3.13, 402 BCE and here belongs also B7.1, 413 BCE).[230] The fragment of the beginning of a contract *TAD* D2.9 (last quarter of the fifth century BCE), drawn up in Syene, includes the place at the top, but the rest of the text is missing. The shift among the Syenian scribes between the two trends of writing the place of execution is shown in the Nabuzeribni tradition by Nabutukulti in *TAD* B2.11 who, drawing up the document in Elephantine, introduces the double mention of place in his scribal tradition.

The situation at the beginning of the fifth century in the scribal practices from Elephantine is different. Consider Table V.

230 See Folmer, *Aramaic Language*, 773–75.

Table V: Elephantine: Mention of the Place of Production of the Document

Date BCE	Ahio's Tradition	Hodaviah's Tradition	Ananiah's Tradition	Shemaiah's Tradition	Unidentified
Beginning of 5th cent.					B4.1[231]
495					B5.1
488/87	B4.2				
483		B4.3			
483		B4.4			
471	B2.1				
459 or 449			B2.5		
456			B3.1		
First Half of 5th cent.					B5.3[232]
449			B3.3		
Mid 5th cent.			B2.5		
Mid 5th cent.			B5.4		
Mid 5th cent.			D2.22		
Second half of 5th cent.					B6.2[233]
Late 5th century			D2.25		
446			B6.1		
446			B2.7		
Third quarter of 5th cent.					B6.3[234]
437				B3.4	
434			B3.5		
Last third 5th cent.			B6.4		
427				B3.6 **B**	
420			B2.9 **T**		B3.7 **T**[235]
420			B3.8 **T**		
Last quarter 5th cent.					B5.2 **T**[236]
416			B2.10 **T**		
413			B7.1		
407					B4.5 **T**[237]
404				B3.10 **B**	
402				B3.11 **B**	
402				B3.12 **B**	
400				B4.6	
400					B5.5 **T**

[shaded] Documents with place of execution:
T = at the top; **B** = at the bottom.

None of the documents written before 427 BCE includes the place of execution. The first document with the place of execution is written by Haggai b. Shemaiah in 427 BCE, who altered his previous practice of not

231 Fragmentary receipt of cancellation of debt, bottom missing.
232 Fragment from end of conveyance, beginning missing.
233 Dowry fragment from a document of wifehood, beginning and bottom missing.
234 End of document of wifehood, beginning missing.
235 Bottom missing.
236 Fragment from document of withdrawal, place restored, bottom missing.
237 Fragmentary deed of obligation, bottom missing.

writing the place of execution in his documents. It is interesting that Haggai b. Shemaiah is mentioned in the disbursement of barley to the *Syenian* garrison in an account dated 401–400 BCE (*TAD* C3.14:3). Was the change in his formulary a consequence of a change of garrison? Mauziah b. Nathan followed in the same direction, and all of the documents that both scribes produced afterwards include the place of execution. Haggai b. Shemaiah wrote the date at the bottom and Mauziah b. Nathan at the top. In the Samaria sales of slaves, the date and place of execution always come together either at the top of the documents (Samaria Papyri 1, 4, 5, and 6), or at the bottom (Samaria Papyri 2, 3, 7, 8, and 9). The tendency to including the place of execution in the legal document seems to be an Aramaic influence on the Jewish scribes of Elephantine.

2.2.3.3. *Parties*

The third component of the Aramaic legal documents is the mention of the parties involved in the transaction. The mention of the parties can be schematized as follows:[238]

a. Including only the names and patronymics of the parties. As opposed to the Egyptian documents, which include the matronymic in the name of the parties,[239] the Aramaic documents include only the name of the father.[240]
b. Including the name and patronymic of the parties and a description (occupational). These are the cases of Esḥor son of Djeḥo, builder of the king (*TAD* B2.6), Peu son of Paḥi, builder of Syene (*TAD* B2.8), and Ananiah son of Azariah, servitor of YHW (*TAD* B3.3; B3.5; B3.7; B3.10; and B3.12).
c. Including the name and patronymic of the parties, a description (ethnic-administrative), and the detachment to which the person belongs. This is the most common way of designating a person in the Aramaic documents.

A problem arises when the same person is described as an Aramaean in one document and as a Jew in another. Consider the evidence in Table VI.

238 See Yaron, 'Schema', 37–39; idem, *Introduction*, 9–10.
239 But not in the witnesses list, where they include only the patronymic.
240 With the exception of *TAD* B2.9-10.

Table VI: Ethnic Designation
Mahseiah b. Jedaniah

TAD	Name	Ethnic	Place of origin	Degel	Date BCE
B2.1	Mahseiah	Aramaean	Syene	Varyazata	12 Sept. 471
B2.2	Mahseiah	Jew	Fortress of Elephantine	Varyazata	2 Jan. 464
B2.3	Mahseiah	Jew	Elephantine the Fortress	Haumadata	1 Dec. 459
B2.4	Mahseiah	Jew	Elephantine	Haumadata	1 Dec. 459
B2.6	Mahseiah	Aramaean	Syene	Varyazata	14 Oct. 449
B2.7	Mahseiah	Aramaean	Syene	Varyazata	17 Nov. 446

Meshullam b. Zaccur

TAD	Name	Ethnic	Place of origin	Degel	Date BCE
B3.1	Meshullam	Jew	Elephantine the Fortress	–	13 Dec. 456
B3.3	Meshullam	Aramaean	Syene	Varyazata	9 Aug. 449
B2.7	Meshullam	Aramaean	Syene	–	17 Nov. 446
B3.6	Meshullam	Jew	Elephantine the Fortress	Iddinnabu	12 Jun. 427

Ananiah b. Haggai

TAD	Name	Ethnic	Place of origin	Degel	Date BCE
B3.8	Ananiah	Aramaean	Elephantine the Fortress	Iddinnabu	2 Oct. 420
B3.13	Ananiah	Jew	–	Nabukudurri	2–31 Dec. 402
B3.12	Ananiah	Aramaean	Elephantine the Fortress	Nabukudurri	13 Dec. 402

In 1923, A. Cowley provided what has become the accepted solution for the apparent contradiction. Commenting on *TAD* B2.1 he stated that, 'the terms seem to be used indiscriminately, but it is noticeable that, although we have six instances of Jews of Yeb we never find Jews of Syene, and though there are ten cases of Arameans of Syene, there are only three of Arameans of Elephantine'.[241] 'This can hardly be accidental and points to Elephantine as the specially Jewish settlement.'[242]

This view was challenged by E. Volterra. In his review of Kraeling's edition of the Brooklyn papyri and in later more detailed articles,[243] Volterra considered the Aramaeans and Jews as two distinctive groups. Whenever a person is described as 'Jew' in one document, but as

241 Referring only to the corpus translated by him.

242 Cowley, *Aramaic Papyri*, 12.

243 E. Volterra, 'Review of E. Kraeling, *The Brooklyn Museum Aramaic Papyri*', *Iura* 6 (1955): 349–60. Idem, 'Le affrancazioni di schiavi', 675 ff.; idem, 'YHDW', 131–73.

'Aramaean' in another, he questioned his identity, suggesting that the case may be one of homonymity. The persons referred to as Aramaeans would be different from the ones called Jews, even if the names are identical. This separation would find expression in their respective religious beliefs and practices. These articles spurred a controversy with R. Yaron,[244] who rejected most of Volterra's arguments and defended the traditional view. Yaron included a very important factor regarding the ethnic qualifications in his argument, its relational character. We can cite him *in extenso*:

> Why are the same persons sometimes described as 'Arameans', sometimes as 'Jews'? No satisfactory answer has so far been given, nor do I have one that will explain all cases. However, it ought to be noted that the description 'Jew' tends to occur especially in documents in which some non-Jewish factor is involved. Amongst themselves they are 'Arameans', but when they come into contact with outsiders, they tend to describe themselves as 'Jews' (or are so described by others). (...) However, this is no hard and fast rule, rather merely a tendency. There are no apparent 'foreign' factors in C. 10 and K. 5. On the other hand, we find 'Arameans' in C. 7, 14, and 15 in spite of non-Jewish factor present; note further C. 28 and K. 8, written by non-Jewish scribes.
>
> Contrary to Volterra's hypothesis, it is reconfirmed that the description 'Aramean' and 'Jew' are not mutually exclusive. Nor indeed are they equivalents. The one is generic, the other specific. In other words, – in view of his provenience, even if already some generations remote, from Judaea (or some part of the Syrian sphere), every Jew can be described as Aramean, but not every Aramean is in turn a Jew.[245]

J. Johnson has suggested that the ethnic term served the administrative function of identifying one's position in the Elephantine bureaucracy, and that these terms seem to reflect an organizational scheme imposed with the purpose of providing an administrative structure.[246] This proposal opens a new direction for understanding the Jew–Aramaean 'ethnic' problem. We would expect that in documents not related to any administrative matter they would refer to themselves as Jews. That is the case in the private letters among Jews, as mentioned above. The letter in which they refer to themselves as 'Syenians who are hereditary property holders in Elephantine the Fortress' (*TAD* A4.10) is an offer of payment for the reconstruction of the temple, i.e. it has some administrative aspect to it.

244 Yaron, 'Identities', 344–54; idem, 'Who is Who in Elephantine?', *Iura* 15 (1964): 167–72, and the response in Volterra, 'Osservazioni sul divorzio', 173–80.

245 Yaron, 'Who is Who', 172.

246 J. Johnson, 'Ethnic Considerations in Persian Period Egypt', in E. Teeter and J. Larson, eds., *Gold of Praise: Studies on Ancient Egypt in Honor of Edward F. Wente* (Chicago: University of Chicago Press, 1999), 218.

Following this reasoning, ‘Aramaean’ would be an ethnic-administrative term used by the Persian administration while ‘Jew’ would be an ethnic-communitarian term. Administratively speaking, all Jews were Aramaeans. The administrative character of this identification is apparent when we relate the ethnic administrative qualification of Aramaeans to the mention of their membership in a certain detachment. None of the people described by their occupation is additionally described as a member of any of the detachments. The case of Miptahiah as a Jewess of Elephantine (and) an Aramaean according to her detachment (*TAD* B5.5:1-2) can be better explained considering ‘Aramaean’ as an ethnic-administrative designation and ‘Jew’ as an ethnic-communal designation.[247] Later on, the ‘Satrapenstele’ (311 BCE) seems to use the term *Irm3w*  to refer to the land of Judah.[248]

2.2.3.4. *Scribe and Witnesses*

Including the name of the scribe was a common feature of ancient Near Eastern legal documents. Among the Aramaic documents, the Samaria papyri constitute an exception to this trend by not including the name of the scribe as such in their schema.[249] The general practice in the Aramaic documents from Egypt is to state the name of the scribe before the list of witnesses,[250] as is the case with Demotic documents. The usual expression in the Egyptian Aramaic papyri is ‘כתב + Name of the Scribe + ספרה זנה כפם + Party’[251] followed by the list of witnesses. As Porten pointed out, כפם does not mean that the party ‘dictated’ the document to the scribe, but rather that he ‘instructed’ the scribe to draw it up.[252] An exception to the sequence of scribe-witnesses is found in five documents from Elephantine: *TAD* B4.2; B4.4 (second copy of B4.3); B5.1; B6.3; and *TAD* B1.1 from Korobis, all of which follow the Babylonian practice of listing the witnesses before the name of the scribe.[253] Yaron rightly attributed this variation to the fact that when the witnesses signed by themselves, the scribe would finish his task by writing his name and then leaving the document for the witnesses to sign. This is the case, also, for

247 The same explanation can be applied to the use of the term ‘Jew’ in *TAD* A3.8.

248 D. von Recklinghausen, ‘Ägyptische Quellen zum Judentum’, *ZÄS* 132 (2005), 149–53.

249 Gropp, ‘Samaria Papyri’, 37.

250 With the exception of court records *TAD* B8.1-12 and Judicial Oaths *TAD* B7.1-4.

251 The expression ספרה זנה was not indispensable and was omitted in some of the documents.

252 Porten, *Elephantine Papyri*, 156 n. 35.

253 As pointed out already by San Nicolò, *Die Schlußklauseln der altbabylonischen Kauf- und Tauschverträge, Ein Beitrag zur Geschichte des Barkaufes* (Munich: C. H. Beck, 1922), 23.

the documents from Naḥal Ḥever and Dura Europos.[254] When the witnesses did not sign, the scribe would write their names and add his name afterwards. No special legal significance is attributed to this variation,[255] although it implies a different approach to the formal procedure of drawing up the document. It is worth mentioning, nonetheless, that five out of six documents which follow the pattern witnesses-scribe are deeds of obligation, and the sixth one is a wifehood document. The pattern of witnesses-scribe is not attested in documents involving transfers or litigation. It is thus possible that in these transactions the witnesses were required to sign by themselves.

The list of witnesses usually begins on the *recto* with the words שהידא בגו 'the witnesses herein'.[256] Rabinowitz realized that this expression is not casual but has a legal meaning. After demonstrating that the traditional Hebrew practice was to list the witnesses in the *verso*,[257] Rabinowitz suggested that the inclusion of the expression שהידא בגו was meant to make special mention of the deviation from the traditional Hebrew practice to forestall any possible argument as to the validity of the document.[258] Yaron agreed as to the purpose of the expression, but suggested that instead of pointing out a contrast between the traditional Jewish practice and that of Elephantine, this expression implies a voluntary departure from the standard Demotic formulary that most commonly included the witnesses on the *verso* of the documents.[259] The fact that both Jewish scribes from Elephantine and Aramaean scribes from Syene used the expression שהידא בגו and listed the witnesses on the *recto* could imply (a) that both Jewish and Aramaean scribes belonged to the same West Semitic formulary tradition of listing the witnesses on the *verso* and felt the need to signal their departure from former practices, or (b) that, as Yaron suggested, the formulary tradition the scribes were departing from when specifying שהידא בגו was the local Egyptian

254 H. M. Cotton and A. Yardeni, *Aramaic, Hebrew and Greek Documentary Texts from* Naḥal Ḥever *and Other Sites*, DJD 27 (Oxford: Clarendon Press; New York: Oxford University Press, 1997), 17.

255 See Yaron, 'Schema', 38–39; idem, *Introduction*, 11–14.

256 With the exception of *TAD* B1.1, which uses אלה שהדיא; B2.2, B2.9 and B3.12, which list the witnesses directly; B4.2, B4.3-4, and B5.1, which list the witnesses before the scribe and begin the list with שהדיא.

257 Late Jewish practice will accept both ways: 'plain documents whose witnesses signed within and tied-up documents in which they signed on the back'. Bab.Bath. 10.1, cited by Porten, *Archives from Elephantine*, 198.

258 Rabinowitz, *Jewish* Law, 156–57 and also in 'Some Notes on an Aramaic Contract from the Dead Sea Region', *BASOR* (1954): 15–16. Rabinowitz's suggestion (*Jewish Law*, 157) that the practice of writing the witnesses' names on the *verso* was first introduced among Jews cannot be sustained in the light of earlier Egyptian documents that attest to this practice.

259 Yaron, 'Schema', 45; idem, *Introduction*, 16.

tradition.[260] The number of witnesses listed in the document was either four (as in *TAD* B2.6, B2.8, B2.9, B2.11, B3.1, B3.4, B3.5, B3.6, B3.12, B3.13, B4.2, B4.6, B5.5, and B6.4), eight (as in *TAD* B2.2, B2.10, B3.2), or twelve (as in *TAD* B2.3 and B2.4). There are also cases with three (*TAD* B3.3), six (*TAD* B2.7) and nine (*TAD* B4.3-4). Pritsch already noticed that four was a key number in the witnesses list,[261] and Yaron further elaborated on this issue looking for a general pattern of the number of witnesses in relation to the kind of legal transaction.[262] The predominance of four- or eight-witness documents is also apparent in the Demotic tradition shortly after the Persian conquest.[263]

2.2.4. *Transfer of Property*

As expected, the majority of documents left by the Elephantine colonists deal with issues related to property rights. The documents are drawn *ex latere alienatoris*. Documents of transfer of property from Elephantine include sales, bequests, and inheritances.

2.2.4.1. *Sales*

The complete documents of sales comprise a sale of abandoned property (*TAD* B3.4) and a sale of apartment to a son-in-law (*TAD* B3.12), both from the archive of Anani b. Azariah. Sales followed the principle of *notwendige Entgeltlichkeit* ('necessary consideration') proposed by E. Seidl for Egyptian Law.[264] The documents are composed following a standard formulary that includes the date, parties, and abstract of the transaction, description of the performance (in sales, the amount of the payment), a declaration of satisfaction by the seller with the price received, a description of the property, a formula of transfer, the declaration of rights of the buyer (investiture), a quitclaim by the seller, a general warranty against suits by third parties, the name of the scribe, a dictation clause, the name of the witnesses, and an endorsement. The endorsement of the document of sale will make clear that the conveyance is precisely that by stating 'Document of a house which PN sold (to PN)' (*TAD* B3.4:25; *TAD* B3.12:35).

260 Although the Egyptian tradition was not uniform in this respect – the cursive Hieratic documents listed the witnesses on the *recto* and the Early Demotic documents listed witnesses on both the *recto* and/or the *verso*. Seidl, *Ägyptische*, *Rechtsgeschichte*, 14.

261 E. Pritsch, 'Jüdische Rechsturkunden aus Ägypten', *ZVRW* 26 (1922): 17.

262 Yaron, *Introduction*, 17–23.

263 Yaron, *Introduction*, 19.

264 See Seidl, *Ägyptische Rechtsgeschichte*, 40.

2.2.4.2. *Bequests*

The corpus includes the following complete documents of bequest, a bequest in contemplation of death of a house by Mahseiah b. Jedaniah to his daughter Mibtahiah (*TAD* B2.3),[265] an apartment by Ananiah b. Azariah to his wife Tamet (*TAD* B3.5), and another bequest in contemplation of death by Anani b. Azariah to his daughter Jehoishma (*TAD* B3.10).

2.2.4.3. *Inheritance*

There are no wills or testaments in the Elephantine corpus. Inheritance was regulated by custom law and provisions in wifehood documents and gifts. Hereditary property is conveyed including the formula ובניכי אחריכי 'and your sons after you' (*TAD* B2.3:9 *passim*) in the Investiture Clause after the rights of the alienor are stated (either using the שליט formula or the זילך הו formula). The formula ובניכי אחריכי, however, does not specifically limit the right of the alienor to transfer property (for such limitations see B2.4:6-8). Only one document deals with a division of inheritance (*TAD* B2.11), where the brothers Mahseiah and Jedaniah, sons of Nathan, divide between themselves two Egyptian slaves which were formerly property of their mother Mibtahiah. The fact that the whole Mibtahiah archive ended up in the hands of Jedaniah suggests that he was the first-born and had preferential hereditary rights. In addition, the formula ובניכי אחריכי seems to imply that sons and not daughters were the primary inheritors. It can be assumed that daughters had a right to inheritance in case the property holder died without sons (cf. Num. 27.8), as they appear as possible claimants in the Covenant of Non-claim formula (*TAD* B2.2:32-34). It seems that in case there were sons, daughters received property by bequests while the father was alive. These bequests could take effect immediately. In this case they used the formula בחיי ובמותי 'in my lifetime and at my death' (*TAD* B2.3:3). After the death of the father, they used the formula במותי (*TAD* B3.10:18). In the case of the death of a husband without children the wife received control (שליט) over the property. In the case of the death of the wife, the husband received full proprietary rights and inherited (ירת) the wife's property (*TAD* B2.6:21).[266] In this aspect, the Elephantine documents seem to reflect a different position from Mesopotamian legal traditions, where in the aforementioned case, the property would revert to the family of the wife (Hammurabi, §163, §164; Neo-Babylonian Laws, §10). The rights of the widow without children are usually established in the marriage

265 Such gifts were to take place immediately. See H. Z. Szubin and B. Porten, 'Testamentary Succession at Elephantine', *BASOR* 252 (1983): 39.

266 Already noted by L. Freund, 'Bemerkungen zu Papyrus G des Fundes von Assuan', *WZKM* 21 (1907): 177.

contracts. In *TAD* B3.8, the document of wifehood between Ananiah b. Haggai and Zaccur b. Meshullam regarding Jehoishma, in case of the death of the husband (Ananiah), without children her rights are limited to the usufruct of his property as long as she does not remarry (*TAD* B3.8:33). In the case that she died, all of her property would become her husband's.

2.2.5. *Obligations*

Documents related to obligations include those related to sums of money or to objects left in deposit.

2.2.5.1. *Loans*

Lending and borrowing was an integral activity in the ancient Near East and it is possible to assume that it was also a component of the socio-economic dynamic of the Elephantine-Syene colonists. The papyri attest to the loan of small sums of money (*TAD* B3.1; *TAD* B4.2, four shekels each) and grain (*TAD* B3.13). The operative section of *TAD* B3.1 begins with the statement יהבת לי זפת 'you have given me a loan'. The interest rate for money loans was as high as 60 per cent per year. When a loan was considered repaid the lender would transfer the deed attesting to the loan to the borrower. In some cases, when loans of grain were not repaid, the lender would threaten to convert the loan into a money-loan. In contrast to the grain-loan, the money-loan was a type of loan that could accrue interests (*TAD* B3.12). When loans were not repaid in a timely manner the lender would take a pledge from the borrower (*TAD* B3.1; *TAD* B3.13). The loan documents usually list the objects that could be taken as a pledge by the lender if such a situation arises (*TAD* B3.13; see also *TAD* B3.13:2-4; *TAD* B3.1:3; *TAD* B4.2:1). Debts arising from previous transactions are declared by the statement יתיא לך עלי 'You have upon me' (*TAD* B4.5:2; B4.6:3) followed by the amount owed.

2.2.5.2. *Deposit*

The only occurrence of goods left in deposit is mentioned in *TAD* B2.9, where they were cause for litigation. The brothers Menahem and Ananiah b. Meshullam sued the brothers Jedaniah and Mahseiah b. Esḥor regarding 'woollen, and linen garments, bronze and iron utensils, wooden and palm-leaf utensils, grain and other (things)' (*TAD* B2.9:5-6). These goods had been taken by Esḥor from their grandfather Sheloman b. Azariah in deposit (פקד) and were not returned. It is not clear why the goods ended up with Esḥor.

2.2.6. *Family Law*

The documents that address marriage and divorce are mostly concerned with the pecuniary consequences of the union (and divorce), for both the parties and their children.

2.2.6.1. *Marriage*

The Elephantine corpus includes three complete documents of wifehood (*TAD* B3.3; B2.6 and B3.8) and a few fragments (*TAD* B6.4; B6.3; B6.1; and B6.2). The documents are drawn between the bridegroom and the head of the family of the bride, or, in the case of the handmaiden Tamet, her master. The main purpose is to regulate the pecuniary rights resulting from the union. It does not seem that the bride had a voice in the contracts. However, considering the evolution of Egyptian marriage documents from contracts between the bridegroom and the bride's guardian to the documents from the Saite period (where the documents are drawn between the bride and the bridegroom),[267] R. Yaron has suggested that the bride might actually have had some veto power. This is based on the assumption that the Elephantine documents might reflect an old formulary tradition, while in reality 'the situation is one of material equality disguised as formal inferiority'.[268] There is no reason, however, to assume that the formulary of the Aramaic documents could not have evolved to reflect a different legal situation of the bride in the same way the Egyptian documents did.

The documents record the request of the bridegroom to the guardian to receive the bride as his wife, the *verba solemnia* 'she is my wife and I am her husband from this day and forever', the payment of a *mohar* by the bridegroom to the bride's guardian which became part of the bride's dowry; the description of the dowry, which consisted of cash, clothes, utensils, and various goods; stipulations in case of divorce; and regulation of some marital duties, like not taking another spouse (*TAD* B3.8:33-34) or the denial of conjugal rights (*TAD* B3.8:37).

2.2.6.2. *Divorce*

All the documents of wifehood include divorce clauses that allow both spouses to end the marriage. The spouse that wants to initiate the divorce 'stands up in the congregation (עדה)' and declares 'I hate (שנה)' the other spouse (*TAD* B2.6:23, 27; B3.3:7, 9; B3.8:21, 24). The party that initiates the divorce is liable to pay a penalty, כסף שנאה 'money of hatred' (*TAD* B2.6:23; B3.3:8, 9, 22, 25). B. Porten and H. Szubin have proposed that

267 See Lüddeckens, *Ägyptische Eheverträge*, docs. 1–4, where the documents are drawn between the bridegroom and the bride's guardian, and doc. 5, where the contract takes place directly between the bride and the bridegroom.

268 Yaron, *Introduction*, 46.

שנה actually does not carry the legal meaning of divorce but of demotion in status,[269] and more recently H. Nutkowicz concluded that 'the declaration of hatred heralds separation, marks a break but not the marriage's dissolution. It is a preliminary stage *before* the separation.'[270] In case it is the wife who initiates the divorce, she would lose the *mohar*, but in any case is entitled to keep the property that she brought with her at the time of the agreement. After the divorce, the woman is free to return to her father's home or to go wherever she pleases (*TAD* B2.6:25, 29; B3.8:26, 28). Tamet, being Zaccur's handmaiden, did not enjoy that right (*TAD* B3.3).

2.2.7. *Litigation*

2.2.7.1. *The Courts*

The 'Chief' *fratarka*[271] and the 'Troop Commander'[272] or 'Troop Commander of Syene'[273] had jurisdiction over legal and military matters. A body of 'judges'[274] (*TAD* B5.1:3; *TAD* B2.2:6), 'judges of the king' (*TAD* B5.1:3), 'judges of the province'[275] or 'judges, overseers and hearers' (*TAD* A4.5:8-10) was present in judicial decisions. The documents refer to them as the judicial instance to which complaints and suits are addressed. The עדה ('assembly') mentioned in the documents of wifehood as the body to whom a declaration of repudiation/divorce should be addressed does not seem to have any adjudicatory judicial function. Rather, it serves as a means of making the dissolution of the marriage public, thereby preventing any future charge or suspicion of adultery.[276]

2.2.7.2. *Procedure*

The Elephantine documents do not provide detailed evidence of court procedures, but it is possible to see three instances in a suit: (a) Plaintiff

269 B. Porten, 'Elephantine', 875–6; and H. Szubin and B. Porten, 'The Status of a Repudiated Wife: A New Interpretation of Kraeling 7 (*TAD* B3.8)', *ILR* 35 (2001): 46–78.

270 H. Nutkowicz, 'Concerning the Verb śn' in Judaeo-Aramaic Contracts from Elephantine', *JSS* 52 (2007): 225. However, there are several reasons to believe that, in Elephantine, שנה 'to hate' was indeed equivalent to 'to divorce'. See A. B. Botta, 'שנה in Elephantine: A "Reevaluation"', forthcoming.

271 Ramnadaina served in this position (*TAD* B2.9:4).

272 Vidranga served in this position (*TAD* B3.9:2; B2.10:2, 4; B2.9:4-5), and later his son Nafaina after he was promoted to Chief.

273 Rauka served in this position (*TAD* B5.1:3).

274 'Damidata and his colleagues the judges' (*TAD* B2.2:6).

275 *TAD* A5.2.

276 See, however, H. Nutkowicz, 'Note sur une institution juridique à Eléphantine, *'dh*, «la cour»', *Transeuphratène* 27 (2004): 181–85, who suggests that the עדה refers to the Egyptian *knbt*. Sir. 7.7 and 42.11 uses עדה to refer to the legal community. Cf. L. Kohler, *Der hebräische Mensch* (Tübingen: Mohr, 1953), 147f.

brings his claim before the courts; (b) Defendant responds by claiming his innocence by an oath to a deity[277] or making restitution;[278] (c) Plaintiff withdraws his claim.[279] It was common procedure in Egypt to interrogate witnesses and both the plaintiff and the defendant in civil disputes. The same is true for the Elephantine papyri where there are several mentions of one of the parties being interrogated.[280] The resolution of the dispute demanded a relinquishment of rights or a withdrawal of claims to prevent additional litigation. Egyptian literature provides a nice example of a never-ending dispute in the story of Horus and Seth.[281] It was the role of the judicial authority to convince the party to draw such a document. *P. Rylands* 9 reports the resolution of a dispute in that way.[282]

2.3. *Legal Traditions in Contact: Methodological Considerations*

As we mentioned before, there are four possible explanations for the intriguing similarities between the Aramaic and Demotic formulae: first, the Aramaic scribes borrowed from the Demotic legal tradition; second, the Demotic scribes borrowed from the Aramaic legal tradition; third, the existence of a common source for both legal traditions; and fourth, the Demotic and Aramaic scribes developed formulae independently of each other. These four options could be reduced to the fundamental question of independent development or diffusion of the legal formulae and legal concepts involved. Any attempt to discuss and interpret this question must consider the long-standing controversy between diffusionist and evolutionist theories of explanation of human development.[283]

Grounded in the Enlightenment and natural evolution proposed by

277 *TAD* B2.2:4.

278 In *TAD* B2.9 Jedaniah and Mahseiah, sons of Esḥor make restitution to Menahem and Ananiah.

279 *TAD* B2.9:9-10; B2.2:12-13.

280 The Aramaic שאל ('to ask') carries a legal meaning here (*TAD* A5.2:3; 5.4:5; B7.2:6; 8.7:2, 9; 8.8:5, 8; 8.10:6). The Talmud B. Mishnah Shevuot 7.1 4 reflects a similar way of resolving disputes.

281 A. H. Gardiner, *The Chester Beatty Gift* (London: British Museum, 1935), vol. 1, pp. 8–26, pls. 1–16. See M. Broze, *Les aventures d'Horus et Seth dans le Papyrus Chester Beatty I: mythe et roman en Egypte ancienne* (Leuven: Peeters, 1996) and the insightful reading of M. Campagno, *La contienda entre Horus y Seth* (Buenos Aires: Del Signo, 2004), esp. 'Prácticas judiciales en el Reino Nuevo', pp. 115–18, and 'Prácticas judiciales en la contienda entre Horus y Seth', pp. 118–35.

282 P. Rylands 9 20.19.

283 See J. S. Slotkin, ed., *Readings in Early Anthropology* (New York: Wenner-Gren Foundation for Anthropological Research, 1965). E. A. Hammel, 'The Comparative Method in Anthropological Perspective', *Comparative Studies in Society and History* 22 (1980): 145–55; and M. Harris, *The Rise of Anthropological Theory: A History of Theories of Culture*, updated edition (Walnut Creek, Calif.: AltaMira Press, 2001), 142–216 and 373–92.

Darwin, the cultural evolutionists believed that all human groups share a spiritual unity, having essentially the same level of intelligence. As a result of similar ways of thinking, human beings at the same level of development tended to devise the same kind of solutions to their problems, and, hence, they evolved along parallel lines through a universal series of stages.

A reaction against the belief in the independent development of human societies and a growing reliance on diffusion and migration to explain human change is evident in ethnological works of the second half of the nineteenth century.[284] When the above is applied to the development of legal institutions, or to the more specific area of the legal formulae, a diffusionist-based approach will explain the similarities, as reflecting some underlying historical connection and/or involving the process of borrowing-lending. On the other hand, an evolutionist approach will emphasize the unity and creative character of the human spirit that reacts in similar ways to similar challenges.

Diffusionism and evolutionism represent two possible approaches to the process of cross-cultural interaction, and, also legal interaction. A third and more pertinent approach to the borrowing and lending of legal data in the context of wider cultural phenomena is the anthropological study of cross-cultural consumption between two or more groups or societies.[285] This approach takes into account every relevant aspect in the process of transmission and reception of an ideological or material product: the function of the product in the donor society, the semantic charge which is attempted to be transmitted with the product, the necessity (real or created) of the product in the receptor, the posterior function of the product in the receptor, and the product's assimilation as a new part of the receptor's culture. In this context, a legal formula could be understood as a tool or a 'product' that can be exported and imported as necessary; that is, another tool to solve a certain problem, in this case, a legal one, in the context of a transaction. But, even when considered in its more 'material' aspect, any assimilation of a foreign element into a new culture involves an active process of symbolic transformation and

284 See F. Egan, 'Anthropological and Comparative Studies: Some Early Developments', in A. Etzioni and F. L. DuBow, eds., *Comparative Perspectives: Theories and Methods* (Boston: Little, Brown, 1969), 72–79 and the bibliography cited there.

285 Cf. M. Dietler, 'Consumption, Agency, and Cultural Entanglement: Theoretical Implications of a Mediterranean Colonial Encounter', in J. Cusick, ed., *Studies in Culture Contact: Interaction, Culture Change and Archaeology* (Carbondale: Center for Archaeological Investigations, Southern Illinois University, 1998), 288–315; idem., 'Consumption, Cultural Frontiers, and Identity: Anthropological Approaches to Greek Colonial Encounters', in *Confini e frontiera nella Grecità d'Occidente*. Atti del trentasettesimo Convegno di studi sulla Magna Grecia, Taranto, 3–6 ottobre 1997 (Taranto: Istituto per la storia e l'archeologia della Magna Grecia, 1999), 475–501.

adaptation.[286] The object is the same, yet it is not the same. As such cultural transformation similarly applies to the process of transmission/reception of legal formulae, it is necessary to keep in mind the consequences of this process. The legal formulae did not belong to an isolated realm, but were conceived using the language of daily life. Such formulae as those based on the verbs 'to clean', 'to hate', 'to withdraw', became legal metaphors, yet had very concrete reference to the lay reality. The legal formulae went through a process of progressive semantic specialization from their original *Sitz im Leben* to their fixation as legal terms and, also, through the necessary transformations in the process of cross-cultural consumption.

2.3.1. *The Evolution of Legal Systems*

Law is a fundamental feature of human society. It reflects the way societies judge what is right and what is wrong, what is an acceptable social behaviour as opposed to what is not acceptable and subject to punishment. The legal system in any given society is one of the mediums of social control, which protects that society from disruption and chaos; but at the same time, a legal system also sanctions and legitimizes asymmetrical power relationships. Moreover, a legal system is a social construction and an historical entity, which is represented at any given time by certain sets of component elements in close mutual relationship, such as institutions, laws, and procedures. Through societal development, all of these elements are subject to variation and diversification. Classical theories of legal evolution reflect in certain aspects the debate among evolutionists and diffusionists.

As the study of the evolution of legal systems shows, legal transplants, defined as 'the moving of a rule or a system of law from one country or people to another',[287] are the most common way through which Western legal systems have developed.[288] When facing a new legal problem, a variety of solutions would be available for the lawgiver, scribe, judge, or court of law, some of them of local origins, and some of them known to be in use in foreign cultures. It is left up to them to decide what will be the better solution.

When a local solution is not available, the society is faced with the option of having to create a new solution, or borrow a foreign one; the history of legal systems shows that the latter option is preferred. Alan Watson has provided some principles regarding legal transplants and the

286 See A. Alexander and B. McCay, 'The Concept of Adaptation in Biological and Cultural Evolution', in John J. Honigmann, ed., *Handbook of Social and Cultural Anthropology* (Chicago: Rand McNally, 1973), 143–78.

287 Watson, *Legal Transplants*, 21.

288 Watson, *Legal Transplants*, 95–101.

evolution of legal systems, which offer useful insights for our methodological discussion. First, 'the transplanting of individual rules or of a large part of a legal system is extremely common'.[289] This is not an *a priori* formulation, but is supported by many examples of Western legal systems. Watson presents the ancient Near East provisions regarding the goring ox as one of the earliest examples of such a dynamic.[290] Secondly, 'transplanting is, in fact, the most fertile source of development. Most changes in the majority of systems are the result of borrowing.'[291] Watson's third proposition describes the way in which lawgivers relate to legal history. He states that, 'to a truly astounding degree, law is rooted in the past'.[292] This affirmation is related to Watson's opinion about the relationship between law and society:[293] the law would be more dependent on legal tradition than on the dynamic of social change. It is possible to assert, however, that the social dynamic determines the kind of problems to be resolved by the legal elite, and that the legal tradition provides the stock of available solutions at hand.

The final result will display, therefore, a very close relationship between the solutions adopted and the legal tradition; nevertheless, the role that societal factors played throughout the entire process should not be dismissed. The 'social factor' in legal transplants helps to understand why, in Watson's fourth and fifth propositions, 'legal rules move easily and are accepted into the system without too great difficulty',[294] and 'a voluntary reception or transplant almost always involves a change in the law'.[295] Society, therefore, plays an active role by creating the demand for a solution and adapting it to its new context. Finally, the fact that 'no area of private law can be designated as being extremely resistant to change as a result of foreign influence',[296] Watson's sixth proposition, should be qualified in the same way as his third proposition. The need of a change in any area of private law is not the consequence of foreign influences, it is what causes the demand for a new solution, or a 'foreign influence', namely, the necessity of adaptation of the legal system to a new situation.

In this dynamic of supply and demand, one of the *foci* will be on how the Aramaic legal formulary, especially in the realm of our topic, could have developed by keeping or adapting legal formulae from its own

289 Watson, *Legal Transplants*, 95.

290 Watson, *Legal Transplants*, 22–24. Cf. M. Malul, *The Comparative Method in Ancient Near Eastern and Biblical Legal Studies* (Kevelaer: Butzon & Bercker; Neukirchen-Vluyn: Neukirchener, 1990), 113–52.

291 Watson, *Legal Transplants*, 95.

292 Watson, *Legal Transplants*, 95.

293 A.Watson, *Society and Legal Change* (Edinburgh: Scottish Academic, 1977).

294 Watson, *Legal Transplants*, 95.

295 Watson, *Legal Transplants*, 97.

296 Watson, *Legal Transplants*, 98.

history. The other focus will be centred on the intrinsic logic of legal consumption, i.e. how the Aramaic scribes imported, adapted, and integrated Egyptian legal formulae into their own system.[297]

2.3.2. *The Pilgrimage of Legal Formulae*

The study of the evolution and migration of legal formulae presents its own specific problems within the wider field of comparative law. The character of interactions between cultures, which have been in contact for a long period, is very complex and can operate on multiple levels: political, religious, economic, technical, linguistic, and legal. Contact and mutual influence in one of these areas do not necessarily imply contact and mutual influence of legal systems. In the realm of legal cross-cultural interaction, we could find that culture 'A' has borrowed the basic elements of its constitution[298] from culture 'B', but relies on previous local laws in regard to its civil code. It can borrow particular laws and make them operate in a completely different constitutional context, or it can adopt legal formulae, but not the legal instrument associated with them.

To be able to deal in a more specific manner with this problem, a clear definition of the levels of analysis of the lending-borrowing dynamics is in order.

2.3.3. *Levels of Analysis*

The fundamental methodological principle of comparative law is that of functionality: only what fulfils the same function may be comparable.[299] The following ascending list is an attempt to circumscribe such levels of comparison according to their function in our study of the interrelationships between the Aramaic and Demotic legal traditions:

1 The Abstract Concept: a concept that can be concretely expressed in more than one legal term. For example, the concept of cleaning, of satisfaction, of removal by physical distance. The concept of removal by physical distance is expressed in Egyptian by two legal terms *wy* and *ḫ3y*; in Aramaic, it is expressed by רחק.

2 The Legal Term: the basic concrete unit, which refers merely to words with legal meaning or nuances. Legal terms are, for example, 'to be far', 'to remove', 'to give'.

3 Legal Formulae: a sentence incorporating the legal term. For

297 See below Chapter 7, 'A Comparison of the Aramaic and Egyptian Uses of Withdrawal Formulae'.

298 See for example the case of the United States Constitution and the British, and the similar relationship between the constitution of Latin American countries and the US Constitution.

299 Zweigert and Kötz, *Introduction*, 31.

example, the Demotic removal formula, 'I will cause him to be far from you.'

4 Legal Clause: a legal formula or a combination of legal formulae, which fulfils a specific legal function within the legal instrument. For example, a defension clause composed in Demotic by a removal formula as apodosis and the phrase, 'if someone comes and makes a claim against you' as protasis.

5 Legal Formulary: the combination of legal clauses that build up in the legal instrument.[300]

6 Scribal Tradition to which the document belongs: A scribal tradition is defined by the transmission of the skills to produce a legal instrument from father or teacher to son or student.[301] Variations in the formulary could be attributed to different scribal schools.

7 Formulary Tradition: Different scribal schools or traditions can produce legal instruments according to certain common patterns and criteria, which results in a common formulary for the various scribal traditions or schools. A formulary tradition can encompass several scribal traditions.

8 Type of Legal Instrument: for example, purchase, sale, wifehood, or gift.

9 Legal Procedure in which the document is involved: for example, a suit, a marriage ceremony, or a conveyance.

10. Institutions related to the procedures: In this level, we approach the public character of the transaction or legal process. For example, institutions related to suits are the functionaries or the assembly.

11. Individual Laws: customary or written laws, which provide the framework for legal decisions and for social behaviour.

12. Legal Tradition: This is the widest category, which means the sum of individual laws and the types of institutions created to enforce them.

Similarity has different consequences for the question of historical connection or borrowing depending upon the level at which it is found. To find some parallels in the substance of legal institutions (no. 10) that might arise as a result of independent development is no surprise. The existence of the concepts of 'sale' or 'suit' are good examples, as attested in many legal systems, as are the existence of written records of transactions,

300 For the Demotic formulary of the *sẖ n wy* and *sẖ n ḏbꜣ ḥḏ* see below 6.2.1.3, 'Sales: The *sẖ ḏbꜣ ḥḏ* and the *sẖ n wy*'.

301 We are here assuming that the father was mostly responsible for training the son. We have a case of a scribal family in the Hebrew Bible, 'the families of scribes who lived in Jabes' (1 Chron. 2.25); See Ahiqar, *TAD* C1.1:18, [20], [27]. This was the case also for the Egyptian scribes. Family archives usually provide information regarding genealogic trees of scribal families, see M. el-Amir, *A Family Archive from Thebes* (Cairo: Government Printing Office, 1959), 95. See *TAD* B, p. 189, for the Aramaean scribes.

or of the settlement of disputes. Even the necessary legal clauses (no. 5), components of such records, could also be attributed without question to a similar development in both societies without needing to argue about a possible borrowing. In this study we shall deal with the first four levels of analysis.[302]

As obvious as it may seem, the implications of temporal precedence should be clearly specified. Mainly due to the fortune of discoveries, we should bear in mind that our picture of ancient Near Eastern legal history is based primarily on what has reached us and that every picture we draw based on that evidence is necessarily provisory. Temporal precedence may be considered to be definitive evidence in order to prove the lender character of a legal system only when other factors are considered.

Table VII: Definition of Legal Terms[303]

Legal Terms	Definition
Abstract	Summary or epitome, or that which comprises or concentrates in itself the essential qualities of a larger thing or of several things.
Action	A lawsuit brought in a court, a formal complaint within the jurisdiction of a court of law.
Actual Possession	Exists where the thing is in immediate occupancy and physical control of the party.
Adjudication	The legal process of resolving a dispute. The formal dispensing of, or pronouncing a judgment or decree in a court proceeding; also the judgment or decision given.
Adverse Possession	A method of acquisition of title to real property by possession for a statutory period.
Alienation	In real property law, the transfer of the property and possession of lands from one person to another.
Alienee	One to whom a conveyance or transfer is made.
Alienor	One who makes a grant, transfer of title, or conveyance.
Arbitration	A method of dispute resolution involving a neutral third party. The results of arbitration are binding.

302 See below 7.1, 'The Legal Metaphor and the Legal Term'; 7.2, 'Legal Formulae'; 7.3, 'Legal Clause'.

303 Based on H. C. Black, *Black's Law Dictionary*, 6th edn. (St Paul, Minn.: West, 1990), and B. A. Garner, *A Dictionary of Modern Legal Use*, 2nd edn. (Oxford: Oxford University Press, 1995).

Legal Terms	Definition
Certificate	A written assurance that some act has or has not been done, or some event occurred, or some legal formality has been complied with.
Clausula	A clause; a sentence or part of a sentence in a written instrument of law.
Clausula Salvatoria	A Clausula which guarantees the continuous right of the alienee to the property after a third party contest.
Clear Title	Meaning that the land is free from encumbrances.
Conclusive Evidence	That which is incontrovertible and establishes the proposition in question beyond any reasonable doubt.
Contingent	When applied to a legal right or interest, this term implies that no present interest exists, and that whether such interest or right ever will exist depends on a future uncertain event.
Conveyance	Transfer of title to land from one person, or class of persons, to another by deed.
Covenant	An agreement, convention, or promise of two or more parties, by deed in writing, signed, and delivered, by which either of the parties pledges himself to the other that something is either done, or shall be done, or shall not be done, or stipulates for the truth of certain facts. The term is currently used primarily with respect to promises in conveyances or other instruments relating to real estate.
Covenant of Non-claim (personal)	A covenant that the alienor shall not claim any title in the premises conveyed.
Covenant of Non-claim (special)	A covenant that neither the alienor, nor his heirs, shall claim any title in the premises conveyed.
Covenant of Non-claim (general)	A covenant that neither the alienor, nor his heirs, nor any other person, etc. shall claim any title in the premises conveyed.
Decisive Oath	When one of the parties to a suit, not being able to prove his charge, offered to refer the decision of the cause to the oath of his adversary.
Defend	To contest and endeavour to defeat a claim or demand against one in a court of law.

Legal Terms	Definition
Defension Clause	A Clause in which the alienor promises to defend the right of the alienee to the property against third party claims.
Demonstratio	One of the formulae in Roman legal procedure, wherein the plaintiff stated the facts upon which his claim was based.
Encumbrance	A claim, lien, charge, or liability attached to and binding real property.
Entitlement	Right to benefits, income, or property, which may not be abridged without due process.
Exchange	Mutual transfer of property other than for money although one of the parties may pay a sum of money in addition to property.
Formed Action	An action for which a set form of words is prescribed, which must be strictly adhered to.
Formula	In common-law practice, a set form of words used in judicial proceedings.
Formulary	The set of formulae used in a legal instrument.
General Warranty	The name of a covenant of warranty inserted in deeds, by which the grantor binds himself, his heirs, etc., to 'warrant and forever defend' to the grantee, his heirs, etc., the title thereby conveyed against the lawful claims of all persons whatsoever.
Good Title	Title which is free of defects and litigation.
Instrument	A document of writing which gives formal expression to a legal act or agreement as means of affording evidence.
Investiture	Delivery of possession in the presence of witnesses.
Mediation	A private, informal dispute resolution process in which a neutral third person, the mediator, helps disputing parties to reach an agreement. The mediator has no power to impose a decision on the parties.
Occupant	One who has actual use, possession, or control of a thing.
Occupying Claimant	An occupant claiming right under statute to recover for improvements he has placed on the land subsequently found not to be his.

Legal Terms	Definition
Occupying Claimant Acts	Statutes providing for the reimbursement of a bona fide occupant and claimant of land, on its recovery by the true owner, to the extent to which lasting improvements made by the occupant have increased the value of the land, and generally giving him a lien therefore.
Ownership	Collection of rights to use and enjoy property, including right to transmit to others. The complete dominion, title, or proprietary right in a thing or claim.
Performance	The fulfilment or accomplishment of a promise, contract, or other obligation according to its terms, relieving such persons of all further obligation or liability thereunder.
Possession	The detention and control, or the manual or ideal custody, of anything which may be the subject of property, for one's uses and enjoyment, either as owner or as the proprietor of a qualified right in it.
Presumptive Title	A title which arises out of the mere occupation or simple possession of property (*jus possessionis*).
Quitclaim	A release or acquittance given to one person by another, in respect of any action that he has or might have against him.
Release	The relinquishment of claim or right to person against whom the claim exists. It may be gratuitous or for consideration.
Renunciation	The act by which a person abandons a right acquired without transferring it to another.
Right of Possession	Right which may reside in one person while another has actual possession, being the right of the owner to enter the property and evict such actual occupant.
Special Warranty	A clause of warranty inserted in a deed of lands, by which the grantor covenants, for himself and his heirs, to 'warrant and forever defend' the title to the same, to the grantee and his heirs, etc., against all persons claiming 'by, through, or under' the grantor or his heirs.
Title	In Real Property Law, the formal right of ownership of property.

Legal Terms	Definition
Transfer	An act by which the title to property is conveyed from one person to another. Transfer means every mode of disposing of or parting with property.
Vacant Possession	An estate which has been abandoned, vacated or forsaken by the tenant. The abandonment should be complete in order to make the possession vacant.

3

The Egyptian Formulary Tradition

The study of Egyptian legal history has not been given the same attention by Egyptologists as have linguistics, art history, and literature. Perhaps one reason for this situation is that nothing similar to the Mesopotamian codes has been preserved from ancient Egypt. Legal documents, royal decrees, contracts, and private letters have been the main sources upon which the history of Egyptian law has been based. The fact that legal codifications were not preserved does not imply, however, that they did not exist.[1] Diodorus Siculus[2] lists six lawgivers who supposedly were responsible for the laws and customs of the Egyptians: Mneves (Μνεύην = Menes),[3] Sasychis (Σάσχιν),[4] Sesoösis (Σεσόωσιν),[5] Bocchoris (Βόκχοριν),[6]

1 See E. Seidl, *Einführung in die ägyptische Rechtsgeschichte bis zum Ende des Neuen Reiches*, 2nd edn. (Glückstadt; New York: J. J. Augustin, 1957), 19–21; D. Lorton, 'Treatment of Criminals in Ancient Egypt through the New Kingdom', *JESHO* 20 (1977): 5; Lurje, *Studien zum altägyptischen Recht*, 126–29. See also, R. Jasnow, 'Old Kingdom and First Intermediate Period', in *A History of Ancient Near Eastern Law*, R. Westbrook, ed. (Leiden: Brill, 2003), 93; idem, 'Middle Kingdom and Second Intermediate Period', 255–56; idem, 'New Kingdom', 289–90; and the survey by R. VerSteeg, *Law in Ancient Egypt* (Durham, N.C.: Carolina Academic Press, 2002).

2 C. H. Oldfather, *Diodorus of Sicily I*, Loeb Classical Library 279 (Cambridge, Mass.: Harvard University Press, 1933), I, 94–95. See also: A. Burton, *Diodorus Siculus Book I, A Commentary* (Leiden: Brill, 1972); and Seidl, *Einführung*, ch. 5: 'Die geschichtliche Entwicklung', 59–62.

3 The traditional founder of the first Dynasty according to Herodotus, who might be identified with Narmer or Aha. See B. J. Kemp, 'Old Kingdom, Middle Kingdom and Second Intermediate Period c. 2686–1552', in B. G. Trigger *et al.*, eds., *Ancient Egypt: A Social History* (Cambridge: Cambridge University Press, 1983), 50.

4 The Asyxhis of Herodotus (2, 136). He has been identified with Shepsekaf of the 4th Dynasty by H. R. Hall, *Ancient History of the Near East*, 8th edn., rev. (London: Methuen, 1932), 127; and F. J. Lauth, 'Zur Verständigung', *ZÄS* 6 (1868): 41–44, but there is no conclusive evidence. See Burton, *Diodorus*, 273.

5 The Sesostris of almost all Greek and Latin writers. Perhaps Sesostris III, fifth king of the 12th Dynasty (1878–1842 BCE).

6 Bocchoris is the Greek name for 'King Wahkare, Son of Re, Bakenranef'. He was the successor of Tefnakht (24th Dynasty) in Sais and ruled at Memphis ca. 720–715 BCE. The precise extent and facts of his rule are unknown. Kitchen, *Third Intermediate Period*, 376.

Amasis (Ἄμασιν),[7] and Darius (Δαρεῖον).[8] He also affirms that Menes had already 'persuaded the multitudes to use written laws',[9] and 'claimed that Hermes had given the laws to him'.[10]

Nothing remains of the legislation attributed to these kings, but it is natural to assume that the Egyptians were familiar with corpora of written legislation.[11] Diodorus also mentions that, during a trial, 'the entire body of the Laws was written down in eight volumes which lay before the judges'.[12] This description seems to be confirmed by the tomb inscription of Rekhmire, a Vizier of the 18th Dynasty under Tuthmosis III (ca. mid-fifteenth century BCE), where forty leather parchments are shown in front of the Vizier (40 *sš.w m-bꜣḥ=f*).[13] In that inscription, the

7 The successor of Apries, 26th Dynasty, ca. 570–526 BCE.

8 The Demotic Chronicle (end of third century BCE) col. C, 8–16, confirms this testimony. It seems that the intention of Darius was to codify all Egyptian law prior to the Persian Conquest. The texts had been composed in Aramaic and Demotic and it is the most plausible way in which the Egyptian legal formulae were translated into Aramaic. W. Spiegelberg, *Die sogenannte 'Demotische Chronik'* (Leipzig: J. C. Hinrichs, 1914), 30–32. See also: J. Johnson, 'The Demotic Chronicle as an Historical Source', *Enchoria* 4 (1974): 1–17; idem, 'The Demotic Chronicle as a Statement of a "Theory of Kinship"' *JSSEA* 13 (1983): 61–72; idem, 'Is the Demotic Chronicle an Anti-Greek Tract?' in *Grammata Demotica: Festschrift für Erich Lüddeckens zum 15. Juni 1983* (Würzburg: Gisella Zauzich Verlag, 1984), 107–24.

9 Diodorus Siculus I, 94.1. The attribution to Menes of the creation of Egyptian civilization is well attested from the 18th Dynasty onwards. See H. Brunner, 'Menes als Schöpfer', *ZDMG* 103 (1953): 22–26; S. Morenz, 'Traditionen um Menes', *ZÄS* 99 (1972): 10–16.

10 Diodorus Siculus I, 94.1.

11 So Seidl, *Einführung*, 19. H. Frankfort, *The Birth of Civilization in the Near East* (Garden City, N.Y.: Doubleday, 1956), 99 n. 15, and J. A. Wilson, *Authority and Law in the Ancient Orient* (Baltimore: American Oriental Society, 1954), 5 ff., denied the existence of legal codes in ancient Egypt, but the present evidence seems to prove the actual existence of such codes. See W. C. Hayes, *A Papyrus of the Late Middle Kingdom in the Brooklyn Museum (Papyrus Brooklyn 35.1446)* (New York: Brooklyn Museum, 1955), 49–52, for references to literary sources which refer to written law and the appendix 'Codified Law in Ancient Egypt', in D. Lorton, 'The Treatments of Criminals in Ancient Egypt', *JESHO* 20 (1977): 53–64. For additional discussion see V. Arangio Ruiz, 'La codification dans l'Égypte ancienne', *JJP* 11–12 (1957–58): 25–46. For Mesopotamian and biblical codes see R. Westbrook, 'Biblical and Cuneiform Law Codes', *RB* 92 (1985): 247–64.

12 Diodorus I, 75.5-6. In the following paragraphs (I, 75–80) Diodorus presents a description of several Egyptian laws.

13 Urk. IV, 1111/1–2. See Seidl, *Einführung*, 19; S. Allam, 'La problématique des quarante rouleaux de lois', in *Studien zu Sprache und Religion Aegyptens*, Fs. W. Westendorf (Göttingen: F. Junge, 1984), 447–52. But see also G. Posener, 'Les quarante rouleaux de lois', *GM* 25 (1977): 63–66, and N. de Garis Davies, *The Tomb of Rekhmi-Re at Thebes* (New York: Metropolitan Museum of Art Egyptian Expedition Publications, 1943), 31ff., who opposed this view, followed by J. Mélèze Modrzejewsky, 'Law and Justice in Ptolemaic Egypt' in M. J. Geller and H. Maehler, eds., *Legal Documents of the Hellenistic World:*

Vizier[14] is admonished to act in accordance with the *hp* and to listen to every petitioner 'in accordance with the *hp* that is in your hand'.[15] A papyrus from the Middle Kingdom also provides evidence of different 'laws' (*hpw*) applied to fugitives,[16] and P. Turin 2021 (end of 20th Dynasty to beginning of 21st Dynasty, ca. 1070 BCE) possibly cites from a legal code.[17]

The Legal Manual of Hermopolis[18] is the closest example of codification. This manual of procedure offers a collection of models for contracts, public protests, receipts, and judicial decisions,[19] which were probably collected in the 'House of Life'.[20] According to the script, the text can be

Papers from a Seminar Arranged by the Institute of Classical Studies, the Institute of Jewish Studies and the Warburg Institute, University of London, February to May 1986 (London: Warburg Institute, 1995), 2–3.

14 For the function of the Vizier in the judicial system see G. P. F. van den Boorn, *The Duties of the Vizier: Civil Administration in the Early New Kingdom* (London and New York: Kegan Paul International, 1988), 166–69.

15 An identical expression is found in Ezra 7.14: 'For you are commissioned by the king and his seven advisers to regulate Judah and Jerusalem according to the law (בְּדָת) of your God, which is in your hand (בִּידָךְ).' In Egyptian, *hp* 'legal right' has a variety of meanings including 'custom, duty, law, right, obligation'. C. Nims, 'Hp, Law, Right in Demotic', *JNES* 7 (1948): 243–60; M. Bontty, 'Concerning *hp*', *JSSEA* 27 [1997 (2000)]: 1–8. The decree of the king Haremhab attests the first act of legislation that has been preserved from an Egyptian king. The stela is preserved at Karnak. For the edition, see J. M. Kruchten, *Le Décret d'Horemheb. Traduction et commentaire épigraphique, philologique et institutionnel* (Brussels: Editions de l'Université de Bruxelles, 1981).

16 For example, *hp … n tšw* 'the laws pertaining to those who desert'. P. Brooklyn 35.1446, 10, *passim*. Hayes, *Papyrus*, 47 ff.

17 S. Allam, *Hieratische Ostraka und papyri aus der Ramessidenzeit* (Tübingen: Allam, 1973), 320–27 and the bibliography cited there.

18 P. Cairo dem J. d'E. 89127–89130 and 89137–89143. G. Matta and G. R. Hughes, *The Demotic Legal Code from Hermopolis West* (Cairo: Institut Français d'Archéologie Orientale du Caire, 1975); K. Donker van Heel, *The Legal Manual of Hermopolis* [P. Mattha] (Leiden: Leiden Papyrological Institute, 1990); S. Grunert, *Der Kodex Hermopolis und ausgewählte private Rechtsurkunden aus dem ptolemäischen Ägypten* (Leipzig: Reclam, 1982); A. Martin, 'Der Rechtskodex von Hermupolis (P. Kairo JE 89.127-30 + 89.137-43)', in *Dokumente zur Rechts- und Wirtschaftsgeschichte. Texte aus der Umwelt des Alten Testaments*, new edn. (Gütersloh: Mohn, 2004), 196–218. See also P. W. Pestman, 'Le manuel de droit d'Hermoupolis. Les passages transmits en démotique et en grec', in *Textes et études de papyrologie grecque, démotique et copte*, Pap.Ludg.Bat. 23 (Leiden: Brill, 1985), 116–43. For an updated survey and typological analysis of Demotic legal manuals see S. L. Lippert, *Ein demotisches juristiches Lehrbuch. Untersuchungen zu Papyrus Berlin P 23757 rto* (Wiesbaden: Harrassowitz, 2004), 147–75.

19 The text was considered to be a commentary on legal procedures, by E. Seidl, 'Eine demotische Juristenarbeit', *Zeitschrift der Savigny-Stiftung, romanististische Abteilung* 96 (1969): 17–30; and to be a manual of Egyptian Law, by P. W. Pestman, 'Een juridisch "Hanboek" uit het oude Egypte in twe talen', *Phoenix* 25 (1979): 25–31.

20 Quaegebeur, 'Sur la "loi sacrée"', 227–40, also followed by Mélèze-Modrzejewsky, 'Law and Justice', 1–19.

dated to the first half of the third century BCE,[21] but its composition should be dated at least two centuries earlier.[22] As J. Mélèze-Modrzejewski suggests, 'the Case-Book seems to be the end-product of a long series of partial collections drawn up by Egyptian priests and preserved in the archives of their temples'.[23] The Legal Manual of Hermopolis would be one of these many Case-Books existing in Ptolemaic Egypt dating back to previous periods.[24] Late Ptolemaic lawsuit records also make reference to legal codes (*iw=f sẖ (n) pꜣ hp*),[25] which determine the verdict of the litigations.

Diodorus expresses his admiration for the Egyptian legal order, commenting that even the kings 'were not allowed to render any legal decision or transact any business at random or to punish anyone through malice or in anger or for any unjust reason, but only in accordance with the established laws (κείμενοι νόμοι) relative to each offence'.[26] This declaration assumes an established codification of the laws.

These codifications were not merely the individual product of an inspired legislator but, rather, the attempt to unify the different traditions that ruled the legal transactions of the individuals.[27] In the course of human history there have been many such efforts to systematize

21 P. W. Pestman, 'L'Origine et l'extension d'un manuel de droit Egyptien', *JESHO* 26 (1983): 16.

22 Pestman, 'L'Origine', suggests that the compilation was made under Bochoris at the end of the eighth century BCE, while J. Johnson sees the legal manual as the result of Darius' compilation of Egyptian laws as recorded in the Demotic Chronicle (column c, lines 6–16). J. Johnson, 'The Persians and Continuity of Egyptian Culture', in H. Sancisi-Weerdenburg, A. Kuhrt, and M. Cool Root, eds., *Continuity and Change: Achaemenid History VIII* (Leiden: Brill, 1994), 157.

23 Mélèze-Modrzejewsky, 'Law and Justice', 6.

24 As, for example, E. Bresciani, 'Frammenti de un "prontuario legale" demotico da Tebtuni nell'Instituto Papirologico "G. Vitelli" di Firenze', *EVO* 4 (1981): 201–15; M. Chauveau, 'P. Carlsberg 301: Le manuel juridique de Tebtunis', in P. J. Frandsen, ed., *The Carlsberg Papyri I. Demotic Texts from the Collection* (Copenhagen: Carsten Niebuhr Institute of Ancient Near Eastern Studies, University of Copenhagen, Museum Tusculanum Press, 1991), 103–29; W. J. Tait, 'P. Carlsberg 236: Another Fragment of a Demotic Legal Manual', in P. J. Frandsen, ed., *The Carlsberg Papyri I* (Copenhagen: Museum Tusculanum), 93–101; *P. Berlin* 13621, E. Seidl, *Ptolemäische Rechtsgeschichte*, 2nd edn. (Glückstadt and New York: J. J. Augustin, 1962), 3–4; in her study of P. Berlin 23757, S. Lippert also concludes that the text is based on an early Demotic source, Lippert, *Ein demotisches juristiches Lehrbuch*, 177.

25 P. Köln 7676. See H. J. Thissen, 'Zwei demotische Prozeßprotokolle', in E. Bresciani, ed., *Acta Demotica. Acts of the Fifth International Conference for Demotists* (Pisa, 1994), 286 = *EVO* 18. See also the reference to the 'law (*hp*) of year 21', in Thompson, *Family Archive*, P. BM. 10591 B, i.17; ii.20 and x.7.

26 Diodorus I, 71.1.

27 A. Theodorides, 'The Concept of Law in Ancient Egypt', in J. Harris, ed., *The Legacy of Egypt* (Oxford: Clarendon Press, 1971), 320–21.

customary laws.[28] The success and permanence of such codes tended to be determined by their capacity to relate to the variety of customary laws of the people to whom they were to be applied and by the strength of the political power behind them.[29]

The history of Europe exhibits many attempts at codification and shows the persistence of local laws based on customary law until the nineteenth century.[30] In France, the customary laws took their particular name from their locality, such as, 'the Custom of Paris', 'the Custom of Orléans', and 'the Custom of Normandy'. In Voltaire's time, there were so many of these sets of laws that in travelling through France, he claimed, 'one changes law more often than one changes horses'.[31] The fact that local laws were able to persist in Western Europe as late as the nineteenth century makes it reasonable to assume that local laws were able to endure for centuries in the no less diverse context of the ancient Near East and Egypt. In fact, we see in the Hellenistic period that the official recognition of regional custom (ἔθος) is a source for private, penal, and administrative law as well.[32] Many aspects of this customary law were not necessarily reflected in the legal formulary.[33]

The continuity of the ancient legal traditions, varying from place to place, was very closely associated with the continuity of the ways of life of

28 Theodosius II ordered the compilation of a Code published in 438 CE. Evaric, king of the Visigoths (466 CE – 484 CE) ordered the Visigothic laws to be compiled. His son Alaric preceded Justinian in the attempt to compile Roman Law and published his compilation in 506 CE. The Digest of Justinian was published in 533 CE. See W. L. Burdick, ch. 1, 'The World Wide Extension of Roman Law', 1–3, and chs. 4–5, 'Outlines of Roman Law History', 87–154, in *Principles of Roman Law and their Relation to Modern Law* (Holmes Beach, Fla.: Wm. W. Gaunt, 1989).

29 The genius of Roman Law is best appreciated in the universality of its application. The Twelve Tablets mark the real beginning of Roman Law (450 BCE), which developed from a law for the Romans alone (*jus civile*) to a law applied to the whole Roman empire (*jus gentium*) and later became the basis of Western laws.

30 When studying the legal development of the ancient Near East, it is necessary to keep in mind that most Western countries, after some fruitless attempts, managed to codify their laws only at the end of the nineteenth century. The first Civil Code was promulgated by Napoleon (le Code Civil des Français) in 1804. The present Spanish Civil Code was promulgated in 1889, the German in 1900, etc.

31 Cited by Burdick, *Principles of Roman Law*, 10–11.

32 As expressed in a decree of the third century BCE: BGU. 1185 II, 28ff., cited by R. Taubenschlag, 'Customary Law and Custom in the Papyri', *JJP* 1 (1944): 41–42.

33 Some documents point to this customary law when including the clause *tp n + legal transaction* (P. Louvre E 3228e, Thebes, 707 BCE) translated by Malinine as 'manière convenue', *Choix de textes juridiques en hieratique anormal et en demotique* (Paris: H. Champion, 1953), 39 n. 11; and by B. Menu as 'manière habituelle', B. Menu, 'Cession de services et engagements pour dette sous les Rois Kouchites et Saïtes', *RdE* 36 (1985): 76 n. a.

these conservative societies.[34] Variations in customary laws had their consequences in the legal formularies used in the various transactions[35] and the study of the Egyptian legal formularies must take into account these geographical variations.[36]

Another fact to take into account in the study of the legal formularies in the ancient Near East is that agreements, claims, legal procedures, and court decisions were originally expressed verbally. The people of ancient societies established the spoken word as the firm basis for any legal transaction long before writing was invented. The use of both written and oral contracts was still a common feature among the Greek population of Egypt, where we find oral contracts to have been valid in a court of law. Roman practice likewise recognized oral contracts[37] and this custom still survives among some groups in the Middle East and Western legal systems.[38] Legal formulae were certainly to be found in the oral realm long before they were written down in documents.

The formulae of the Egyptian legal instruments contain many expressions referring to the oral character of business practices: 'party A *said* to party B',[39] 'the one who will come against you *saying* X',[40] 'his claim will not be *heard* in any house of writing'.[41] All of these expressions reflect the *verba solemnia* that later developed in *scripta solemnia*.[42] When studying the legal instruments of this period, it is necessary to keep in mind the customary and oral legal practices in which they originated. It is there that we find the *realia* of the legal transaction while the purpose of the contract

34 S. von Bolla, 'Zur Rechstkontinuität der Volksreschte in Aegypten', *JJP* 7–8 (1953–54): 155. Bedouin courts still apply customary law for the solution of certain individual or tribal problems; such law is also recognized in Islamic countries, where private and legal customs sometimes prevail over general laws as provided by the Civil Codes. See S. H. Amin, *Middle East Legal Systems* (Glasgow: Royston, 1985).

35 See B. Menu, 'Les actes de vente en Egypte Ancienne particulièrement sous les Rois Kouchites et Saïtes', *JEA* 74 (1988): 165–68, who relates the evolution of the Egyptian legal formulary to substantive variations in the concept of sale.

36 K. Th. Zauzich provides a list of the various legal formularies of the *sẖ ḏbꜣ ḥḏ* and *sẖ n wy* associated with different regions of Ptolemaic Egypt. *Schreibertradition*, 115–24.

37 Taubenschlag, *Law*, 301–03.

38 See *Black's Law Dictionary* s.v. 'Parol conract', and s.v. 'Oral contract'.

39 *ḏd A n B*: the usual initial formula to introduce the parties of the document.

40 *pꜣ nt iw=f iy r-r=k r-ḏbꜣ.ṯ=s r ṯ. ṯ mtw=k r ḏd* as for example in P. Rylands 8 (El-Hibeh, 563 BCE), line 5.

41 *bn sḏm=f rꜣ=f* as for example in P. Louvre E 3228e (Thebes, 707 BCE).

42 Besides the *verba solemnia*, symbolic acts were also used in the ancient Near East to materialize the transaction. See M. Malul, *Studies in Mesopotamian Legal Symbolism* (Kevelaer: Butzon & Bercker; Neukirchen-Vluyn: Neukirchener Verlag, 1988), esp. ch. 7: 'Ratifications of Deeds of Sale', 346–78; and E. Cassin, 'Symboles de cession immobilière dans l'ancien droit Mésopotamien', *L'Année Sociologique*, 3rd series (1952–55), 107–61. For Ancient Egypt see N. Shupak, 'A New Source for the Study of the Judiciary and Law of Ancient Egypt: "The Tale of the Eloquent Peasant"', *JNES* 51 (1992): 6–8.

was to define the arrangement intended by the parties. The written instrument was solely a proof for both parties that the transaction indeed took place and was produced in light of potential litigation to obtain enforcement of the contract.[43] The transaction, therefore, expresses in the procedure of sale a different step from that of the writing of the document that registered the transfer (the sale document).[44]

We have written evidence of commercial transactions in the history of Near Eastern civilization dating back to the third millennium.[45] Furthermore, archaeological evidence of commercial activity in the ancient Near East dates back as far as Neolithic times.[46] How ancient Near Eastern societies reflected these commercial activities in writing varies from region to region.

The progressive introduction of notarized acts in Egyptian legal history has been schematized by B. Menu as follows:[47]

1. Old Kingdom through the 18th Dynasty: evolution from pure verbal agreements to the transcription of the transaction.
2. Between the 23rd and the 25th Dynasty: evolution from dialogic acts to unilateral declarations by one of the parties.
3. Between the 25th Dynasty and year 8 (or 4) of Psammetichus: from the material nature of the reciprocal legal performances to conceptualization of the acquired rights.

The most ancient evidence of a conveyance in ancient Egypt is the sale of a house[48] from Giza, roughly dated during the 4th–6th Dynasties (2575–

43 The notarized general character of the Egyptian instruments was recognized long ago by W. Spiegelberg, 'Ägyptologische Mitteilungen' V. Der Ursprung und das Wessen der Formelsprache der demotischen Urkunden, in *Sitzungsberichte der Bayerischen Akademie der Wissenschaften, Philosophisch-philologische und historische Klasse*, 2 Abhandlung, (1925), 29.

44 R. H. Pierce made the same distinction between a *contract* and an *instrument* that documented it. R. H. Pierce, *Three Demotic Papyri in the British Museum: A Contribution to the Study of Contracts and their Instruments in Ptolemaic Egypt* (Oslo: Universitetsforlaget, 1972), 83.

45 See I. J. Gelb, P. Steinkeller, and R. M. Whiting Jr, *Earliest Land Tenure Systems in the Near East: Ancient Kudurrus* (Chicago: Oriental Institute of the University of Chicago, 1991), 1–4; D. O. Edzard, *Sumerische Rechtsurkunden des III. Jahrtausends aus der Zeit vor der III Dynastie von UR* (Munich: Verlag der Bayerischen Akademie der Wissenschaften; Beck in Kommission, 1968); U. Hartnung, 'Zur Entwicklung des Handels und zum Beginn wirtschaftlicher Administration im prädynastischen Ägypten', *SAK* 26 (1998): 35–50.

46 See T. Earle, ed., *Context for Prehistoric Exchange* (New York: Academic Press, 1982). Cf. J. M. Postgate, *Early Mesopotamia: Society and Economy at the Dawn of History* (New York: Routledge, 1994), 207ff.

47 Menu, 'Les Actes de Ventes', 181.

48 Musée du Cairo, Jd'E. 42 787. See Goedicke, *Die privaten Rechtsinschriften*, 149–73, and the bibliography cited there. In this work and in a later article, Goedicke proposed that the inscription is not a conveyance but an 'unsecured statement to deliver a certain matter for a rent'; idem, 'Bilateral Business in the Old Kingdom', *DE* 5 (1986): 78; but see the new

2150 BCE). The stela, discovered beside the funerary temple of the Khephren pyramid, is, according to B. Menu, a copy of a document written previously on papyrus.[49] It includes the essential elements of a deed of conveyance: (1) the parties; (2) the mention of the property sold; (3) the payment; (4) the satisfaction clause; (5) the witnesses.

The formulary is built up according to the following pattern:

Musee du Cairo, Jd'E 42787

I.	The buyer, PN1, says:
II.	I have bought for the price (*ỉn n=(y) r ỉsw*)[50] this house (*pr pn*) from PN2.
III.	I gave (*rdỉ*) 10 *shatis*.
IV.	The seller PN2 takes an Oath: For the life of the King (*ʿnḫ njsw.t*): I will give you what is right and you will be satisfied (*ḥtp*) regarding this, as exchange (*m wḏb*).[51]
V.	PN2 declares that he received the payment in full (*mḥ.n=k ḏbꜣ <.w> ipn*).
VI.	List of Witnesses (Nine).

What we have here is not a full contract but an abridged notarized abstract of its essential components. The intention of such stelae was to make public the contract and the transfer of property.[52] Through the brevity of the content, we can appreciate the incipient occurrence of legal formulae that will be well documented in later periods, e.g. 'to give' (*rdỉ*)

treatment by B. Menu, 'Ventes de maisons sous L'Ancien Empire Egyptien', in *Mélanges offerts à Jean Vercoutter* (Paris: editions Recherche sur les civilisations, 1985), 249–65; and also Gödecken, *Betrachtung*, 174f., 203ff., 223ff.

49 Menu, 'Ventes de maisons', 251. The use of legal documents in this early period in Egypt is also attested by a 6th Dynasty record of lawsuit from Elephantine where reference is made to a hereditary disposition. K. Sethe, 'Ein Prozessurteil aus dem alten Reich', *ZÄS* 61 (1926): 67–79.

50 For this formula in the Old Kingdom see H. Goedicke, 'The expression *ỉnỉ r ỉsw*', *DE 6* (1986): 67–78.

51 There is not much agreement about how to translate *ḏbꜣw ipn m wḏb*. Sethe and von Bissing translate it as 'Zuwendung' (K. Sethe, 'Aegyptische Inschrift auf den Kauf eines Hauses aus dem alten Reich', *Berichte über die Verhandlungen der König., Sächsischen Gesellschaft der Wissenschaften zu Leipzig, Philol.-hist. Kl.* 63 (1911); W. von Bissing, 'Ein Hausverkauf im IV. Jahrtausend vor Chr.', *Sitzungsbericht der Bayerischen Akademie der Wissenschaften, Philos.-philol. u. hist. Kl. 14* (1920). Sottas has 'virement' (*Etudes critique sur un acte de vente immobilière du temps des pyramides* (Paris: Paul Geuthner, 1913), 17), and Pirenne-van de Walle 'soit vire' (*AHDO* 1 (1937): 6). B. Menu on the other hand translates 'en échange' (Menu, 'Ventes de maisons'), which is in agreement with our understanding of this expression as a derivation of the sense given by Hannig in *HWB*, 235: 'Zuwendung von Naturalien'.

52 For a stela made for the purpose of protecting office and shares, see P. Rylands 9, 13.17-20.

in the sense of transfer of ownership,[53] the oath as a warranty of the transaction,[54] the clause of satisfaction,[55] and the receipt of the payment.[56] This stela demonstrates that at the earliest stage in Egyptian legal history a well-developed formulary tradition was already present.[57]

53 Attested since the Old Kingdom through the Ptolemaic Period. Cf. for the Late Period Menu, 'Les Actes de vente', 174–76; Ritner, 'Third Intermediate Period Antecedents', 344.

54 The oath as warranty will still be used in the Demotic documents. See Zauzich, *Schreibertradition*, 146–48. Cf. for the Late period, Menu, 'Les Actes de Vente', 178.

55 From the Old Kingdom through the 20th Dynasty, the satisfaction clause was built with *sḥtp*. For early examples, see Goedicke, 'Bilateral Business', 74–75; cf. Ritner, 'Third Intermediate Period Antecedents', 348–49.

56 For the Late period, Menu, 'Les Actes de vente', 174.

57 For the legal formulary during the Old Kingdom, see Mrsich, *Untersuchungen*, 1–13; and Gödecken, *Betrachtung*, 172–80. For other legal formulae in this period see H. Goedicke, 'Juridical Expressions of the Old Kingdom', *JNES* 15 (1956): 27–32.

4

Challenging the Consensus: The שליט Clause

As we already stated, the case for a Mesopotamian origin of the Aramaic legal formulae used in Elephantine was supported mainly by the evidence and conclusions presented in two in-depth studies of the function and origins of two of the Aramaic legal formulae: The שליט (investiture) clause and the טיב לבבי (satisfaction) clauses. In this chapter we present evidence that points to the Egyptian origins of the שליט clause.[1]

Among the legal formulae attested in the Aramaic papyri from Elephantine, besides the satisfaction clause טיב לבבי,[2] the שליט-based clause is perhaps the one that has received the most attention.[3] It is

1 Some of this material was presented in lectures at the Oriental Institute, University of Chicago ('Tracing Ancient Near Eastern Legal Formulae: Methodological Issues', 5 March 2003) and at the Aramaic Studies Section of the Society of Biblical Literature ('The Origins of the שליט Clause: A Reevaluation', Annual Meeting in Atlanta 23 November 2003). I wish to thank Profs. Janet Johnson, Robert Ritner, and Bezalel Porten for their valuable comments. This chapter is a modified version, including additional evidence, of our article. 'The Legal Function and Egyptian Background of the שליט Clause: A Reevaluation', *Maarav* 13.2 (2006), 193–209.

2 Reevaluations of the function of the טיב לבבי clause followed Muffs's study. In his review of Muffs, Yaron disagreed with his interpretation of טיב לבבי as quittance formula and regarded it as a volitional statement (R. Yaron, 'Review of *Studies in the Aramaic Legal Papyri from Elephantine*, by Y. Muffs', *RB* 77 (1970): 408–16); Levine defended Muffs's views (B. Levine, 'On the Origins of the Aramaic Legal Formulary at Elephantine', in *Christianity, Judaism and other Greco-Roman Cults*, J. Neusner, ed. (Leiden: Brill, 1975)), 37–54. R. Westbrook, on the other side, regarded it as a receipt clause (R. Westbrook, 'The Phrase "His Heart is Satisfied", on Ancient Near Eastern Legal Sources', *JAOS* 111 (1991): 219–24).

3 See A. Ungnad, *Aramäische Papyrus aus Elephantine. Kleine Ausgabe unter Zugrundlegung von Eduard Sachau's Erstausgabe Aramäische Papyrus aus Elephantine* (Leipzig: Hinrichs, 1911), 47 n. 8; L. Blau, 'Zur demotischen und griechischen Papyrusurkunde', in *Judaica, Festschrift zu H. Cohens Siebzigsten Geburstage* (Berlin: Cassirer, 1912), 148; E. Y. Kutscher, 'New Aramaic Texts', *JAOS* 74 (1954): 239; J. J. Rabinowitz, 'Brooklyn 12 and the Kyreia Clause of the Graeco Egyptian Papyri', in *Jewish Law: Its Influence on the Development of Legal Institutions* (New York: Bloch, 1956), 124–40; idem, 'Neo-Babylonian Legal Documents and Jewish Law', *JJP* 13 (1961): 150–57; R. Yaron, 'Aramaic Deeds of Conveyance', *Bib* 41 (1960): 257; idem, 'Aramaic Marriage Contracts from Elephantine', *JJS* 3 (1958): 9–10; A. Goldstein, 'The Syriac Bill of Sale from Dura-Europos', *JNES* 25 (1966): 11–12; Muffs, *Studies*, 152, 176ff.; S. Kaufman, *The Akkadian Influences on Aramaic* (Chicago: University of Chicago Press, 1974), 98. See also J.

generally accepted that the שליט clause 'affirms or denies the authority of a legal participant over some object concerned in a legal transaction'.[4] In addition to the Elephantine papyri, the formula is also attested in the Samaria papyri,[5] at Palmyra,[6] and in the Dura Europos bill of sale.[7] רשי,[8] a synonym of שליט, is attested with a similar meaning in the Murabbaʿat [9] and Naḥal Ḥever[10]documents. Uses of שליט are also attested in Hebrew and Aramaic in the Bible, though it is now accepted[11] that those attestations of שליט are due to Aramaic influence.[12] The original Hebrew word to cover the same semantic field of שלט is משל, which is followed by -ב to mean 'to rule, to exercise authority over' regarding property, as in the case of Abraham's slave in Gen. 24.2, or political authority, as Joseph had over Egypt in Gen. 45.8, 26. Followed by -ל, it is used in the same way

C. Greenfield, 'Studies in the Terminology of the Nabatean Funerary Inscriptions', in *Henoch Yalon Memorial Volume*, E. Y. Kutscher, S. Lieberman, and M. Z. Kaddari, eds. (Ramat Gan: Kiryat Sefer, 1974), 67–68 (Hebr.); idem, 'The Genesis Apocryphon: Observations on Some Words and Phrases', in *Studies in Hebrew and Semitic Languages Dedicated to the Memory of Prof. Eduard Yechezkel Kutscher*, G. B. Sarfatti *et al.*, eds. (Ramat Gan: Bar Ilan University, 1980), xxxii–xxxiii; E. Cussini, 'The Aramaic Law of Sale and the Cuneiform Legal Tradition' (Ph.D. diss., Johns Hopkins University, 1993), 180–85; D. M. Gropp, 'The Origin and Development of the *šalliṭ* Clause', *JNES* 52 (1993): 31–36; Porten, 'Aramaic-Demotic Equivalents', 260 no. 6; Ritner 'Third Intermediate Period Antecedents', 341–59.

4 Gropp, 'The *šalliṭ* Clause', 31.

5 See Gropp, *Wadi Daliyeh II* (WDSP 1.4; 4.5; 10.8); Gropp, 'The *šallīṭ* Clause', 32 n. 10. The rest of the שליט formulae in the operative clause are restored based on those three cases. The particularity of this construction שליט + noun was noted by Porten in his review of Cross's publication of SP 1. See B. Porten, 'Review of *Eretz Israel: Archaeological, Historical, and Geographical Studies. Volume 18*', *BASOR* 271 (1988): 85–86; שליט + noun is attested in a similar construction in 4QAram d Frag. 1.2 (J. T. Milik, '4Q Visions de 'Amran et une Citation d'Origène', *RB* 79 (1972): 84; cited by Gropp, 'The *šallīṭ* Clause', 34 n. 26).

6 See D. R. Hillers and E. Cussini, *Palmyrene Aramaic Texts* (Baltimore and London: Johns Hopkins University Press, 1996), 415.

7 Goldstein, 'Syriac', 1–16.

8 See Greenfield, 'Studies in the Terminology', 79–82.

9 P. Mur. 19.17–18, a divorce document where the woman is addressed with בנפשכי רשיא ('having control over yourself'); P. Benoit, J. T. Milik and R. de Vaux, *Les grottes de Murabbaʿat*, DJD 2 (Oxford: Clarendon, 1961), 104–09.

10 The entitlement clause of XḤev/Se pap Deed of Sale D ar l. 6 reads PN לעלם רשי ושלט ('Forever entitled and empowered are PN'); H. M. Cotton and A. Yardeni, *Aramaic, Hebrew and Greek Documentary Texts from* Naḥal Ḥever *and Other Sites*, DJD 27 (Oxford: Clarendon, 1997), 40.

11 See *KB*, 4.1521 s.v. שלט and 4.1524 s.v. שלט and M. Wagner, *Die lexikalischen und grammatikalischen Aramaismen im alttestamentlichen Hebräisch* (Berlin: Töpelmann, 1966): #306 and #309.

12 Also pointed out by Kutscher, 'New Aramaic Texts,' 239. See *KB*, 2.647–648 s.v. II משל; N. Lohfink, 'Melek Šallîṭ und Môšēl bei Kohelet und die Abfassungszeit des Buchs,' *Bib* 62 (1981): 535–43; C. L. Seow, 'Linguistic Evidence and the Dating of Qohelet,' *JBL* 115 (1996): 653–54.

as שלט, 'to give or deny right to do something', as in Exod. 21.8 'the master . . . shall not have the right to sell her (לֹא־יִמְשֹׁל לְמָכְרָהּ) to outsiders'; cf. *TAD* B2.4:6 לא שליט אנת לזבנה ולמנתן 'you do not have right to sell it or give it'. In Hebrew, שליט is attested fifteen times. It is used as a verb in the constructions -שליט ב with the meaning of 'having dominion over people – subjugate' (Est. 9.1); or 'having control/possession over things' (Eccl. 2.19). In the political realm -שלט על is used to mean 'to have control over people' as in Neh. 5.15 and Gen. 42.6. It is also used with ל + infinitive (Eccl. 5.18; 6.2). שלט is attested some 33 times in various Aramaic contexts in similar constructions, but as a verb it is mostly used with -ב (Dan. 2.38, 39; 3.27; 5.7, 16; 6.25) and once with -על in Dan. 2.48. Rabinowitz pointed to the similar formulation of Dan. 4.14, 'the Most High is sovereign (-שַׁלִּיט ב) over the realm of man, and He gives it to whom He wishes (ו...לְמַן־דִּי יִצְבֵּא יִתְּנִנַּהּ...)', and the Aramaic investiture and right of disposal formulae.[13] The root ש-ל-ט is also attested in Ugaritic, Ethiopic and Arabic. The wide geographical attestation of the שליט clause, however, does not imply uniformity in its construction or in its particular legal meaning for the different contexts.

The connections of the שליט clause with the Mesopotamian *ul išallat* ('to rule, be in authority, have control') and with the Demotic *ir sḫ.t* ('control') were already noticed by A. Ungnad[14] and J. J. Rabinowitz respectively.[15] This situation immediately raised the question of which is the borrowing and which is the lending legal tradition. There are two essential aspects of the discussion about the שליט clause that we will address here in pursuit of an answer to that question: first, its precise legal function in each context, and second, its origins.

4.1. *The Legal Function of the* שליט *Clause*

The general legal purpose of the שליט clause in the Elephantine Aramaic documents is to affirm or to deny a legal right, which is usually further specified in different contexts by means of complementary infinitives. For example, the right to build upon a wall, the right to open a gateway (*TAD* B2.1:11, 14); the right to sell a property (*TAD* B2.4:6, 9); the right to take/seize a security (*TAD* B4.4:19; B3.1:8, 16; B3.13:10); the right to take

13 Rabinowitz, 'Brooklyn 12', 128–29. שליט על is also used in *Genesis Apocryphon* 20.13. For later Aramaic usages see M. Sokoloff, *A Dictionary of Jewish Palestinian Aramaic of the Byzantine Period* (Ramat Gan: Bar Ilan University, 1990), 552b; idem, *A Dictionary of Jewish Babylonian Aramaic* (Ramat Gan: Bar Ilan University, 2002), 1149; and M. Jastrow, *A Dictionary of the Targumim, the Talmud Babli and Yerushalmi, and the Midrashic Literature*, 2 vols. (Brooklyn: Shalom, rpt. 1967), 2.1581a.

14 Ungnad, *Aramäische Papyrus*, 47 n. 8.

15 Rabinowitz, 'Brooklyn 12', 136 and the bibliography cited there.

another husband (*TAD* B3.8:33).[16] In those cases, there is little doubt about its legal meaning. The meaning of the clause is more ambiguous, however, when שׁליט is not specified by infinitives but is used in the positive construction אנת שׁליט ב- + property or its negative counterpart ב/ל PN לא שׁליט. This construction is attested four times in Elephantine:

לאם לא שליט]ה אנתי בביתה זי שלומם ונכסוהי וקנינה]

'[You] do not have right [to the house of Sheloman and his goods and his property]' (*TAD* B6.3:8)

גבר אחרן אמי ואבי אח ואחה ואיש אחרן לא ישלט בביתה כלה
להן בני זי ילדתי לי

'Another person – my mother or my father, brother or sister or another man – shall not have right to the whole house but [only] my children whom you bore me' (*TAD* B3.5:19–20)

בר לי וברה ואח לי ואחה קריב ורחיק הנגית והנבג לא שליט בכי
וביהישמע ברתכי זי לידתי לי

'Son or daughter of mine or brother of mine or sister, near or far, partner-in-chattel or partner-in-land does not have right to you or to Jeh(o)ishma your daughter, whom you bore me' (*TAD* B3.6:5–6)

וגבר אחרן לא שליט עליכי ועל יהישמע ברתכי

'another person does not have right to you and to Jeh(o)ishma your daughter' (*TAD* B3.6:9–10)

In his analysis of the uses of the שׁליט clause in the Samaria papyri, Gropp defined its legal purpose as 'something like the right of alienation'[17] and labelled it 'the right of disposal'.[18]

The Samaria papyri attest the שׁליט clause in the expressions PN-ל + PN + שׁליט and in its negative counterpart PN_2- ל + PN_1 + לא שׁליט (the PN_2 are slaves, i.e. the property conveyed).[19] It is used in both the transfer clause and the warranty clause to affirm the rights of the alienee to the property and to deny the rights of others to it. It is interesting that in the restorations of the Samaria papyri provided by F. M. Cross and Gropp,[20] they do not include a specific clause to express the right of alienation of the property (slaves in all cases), which is expressed, therefore, according

16 See also Muffs, *Studies*, 41 n. 2; Gropp, 'The *šallīṭ* Clause', 34.

17 Gropp, 'The *šallīṭ* Clause', 32.

18 Gropp, 'The *šallīṭ* Clause', 32.

19 Its clearest attestation is WDSP 7.16 (Gropp, *Wadi Daliyeh II*, 82). For a new edition of the Wadi Daliyeh corpus see J. Dušek, *Les manuscripts araméens du Wadi Daliyeh et la Samarie vers 450–332 av. J.-C.* (Leiden: Brill, 2007).

20 F. M. Cross, 'Samaria Papyrus I: An Aramaic Slave Conveyance of 335 BCE found in Wadi ed Daliyeh', *ErIsr* 18 (1985): 8–9; Gropp, *Wadi Daliyeh II*, 34 (WDSP 1).

to Gropp, by the שליט clause.[21] In the Elephantine documents, on the other hand, a division of slaves registers the right of alienation after the שליט clause: 'you, Jedaniah, have right to (שליט ב-) Petosiri, [...] and you may give [him] to whomever you desire' (*TAD* B2.11:6). Was the right of disposal concerning the slaves so obvious in Samaria that it was not necessary for it to be expressed? Are we to infer that the slave still had some rights which could limit the rights of the lord as described in Lev. 25.39–55?[22] The available material from Samaria does not warrant a definitive answer. Even if the right of disposal is a right that could be inferred from the use of שליט in the Samaria papyri, it does not necessarily follow that this is the legal meaning of the term. The semantic field of שליט and its cognates is related to that of 'control, dominion, and political authority'. In some contexts, the sole declaration that 'PN has control over X' could imply that PN will have both the right of usufruct and of disposal. It is also possible that in other contexts the right of disposal must be explicitly mentioned in the document in order for it to be effective, as seems to be the case in Elephantine.

In all the cases in the Bible where שליט ב- is used, its meaning is clearly related to the semantic field of 'dominion', 'control', and 'possession' without specific restrictions. In other cases, however, it is possible to specify this right further as in *TAD* B3.7:10 שליט ב- where it can be understood as 'right to usufruct'. It is not clear if this dominion/control could mean something slightly different in Gen. 42.6 where Joseph can 'dispense rations' and, therefore, has 'right of disposal' (שליט על-), but the ultimate owner of them is Pharaoh, which surely implied a limitation in Joseph's authority. This distinction, however, might not be applied to משל ב (cf. Gen. 45.8 and 45.26). The other case with שליט על is *TAD* B3.6, where Tapmet is set free (שביקה) and as a consequence no one will have right to/control over/right of disposal over her (לא שליט עליכי). In this case, however, there is no superior authority as is Pharaoh in Gen. 42.6.

The use of the שליט clause in Elephantine is less uniform and more complex than its Samarian counterpart. It can be summarized as follows:

Documents of Obligation (*TAD* B4.3:19 (483 BCE); B4.4:16 (483 BCE); B3.1:8, 16 (456 BCE); B3.13:10 (402 BCE)). The שליט formula functions as a component of the warranty clause covering the case of non-fulfilment of an obligation and non-indemnification,[23] such that the obligor has the

21 Gropp, *Wadi Daliyeh II* (WDSP 10). In Naḥal Ḥever, on the other hand, a legal clause recording the right of disposal of the alienee follows the שליט clause. See XḤev/Se pap Deed of Sale D ar l. 7 (Cotton and Yardeni, *Aramaic*, 40).

22 See R. de Vaux, *Ancient Israel: Its Life and Institutions*, 2nd edn. (New York and Toronto: McGraw-Hill, 1965), 82.

23 Indemnify means to restore the victim of a loss, in whole or in part, by payment, repair, or replacement: *Black's Law Dictionary* (St. Paul, Minn.: West, 1990), 769 s.v. 'Indemnify'.

right to take a security from among the property of the obligee. It seems an essential clause in these documents.

Documents of Wifehood (*TAD* B6.3:8 [third quarter of fifth century BCE]; B2.6:18 [449 BCE]; B3.3:11, 12 [449 BCE]; B3.8:33 [420 BCE]). In the marriage documents the clause is used within testamentary stipulations regarding the individual property of the spouses in case one of them dies when there are no children from the marriage.[24]

According to the stipulations stated in *TAD* B2.6 and B3.8, there is a difference between the rights of the woman and the rights of the man. While the woman will 'have right' (שליטה ב-) to the husband's property (*TAD* B2.6:18) or will '[hol]d on to it' ([א]חדתה) (*TAD* B3.8:29) the husband will 'inherit' (ירתנה) (*TAD* B2.6:21; B3.8:35). While to inherit the property implies full proprietary rights, to have control over it can be understood as something less than full ownership. This difference is confirmed in *TAD* B3.3:12 where, since the wife is a slave, the husband cannot aspire to gain full proprietary rights to her property, which should certainly remain in the hands of her master.[25] Therefore, he only gets 'control' or 'possession' (שליט).

The different legal implications of the use of the terms 'to control' and 'to inherit' could point to two different ways of assessing the rights of a person regarding property. These rights can be identified as 'possession' and 'ownership'. 'Possession' may be legally defined as 'the detention and control, or the manual or ideal custody, of anything which may be the subject of property, for one's uses and enjoyment, either as owner or as the proprietor of a qualified right in it'.[26] 'Ownership', on the other hand, may be legally defined as the 'collection of rights to use and enjoy property, including the right to transmit to others', and 'the complete dominion, title or proprietary right in a thing or claim'.[27]

This distinction between possession and ownership was a dominant characteristic of Ptolemaic law.[28] The terminology used was κυριεία or δεσπόζειν denoting possession, and κράτεσις denoting ownership.[29] As Taubenschlag remarks, however, 'the term κύριος is applied in a sense

24 See Yaron, 'Aramaic Marriage Contracts from Elephantine', 7–10.

25 See B. Porten and Z. Szubin, 'The Status of the Handmaiden Tamet: A New Interpretation of Kraeling 2 (*TAD* B3.3)', *ILR* 29 (1995): 43–64.

26 *Black's Law Dictionary*, 1163, s.v. 'Possession'.

27 *Black's Law Dictionary*, 1106, s.v. 'Ownership'.

28 It seems not to be the same case for ancient Egyptian law; see T. Mrsich, 'Besitz und Eigentum', in *Lexikon der Ägyptologie*, 7 vols., W. Helck and W. Westendorf, eds. (Wiesbaden: Harrassowitz, 1975–86), 1.732–43.

29 In the Roman era, these terms were replaced by νομή and δεσποτεία, which equalled the Roman *possessio* and *dominium*. See R. Taubenschlag, *The Law of Greco-Roman Egypt in the Light of the Papyri* (New York: Herald Square, 1944), 173–74.

transcending the meaning of "a possessing owner"; it indicates anyone with real rights, however restricted'.[30]

These considerations about the distinction between possession and ownership serve well as preface to the discussion about the function of שליט in conveyances.

Conveyances. Here we have the most complex cases for the understanding of the שליט clause. The formula is attested in sales (*TAD* B3.4:11 [437 BCE] and B3.12:23 [402 BCE]) and bequests (B2.3:9, 11 [460 BCE]; B3.7:9, 10 [420 BCE]; B3.10:13, 14, 21 [404 BCE]; B3.11:8, 11, 14 [402 BCE]).

If we assume that the function of the שליט formula is to affirm the rights of possession or that it 'indicates anyone with real rights, however restricted',[31] and that a similar distinction between 'possession' and 'ownership' is valid for the Aramaic documents, the question that immediately arises is whether there is another term in the Aramaic documents from Egypt that can account for full ownership, i.e. 'the complete dominion, title, or proprietary right in a thing or claim'.[32] If we consider the components of the investiture clause, the obvious candidate for such a function is the formula זילך הו, 'it is yours'. It is tempting, therefore, to propose that two different legal rights, i.e. possession and ownership, are expressed in the Aramaic documents by two different formulae within the investiture clause: the שליט clause and the זילך הו clause.[33]

The following logical step would be to assume that full ownership can only be conveyed in cases of a clear title. If this is true, the זילך הו clause should only be attested in the transfer clause of documents when the alienor had a clear title. This is exactly the case in *TAD* B2.7:7; B3.5:4; B3.10:11 where the זילך הו clause is included in documents where the alienor can declare that the property was bought, providing evidence of a clear title.[34] On the other hand, the omission of the זילך הו clause in cases of clear title would imply certain restrictions for the alienee.

The transfer clause of the sale of abandoned property (*TAD* B3.4:3, 10

30 Taubenschlag, *Law*, 174.

31 Taubenschlag, *Law*, 174.

32 *Black's Law Dictionary*, 1106, s.v. 'Ownership'.

33 For a similar approach see B. Porten, with J. Joel Farber *et al.*, *The Elephantine Papyri in English: Three Millennia of Cross-Cultural Continuity and Change*, DMOA 22 (Leiden: Brill, 1996), 153 n. 9, and B. Porten and H. Z. Szubin, 'An Aramaic Deed of Bequest (Kraeling 9)', in *Community and Culture: Essays in Jewish Studies in Honor of the Ninetieth Anniversary of the Founding of Gratz College*, N. Waldman, ed. (Philadelphia: Gratz, 1987), 185–86.

34 That Ananiah son of Azariah had a clear title when he bequested an apartment to his wife (*TAD* B3.5) may be open to discussion. His property, after all, was a purchase of abandoned property to Bagazushta and *Wbyl*, of which they had possession but not ownership and that could still be contested by the original owner, *ʾpwly* son of Misdaya, or any legitimate heir as stated in *TAD* B3.4:21–22.

11) seems at first to confirm this hypothesis. In this case, where no evidence of clear title is available, the transfer clause includes the elements: אנחן זבן ויהבן 'we sold and gave'; אנחן ... ורחיקן 'we withdrew'; אנת ... שליט 'you have control'. There is no זילך הו clause in the transfer clause. A few lines later, however, we have a *clausula salvatoria* that reads:

> הן גרינך דין ... אנחן ננתן לך כסף כרשן ... וביתא זילך אם
> וזי בניך מן אחרין
>
> 'if we institute suit ... we shall give you X karsh ... and the house is moreover yours and your children's after you'.[35]

What is the relation between the statement in the *clausula salvatoria* and that of the investiture? It is hard to accept that because of a suit the alienee will gain full ownership rights upgrading his previous right from control/ possession to full title.[36] Moreover, the defension clause of the document states that if the alienor should not be able to defend the property against the claims of a son or daughter of *ʾpwly*, the property would be returned. We need to conclude that the formula זילך הו placed in the *clausula salvatoria* is not a declaration of full ownership and, therefore, that the proposed distinction does not work in this document.[37]

Another problem is posed by the apportionment of slaves (*TAD* B2.11). In this case, there is evidence of clear title (the slaves are part of the inheritance), the right of disposal is spelled out, but no זילך הו is attested in the investiture, where only the שׁליט formula is included. Again, in the quitclaim (*TAD* B2.11:9-12) it is stated that:

> הן רשינך דינא ... ננתן לך אבינרנא ... ורחיקן אנחנה מנך ומן
> בניך מן דין עלדבר פטוסירי זך ... לך יהוה וזי בניך אחריך
>
> 'if we bring suit ... we shall give you (penalty) ... and are withdrawn from you and from your children from any suit on account of that Petosiri ... Yours shall he be and your children's after you.'[38]

A similar case is that of *TAD* B3.12, a sale of an apartment to a son-in-law. Here the transfer clause זבן ויהבן 'we sold and gave' is followed by the

35 *TAD* B3.4:14–16 and again in 19. It would be possible to think that the scribe had to use a *clausula salvatoria* and the only one at hand included the investiture clause זילך הו. In *TAD* B3.10:21, however, the *clausula salvatoria* reads, 'and you moreover have right and your children have right after you and you may give [it] to whomever you love'.

36 A similar situation occurs in the apportionment of slaves *TAD* B2.11:6, 12.

37 P. BM 10782, a Demotic lease of land dated 119 BCE., uses 'it is yours' and then specifies different rights. In this case (a lease) 'it is yours' should not be understood as a term for full ownership. C. Andrews, *Catalog of the Demotic Papyri in the British Museum*, vol. 4: *Ptolemaic Texts from the Theban Area* (London: British Museum, 1990), no. 22.

38 The opinion of Porten is that in this clause 'the scribe has reiterated and expanded the investiture clause (lines 6–7) – "not only do you have right of possession over (שׁליט ב-) that slave but also title to him (לך יהוה)"' (*Elephantine Papyri*, 201 n. 28). As stated above, an upgrade of the rights of the alienee in the warranty clause seems unlikely.

שליט clause 'you have right', and an alienation clause without the investiture clause זילך הו, albeit in this case there is evidence of a clear title. In this case, moreover, it is clear that the שליט clause is conveying full proprietary rights, since the document of acquisition is also transferred to the buyer.

These difficulties in defining the use of the legal formulae, according to modern legal use, say more about our limits in understanding the legal reality of that time than about the lack of precision of the scribes in their use of the legal formulae. We tend to think in absolute terms, i.e. ownership is an 'absolute' right, universal and independent of circumstances. The perspective of the ancient Egyptians and Aramaeans and of most of the Mediterranean peoples was different. In those 'face-to-face' societies, the affirmation that something 'is yours' is more of a strong affirmation of your right to the property in opposition to my rights to it than a universal right of ownership. When I say 'it is yours' it implies that it is not mine anymore, but I am transferring to you 'my' ownership rights, namely not a universal right to the property, but the previous rights to it that I held. Thus, the investiture clause is not a transfer of universal rights of ownership but a transfer of the alienor's rights. Therefore, a transfer of title from the alienor to the alienee should be expressed in the transfer clause, i.e. 'it is yours in respect to me'. When we have an investiture clause as part of the *clausula salvatoria* it means: 'the property will still be yours in respect to them'.[39]

The legal meaning of 'ownership' was not precisely defined in ancient legal systems. In both Mesopotamia and Egypt, it seems to have been associated with the concept of 'control' or 'authority' over property.[40] This terminology would have been reminiscent of times when communal property was the predominant type of ownership and the various members of a group received 'control' over a determined property while the ownership and right of alienation remained with the whole group (Lev. 25.23).

The study of the uses of the of שליט and זילך הו clauses leads to the conclusion that it is not possible to ascribe to each term a clear and differentiated legal meaning. There is, however, another approach to the problem of the meaning of שליט and זילך הו, and this is to understand both as conveying similar rights but originating in different scribal traditions.[41]

39 The investiture in *TAD* B2.3:19 works as apodosis of the affirmation of Mahseiah that he will not reclaim the property.

40 See G. Cardascia, '*Le concept babylonien de la propriété*', *RIDA*, 3rd series, 6 (1959): 19ff. and cf. É. Szlechter, 'Le Droit de propriété et la «Possession» (Codex Hammurapi)', *RIDA*, 3rd series, 34 (1987): 12–23.

41 See A. F. Botta, 'Scribal Traditions and the Transmission of Legal Formulae in the Aramaic Papyri from Elephantine', *RIHAO* 12 (2006): 153–68; P. Joüon, 'Notes grammaticales, lexicographiques et philologiques sur les papyrus araméens d'Égypte',

We know other cases in the ancient Near East where several scribal traditions were present in the same city; and, even if they belonged to the same legal tradition, their legal formularies included some variations.[42]

If we consider how the Elephantine scribes spelled out the investiture clause we observe that in the Ananiah tradition the investiture clause is always built up with זילך הו.[43] On the other hand, in the Shemaiah tradition the investiture is always built up with שליט [44] and once with both שליט and זילך הו.[45] In Syene, the Nabuzeribni tradition seems to follow a pattern similar to that of Shemaiah and builds the investiture clause with שליט.[46] We have, therefore, another example of the relevance of the variations of scribal traditions for the study of the legal formulary in Elephantine.

After all these considerations, we define the שליט clause as a clause conferring a 'right (...) to property, which may not be abridged without due process',[47] and that could be properly translated, 'you have authority/control'. Depending on the scribal tradition, the שליט clause could fulfil the same function as the זילך הו clause.

4.2. *The Origins of the* שליט *clause*

We want to turn to our second concern, the origin of the שליט clause. In this task it is necessary to keep in mind the two expressions of the clause in the Aramaic documents, the positive and the negative. Previous studies of the שליט clause have provided examples of similar formulae in the

---

MUSJ 18 (1934): 3–89; and M. L. Folmer, *The Aramaic Language in the Achaemenid Period: A Study in Linguistic Variation* (OLA 68; Leuven: Peeters, 1995), are the only linguistic studies that took into account the various scribal traditions attested in the Aramaic documents. The implications of the different origin of the scribes from Elephantine-Syene for the legal formulary, however, did not pass unnoticed in R. Yaron, *Introduction to the Law of the Aramaic Papyri* (Oxford: Clarendon, 1961), 12–13.

42 Nuzi is one of the best documented cases; see A. H. Friedman, 'Economic Geography and Administration at Nuzi' (Ph.D. diss., Hebrew Union College, Jewish Institute of Religion, Ohio, 1982): ch. 5, 'Notes on Scribal Activity at Nuzi', pp. 199–211. Differences in style between two of the Elephantine scribes, Mauziah b. Nathan, and Haggai b. Shemaiah, were noted by B. Porten, 'The Jews in Egypt', in *The Cambridge History of Judaism*, 5 vols., W. D. Davies and L. Finkelstein, eds. (Cambridge: Cambridge University Press, 1984), 1.396.

43 *TAD* B2.7; B3.5; B2.10.

44 *TAD* B3.4; B3.6; B3.10; B3.11; B3.12.

45 *TAD* B3.10. The Shemaiah tradition also distances itself from the rest of the Elephantine scribes in writing the place of execution of the document on the bottom as opposed to the usual practice in Elephantine of writing it at the top.

46 *TAD* B2.11 and B2.3. A second 'investiture' in B2.3:19, however, is built up with זילך הו.

47 *Black's Law Dictionary*, 532 s.v. 'Entitlement'.

Mesopotamian realm. Ungnad[48] pointed out the relationship between שליט and Mesopotamian legal terminology. Later, the negative שליט clause was well documented in Neo-Babylonian documents. A Neo-Babylonian conveyance reads:[49]

> *ul išallaṭ-ma PN [item] šuâtu ana kaspi ana rîmûti ana nadunnû ana epêš ṣubûtu ana mimma gabbi ana mamman šanamma gabbi elat* PN_2 *ul iddin u ul inamdin*
>
> 'PN (donor/seller) has no power of disposition, and has not given nor shall give that [item] for sale, as a gift, as a dowry, for disposal, for any other purpose to anyone else except PN_2 (recipient).'[50]

The similarities between the Neo-Assyrian and Neo-Babylonian usage and the Aramaic documents are striking: *ina muḫḫi memēni ina bīt bēliya la šal-ṭa-ak* 'I no longer have control over anything in my lord's house.'[51] A Neo-Babylonian deed reads: '[any of various officials] *ana muḫḫi* ^{f}PN *u mārīšu ul i-šal-aṭ* will not have control of ^{f}PN and her children';[52] which is very similar to the formula used in the testamentary manumission *TAD* B3.6:9–10 that reads:

> וגבר אחרן לא שליט עליכי ועל יהישמע ברתכי
>
> 'another person does not have control over you and over Jehoishma your daughter'.

More examples of the use of *šalaṭu* are attested in private votive donations to the temples from the Neo-Assyrian period: *man-nu ša ina UGU UN.MEŠ š[u-na-tu-nu] i- da-bu-bu i-šal-liṭ-ṭ[u-u-ni]* 'Whoever raises a claim against t[hose] people and tries to assert his contr[ol over them]'[53] (followed by a curse).

This convergence of legal formulae cannot be attributed to independent development but to interaction and borrowing and raises the question of who is the borrower and who is the lender. Gropp, following Muffs's approach,[54] assesses that 'Aramaic scribes creatively converted an

48 Ungnad, *Aramäische Papyrus*, 47 n. 8.

49 O. Krückmann, *Babylonische Rechts- und Verwaltungsurkunden aus der Zeit Alexanders und der Diadochen* (Weimar: Hof-Buchdruckerei, 1931), 4ff.

50 Krückmann, *Babylonische*, 42–43.

51 R. Harper, *Assyrian and Babylonian Letters Belonging to the Kouyunjik Collection of the British Museum*, 14 vols. (Chicago: University of Chicago Press, 1892–1914), 84 r. 7 (NA) cited in *CAD* Š, I, 238.

52 G. Contenau, *Contrats Néo-Babyloniens*, Textes Cunéiforms du Louvre 12 (Paris: Geuthner, 1927–29), 12 36.14 cited in *CAD* Š, I, 239.

53 L. Kataja and R. Whiting, *Grants, Decrees and Gifts of the Neo-Assyrian Period*, SAAS 12 (Helsinki: Neo-Assyrian Text Corpus Project of the University of Helsinki, 1995), #97.4–5. See also #69r.28; #86.35; #95.10; #96e.20; B. Menzel, *Assyrische Temple* (Rome: PBI, 1981), 2.23 n. 254 and documents #65.10; #66.14–20; #67.

54 Muffs, *Studies*, 41 n. 2.

Akkadian negative formulation into a positive transfer/investiture.'[55] Rabinowitz[56] and S. Kaufman, on the other hand, proposed that the Mesopotamian formula was 'modeled after Aramaic usage, not the reverse'.[57]

E. Kraeling also proposed a Babylonian origin[58] and denied that the Aramaic שליט formula was an 'Egyptianism'.[59] What is surprising is that no serious treatment of the Egyptian evidence was used to determine the origin of a legal formula found on Egyptian soil, and which is, moreover, widely attested in Egyptian legal documents. We wish to show that there is Egyptian evidence going back to the earliest stages of Egyptian history of the use of this formula that argue for an Egyptian origin of the שליט clause.

Referring to the Mesopotamian material, Gropp was willing to admit that 'it is true that the specialized usage we are most interested in is not attested until the seventh century',[60] but he was also willing to accept that 'the specialized usage derives easily from the general meaning of the root'.[61] This, however, could be said for the Egyptian evidence discussed below. The negative form of the שליט clause is clearly attested in seventh-century BCE Egypt, and its legal meaning could also have been derived from the general meaning of the root *sḫm*. Consider the following evidence for the negative use of the שליט clause in Egypt:

> Florence Stela 1639 (2507) (659 BCE):[62] (10) *bn iw rḫ rmt nb.t [n] pꜣ tꜣ ir sḫj [n] im=f* 'No man in the land will be able to exercise authority over it.'

> P. Rylands I (Demotic, 641 BCE):[63] (4) *bn iw rḫ ḫrṯ.w sn.w rmt nb pꜣ tꜣ*

55 Gropp, 'The *šallīṭ* Clause', 35; and also Dušek, *Les manuscrits araméens*, 76–77, who follows Gropp's conclusions.

56 Rabinowitz, 'Neo-Babylonian Legal Documents', 152.

57 Kaufman, *Akkadian*, 98–99.

58 Kraeling reached the conclusion that the שליט clause was Babylonian in origin by citing only one example of the late *ul išallaṭ* formula and without considering any Egyptian evidence; E. Kraeling, *The Brooklyn Museum Aramaic Papyri: New Documents of the Fifth Century B.C. From the Jewish Colony at Elephantine* (New Haven: Yale University Press, 1953), 148. Kutscher replied that although 'it figures prominently with the same meaning in Neo-Babylonian documents, ... this fact in itself does not prove anything' (Kutscher, 'New Aramaic Texts', 239).

59 Kraeling, *Brooklyn*, 148, citing J. Leibovitch, 'Quelques egyptianismes contenus dans les textes araméens d'Égypte', *BIE* 18 (1936): 10; but there is no indication in Leibovitch's article that he sustained such an opinion.

60 Gropp, 'The *šallīṭ* Clause', 34 n. 34.

61 Ibid.

62 M. Malinine, 'Ventes de tombes à l'époque saïte', *RdE* 27 (1975): 164–68.

63 F. L. Griffith, *Catalogue of the Demotic Papyri in the John Rylands Library Manchester*, 3 vols. (Manchester: John Rylands Library, 1909), trad. 3.44–45; transcription, 3.201–06.

> *ink ḥʿtj iw ir.t sḫ.t n.im n pꜣy=k bl* 'Neither children nor brothers nor any man in the land, including myself, will be able to exercise authority over it, except you.'

> P. Turin no. 248 (Abnormal Hieratic, 617 BCE):[64] (8*) mn rm nb n pꜣ tꜣ ḏr.f iw.f rḫ* (9*) ir sḫj.t.w pꜣj.k bl* 'No man in the whole land will be able to exercise authority [over it] except you.'

Due to the generally accepted opinion that the Aramaic legal formulary was brought to Egypt during the Assyrian conquest (671–664 BCE), proving the Egyptian roots of the שליט formula would necessitate providing examples of its use in Egypt prior to the seventh century BCE.

The quantity of Egyptian legal documents that have reached us is in no way comparable to the thousands of cuneiform tablets from the Mesopotamian realm. The scarcity of the material makes it necessary, therefore, to turn to other sources in order try to find the שליט formula. In the absence of documentary papyri, other types of legal and literary texts can provide evidence of legal practices and legal formulae. In order to decide the question of the origins of the שליט clause it is necessary to provide additional evidence of the usage of the שליט clause from such sources attested before the seventh century. While Mesopotamian evidence preceding this date has not been found so far, evidence of the Egyptian formula is clearly attested before the seventh century BCE.[65]

In order to claim his right to transfer his property to his daughter, Nakhtef-Mut cites a decree of the God (the king):

> Statute of Nakhtefmut (Osorkon II) (874–850):[66] *ir s nb sḫr.w n iš.t=f* 'Let every man exercise control over his property.'

64 M. Malinine, *Choix de textes juridiques en hiératique 'anormal' et en démotique* (Paris: Bibliothèque de l'École des Hautes Études, Sciences historiques et philologiques, 1953): 117–24.

65 The use of *sḫr* 'have power, authority' in the Decree of Amonrasonther for Neskhons (21st Dynasty, ca. 1075–945 BCE.) line 67 cited by Ritner is not related to the legal but to the magical-religious realm. Cf. Ritner, 'Third Intermediate Period Antecedents', 352. See W. Golésnicheff, *Papyrus Hierátiques* (Cairo: Institut Français d'Archéologie Orientale, 1927), 182; B. Gunn, 'The Decree of Amonrasonther for Neskhons', *JEA* 41 (1955): 85 and 91 n. 4. The same use of *sḫm* is widely attested in the Coffin texts (e.g. Coffin Text I.196h; III 224b, c; III 226a, b, d; III 228a, b, c; III 230a). The Maatkare Decree, also cited by Ritner, 'Third Intermediate Period Antecedents', p. 352, is not related to legal issues but political authority. The text appears in G. Maspero, *Les momies royales de Deir-el-Bahar*, 2 vols. (Mémoires publiées par les membres de la Mission archéologique française au Caire; Paris, 1889), 1.694–95; translation and comments in A. Gardiner, 'The Gods of Thebes as Guarantors of Personal Property', *JEA* 48 (1962): 64–67; biographical references in K. A. Kitchen, *The Third Intermediate Period in Egypt (1100–650 BC)* (Warminster: Aris & Phillips, 1995), 60–61.

66 Cairo 42208, cf. Ritner 'Third Intermediate Period Antecedents', 352; see G. Legrin, *Statues et statuettes des rois et de particuliers* 4 vols., CGC (Cairo: Institut Français

Going still further back in time, we find additional evidence of the legal use and meaning of the positive formula in the Coffin texts:

> Coffin Texts VII, 235 (Spell 1016) (early second millennium BCE): *ṯ3.n=i Ḥu sḫm.n=i m šiꜥ* ‘I have taken possession of Ḥu I have control over Sia.’

Here we have a clear synonymous parallelism between two words equally used in legal contexts: *ṯ3* ‘to take’ and *sḫm* ‘to have authority over’. The quite conservative character of the funerary spells strongly suggests that we are dealing here with a text probably composed much earlier than the Middle Kingdom. The evidence of the Egyptian formula does not go back to only the second millennium. The *imyt-pr* conveyances from the Old Kingdom provide more examples of the negative expression of the formula.[67]

In the testamentary enactment of *šnnw-ꜥnḫ* (ca. 2470 BCE) we read: *n rdi.n(.i) sḫm.s[n m rdi]t r isw, m imyt-pr n rmṯ nb igr ḏd.sn n msw.sn nw* ‘I have not given them authority to sell it (lit., give it for a price) or through *imyt-pr* to anyone but to their son.’[68]

The use of the *sḫm* clause in the testamentary enactment of *šnnw-ꜥnḫ* follows closely the formulation of the use of the שליט clause in the grant of usufruct *TAD* B2.4 that reads:

> ביתא זנך לא שליט אנת לזבנה ולמנתך רחמת לאטרנן
> להן בנין מן מבטחיה ברתי המו שליטן בה אחריכם
>
> ‘But that house – you do not have right to sell it or to give [it] affectionately to others but it is your children by Mibtahiah my daughter [who] have right to it after you [both].’

Another expression of the Egyptian *sḫm* formula is also similar to the expression -שליט ב in the Aramaic documents. Referring to a property

---

d’Archéologie Orientale, 1914), 3.22; E. Otto, *Die biographischen Inschriften der ägyptischen Spätzeit* (Leiden: Brill, 1954), 141; J. Johnson, ‘The Legal Status of Woman in Ancient Egypt’, in *Mistress of the House Mistress of Heaven*, A. K. Capel and G. E. Markoe, eds. (New York: Hudson Hills Press, 1997), 182.

67 See the ‘*Machtreservationklausel*’ in the documents collected in T. Mrsich, *Untersuchungen zur Hausurkunde* (Berlin: Hessling, 1968), 40, 49, 56, 72, 75; T. Logan, ‘The *Jmyt-pr* Document: Form, Function, and Significance’, *JARCE* 37 (2000): 49–73. I am indebted to J. Johnson for this reference.

68 *Urk*. I 36–37, translated by J. H. Breasted, *Ancient Records of Egypt* (Chicago: University of Chicago Press, 1906), I §23; Mrsich, *Untersuchungen*, §59; H. Goedicke, *Die privaten Rechtsinschriften aus dem Alten Reich* (Vienna: Notring, 1970), 75–80. Cf. Exod. 21.8 ‘the master … shall not have the right to sell her (לֹא־יִמְשֹׁל לְמָכְרָהּ) to outsiders’; and *TAD* B2.4:6 ‘you do not have right to sell it or give it’ לא שליט אנת לזבנה ולמנתן.

(slaves) received from his father, *Ppj* (5th Dynasty ca. 2487–2348 BCE)[69] says in his testamentary enactment: *nn rdj.n.j sḫm rmt nb im.sn* 'I have not given to any man control over them.'

The wide attestation of the *sḫm* formulae, with some variants,[70] during the Old Kingdom should certainly be enough proof of how deeply the שליט clause is rooted in the Egyptian legal tradition.[71]

The evidence provided above strongly supports the native Egyptian origins of the Aramaic שליט clause and suggests that the Aramaic clause was patterned after the Egyptian. If we accept the conclusion of Kaufman and Rabinowitz cited above as we do that the Mesopotamian *šalātu* clause was modelled after Aramaic usage, the conclusion should be, therefore, that Aramaic was in this case the bridge through which the Egyptian legal formulae reached Mesopotamia.

69 *Urk.* I 35, 13. Goedicke, *Privaten Rechstinschriften*, 108–12, Mrsich, *Untersuchungen*, 36–37; K. B. Gödecken, *Eine Betrachtung der Inschriften des Meten im Rahmen der sozialen und rechtliche Stellung von Privatleuten im ägyptischen Alten Reich* (Wiesbaden: Harrassowitz, 1976), 176.

70 For the various expressions see Gödecken, *Betrachtung*, 181.

71 It is attested in the testamentary enactments of *K3-m-nfrt* – 5th Dynasty, ca. 2487–2348 BCE – (*Urk.* I 11–15; Goedicke, *Privaten Rechtsinschriften*, 44–67; Logan, 'The *Jmyt-pr* Document', 54); in that of *Pn-mrw* – end of 5th Dynasty, ca. 2360 BCE – (B. Grdseloff, 'Inscription de Penmerou', *ASAE* 42 (1943): 39–63; Mrsich, *Untersuchungen*, 40–41; Goedicke, *Privaten Rechtsinschriften*, 68–74; Gödecken, *Betrachtung*, 178); in the inscription of – the end of the 5th Dynasty, ca. 2360 BCE – (*Urk.* I 24–31; Breasted, *Ancient Records*, §213–30; Mrsich, *Untersuchungen*, 70–84; Goedicke, *Privaten Rechtsinschriften*, 131–43; Logan, 'The *Jmyt-pr* Document', 52–53); in the testamentary enactment of *Nb-kw3-Ḥr* – the beginning of the 6th Dynasty, ca. 2320 BCE – (Goedicke, *Privaten Rechtsinschriften*, 81–103); and in the inscription of *Snnj* – late 6th Dynasty, ca. 2250 BCE – (*Urk.* I 115–117; Breasted, *Ancient Records*, §337–38; Goedicke, *Privaten Rechtsinschriften*, 186–89).

5

The 'Withdrawal' and Related Formulae in the Aramaic Legal Tradition

5.1. *The Use of* רחק *in the Aramaic Legal Documents from Elephantine*

The withdrawal clause was recognized as a legal formula soon after the first Aramaic papyri came to light.[1] Widely attested in the Semitic languages,[2] the general meaning of the root רחק was never a mystery and its legal function in the Aramaic documents was promptly defined as a technical term for quittance. Cowley translated יהבתה לכי ורחקת מנה ביתא זנה (*TAD* B2.7:7) as 'this house I give to you and I resign all claim to it';[3] and Kraeling translated אנחן זבן ויהבן לך ורחקן מנה מן יומא זנה ועד עלמן (*TAD* B3.4:10-11) as 'we have sold and given (over) to thee and have removed from it from this day unto forever'.[4] Later on, legal studies by Muffs and Yaron[5] provided more precision regarding its specific function in different contexts within the Aramaic corpus, setting the actual standard interpretation of the withdrawal formula. As recently defined by Porten, 'the technical term רחק indicates that the alienor had relinquished all rights to the object (...). Withdrawal was either from the alienee (...), from the object (...), or from both (...).'[6] This definition already points to some variation in the usage of the withdrawal formula in Elephantine which deserves a closer look. Our intention in this chapter is to explore the different expressions of the withdrawal formula in order to determine its

1 Some of the material of this chapter was presented in lectures at the University of Chicago ('Sojourners in Egypt: The Jewish-Aramaic Legal Formulary at Elephantine'. Workshop on Ancient Societies, 9 March 1999) and at the Aramaic Studies Section of the Society of Biblical Literature ('"Get away from me!" An Egyptological Approach to the Withdrawal Clause in the Elephantine Papyri', Annual Meeting in Boston, November 21–23, 1999).

2 *DNWSI* II, 1072–74.

3 Cowley, *Aramaic Papyri*, 38.

4 Kraeling, *Brooklyn*, 155.

5 Muffs, *Studies*, 24ff., 47–50, 118ff., 158ff.; and Yaron, 'Aramaic Deeds of Conveyance', 383–86.

6 Porten, *Elephantine Papyri*, 185 n. 17.

particular legal function in each context, and from them, to propose a coherent picture of the withdrawal formula that could account for both its particular function in the various documents and its absence in others. We are aware that, in some cases, such achievement would not be possible without some degree of speculation. The documents provide rich information regarding the usage of legal formulae; however, many facets related to the documents are hidden from us and some questions remain unresolved.

The withdrawal formula is attested sixteen times in the Aramaic documents from Elephantine, as chronologically displayed in Table VIII.

Table VIII: Occurrences of רחק in the Aramaic Legal Documents from Elephantine

	TAD **Scribe** **Date**	**Archive and type of document**	**Aramaic text and translation**
1	*TAD* B2.2:15 Itu son of Abah 464 BCE	Mibtahiah – Release after Judgment	ואנת רחיק מן כל דין זי יקבלון עליך עלדבר ארעא זך And you are far from every suit that they shall complain against you on account of that land
2	*TAD* B3.2:7 Bunni son of Mannuki 451 BCE	Ananiah – Release after Judgment	ויהבת לי דמוהי כסף שקלן 5 ורחקת מנך And you gave me its payment silver 5 shekels and I withdrew from you
3	*TAD* B2.7:7 Nathan son of Ananiah 446 BCE	Mibtahiah – Exchange	זנה ביתא יהבתה לכי ורחקת מנה This house, I gave it to you and withdrew from it
4	*TAD* B2.7:16 Nathan son of Ananiah 446 BCE	Mibtahiah – Exchange	זך ביתא יהבתה לכי ורחקת מנה That house, I gave it to you and withdrew from it
5	*TAD* B2.8:5-6 Peṭeese son of Nabunathan 440 BCE	Mibtahiah – Release after Judgment	וטיב לבבי במומאה דכה זי עבדתי לי על נכסיא אלך ורחקת מנכי מן יומא זנה ועד עלם And my heart was satisfied with that oath which you made for me about those goods and I withdrew from you from this day and forever

	TAD **Scribe Date**	**Archive and type of document**	**Aramaic text and translation**
6	*TAD* B2.8:11 Peṭeese son of Nabunathan 440 BCE	Mibtahiah – Release after Judgment	ואנה רחיק מן כל דין ודבב And I am far from every suit or process
7	*TAD* B3.4:10-11 Haggai son of Shemaiah 437 BCE	Ananiah – Sale	אנחן זבן ויהבן לך ורחקן מנה מן יומא זנה ועד עלמן We sold and gave (it) to you and withdrew from it from this day and forever
8	*TAD* B3.4:13 Haggai son of Shemaiah 437 BCE	Ananiah – Sale	אנחן זבן ויהבן לך ורחקן מנה We sold and gave (it) to you and withdrew from it
9	*TAD* B2.9:8-10 Mauziah son of Nathan 420 BCE	Mibtahiah – Release after Judgment	הוטבתם לבבן באלך נכסיא וטיב לבבן בגו מן יומא זנה עד עלם אנה מנחם ועניה רחיקן אנחנה מנך מן יומא זנה עד עלם (and) you satisfied our heart with those goods, and our heart was satisfied herein from this day forever. I Menahem and Ananiah, we are far from you from this day forever.
10	*TAD* B2.9:15 Mauziah son of Nathan 420 BCE	Mibtahiah – Release after Judgment	והו אפם רחיק מן אלה נכסיא And he is likewise far from these goods
11	*TAD* B5.2:7-8 Scribe unknown Last quarter of the 5th century BCE	Unknown – Release after Judgment	וטיב בבל[י . . .] [. . . אנה מתן] רחקת מנך מן י[ומא זנה ועד עלם . . .] and [my] heart was satisfied [. . . . . . I, Mattan], withdrew from you from [this] d[ay and forever]
12	*TAD* B5.5:4 Scribe unknown 420–400 BCE	Unknown – Exchange	יהבת לכי כסף . . . [ורח]קת מנכ[י] מן יומא זנה ועד עלם I gave you silver . . . and I [with]drew from yo[u] from this day and forever

TAD **Scribe Date**	**Archive and type of document**	**Aramaic text and translation**
13 *TAD* B5.5:7-8 Scribe unknown 420–400 BCE	Unknown – Exchange	יהבתהי לי וטיב לבבי [בגו מן יומא זנה ועד עלם ורחקת מנכי מן כס]פא זנה you gave it to me and my heart was satisfied [herein from this day and forever and I withdrew from you from] this [sil]ver
14 *TAD* B2.10:4 Mauziah son of Nathan 416 BCE	Mibtahiah – Document of Withdrawal	רחקת מנכם מן בית יזניה בר אוריה I withdrew from you from the house of Jezaniah son of Uriah
15 *TAD* B2.11:11 Nabutukulti son of Nabuzeribni 410 BCE	Mibtahiah – Division	ורחיקן אנחנה מנך ומן בניך מן דין עלדבר פטוסירי And we are far from you and from your children from (any) suit on account of that *Pet*[*osiri*
16 *TAD* D2.21:6 Scribe unknown End of 5th century BCE	Unknown – Fragmentary	...] ורחקת [מנכם ומן ב]ניכם ......[[... and withdrew] from you and from [your] c[hildren ...][7]

A close look at the various uses of the withdrawal clause shows that we are not dealing with a fixed legal formula that is always used in the same way. The use of the verb רחק is actually far from uniform. Yaron offered a basic classification of the withdrawal formula into two groups, the one 'expresses the idea of separation of the parties',[8] which derives from procedure and carries a legal meaning; the other 'expresses the idea of a man withdrawing from a piece of property'[9] (physical withdrawal) and is 'probably expressive of the fact that in the conveyance of land what actually happens is that the transferor abandons the land'.[10] Yaron's

7 Here we differ from the reconstruction proposed by Porten and Yardeni who reconstructed the formula 'and from that house'. The withdrawal formula 'I withdrew from you and from that house' is not attested elsewhere (what is attested is 'I withdrew from you from the house of PN – as in *TAD* B2.10:4). The withdrawal formula here should be read, therefore, 'and withdrew from you and from your children' ...] ורחקת [מנכם ומן ב]ניכם ......[as in *TAD* B2.11:11.

8 Yaron, *Introduction*, 81.

9 Ibid.

10 Yaron, *Introduction*, 82.

proposal rightly points to the *Sitz im Leben* in which the two formulations of the withdrawal clause would have originated.

Regarding the withdrawal from property, the fundamental question is, however, whether the withdrawal clause denoted the physical act of abandonment of the property or, instead, whether it indicated a final renunciation of rights based on a well-known ancient Near East legal metaphor.[11] Indeed, in a sale transaction of real property we expect both: for the seller to leave the property to allow the buyer to take possession of it and, at the same time, to renounce any claim on the property. Three objections may be posed against the former interpretation. First, in the ancient Near East during the second millennium and perhaps earlier,[12] the various uses of withdrawal clauses already had a metaphoric sense. Second, the physical interpretation of the formula does not have antecedents in the legal formulary of the Persian period, neither in the Semitic nor in the Egyptian realm.[13] Third, at least in one case (*TAD* B3.4, nos. 7 and 8), it is most likely that the property to be conveyed was abandoned and the alienors were not living there.[14] We assume, therefore, that by this period, the withdrawal formula had already reached a metaphoric meaning, indicating a legal and not a physical withdrawal. The fact that the second part of the Aramaic formula (מן בית) is built up with מן instead of עלדבר[15] might be explained in light of the Semitic use of the withdrawal formula as a withdrawal from property.[16]

Based on the function of the רחק formulae and the classification proposed above in 2.3.3, 'Levels of Analysis', we can arrange the occurrences of the רחק formulae in four groups. The withdrawal formula appears as:

1. **A withdrawal clause** in: 'I withdrew from you from the X property' (example 14). A release clause regarding the property.
2. **A central component of the release clause** in the documents of release

11 See below chapter 7, 'A Comparison of the Aramaic and Egyptian Uses of Withdrawal Formulae'.

12 The use of the withdrawal formula referring to movable goods (cf. example 10 above) and suits (cf. examples 1 and 6 above) supports the opinion that we are dealing here with a legal metaphorical use of the withdrawal formula.

13 The cases mentioned in 4.2.2.5, where the withdrawal is from the object, are not included in the standard formulary of any kind of legal document.

14 The property is described as lacking beams (נשרן) and therefore unlikely to have been inhabited. See Porten, *Archives from Elephantine*, 97; B. Porten and H. Z. Szubin, '"Abandoned Property" in Elephantine: A New Interpretation of Kraeling 3', *JNES* 41 (1982): 123–31.

15 עלדבר would convey the same meaning as Demotic *n*, as can be inferred from the endorsement of *TAD* B2.10.

16 See, for example, the use of רחק in the *Marzeaḥ* papyrus, below 5.1.3, 'The Use of רחק in North West Semitic', and the use of *rêqu* in *JEN* 221 from Nuzi, see below, pp. 167ff.

after judgment is found in examples 2, 5, 9, and 11 in the expressions:

a. 'You gave me X and I withdrew from you' (example 2).
b. 'My heart was satisfied ... and I withdrew from you' (examples 5 and 11).
c. 'You satisfied our heart, our heart was satisfied, we are far from you' (example 9).

3. **Two different components of the transfer clause** are found in examples 3, 4, 7, 8, 12, and 13 in the expressions:

   3.a. Legal withdrawal based on the metaphor of vacancy of property as in examples 3, 4, 7, and 8.[17]

   a. 'I gave it to you and withdrew from it' (examples 3 and 4).
   b. 'We sold and gave it to you and withdrew from it' (examples 7 and 8).

   3.b. Release

   'I gave it to you/You gave it to me, and I withdrew from you' (examples 12 and 13).

4. **Two different complements of the waiver of suit clause:**

   4.a. Withdrawal from suit or from persons from suit, a particularity of the Syene-Aramaean scribes, in examples 1, 6, and 15 in the expressions:

   a. 'You are far from any suit that they shall complain' (example 1)
   b. 'I am far from any suit or process' (example 6).
   c. 'We are far from you and from your children from any suit' (example 15).

   4.b. Withdrawal from object or from person, as in examples 10 and 16 in the expressions:

   a. 'And he is likewise far from these goods' (example 10).
   b. '[And withdrew] from you and from [your] c[hildren ...]' (example 16).

It is thus clear that the withdrawal clause in the Elephantine papyri is not an absolutely fixed formula. Instead, we find different uses of the withdrawal clause, i.e. different realizations of the metaphor of removal by physical distance applied to different contexts. These variations in the use of the withdrawal formula could be attributed both to the presence of different scribal traditions (see 4.a above) and to the fact that the Aramaic legal formulary in Elephantine was not rigid at that time. We will see in the next chapter that the situation is different in the Demotic legal documents where although the uses of the withdrawal clause are more diversified (i.e. it is used in a wide variety of documents), they are uniform in their expression (i.e. either *tw=y wy.k r-r=k n* X Property, 'I am far from

17 See the discussion below.

you regarding the X Property', or *iw=y r di.t wy=f r.r=k n.im=s* 'I will cause him to be far from you regarding it.').[18]

In regard to the morphological distribution, the root רחק is attested in the Elephantine legal documents ten times in Peal Perfect:[19] three times in the construction רחק + מן + Pronominal Suffix, referring back to the aforementioned object of the transaction (numbers 4, 7, and 8); five times in the construction רחק + מן + Pronominal Suffix, referring to a person (numbers 2, 5, 9, 11, and 12); and two times in the construction רחק + מן + Pronominal Suffix, referring to a person, + מן + independent noun referring back to the aforementioned object of the transaction (numbers 13 and 14). It is attested, also, five times as adjective: twice (numbers 1 and 6) in the construction Independent Personal Pronoun + רחק + [Action-noun] (Suit); once in each of the constructions, Personal Name(s) + רחק + Independent Personal Pronoun + מן + Pronominal Suffix, referring to a person (number 9); רחק + Independent Personal Pronoun + מן + Pronominal Suffix + מן + Other persons + מן + [Action-noun] (Suit) (number 15); and Independent Personal Pronoun + אפם + רחק + מן + Object (number 10). Moreover, the root רחק is attested eight times as a noun in מרחק 'withdrawal'.[20] We have chosen to translate the adjective cluster as 'I am far from ... ' and the active as 'I withdrew from'.

Related to the study of the withdrawal clause is the analysis of the functions of the ספר מרחק. Based on the same root רחק, we also have in Elephantine eight references to the document of withdrawal ספר מרחק. Two of them are in the body of the document (2 and 3) and the other six are dockets referring to the legal content of the document (1, 4–8). Table IX displays the references to the ספר מרחק arranged in chronological order.

18 See below 6.2, 'The Uses of *wy* in the Saite and Persian Periods (664–332 BCE)' and 6.3, 'Further Developments of *wy*-Based Formulae in the Ptolemaic Period'.

19 J. A. Fitzmyer regards it as a 'contractual' perfect. J. A Fitzmyer, 'The Syntax of Imperial Aramaic based on the Documents Found in Egypt' (Ph.D. diss., Johns Hopkins University, 1956), 176. See also Muraoka and Porten, *Grammar*, 193–94, §51.

20 See Table IX: Documents of Withdrawal.

Table IX: Documents of Withdrawal

TAD **Scribe Date**	**Archive and type of document**	**Aramaic text and translation**
1 *TAD* B2.2:22 Dargamana son of Khvarshaina 464 BCE	Mibtahiah – Release after Judgment	ספר מרחק זי כתב [דרגמ]ן בר חרשין ל מחסיה Document of withdrawal which [Dargama]n son of Khvarshaina wrote for Mahseiah.
2 *TAD* B2.3:23 Attarshuri son of Nabuzeribni 460 BCE	Mibtahiah – Bequest	אף איתי ספר מרחק 1 זי דרגמן בר חרשין חרזמיא כתב לי Moreover, there is 1 document of withdrawal which Dargamana son of Khvarshaina, the Khwarezmian, wrote for me.
3 *TAD* B2.3:25 Attarshuri son of Nabuzeribni 460 BCE	Mibtahiah – Bequest	וספר מרחק כתב ויהב לי And he wrote a document of withdrawal and gave (it) to me.
4 *TAD* D2.5:4 Unknown Middle of 5th century BCE	Unknown	ספר מרחק [זי כתב בר ל ה ברת גמריה] Document of withdrawal [which PN son of PN wrote for PN daughter of Gemariah].
5 *TAD* B2.8:14 Peṭeese son of Nabunathan 440 BCE	Mibtahiah– Release after Judgment	ספר מרחק זי כתב פיא למפטח[י]ה Document of withdrawal which Peu wrote for Miptah[ia]h.
6 *TAD* B3.6:18 Haggai son of Shemaiah 427 BCE	Ananiah – Testamentary Manumission	[ספר] מרחק זי כתב משלם בר זכור לתפמת ויהישמ [Document] of withdrawal which Meshullam son of Zaccur wrote for Tapmet and Jeh(o)ishm(a).
7 *TAD* B2.9:19 Mauziah son of Nathan 420 BCE	Mibtahiah– Release after Judgment	ספר [מרחק] זי כתב מנחם ועניה כל 2 בני מנחם בר שלומם [לידני]ה ומחסיה כל 2 בני אסחור בר צחא Document of [withdrawal] which Menahem and Ananiah, all (told) 2, sons of Menahem son of Shelomam wrote [for Jedania]h and Mahseiah, all (told) 2, sons of Esḥor son of Djeḥo.
8 *TAD* B2.10:20 Mauziah son of Nathan 416 BCE	Mibtahiah – Document of Withdrawal	ספר מרחק זי כתב ידניה בר הושע על בית יזניה בר אוריה לידניה בר נתן ומחסיה אחוהי כל 2 Document of withdrawal which Jedaniah son of Hosea wrote about the house of Jezaniah son of Uriah for Jedaniah son of Nathan and Mahseiah his brother, all (told) 2.

The ספר מרחק and its Egyptian linguistic and functional counterpart, the Demotic document of withdrawal *sẖ n wy*, were considered by Muffs later developments of the cuneiform *ṭuppi lā ragāmim* 'document of no-contest'.[21] The cuneiform origin of the ספר מרחק, however, cannot explain the reason why *TAD* B3.6 (Kraeling 5), a testamentary manumission, is also called ספר מרחק. However, what cannot be explained in the light of the cuneiform legal tradition can be explained in the light of the Egyptian uses of the verb *wy* 'to be far'. We will see later that in the Rosetta Stone[22] the withdrawal formula is used in the context of liberation of prisoners, a situation similar to the liberation of a slave in *TAD* B3.6.

In what follows, we describe and analyse the various types of documents containing רחק formulae. The classification is based on the legal function of the document. In section 5.1.1, we will analyse רחק in transfer, including different types of conveyances, which include some form of the withdrawal formula (*TAD* B2.7; B3.4; B2.10; B2.11; and B5.5).[23] In section 5.1.2, רחק in litigation, we will analyse the documents of release after judgment (*TAD* B2.2; B2.8; B2.9; B3.2; and B5.2).

As we mentioned above, the main purpose of this chapter is to describe the function of the withdrawal formula in the various documents and not to produce a detailed analysis of the whole Aramaic formulary. Some of the Aramaic formulae have been studied in detail and it is not our purpose to repeat previous discussions. In some cases, however, when our interpretation of a particular legal formula differs from the accepted scholarly opinion, we will briefly state our dissenting view regarding it. Finally, at the end of the each section ('רחק in Transfer' and 'רחק in Litigation'), we will present a summary of the function of the withdrawal formula for the various types of documents.

5.1.1. רחק *in Transfer*

We adopted the definition of transfer as 'an act by which the title to property is conveyed from one person to another, meaning every mode of disposing of or parting with property'.[24] The Aramaic documents from Egypt attest five types of transfers: (a) sale (*TAD* B3.4; B3.12; and B5.6); (b) bequest (*TAD* B3.5; B3.7; B3.10; B3.11; and B2.3[25]); (c) exchange (*TAD* B2.7; B5.1; and B5.5); (d) withdrawal (*TAD* B2.10); (e) division

21 Muffs, *Studies*, 25 n. 3; 81.

22 See below 6.3.12, 'The *wy* Formula in Release of Prisoners'.

23 For documents of transfer that do not include a רחק formula see below 5.1.1.6, 'Summary: רחק in Transfer'.

24 *Black's Law Dictionary*, s.v. 'Transfer'.

25 *TAD* B2.4 enters into the category of 'additionales', i.e. 'additional terms or propositions to be added to a former agreement' (*Black's Law Dictionary*, s.v. 'Additionales'). The former agreement to which *TAD* B2.4 refers is *TAD* B2.3, a bequest by Mahseiah to her daughter Mibtahiah drawn up on the same day as *TAD* B2.4 (1 December 459 BCE). *TAD* B2.4 records the permission by Mahseiah to Mibtahiah's husband, Jezaniah, to make improvements in the property he bequeathed to her daughter. In exchange for his investment in improving the house, Jezaniah receives right to half of it, but

(*TAD* B2.11). A withdrawal formula, however, is not attested in all of them. It is absent from (a) two deeds of sale (*TAD* B3.12 and B5.6), (b) all the bequest documents, (c) exchange (*TAD* B5.1). Documents recording a withdrawal formula are: (a) sale (*TAD* B3.4) as a component of the transfer clause;[26] (c) exchange (*TAD* B2.7; and B5.5) also as a component of the transfer clause;[27] (d) withdrawal (*TAD* B2.10) as a withdrawal clause;[28] (e) division (*TAD* B2.11) as complement of the waiver of suit clause.[29] The question naturally arises, therefore, why the withdrawal formula is absent from these documents.[30]

In what follows, we present a complete outline of each of the five transfer documents so that we may see how the withdrawal formula functions in the larger context. References to Demotic parallels are cited where pertinent. The documents are arranged in chronological order.

5.1.1.1. *Exchange:* TAD *B2.7 (Cowley 13) November 17, 446 BCE*
This document records the grant of a house by Mahseiah son of Jedaniah to his daughter Mibtahiah. It was drawn up by the scribe Nathan son of Ananiah on 17 November 446 BCE, in Elephantine. Mibtahiah had provided goods for her father Mahseiah while he was 'garrisoned'[31] in the fortress. In exchange for those goods, Mahseiah gave to Mibtahiah a house he bought from Meshullam son of Zaccur son of Ater. In this case, the goods received by Mahseiah (5 karsh = 50 shekels) largely exceeded the value of the house (certainly no more than 20 shekels).[32] This document is classified in the Endorsement as a Document of a House (ספר בי).

The structure of the document reads as follows:

with the restriction that he is not allowed to sell it to others but to keep it for the couple's children who will have 'right to it after you' (*TAD* B2.4:12). See Porten, *Elephantine Papyri*, 172–75.

26 See Table IX, examples 7 and 8.

27 See Table IX, examples 3 and 4 for *TAD* B2.7 and examples 12 and 13 for *TAD* B5.5.

28 See Table IX, example 14.

29 See Table IX, example 15.

30 See below 5.1.1.6, 'Summary: רחק in Transfer'.

31 *TAD* B2.7:5. For the meaning of הנדיז see Porten, *Elephantine Papyri*, 136 n. 14; *DNWSI*, 288 s.v. hndyz.

32 See Porten, *Elephantine Papyri*, 185 n. 9. There is not enough evidence in the document to understand how Mibtahiah acquired such an amount of property and why she would accept a house in exchange valued at only a fraction of the goods she delivered. See Porten, *Archives from Elephantine*, 244–45.

TAD B2.7: Grant of a House in Exchange for Goods

I. **Date:** Babylonian and Egyptian
II. **Parties:** Mahseiah speaks to Miptahiah
III. **Abstract**
  A. **Certificate of Transaction:** 'I gave to you ...'
  B. **Object:** a house,
  C. **Pedigree:** 'which Meshullam son of Zaccur son of Ater (...) gave me for its value'
IV. **Performance:** Exchange: goods given previously by Miptahiah to Mahseiah; house given by Mahseiah to Miptahiah
V. **Document Transfer:** 'and I gave you the old document which that Meshullam wrote for me concerning it'
VI. **Transference**
  A. **Transfer:** 'I gave it to you'
  B. **Withdrawal:** 'and withdrew from it'
VII. **Investiture**
  A. **Personal:** 'it is yours'
  B. **Heirs:** 'and your children after you'
  C. **Right of Disposal:** 'and to whomever you love, you may give it'
VIII. **Quitclaim**
  A. **Covenant of Non-claim (general):** 'I shall not be able – I or my children, or seed of mine or another person – to bring against you suit or process in the name of that house'
  B. **Provisions in case of Violation of Covenant of Non-claim (general):**
    1. **Penalty:** 'Whoever shall institute against you suit or process shall give you silver 10 karsh'
    2. **Clausula Salvatoria:** 'and moreover (the) house is yours'
IX. **Invalidity of other Documents:** 'Moreover another person shall not be able to take against you a new or old document, but (only) this document which I wrote and gave you. Whoever shall take out against you a document, I did not write it'
X. **Boundaries:** above, below, east, west
XI. **Transference (bis)**
  A. **Transfer:** 'I gave it to you'
  B. **Withdrawal:** 'and withdrew from it'
XII. **Investiture (bis)**
  A. **Personal:** 'it is yours forever'
  B. **Right of Disposal**: 'and give it to whomever you desire'
XIII. **Scribe:** Nathan son of Ananiah
XIV. **Dictation:** 'at the instruction of Mahseiah'
XV. **Witnesses:** 6
XVI. **Endorsement:** Document of a House (ספר בי)

As usual in the transfer documents, *TAD* B2.7 begins with an abstract. As was noticed by Porten,[33] the scribe Nathan son of Ananiah arranged the abstract, the performance, and the transference clauses in a chiastic structure:

> a. I gave to you the house, which Meshullam son of Zaccur son of Ater gave me
>> b. and a document he wrote for me about it
>>> c. and I gave it to Mibtahiah in exchange for her goods
>>>> d. which she gave me. I consumed them but did not find silver or goods to repay you.
>>>
>>> c^1. I gave to you this house in exchange for your goods worth 5 karsh.
>>
>> b^1. And I gave you the old document, which Meshullam wrote for me.
>
> a^1. This house I gave it to you and withdrew from it.

To keep the chiastic structure, the scribe Nathan son of Ananiah had to alter the structure of the document, displacing the boundaries clause to the end of the document and duplicating the transference clause (VI. and XI.) and the exchange clause (VI.A and B = c and c^1 in the structure). The formula of exchange יהב ל-PN חלף is another Aramaic legal formula with a Demotic equivalent *dy(y) n=PN Object n tꜣ šb(.t) n Object* ('I gave to PN Object in exchange for Object') also attested in documents of exchange.[34]

Because of the duplication of the transference clause, we thus have two

33 Porten, *Elephantine Papyri*, 184; idem, 'Structure and Chiasm in Aramaic Contracts and Letters', in J. Welch, ed., *Chiasmus in Antiquity* (Hildesheim: Gerstenberg, 1981), 172.

34 Beside this text, חלף is attested in *TAD* B2.4:10 and 11; B5.1:3; B7.3:8 and 9. See *DNWSI* 377, s.v. $ḥlp_4$; J. Ribera, 'El doble significado de la partícula aramea *ḥlf*'; *AuOr* 8 (1990). 136–38. In Demotic it is attested in P. Turin 2128, l. 2 = P. Tsenhor 17 (Thebes, 487 BCE). The expression *n tꜣ šbt* is also attested in P. Turin 2139, l. 13–14 = P. Tor Amenothes (Thebes, 118 BCE); following the satisfaction clause in P. Turin 2124 = P. Tsenhor 11, l. 2 (Thebes, 507 BCE); P. Heidelberg 32, 9 (104–100 BCE) = U. Kaplony-Heckel, *Die demotischen Gebelen-Urkunden der Heidelberger Papyrus-Sammlung* (Heidelberg: Carl Winter, 1964), 65–6. P. Vindob. 10.151, 2 (460 or 337/336 BCE); P. BM 10589, 9, 11, 14 = A. F. Shore and H. S. Smith, 'Two Unpublished Demotic Documents from the Asyut Archive', *JEA* 45 (1959): 52–60. See also W. Spiegelberg, *Demotische Grammatik* (Heidelberg: Winter, 1925), § 358; K. Sethe and J. Partsch, *Demotische Urkunden zum aegyptischen Bürschaftsrechte vorzüglich der Ptolemäerzeit*, Abhandlungen der Sächsischen Akademie der Wissenschaften zu Leipzig, Philologisch-Historische Klasse 32 (Leipzig: Teubner, 1920), 365. P. W. Pestman and S. P. Vleeming, *Les Papyrus Démotiques de Tsenhor (*P. Tsenhor*): les archives privées d'une femme égyptienne du temps de Darius 1er* (Leuven: Peeters, 1994), 92, III; idem, *L'Archivio di Amenothes figlio di Horos (*P. Tor. Amenothes*): testi demotici e greci relativi ad una famiglia di imbalsamatori del secondo sec. a* (Milano: Goliardica,1981), 122 n. m.

occurrences of the withdrawal clause type 3 (withdrawal from object) with the same meaning.[35] The withdrawal clause is, in this case, an essential part of the transfer clause which precedes the investiture. We propose that the clause 'I withdrew from X Property' implies legal withdrawal and, therefore, a legal renunciation of rights to the property, based on the metaphoric use of a physical withdrawal i.e. 'to move out, to surrender possession by removal'.[36]

5.1.1.2. *Sale:* TAD *B3.4 (Kraeling 3) September 14, 437 BCE*

The Aramaic sale documents comprise *TAD* B3.4 (437 BCE); B3.12 (402 BCE); and B5.6 (Saqqara, end of fourth century BCE). The characteristic of these documents is that a payment in silver is required in exchange for the property.[37] As we mentioned before, *TAD* B3.4 is the only one of the three where a withdrawal formula is documented. It records the conveyance of a house from Bagazushta and *Wbyl* to Ananiah.[38] It was drawn up by the scribe Haggai son of Shemaiah on 14 September 437 BCE, at the request of Bagazushta and *Wbyl.* The endorsement describes the document as the 'sale of a house' ('Document of a house which Bagazushta and *Wbyl* sold to Ananiah'). As Porten and Szubin demonstrated,[39] Bagazushta and *Ybl* did not have clear title to the property but only possession, and it is for this particular reason that they included an exception in the general warranty clause considering the possibility that the rightful owners might claim the property from Ananiah.

The structure of the document reads as follows:

TAD B3.4: Conveyance of Abandoned Property

I. Date: Babylonian and Egyptian
II. Parties: Bagazushta and lady *Wbyl* speak to Ananiah
III. Abstract
  A. Certificate of Transaction: 'we sold and gave to you'
  B. Object: 'the house of ʾpwly son of Misdaya'

35 See Table IX and the classification following it.

36 *Black's Law Dictionary*, s.v. 'Vacate'.

37 The sequential components of a sale according to the Judaean tradition are well described in the known passage of Jer. 32.9-11. In this passage, we observe the necessity of a verbal agreement, the weighing of the silver, the need for a deed signed by the buyer, the presence of witnesses, and the public character of the transaction. For Jer. 32.9-11 see W. L. Holladay, *Jeremiah 2: A Commentary on the Book of the Prophet Jeremiah, Chapters 26–52* (Minneapolis: Augsburg Fortress 1989), 214–15. The same elements are present in Gen. 23.1-20.

38 See Porten, *Elephantine Papyri*, 212–15; Porten and Szubin, 'Abandoned Property', 123–31.

39 'Abandoned Property', 123–31.

C. **Description:** 'whose walls are standing ... '

IV. **Performance:** Payment: 'We sold and you gave us its payment in silver'

V. **Satisfaction:** 'and our heart was satisfied with the payment you gave us.'

VI. **Boundaries:** above, below, east, west

VII. **Transference**

A. **Sale:** 'we sold, and gave to you'

B. **Withdrawal:** 'and withdrew from it from this day and forever.'

VIII. **Investiture**

A. **Personal:** 'you have authority over that house,'

B. **Heirs:** 'and your children after you,'

C. **Right of Disposal**: 'and to whomever you desire to give it.'

IX. **Quitclaim**

A. **Covenant of Non-claim (personal)**: 'We shall not be able to institute against you suit or process.... '

B. **Provisions in case of Violation of Covenant of Non-claim**

1. **Penalty:** 'If we institute against you suit or process ... we shall give you silver, 20 karsh'

2. **Clausula Salvatoria:** 'and the house is moreover yours ... '

C. **Covenant of Non-claim (special):** 'And son or daughter of ours shall not be able to institute against you suit or process ... '

D. **Provisions in case of Violation of Covenant of Non-claim**

1. **Penalty:** 'If they institute suit against you ... they shall give you 20 karsh'

2. **Clausula Salvatoria:** 'and the house is moreover yours ... '

X. **General Warranty**

A. **Defension:** 'And if another person institute suit against you ... we shall stand up and cleanse (it) and give (it) to you within 30 days'

B. **Provisions in Case of Non-defence:**

1. **For every claim:** 'we or our children shall give you a house in the likeness of your house'

2. **In case of claim by owners:** 'we shall give you your silver 1 karsh, 4 shekels and (the value) of the building (improvements) which you will have built in it'

XI. **Scribe:** Haggai son of Shemaiah

XII. **Dictation:** 'at the instruction of Bagazushta and *Wbyl*

XIII. **Witnesses:** 4

XIV. **Endorsement:** Document of a House (ספר בי) which Bagazushta and *Wbyl* sold to Ananiah, servitor of YH in Elephantine

The operative section of the sale document begins with an abstract, i.e. a summary that comprises, in and of itself, the essential qualities of the document. The abstract includes the basic legal formula involving the notions of sale in the Aramaic documents of Elephantine 'to sell' and 'to give', Aramaic זבן and יהב, that will later appear again in the document in the transfer clause (VII.A.).[40]

Moving out of the abstract to the operative section of the document, we find that the dynamic of the transaction follows the sequence: seller: זבן to the buyer, which is the transaction *per se*; then, we have a bipartite structure: the buyer gives the payment and the seller is satisfied with the payment; the seller withdraws from the property and the buyer has 'authority', i.e. control/possession, which is expressed here by the שליט clause.

The withdrawal formula (VII.B.) is found between the sale-transfer (VII.A.) and the declaration of the right of control/possession of the buyer (VIII. Investiture clause).[41] It is, therefore, an essential part of the transfer in this document. The operative section of the Aramaic documents is usually built up, amid repetitions, by pairs of formulae recording an action and its legal consequence.[42] Here in *TAD* B3.4 we have:

> You gave us its payment ⇒ Our heart is satisfied with the payment
>
> Description of the Property
>
> We withdrew from the house ⇒ You have authority over it

We consider that here too, the withdrawal clause in this context also implies the legal, not necessarily physical, withdrawal from the property and has as its direct consequence the fact that the alienor receives the authority/control over the property. As Porten pointed out, the run-down house was held in adverse possession by Bagazushta and *Wbyl*, probably facilitated by *Wbyl*'s father, Shatibara, whose house was adjacent to the sold property.[43] The legal meaning of this withdrawal formula would be

40 For the meaning of זבן and יהב see A. F. Botta, 'A Reevaluation of the use of זבן and יהב in Elephantine' *Antiguo Oriente* 6 (2008), 99–108.

41 Similar components, but in different order, are to be found in the Ptolemaic P. Lille (Memphis (?), 136 BCE) published by B. Menu, 'Vente d'une vache de labour sous Ptolémée VIII Evergète II', *Cahiers de Recherches de l'Institut de Papyrologie et d'Égyptologie de Lille* 6 (1981): 229–42; where the document reads: *[mtw=k] tꜣy=k iḥ.t tꜣy di=y st n=k (r)-ḏbꜣ ḥḏ tw=y wy.k r-r=k di(=y) st (n=k)* 'it is yours, this cow, I sold it to you, I am far from you, I gave it to you'.

42 For example, *TAD* B.2.2:11-12 'You swore to me by YHW and satisfied my heart about that land'; B2.3:8-9 'That house, land – I gave it to you ... you have right to it', etc.

43 Porten, *Elephantine Papyri*, 212.

the same as in *TAD* B2.7:7, i.e. to metaphorically move out, to surrender possession by metaphoric removal.[44]

5.1.1.3. *Document of Withdrawal:* TAD *B2.10 (Cowley 25) 16 December 416 BCE*

This document records the withdrawal of Jedaniah son of Hoshaiah from the house of Jezaniah son of Uriah in favour of the brothers Jedaniah and Mahseiah sons of Nathan and Mibtahiah. It was drawn up by the scribe Mauziah son of Nathan on 16 December 416 BCE. Jedaniah was a nephew of Jezaniah, Mibtahiah's first husband, and in the absence of sons or daughters of Jezaniah, the natural legal heirs, Jedaniah might have had some rights to the property, which he relinquished to the sons of Mibtahiah and her husband, Nathan.[45] The structure of *TAD* B2.10 reads as follows:

TAD B2.10: Document of Withdrawal

I. **Date:** Babylonian and Egyptian
II. **Place:** Elephantine
III. **Parties:** Jedaniah son of Hoshaiah son of Uriah speaks to Jedaniah and Mahseiah sons of Nathan
IV. **Withdrawal**
  A. **Withdrawal:** 'I withdrew from you . . . '
  B. **Object:** ' . . . from the house. . . . '
  C. **Boundaries:** above, below, east, west
  D. **Description:** 'windows are open'
V. **Investiture**
  A. **Personal:** 'the house . . . is yours forever'
  B. **Heirs**: 'and your children's after you'
  C. **Right of Disposal:** 'and to whomever you love, you may give it'
VI. **Quitclaim**
  A. **Covenant of Non-claim (special):** 'I shall not be able, I or my children, to institute suit or process against you or your children'
  B. **Provisions in Case of Violation of Covenant of Non-claim (special)**
    1. **Penalty:** 'and if I Jedaniah bring suit . . . (excluding liability for suits in the name of son or daughters of Jezaniah son of Uriah) I shall give you 10 karsh, without suit'

44 Based on *Black's Law Dictionary*, s.v. 'Vacate'.

45 Yaron, *Introduction*, 75–76; Porten, *Archives from Elephantine*, 240–45; idem, *Elephantine Papyri*, 195–98.

2. **Clausula Salvatoria:** 'and moreover the house is yours forever and your children's after you'

VII. **Scribe:** Mauziah son of Nathan
VIII. **Dictation:** 'at the instruction of Jedaniah son of Hosea'
IX. **Witnesses:** 8
X. **Endorsement:** ספר מרחק ... על בית יזניה 'Document of withdrawal ... about the house of Jezaniah'

This document and *TAD* B3.9 are the only documents drawn up before the Persian authorities. Muffs classified *TAD* B2.10 as Transfer-*mrḥq* which 'records the transfer and relinquishment of goods without specifying the reason for the transfer'.[46] On the other hand, Kraeling, Yaron, and Cussini have proposed that the document is most likely the result of litigation based on the presence of the Persian authorities.[47] However, the aforementioned *TAD* B3.9 was also drawn up in the presence of Persian authorities and is a Document of Adoption without any traces of either dispute or litigation whatsoever.

Even if *TAD* B2.10 could have come out as a result of litigation between Jedaniah son of Nathan and his brother Mahseiah against Jedaniah son of Hoshaiah the presence of Vidranga is not necessarily substantial evidence of that; however, it could be evidence of the required public character of the transaction involved, or of the use of the Persian authorities as 'privileged' witnesses, similar to the way the king and notables appear in the conveyances from Ugarit.[48] Moreover, all the Documents of Release after Judgment include a clause of Record of Litigation,[49] which is not the case with *TAD* B2.10. Porten and Szubin rightly suggest that 'one should resist the temptation to interpret Yedaniah's act as consequent to the loss of a legal suit'.[50]

This document is a Document of Release-conveyance that follows closely the formulary of the Egyptian *sẖ n wy*.[51] At a later point, we shall discuss more extensively the legal significance of the Demotic *sẖ n wy*.[52] The constitutive element of the *sẖ n wy* is the formula '*tw=y wy.k r-r=k n X property*' 'I am far from you regarding the X property.' We may

46 Muffs, *Studies*, 17.

47 Kraeling, *Brooklyn*, 57; Cussini, 'Aramaic Law of Sale', 201, following Yaron, *Introduction*, 41, 75–76. Yaron, however, does not explicate the basis for his assumption.

48 J. Nougayrol, *Le Palais Royal D'Ugarit III: Textes Accadiens et Hourrites des Archives Est, Ouest et Centrales* (Paris: Imprimerie nationale, 1955), nos. 15.138; 16.256; 16.245.

49 See below 5.1.2, 'רחק in Litigation: Documents of Release after Litigation', p. 120.

50 Porten and Szubin, 'Exchange of Inherited Property', 654.

51 For the variations in the formulary of the *sẖ n wy* see K.-Th. Zauzich, *Die Ägyptische Schreibertradition in Aufbau, Sprache und Schrift der demotischen Kaufverträge aus ptolemäischer Zeit* (Wiesbaden: Harrassowitz, 1968), 119–24.

52 See below 6.2.1.3.2, 'The Document of Withdrawal *sẖ n wy*'.

assume that the Aramaic construction follows the Egyptian model and, consequently, is conveying a similar legal meaning: 'I relinquish my rights to you regarding the property.'

This cession of rights, however, is not made in the context of a sale but of a probate, as Porten and Szubin have demonstrated,[53] i.e. 'the legal process wherein the estate of the decedent is administered'.[54] The presence of the official authorities fulfils the function of the modern probate court, which is responsible for collecting a decedent's assets, liquidating liabilities and distributing property to heirs.

5.1.1.4. *Division of Inheritance:* TAD *B2.11 (Cowley 28) 10 February 410 BCE*

This document was drawn up by Nabutukulti son of Nabuzeribni (son of the scribe Attarshuri son of Nabuzeribni) in Elephantine on 10 February 410 BCE, at the instruction of Mahseiah son of Nathan and his brother Jedaniah. *TAD* B2.11 deals with the division of two slaves inherited by Mahseiah and Jedaniah from their mother Mibtahiah.[55] The structure of the document reads as follows:

TAD B2.11: Division of Inheritance

I. **Date:** Babylonian and Egyptian
II. **Place:** Elephantine
III. **Parties:** Mahseiah and Jedaniah sons of Nathan speak
IV. **Abstract**
   A. **Certificate of Transaction:** 'We have acted as equals as one and divided (between) us'
   B. **Object:** 'the slaves of Mibtahiah our mother'
V. **Transference**
   A. **Share to Jedaniah:** 'and behold this is the share which came to you as a share, you Jedaniah: Peṭosiri by name'
   B. **Share to Mahseiah:** 'and behold this is the share which came to me as a share, I Mahseiah: Bela by name'
VI. **Investiture**
   A. **Personal:** 'You Jedaniah have authority over Peṭosiri ... from this day and forever'
   B. **Heirs**: 'and (so do) your children after you'
   C. **Right of Disposal**: 'And to whomever you desire you may give (him)'
VII. **Quitclaim**

53 Porten and Szubin, 'Exchange of Inherited Property', 651–54.

54 *Black's Law Dictionary*, s.v. 'Probate'.

55 As Porten points out, Mibtahiah 'had probably died at least six years earlier when her house from her first husband Jezaniah passed through probate' (*TAD* B2.10). Porten, *Elephantine Papyri*, 199 n. 7.

A. **Covenant of Non-claim (special):** 'I shall not be able – I, Mahseiah, son or daughter of mine, brother or sister of mine, or an individual who is mine – to bring suit against you or against your children on account of Peṭosiri ... '

B. **Provisions in case of Violation of Covenant of Non-claim (special)**

1. **Penalty:** 'if we, Mahseiah or my children bring suit against you about it or bring (suit) against son etc. we shall give you 10 karsh'
2. **Release Clause:** 'and we are far from you and from your children from (any) suit on account of that Peṭosiri who came to you as a portion'
3. **Clausula Salvatoria:** 'he shall be yours and your children's after you and you may give him to whomever you desire, without suit'

VIII. **Future Apportionment:** 'Moreover there is Taba ... and Lilu ... when it will be time, we shall divide them (between) us and we shall take hereditary possession'

IX. **Scribe:** Nabutukulti son of Nabuzeribni

X. **Place:** Elephantine

XI. **Dictation:** 'at the instruction of Mahseiah and Jedaniah his brother'

XII. **Witnesses:** 4

XIII. **Endorsement:** ספר פלגן 'Document of Division of (the) slave Peṭosiri (which) Mahseiah son of Nathan wrote for Jedaniah son of Nathan his brother'

The document[56] begins with an abstract which summarizes the transaction.[57] It is followed by the Division clause which utilizes the technical vocabulary of inheritance: מטא and בחלק. The verb מטא 'to come' in this sense is attested in *TAD* B5.1:4 and, also, as בוא, in biblical and Talmudic texts.[58] The division clause fulfils the same function as the transfer clause

56 ספר פלגן 'Document of Division'. Cf. the demotic *sẖ dnit pš* 'deed of apportionment', Seidl, *Ägyptische Rechtsgeschichte*, 21; H. Thompson, *A Family Archive from Siut, from Papyri in the British Museum, Including an Account of a Trial Before the Laocritae in the Year B.C. 170* (Oxford: Oxford University Press, 1934), cols. v-viii, pp. 57–62, and also R. A. Parker, 'A Demotic Settlement from Deir el Ballas (MFA 38.2063b)', *JARCE* 3 (1964): 89.

57 A similar formula is also attested in *TAD* B1.1:6. See Porten, *Elephantine Papyri*, 199 n. 5; Porten and Szubin, 'Aramaic Joint Venture', 76.

58 בוא is used in Num. 32.19 and in *Ket*. 83a; *Git*. 77a; *Bab. Bath*. 141b cited by Porten and Szubin, 'Exchange of Inherited Property', 653. In demotic a similar use is applied to the word *pḥ* (Legal Manual IX: 33) 'the share which came to me' *dnit nty pḥ r-ir=y*; W. Erichsen, *Demotisches Glossar* (Copenhagen: E. Munksgaard, 1954), 137. See Parker, 'Demotic Settlement', 95. Similar formulae are also attested in Urk. Hawara XI.6; XV.5; XXI a.5. b 5. E. Lüddeckens, *Demotische Urkunden aus Hawara* (Stuttgart: F. Steiner, 1998); P. BM 10.075.3; P. Louvre 7862.4; P. Dublin 1660.5. See Pestman *et al.*, *Recueil* II, p. 97 r. In this

in conveyances. It is followed by the investiture, which, in this case, adopts the form of the שליט clause[59] as is the norm in Nabuzeribni's tradition.[60] The quitclaim displays the particular formulation of the Aramaean scribes in Syene (רחק + suit [B2.8.11; B2.2.15]). The standard quitclaim follows the pattern: 'I shall not be able to sue you; penalty if I sue; the property is still yours.'[61] In this document, however, we have an expression of the withdrawal formula between the penalty and the *clausula salvatoria*. It reads: 'and we are far from you and from your children from (any) suit on account of that Peṭosiri'. In other documents, the penalty clause often concludes with the formula 'without suit and without process'[62] and there is one case with a double formula, 'without suit and without process, and I am withdrawn from every suit or process'.[63] The legal function of the formula ולא דין ולא דבב has been clearly established. It means that 'the affected party did not have to undertake any further legal action to realize payment'.[64] On the other hand, the meaning of the formula 'far from PN from suit' needs further analysis. A Demotic parallel provides some clarification. The business letter P. Louvre 7850 reads:

> *šp(=y) pꜣy iḥ ntj ḥry ṯꜣj(=y) s ḥꜣ.t(=y) mtr.w n.im=f tw=y wy r-r=f n md nb n rn n pꜣ ḥm-nṯr 4-nw ꜥnꜥ rn n pꜣy=f qs*
>
> 'I have received this bull mentioned above. I have taken it. My heart is satisfied with it. I am far from him (i.e. from Pamety) regarding every suit[65] in the name of the fourth god's servant, regarding his burial.'

P. Louvre E. 9292 (501 BCE) provides another example of the 'withdrawal from suit'. The text reads:

> *pꜣ nt iw=f iy r-r=k r-ḏbꜣ.ṯ=-s [n?] tꜣy=s pš(.t) nt ḥry*
> *iw(=y) r ti wy(=f) r-r=k n mt nb ḳnby nb n pꜣ tꜣ*
>
> '(As for) the one who shall come to you concerning her, i.e. her half

---

legal sense, *pḥ* is also attested in the New Kingdom stela of Senmose (S. Cairo 27815, ll, 16–18; Urk. IV, 1070/1–5 and 1068/10–11). See Wb. I, 534/18. Ritner, 'Third Intermediate Period Antecedents', 354.

59 See our discussion of the שליט clause, 'The Legal Function and Egyptian Background of the שליט Clause: A Reevaluation', *Maarav* 13.2 (2006), 193–209.

60 As in *TAD* B2.3:9 and B2.4:6 (negative formulation) written by Attarshuri, grandfather of Nabuzeribni.

61 Porten, *Elephantine Papyri*, 81.

62 *TAD* B2.3:14; B2.4:15; B2.6:26, 29; B2.8:10; B3.6:15. A shorter form, 'without suit' is used in *TAD* B2.10:17; B2.11:12, 14; B3.5:15, 22; B3.8:32; B3.13:8, 12; B4.7:3, always after the penalty.

63 *TAD* B2.8:10-11.

64 Porten, *Elephantine Papyri*, 167 n. 42.

65 *md* 'dispute, suit', see Allam, *Hieratische Ostraka und Papyri*, 47 n. 13; idem, *JEA* 53 (1967): 47–50; for non-legal contexts see A. Théodorides, *Annuaire de l'Institut de Philologie et d'Histoire Orientales et Slaves* 22 (1978): 77–96.

mentioned above, I will cause him to be far from you regarding any suit, any deed in the land.'

The Demotic examples provide a clearer *Sitz im Leben* and allow us to conclude that the legal function of the Aramaic formula is that of a release clause. It is an absolute relinquishment of rights regarding any property suit.

5.1.1.5. TAD *B5.5 (Cowley 43) Last Quarter of 5th Century BCE*
This document is actually a double document, which registers the transfer of silver from Miptahiah to her sister Eswere as compensation for support through the ration Miptahiah had received on Eswere's behalf. The document records two peculiar instances of the withdrawal formula as components of the transfer and receipt clauses. In both cases the withdrawal formula works as a release clause.

We follow the restoration proposed by Porten.[66]

TAD B5.5: Mutual Quitclaim

I. **Date:** Egyptian
II. **Parties:** Miptahiah speaks to Eswere
III. **Transference**
  A. 'I gave to you silver … '
  B. 'I gave it to you in affection in consideration of support … '
  C. 'I withdrew from you from this day and forever'
IV. **Quitclaim**
  A. **Covenant of Non-claim (special):** 'I shall not be able to bring suit … '
  B. **Provisions in case of Violation of Covenant of Non-claim:** '[whoever shall bring (suit) against you … '
1. **Penalty:** 'shall give you penalty of silver 2 karsh'
II. **Parties:** (Eswere) speaks
III. **Receipt**
  A. '[The ration of mine from the (store-)house of the king and your silver, you Mi]ptahiah, which was in your hand you gave it to me'
  B. **Satisfaction:** 'and my heart was satisfied [with it from this day and forever'
  C. **Withdrawal:** 'and I withdrew from you from] this [sil]ver and (from) the ration which was mine from the house of the king'
IV. **Quitclaim**
  A. **Covenant of Non-claim (special):** 'I shall not be able [I, Eswere to bring against you suit or process … '

66 See B. Porten, 'Fragmentary Aramaic Deeds of Obligation and Conveyance: New Collations and Restorations', *JNES* 48 (1989): 174–77; idem, *Elephantine Papyri*, 259–61.

B. Covenant of Non-claim (general): 'Moreover, son] of mine or daughter of mine. . . . [shall not be able (to sue) in the na] me of this silver'

C. Provisions in case of Violation of Covenant of Non-claim: '[whoever shall bring (suit) against you . . . '

1. Penalty: '[shall give you penalty of silver x karsh]'

V. **Scribe:** missing

VI. **Dictation:** 'at the instruction of Miptahiah . . . '

VII. **Witnesses:** 4

VIII. **Endorsement:** [Document of . . .] which Miptahiah daugh[ter of Gemariah] wrote [for Eswere daughter of Gemariah] her sister.

5.1.1.6. *Summary:* רחק *in Transfer*

After analysing the function of the withdrawal formula in these documents, we can summarize its function as follows:

1. Metaphorical withdrawal from real property: a legal withdrawal from the property. It is akin to vacating the property in modern legal terminology: i.e. to move out, to surrender possession by removing oneself (*TAD* B2.7:7, 16; B3.4:11, 13).
2. Withdrawal from person: a metaphorical use of removal by physical distance. It fulfils the function of a release clause (*TAD* B5.5:4).
3. Withdrawal from person regarding property: another metaphorical use of physical removal. It further specifies the release by mentioning the object of it. It is a release clause regarding the property (*TAD* B2.10:4; B5.5).
4. Withdrawal from person regarding suit: a similar construction as in 3., using the metaphorical sense of withdrawal and adding a specification. It works as a declaration of release (*TAD* B2.11:11).

It is now necessary to turn to the remaining transfer documents where the withdrawal formula is not attested and see if the above proposed interpretation of the withdrawal formulae can be harmonized with its absence in the rest of the documents of transfer. There are three ways to approach this problem: (1) Try to find out reasons for the exclusion of the withdrawal clause in the particularities of the transaction, i.e. had the alienor a clear title? Was he occupying the property or was it vacated? Was a consideration involved? (2) Explore the legal formulary of the scribe responsible for the document to determine whether or not the withdrawal formula was an essential component of his formulary tradition. (3) Try to find out if the withdrawal formula or some of its expressions are related to an ethnic group (i.e. Jews, Aramaeans). These three approaches to the problem ultimately correspond to the three components of the transaction, the transaction *per se*, the scribe, and the parties.

As we mentioned at the beginning of this section, the Aramaic sale documents include two documents that lack a withdrawal formula, the sale of an apartment to a son-in-law (*TAD* B3.12),[67] and a fragmentary conveyance from Saqqara (*TAD* B5.6). The reason why the withdrawal formula is not attested is different for each of the documents. *TAD* B5.6 originated in Saqqara at the end of the fourth century BCE. The formulary of this document is quite different from that of Elephantine and it closely follows the formulary of the Demotic *sẖ ḏbꜣ ḥḏ*.[68]

The structure of the documents reads as follows:

TAD B5.6: Conveyances of Slaves

I.	**Parties:**	'[PN son of PN], his mother (being) Teṭosiri [said to PN] son of Ṣeḥa'
II.	**Satisfaction:**	'You satisfied [my heart in (regard to) my slaves'
III.	**Investiture:**	'They are yours with [... from thi]s [day] forever'
IV.	**Warranty:**	'Whoever shall come to you concerning them [...]'
V.	**Clausula Salvatoria:**	'they are [yo]urs with all [...] they are [yo]urs with their right'
VI.	**Particular clauses to the transaction**	

In this case, therefore, the withdrawal clause, which became the distinctive feature of the document of withdrawal *sẖ n wy*, was not part of the formulary of the sale document. It is necessary to remember that the withdrawal from property in the metaphorical sense, to vacate, as found in the Aramaic documents, was not part of the Demotic formulary.

TAD B3.12, on the other hand, is a regular sale, written by the same scribe as *TAD* B3.4, Haggai son of Shemaiah. After the description of the property, the withdrawal formula is omitted and the document goes directly to the שׁלים clause. The absence of the withdrawal clause responds to the *Sitz im Leben* of the transaction and to the interpretation of the formula 'I withdrew from X property' as the final release formula necessary for the final transfer to take place. *TAD* B3.12 is the last and final division and transfer of the property that Ananiah bought from Bagazushta in 437 BCE. He bequeathed part of it to his wife Tamet in 434 BCE (*TAD* B3.5) and part as a dowry addendum to Jehoishma in 402

67 See Porten, *Elephantine Papyri*, 246–51.

68 See Zauzich, *Schreibertradition*, 114, esp. formulary A8 and A9, p. 117. See also below 6.2.1.3.1, 'The Document in Exchange for Silver, the *sẖ ḏbꜣ ḥḏ*'.

BCE (*TAD* B3.11). In *TAD* B3.12 the couple sold their remaining share in the house to their son-in-law, Anani son of Haggai. The reason that no withdrawal formula is present, such as 'I withdrew from it', can be explained, as Porten pointed out, by the fact that Ananiah (already in his mid-sixties)[69] and Tamet 'no doubt continued to live in the apartments, which they sold to their son-in-law',[70] while Anani son of Haggai and his wife could have kept living in their contiguous house. The transfer, therefore, was not final.

Ancient Egyptian law did not develop an equivalent of Roman testament, and the distribution of the parental estate was done by means of sales *propter mortem*[71] or documents of division.[72] In those cases, no *sẖ n wy* was produced and it is assumed that the final transfer took place after the death of the alienor.[73] It is possible to assume a similar situation for the Aramaic documents. In those cases we do not expect a formal renunciation of rights by means of a document of withdrawal, or a withdrawal formula inserted in the transfer document. Considering that there are no wills left in the archives but divisions of property for the benefit of the heirs, it is possible to discern the real situation behind the legal document as a disposition of inheritance to heirs instead of real sales or gifts. To sell the last owned property to descendants when the person became old is to avoid probate or disputes among heirs, a common practice worldwide.

The same reason is behind the absence of withdrawal formulae from the bequest documents *TAD* B3.5; B3.7; B3.10 and B3.11 belonging also to Ananiah's archive and dealing with the same property bought from Bagazushta in 437 BCE. An explanation might be given for the absence of a withdrawal formula in the bequest *TAD* B2.3.[74] The document is a gift

69 Ananiah was a party to a contract in 451 BCE (*TAD* B3.2) and already had a son by Tamet in 449 BCE (*TAD* B3.3). Porten, *Archives from Elephantine*, 233 n. 93.

70 Porten, *Archives from Elephantine*, 234.

71 See P. W. Pestman, 'Appearance and Reality in Written Contracts; Evidence from Bilingual Family Archives', 80, and C. J. Martin, 'Marriages, Wills and Leases of Land: Some Notes on the Formulae of Demotic Contracts', 60, in M. J. Geller, H. Machler, and A. D. E. Lewis, eds., *Legal Documents of the Hellenistic World* (London: Warburg Institute, 1995).

72 See E. Seidl, 'Die Teilungschrift', *MDAIK* 8 (1939), 198–200; Martin, 'Marriages, Wills and Leases of Land,' 59–60.

73 This seems to be also the case in *TAD* B3.7 and B3.10. Porten, *Archives from Elephantine*, 229.

74 The various bequest documents come from different scribal traditions (*TAD* B3.5 was written by Mauziah b. Nathan – 434 BCE; B3.10 and B3.11 by Haggai b. Shemaiah – 402 BCE; B2.3 by Attarshuri b. Nabuzeribni – 459 BCE; the scribe of B3.7 is not yet identified – 420 BCE) providing evidence that the absence of the withdrawal formula in the bequest documents could also be a feature of the kind of document involved. All the bequests were among the family members of the Jewish community.

in contemplation of death, granted already *inter vivos*,[75] which included the right of possession (B2.3:9), but not the right to transfer the property outside the family (B3.9-10). The property was probably run-down, described as בי 1 ארק in *TAD* B2.3:4 and Mahseiah probably had another house where he was living (*TAD* B2.7).

To explain the absence of a withdrawal formula in the exchange of shares in *TAD* B5.1 is more complicated, because the nature of the shares (מנתא) is not described.[76] In case the shares were not immobilia,[77] this might explain why a legal clause based on the metaphor of vacancy from property was not used, as it is not used also in the division of slaves (*TAD* B2.11). In the case of division of land, as Porten and Szubin[78] propose, it is not clear why no withdrawal formula was used. As we mentioned above, we have another document of exchange (*TAD* B5.5) where a withdrawal formula is present as a component of the transfer clause. In this case, however, the first declaration of withdrawal by Miptahiah is not from the property but from the person.[79]

We have discussed the presence of the withdrawal formula in different clauses and have sought to explain its absence in other documents. In the next section of this chapter, we shall study the function of the withdrawal formula in the context of litigation.

5.1.2. רחק *in Litigation: Documents of Release after Litigation (*TAD *B2.2; B2.8; B2.9; B3.2; B5.2)*

Eventually, conflict arises in all kinds of human organization as a disruptive force that needs to be controlled. Conflicts are an inherent part of every society.[80] Every societal organization has developed a way to deal with disputes among its members so as to keep the social order from disruption and chaos. Being so inherent in every form of social organization, procedures to settle disputes must have appeared very early in the history of humankind and must have been established before the introduction of writing.[81] The process of dispute settlement in ancient

75 Yaron, *Introduction*, 78.

76 See Porten and Szubin, 'Exchange of Inherited Property', 652.

77 So Yaron, 'Aramaic Deeds of Conveyance', 253–54.

78 Porten and Szubin, 'Exchange of Inherited Property', 652.

79 A second withdrawal, from silver and ration, pronounced by Eswere, is restored by Porten-Yardeni in lines 8–9. The whole document is still problematic.

80 K. F. Koch, 'The Anthropology of Law and Order', in S. Tax and L. G. Freeman, eds., *Horizons in Anthropology* (Chicago: Aldine, 1977), 300.

81 For ancient Greece see M. Gagarin, 'The Settlement of Disputes in Early Greek Literature', in *Early Greek Law* (Berkeley: University of California Press, 1986), 19–50. However, Gagarin only deals with Homeric stories. See also §5, 'Arbitrators', in A. R. W. Harrison, *The Law of Athens* (London: G. Duckworth; Indianapolis, Ind.: Hackett, 1998), 64–68. For Mesopotamia, see M. Y. Ishikida, 'The Structure and Function of Dispute

societies would have included four procedures;[82] first, negotiation, a private settlement between the conflicting parties is reached without the intervention of a third party; second, mediation or conciliation, a third party without any official capacity helps the conflicting parties to reach an agreement;[83] third, arbitration, two parties agree to present their case to a recognized member of the society and to accept his *arbitrio*;[84] and fourth, one or both parties present the case to a public court or appointed official. The second and third cases – mediation and arbitration – are typical of pre-state societies where the necessary legitimization comes directly from the social body.[85] The fourth – public courts – is more common in more complex forms of societal organization where the necessary legitimization comes from the state.[86]

Management in the Public Administration of Larsa under Hammurapi', *Orient* 23 (1998): 66–78. For the Hebrew Bible, see P. Bovati, *Re-Establishing Justice: Legal Terms, Concepts and Procedures in the Hebrew Bible*, JSOTS 105 (Sheffield: Sheffield Academic Press, 1994). For ancient Egypt, M. M. Bontty, 'Conflict Management in Ancient Egypt: Law as a Social Phenomenon' (Ph.D. diss., University of California, Los Angeles, 1997).

82 For Egypt in the Ptolemaic period, see G. Semeka, *Ptolemäisches Prozessrecht: Studien zum ptolemäischen Gerichtsverfassung und zum Greichtsverfahren* (Munich: C. H. Beck, 1913), 204ff. and A. Steinwenter, *Die Streitbeendigung durch Urteil, Schiedsspruch und Vergleich nach griechischem Rechte* (Munich: C. H. Beck, 1925), 14, 117ff. For Late Antiquity see T. Gagos and P. van Minnen, *Settling a Dispute: Toward a Legal Anthropology of Late Antique Egypt* (Ann Arbor: University of Michigan Press, 1994), 30–31.

83 For example, in a letter from ancient Mesopotamia, the sender asks his father to settle a dispute 'according to his honorable status'. W. H. Van Soldt, *Letters in the British Museum*, Altbabylonische Briefe XIII Part 2 (Leiden: Brill, 1994), no. 89.35.

84 Exod. 18.16 provides an example of arbitration, presenting Moses settling disputes: 'When they have a matter, they come unto me; and I judge between one and another.' The role of the judge in ancient Israel has been throughly studied. See M. Weinfeld, 'Judge and Officer in Ancient Israel and in the Ancient Near East', *Israel Oriental Studies* 7 (1977): 65–88; A. J. Soggin, 'Das Amt der "kleinen Richter" in Israel', *VT* 30 (1980): 245–48. Arbitration is also the way in which some Bedouin groups settle their disputes today. See A. Kennett, *Bedouin Justice: Laws and Customs Among the Egyptian Bedouin* (Cambridge: Cambridge University Press, 1925), esp. ch. 11, 'Trial by Ordeal', 107–14.

85 For the traditional societal classification in bands, tribes, chiefdoms, and states, see E. R. Service, *Primitive Social Organization: An Evolutionary Perspective*, 2nd edn. (New York: Random House, 1971); idem, *Origins of the State and Civilization: The Process of Cultural Evolution* (New York: Norton, 1975), where he reduced the four types to three: segmental society, chiefdom, and archaic civilization.

86 An example of the coexistence of the private and court-like procedures from the classical world is presented by Plutarch. It is said by Plutarch that Themistocles 'set the story going among the multitude that Aristides had done away with the public courts of justice by his determining and judging everything in private'. Plutarch, *Lives*, Aristides VII, 1–3, trans. B. Perrin, Loeb Classical Library. The anthropological study of contemporary primitive societies has demonstrated the existence of the last two ways of resolving disputes (arbitration and public courts) albeit not necessarily their coexistence. See P. H. Gulliver, 'Dispute Settlement Without Courts: The Ndendeuli of Southern Tanzania', in L. Nader, ed., *Law in Culture and Society* (Berkeley: University of California Press, 1997), 24–68, and

Various examples of the different ways of settling disputes in Ancient Egypt are attested in such literary texts as the Eloquent Peasant,[87] Horus and Seth,[88] and P. Rylands IX.[89] From these examples, it is clear that the jurisdiction of the court or public officials in charge of administrating justice offered more than one possibility for settling a dispute.[90] A similar situation is attested in Elephantine where, when other ways of settling a dispute (negotiation, mediation, and arbitration) had failed, claims could have been brought before 'prefect, lord or judge' (*TAD* B3.12:28). Testimonies of those claims are the documents involved in the litigation process in which an official court or functionary was responsible for asserting the merits of the claimants. They include (1) court records from Saqqarah (*TAD* B8.1-12); (2) obligations to take a judicial oath (*TAD* B7.1 and B7.2); (3) oaths (*TAD* B7.3); and (4) release after judgment (*TAD* B2.2; B2.8; B2.9; B3.2; and B5.2).

The documents of release after litigation were produced when a dispute was resolved by a court decision, a third party arbitration, or private settlement after a public dispute. The party who had initiated the claim and was properly compensated or the party who had initiated a claim and lost it, drew up the necessary document of release for the other party. The technical Aramaic endorsement for these documents is ספר מרחק. We will proceed to examine in chronological order the five documents endorsed as ספר מרחק that function as documents of release after judgment. As earlier, we shall present a complete outline of each document. The documents display the following basic common features in their formulary: I. Date; II. Parties; III. Certificate of Performance; IV. Satisfaction; V. Quitclaim; VI. Scribe; VII. Witnesses; and VIII. Endorsement.

---

also L. Nader and H. F. Todd Jr, eds., *The Disputing Process: Law in Ten Societies* (New York: Columbia University Press, 1978). Matt. 5.25 narrates a case where to appeal to the appointed official is the final resort for settling a dispute, and makes evident the benefits of settling the differences by private negotiation.

87 F. Vogelsang and A. H. Gardiner, *Die Klagen des Bauern*, Literarische Texte des Mittleren Reiches I (Leipzig: J. C. Hinrichs'sche Buchhandlung, 1908); M. Lichtheim, *Ancient Egyptian Literature*, vol. 1: *The Old and Middle Kingdom* (Berkeley and Los Angeles: University of California Press, 1973), 169–84.

88 Gardiner, *Chester Beatty I*, pp. 8–26, pls. 1–16; M. Broze, *Les aventures d'Horus et Seth dans le Papyrus Chester Beatty I: mythe et roman en Egypte ancienne* (Leuven: Peeters, 1996).

89 G. Vittmann, *Der demotische Papyrus Rylands 9*, ÄAT 38 (Wiesbaden: Harrassowitz, 1998), 2 vols.

90 See M. M. Bontty, 'Third Party Dispute Processing Institutions', in 'Conflict Management in Ancient Egypt', 150–75; idem., 'Images of Law and the Disputing Process in the Tale of the Eloquent Peasant', *Lingua Aegyptia* 8 (2000), 93–107; M. A. Light, 'The Power of Law: Procedure as Justice in the Eloquent Peasant', *Lingua Aegyptia* 8 (2000), 109–24.

5.1.2.1. TAD *B2.2 (Cowley 6) 2 January 464 BCE*

This document was drawn up by the scribe Itu son of Abah, in Syene, on 2 January 464 BCE, for Mahseiah son of Jedaniah, at the request of Dargamana son of Khvarshaina. According to its endorsement, *TAD* B2.2 is a ספר מרחק. The document is the result of a dispute, which originated in a complaint made by Dargamana to the authorities, the Persian Damidata, and his colleagues, the judges, regarding a plot of land possessed by Mahseiah. Dargamana attempted to evict Mahseiah, claiming ownership of the property,[91] but a settlement was reached by Mahseiah swearing by YHW that the land was not the property of Dargamana. This decisive oath resulted in a withdrawal by Dargamana. Oaths were one of the ways of resolving disputes under certain circumstances,[92] sometimes involving some extra judicial arrangements not registered in the document.[93] We should not exclude, therefore, the possibility that extra-court compensation was given to Dargamana to make him accept the oath of Mahseiah.

Cowley classifies this document as a conveyance[94] and translates the endorsement as a 'deed of renunciation'.[95] Assuming that the technical legal meaning of a conveyance is a 'transfer of title to land from one person, or class of persons to another by deed',[96] *TAD* B2.2 does not fall under such a category. At the same time, the translation 'deed of renunciation' fails to do justice to modern legal terminology where a renunciation is 'the act by which a person abandons a right acquired without transferring it to another'.[97] Following as closely as possible the Aramaic endorsement, Porten describes this document as a 'withdrawal

91 See Szubin and Porten, 'Litigation concerning Abandoned Property', 282–83.

92 For the legal function of the oath, see: M. Malinine, 'Notes Juridiques', *Bulletin de l'Institut Français d'Archéologie Oriental* 46 (1947): 93–123; J. A. Wilson, 'The Oath in Ancient Egypt', *JNES* 7 (1948): 129–56; P. Kaplony, 'Eid', *LÄ* II (Wiesbaden, 1975), 1188–1200; B. Menu, 'Le serment dans les actes juridiques de L'Ancienne Égypte', in R. Verdier, ed., *Le serment I, Signes et Fonctions* (Paris: Editions da Centre National de la Recherche Scientifique 1991), 329–44; M. Green, 'A Means of Discouraging Perjury', *GM* 39 (1980): 33–40; E. Seidl, *Der Eid im ptolemäischen Recht* (Munich: F. Straub, 1929); idem, *Der Eid in römish-ägyptischen Provinzialrecht*, Münchener Beiträge zur Papyrusforschung und antiken Rechtsgeschichte 24 (Munich: C. H. Beck 1935); Porten, *Archives from Elephantine*, 151–58; idem, *Elephantine Papyri*, 159 n. 17.

93 In this regard, the Petition of *Peṭeese* displays an interesting situation in which those guilty of the crime reach an agreement with the victim. The victim accepts some economic compensation, the criminals swear an oath declaring their innocence, and the claimant accepts the oath and withdraws from them (P. Rylands 9, esp. 20.6-19). The Demotic ostraca provide us with dozens of examples of oaths after judgment including the formula: *iw=f iry pꜣ ꜥnḫ mtw=f wy r-r=f* 'If PN_1 makes the oath PN_2 will withdraw from him'.

94 Cowley, *Aramaic Papyri*, 15.

95 Cowley, *Aramaic Papyri*, 17.

96 *Black's Law Dictionary*, s.v. 'Conveyance'.

97 *Black's Law Dictionary*, s.v. 'Renunciation'.

from land'.[98] We prefer to use the designation 'document of release'. A release is defined as the relinquishment of a right or claim (gratuitous or for consideration) by the person with whom it exists, to the person against whom it might have been demanded or enforced;[99] this is precisely what has happened in the case of *TAD* B2.2. The structure of the document reads as follows:

TAD B2.2: Document of Release after Judgment

I. **Date:** Babylonian and Egyptian.
II. **Parties:** Dargamana speaks to Mahseiah
III. **Performance**
  A. **Defendant's Oath:** 'you have sworn to me by YHW'
  B. **Object of Dispute:** land
  C. **Record of Litigation:** 'on account of which I complained against you.'
  D. **Verdict:** 'they imposed upon you an oath on account of that land'
IV. **Boundaries:** east, west, below, above
V. **Satisfaction:** 'you swore to me by YHW and satisfied my heart about that land.'
VI. **Quitclaim**
  A. **Covenant of Non-claim (special):** 'I shall not be able to institute against you suit or process – I, or son of mine or daughter, brother or sister of mine, near or far, about that land against you or son of yours …'
  B. **Provisions in Case of Violation of Covenant of Non-claim (special)**
    1. **Penalty:** 'Whoever shall institute against you (suit) in my name about that land shall pay 20 karsh …'
    2. **Clausula Salvatoria:** 'and moreover the land is yours.'
    3. **Release:** 'and you are far from any suit (in) which they shall complain against you on account of that land.'
VII. **Scribe:** Itu son of Abah
VIII. **Place:** Syene the fortress
IX. **Dictation:** 'at the instruction of Dargamana'
X. **Witnesses:** 8
XI. **Endorsement:** ספר מרחק

The temporal dynamic of the Elephantine Aramaic conveyances has been described as a tale told in past, present, and future.[100] In this document, however, there is a transition from the perfect mode (here translated as a

98 Porten and Yardeni, *TAD* B2.2, p. 21, and Porten, *Elephantine Papyri*, 158.
99 See *Black's Law Dictionary*, s.v. 'Release'.
100 Porten, *Elephantine Papyri*, 19, 81.

past tense) characteristic of clauses III and V, to the imperfect mode of clause VI (here translated as a future tense). The legal dynamic of the document is built on the tripartite axes constituted by III, the certificate of the performance; V, the satisfaction; and VI, the quitclaim clause.

Let us take a closer look at each of these instances. Clause III is a certification on the part of the plaintiff that the defendant has performed his obligation. We call it a certificate, which is defined technically as a 'written assurance that some act has or has not been done, or some event occurred, or some legal formality has been complied with'.[101] As we already mentioned, the performance by the defendant was a decisive oath,[102] which was accepted by the plaintiff, who expressed his acceptance in the following satisfaction clause. This clause is built upon the technical term והוטבת לבבי (line 11–12) and triggers the quitclaim clause.

The close relationship between the defendant's performance *per se* and the acceptance by the plaintiff is expressed in the prepositional complement to the passive expression of the formula (וטיב לבבי). It is usually followed by the preposition ב, indicating the performance that was accepted, and usually denotes the object that is transferred from one of the parties to the other.[103]

In *TAD* B2.2, however, the prepositional complement is headed by the preposition על followed by the object of dispute. In this case, the land was not conveyed to the plaintiff and, therefore, the satisfaction formula is not constructed with the prepositional complement ב plus the object.

The clause number VI, Quitclaim, is composed with a bipartite structure. The legal purpose of the quitclaim clause is to assure the durability of the agreement reached and to prevent suit and counter suit *ad eternum*.[104] The two parts of the quitclaim are the covenant of non-claim (special) and the provisions in case of violation of the covenant of non-claim (special). The first part establishes the promise or covenant and the second part provides a remedy in case the covenant is violated. In the third clause of this second part, we find a רחק base formula in what we call the release clause. As in other formulary sequences, the three clauses that compose the provisions in case of violation of the covenant of non-claim follow a logical sequence in the context of a hypothetical suit by the

101 *Black's Law Dictionary*, s.v 'Certificate'.

102 'When one of the parties to a suit, not being able to prove his charge, offered to refer the decision of the cause to the oath of his adversary.' *Black's Law Dictionary*, s.v 'Oath'.

103 See for example the document of wifehood *TAD* B2.6 where the preposition ב in the satisfaction clause denotes the mohar transferred from the husband to the father of the wife (lines 5–6), and the dowry transferred from the father of the wife to the husband (line 15). See also E. Jenni, Section B.10, 'Beth Instrumenti', in *Die hebräischen Präpositionen*, vol. 1: *Die Präposition Beth* (Stuttgart, Berlin, and Cologne: Kohlhammer, 1992), 118–49.

104 The common practice of not accepting a verdict is well exemplified in the story of Horus and Seth.

present plaintiff, or his relatives, against the present defendant or the defendant's relatives. In such a case, a penalty is imposed: the person who will dare to bring a case to the court will have to pay the amount stipulated in the document. The second formula, the *clausula salvatoria*, states that even in the event of the future claimant having paid this high amount, the property will remain in possession of the present defendant or his relatives, and he will be released from that suit.[105] The three clauses, the penalty clause, the *clausula salvatoria*,[106] and the release clause, all refer to such a hypothetical situation.

The construction of the Release Clause in *TAD* B2.2 displays a particularity worthy of attention. The text reads:

ואנת רחיק מן כל דין זי יקבלון עליך עלדבר ארע זך

'You are far from any suit that they shall complain against you on account of that land.'

We have already seen in *TAD* B2.11 that 'to be far from person regarding suit' was a particular construction used by the Aramaean scribes where the party who declares, 'we are far from you from any suit . . .' is the party who relinquishes the right to future suits. In this case, however, it is the plaintiff who declares that the defendant 'is far from any suit that they shall complain'. It is clear from the context that the legal sense of this phrase is intended to protect the defendant against future suits. We have here, therefore, a very peculiar use of the רחק formula by Itu son of Abah. The רחק-based formula traditionally has been understood as a declaration of quitclaim from the perspective of the speaker or subject of the action. The one who is far, or the one who withdraws, is the one relinquishing rights. But the opposite is true in this case, the one who is far from suit is the one who is benefiting from the quitclaim.

5.1.2.2. *TAD B3.2 (Kraeling 1) 6 July 451 BCE*

This document records the final settlement of a suit and counter-suit regarding a הירא, a word of uncertain meaning.[107] Porten and Szubin consider it to have been a piece of abandoned property to which neither Mica nor Anani had a clear title,[108] but the absence of the mention of the

105 As Porten points out, the release clause reinforces the *clausula salvatoria*. Cf. *TAD* B2.9:15 ('and moreover he is far from these goods'); Porten, *Elephantine Papyri*, 161 n. 41.

106 For the *clausula salvatoria* see Yaron, 'Aramaic Deeds of Conveyance'; idem, *Introduction*, 79–92; A. Skaist, 'The Clasula (sic!) Salvatoria in the Elephantine and Neo-Assyrian Conveyance Document', in M. Sokoloff, ed., *Arameans, Aramaic and the Aramaic Literary Tradition* (Ramat-Gan, Israel: Bar-Ilan University Press, 1983), 31–41; Porten, *Elephantine Papyri*, 155 n. 19.

107 *DNWSI* 279, s.v. *hyr*.

108 Szubin and Porten, 'Litigation Concerning Abandoned Property', 279–84.

boundaries makes it improbable that the הירא was a piece of immovable property. The object of dispute was more likely a right or a movable good, as the low price paid (5 shekels)[109] and the absence of boundary description suggest. [110] The settlement is reached by the payment of 5 shekels by Anani to Mica, who then declares his withdrawal after the payment is made. The structure reads as follows:

TAD B3.2: Document of Release after Judgment

I. **Date:** Babylonian and Egyptian
II. **Parties**: Mica speaks to Ananiah
III. **Performance**
  A. **Payment:** 'you gave me silver 5 shekels.'
  B. **Object of Dispute:** הירא
  C. **Record of Litigation:** 'you complained against me.'
IV. **Satisfaction:** 'and my heart was satisfied with its payment.'
V. **Quitclaim**
  A. **Covenant of Non-claim (personal):** 'I shall not be able to institute against you suit or process in the name of this הירא'
  B. **Provisions in Case of Violation of Covenant of Non-claim (personal):** Penalty: 'if I complain against you (before) judge or lord in the name of this הירא which I complained against you herein and you gave me its payment (...) and I withdrew from you, I shall give you 5 karsh.'
VI. **General Warranty:** Defension: 'if brother or sister near or far institute (suit) against you in the name of this הירא I shall cleanse (it) and give (it) to you.'
VII. **Scribe:** Bunni son of Mannuki
VIII. **Dictation:** 'at the instruction of Mica son of Ahio'
IX. **Witnesses:** 8
X. **Endorsement:** Missing

The classification of this document as a document of release after judgment deserves some explanation, for if we should define it according to the performance, it would be a receipt. *TAD* B3.2 differs from other documents of release in that there is not a release or withdrawal clause in the operative section. The withdrawal of Mica is mentioned in a subordinate clause, describing the steps of the release: Mica complained, Anani gave the payment, Mica withdrew from him. Based on this clause, it is possible to assume that the legal meaning of the document is one of release, although in lines 4 and 5, it is mentioned that it was Anani who

109 An average woollen garment was between seven and twelve shekels. See Porten, *Archives from Elephantine*, 72–80. *TAD* B2.6:4 and B3.8:4.

110 Every Aramaic or Demotic document involving transfer of real property included the description of the boundaries of the property.

complained. As Porten and Szubin suggest, either we should consider line 6 a scribal error, or we have a document recording a suit and counter-suit.[111] Either way, the withdrawal formula is again a relinquishment of rights, in this case, from Mica to Ananiah.

5.1.2.3. TAD *B2.8 (Cowley 14) 26 August 440 BCE*

This document was drawn up by the scribe Peṭeese son of Nabunathan, at the instruction of Peu, in the fortress of Syene, on 26 August 440 BCE, for Mibtahiah daughter of Mahseiah. It is also a ספר מרחק, as we learn from the endorsement. The document is neither explicit about the causes of the litigation between Peu and Mibtahiah, nor does it tell us who initiated it. The mention of a document of wifehood could point to a situation where Mibtahiah was married to Peu, and after the divorce he kept some goods belonging to her, or that she had taken those goods from the house of Peu when she left.[112] The material available does not provide more information about the dispute. We just know that a settlement was reached and Peu produced this document of release.

The structure of the document reads as follows:

TAD B2.8: Document of Release after Judgment

I. **Date:** Babylonian and Egyptian
II. **Parties:** Peu speaks to Mibtahiah
III. **Performance**
   A. **Record of Litigation:** 'about the suit, which we made in Syene.'
   B. **Object of Dispute:** various goods: silver, grain and clothing and bronze and iron and the wifehood document.
   C. **Verdict:** 'an oath came upon you.'
   D. **Oath:** 'You swore to me about them by Sati the goddess.'
IV. **Satisfaction (of Peu):** 'And my heart was satisfied with that oath[113] which you made to me about those goods.'

111 Porten, *Elephantine Papyri*, 206 n.14.

112 Porten suggests that the dispute involved 'some goods left on deposit' (Porten *Elephantine Papyri*, 189 n.10) and disregards his previous solution (Porten, *Archives from Elephantine*, 245–47) that the dispute referred to a marriage with Peu. The new date provided for *TAD* B2.6, which would imply that Mibtahiah was married to Esḥor at this time, should not be a problem. *TAD* B2.8 just tells us when the suit was settled and not when it began. It is possible that the suit began just after the divorce or that some time passed since Mibtahiah or Peu decided to bring the case to the authorities after other ways of settling the dispute failed. Mibtahiah then married Esḥor before the issue was settled. She was married to Esḥor in 449 BCE, which means that the whole process took about ten years.

113 = P. Louvre E. 7861 (Abnormal Hieratic, 560 BCE): *dy=k mtj ḥ3tj(=y) n p3 ʿnḫ m-b3ḥ ḫnsw-m-W3s.t-nfr-http* 'You satisfied my heart with the oath before Khons.' M. Malinine, *MDAIK* 16 (1958): 221.

V. **Release:** 'I withdrew from you from this day and forever.'
VI. **Quitclaim**
  A. **Covenant of Non-claim (personal):** 'I shall not be able to institute against you suit or process ... '
  B. **Provisions in Case of Violation of Covenant of Non-claim (special)**
    1. **Penalty:** 'if I institute against you suit or process, or a son of mine ... institute (suit) in the name of that oath ... shall give to Mibtahiah 5 karsh ... '
    2. **Release Clause:** 'and I am far from every suit or process.'
VII. **Scribe:** Peṭeese son of Nabunathan
VIII. **Dictation:** 'at the instruction of Peu son of Paḥi'
IX. **Witnesses:** 4
X. **Endorsement:** ספר מרחק

The document follows closely the formulary of the other documents of release after judgment: the certificate of defendant's performance, the satisfaction of the declarant, in this case with the oath, and the release followed by the quitclaim. In *TAD* B2.8, we have another example of the peculiar use of the withdrawal formula by the Aramaean scribes: Peu declares that he 'is far from every suit or process', which equals to a renunciation by Peu of future claims.[114]

5.1.2.4. TAD *B2.9 (Cowley 20), 2–30 September 420 BCE*

This document is the outcome of a suit brought by the brothers Menahem and Ananiah against the brothers Jedaniah and Mahseiah regarding some goods that Menahem and Ananiah's grandfather, Meshullam, had left on deposit with Esḥor, the father of Jedaniah and Mahseiah. Apparently, the goods were never returned, producing the situation that presented the claim by Menahem and Ananiah before the *frataraka* Ramnadaina and before the troop commander Vidranga.[115] The schema of the document reads as follows:

114 The meaning is, therefore, similar to *TAD* B2.11:11 'we are far from you and from your children from (any) suit on account of that Petosiri who came to you as a portion'.

115 That suits were made before the *frataraka* does not necessarily imply that the document was drawn up in their presence. Clause III. A. Record of the Litigation registers the previous actions that led to the drawing up of this document. Some time could have elapsed between the decision and devolution of the goods and the redaction of the document.

TAD B2.9: Document of Release after Judgment

I. **Date:** Babylonian and Egyptian
II. **Place:** Elephantine
III. **Parties:** Menahem and Ananiah speak to Jedaniah and Mahseiah
IV. **Performance**
  A. **Record of Litigation:** 'We brought suit of *np'* against you before Ramnadaina Chief (and) Vidranga, the Troop Commander . . . '
  B. **Object of Dispute:** various goods
  C. **Interrogation:** 'you were interrogated.'
  D. **Restoration:** 'And you . . . satisfied our heart with (ב) these goods.'
V. **Satisfaction**: 'and our heart was satisfied herein from this day forever.'
VI. **Release**: 'We are far from you from this day forever.'
VII. **Quitclaim**
  A. **Covenant of Non-claim (special):** 'we shall not be able, we or our sons . . . to bring against you . . . suit or process in the name of the goods . . . '
  B. **Provisions in Case of Violation of Covenant of Non-claim (special)**
    1. **Penalty:** 'if we or our sons . . . shall bring (suit) against you or your sons . . . shall give you 10 karsh . . .'
    2. **Release**: 'and moreover he is far from these goods . . . without suit or without process.'
VIII. **Scribe:** Mauziah son of Nathan
IX. **Dictation:** at the instruction of Menahem and Ananiah
X. **Witnesses:** 4
XI. **Endorsement:** ספר [מרחק]

Clause IV. D., the Performance, deserves special attention. The preposition ב after the phrase 'you have satisfied my heart' points to what the defendant delivers to the plaintiff in order to satisfy him.[116] In this case, the phrase, 'you satisfied our heart *with* those goods', means that the goods, which were left on deposit by Sheloman with Esḥor, were now to be given back to the plaintiffs, the sons of Sheloman.[117]

116 See our discussion 'The שליט Clause, Its Legal Function and Egyptian Background: A Reevaluation', *Maarav* 13 (2006): 193–209.

117 Contra Porten, *Elephantine Papyri*, 192 n. 23; and idem, *Archives from Elephantine*, 256 who states that the nature of the satisfaction cannot be inferred from the document. A

As Porten[118] has noted, if it had been the case that Jedaniah and Mahseiah (the defendants) had retained possession of the goods in dispute, the qui quitclaim would have included, in addition to the covenant of non-claim and the penalty clause, a *clausula salvatoria* as we have seen in *TAD* B2.2. Instead, the clausula states that whoever will sue Jedaniah, Mahseiah, or their relatives, will pay the penalty and is likewise (אפם) far from these goods. We have, therefore, a new expression of the withdrawal formula in the context of the quitclaim. In this context, this metaphor of physical withdrawal means that 'he has no right to reclaim these goods again from you'.

5.1.2.5. TAD *B5.2 (Cowley 65,3 and 67,3 5) Last Quarter of the 5th Century BCE*

This rather fragmentary text was capable of being reconstructed to some extent by Porten and Yardeni. The sequence, Satisfaction + Release is the same as *TAD* B2.9. The structure reads as follows:

TAD B5.2: Document of Release after Judgment

I. Date: Babylonian and Egyptian (Reconstructed)
II. Place: (Reconstructed)
III. Parties: Mattan son of Jashobiah speaks to NN
IV. Performance
 A. Record of Litigation: 'I] instituted against you suit'
 B. Object of Dispute: ?
V. Satisfaction: 'and [my] heart was satisfied'
VI. Release: '[I Mattan] withdrew from you from [this] d[ay and forever;'
VII. Quitclaim
 A. Covenant of Non-claim (special): 'I shall not be able, I Mattan or son or daughter of mine or] man of mine to institute against you su[it or process...'

The rest is missing.

5.1.2.6. *Summary:* רחק *in Release after Judgement*

The five documents of release after judgment analysed above covered the period from 464 BCE through ca. 420 BCE. One of the documents comes from Elephantine (*TAD* B2.9) and two of them come from Syene (*TAD* B2.8 and B2.2). The provenance of the other two is not expressed in the texts. The documents display the following basic common features in

similar situation is related to the production of P. Cairo 30657 (Gebelein, 547 BCE), where we find the satisfaction clause referring to the goods left in deposit that were afterwards returned.

118 Porten, *Elephantine Papyri*, 193 n. 38.

their formulary: I. Date; II. Parties; III. Certificate of Performance; IV. Satisfaction; V. Quitclaim; VI. Scribe; VII. Witnesses; and VIII. Endorsement. The formulary of the documents, however, is not uniform. The similarities in their formulary and their differences in the particular order of the formulae is shown in Table X.

Table X: Formulary of the Documents of Release after Judgment[119]

Formulary	**B2.2**	**B3.2**	**B2.8**	**B2.9**	**B5.2**
I. Date	E-B	B-E	E-B	B-E	[B-E]
BCE	464	451	440	420	ca. 420
II. Parties	x	x	x	x	x
III. Certificate of Defendant's Performance	x	x	x	x	x
A. Performance	1	1	4	3	-
B. Object	2	2	2	2	2
C. Record of Litigation	3	3	1	1	1
D. Interrogation	-	-	-	3	-
E. Verdict	4	-	3	-	-
IV. Satisfaction	x	x	x	x	x
V. Release	-	in penalty	x	x	x
VI. Quitclaim	x	x	x	x	x
A. Covenant of Non-claim	1	1	1	1	1
B. Provisions in case of Violation	x	x	x	x	missing
1. Penalty	1	1	1	1	missing
2. Defension	-	2	-	-	missing
3. *Clausula Salvatoria*	2	-	-	-	missing
4. Release	3	-	2	2	missing
VII.Scribe	Itu b. Abah	Bunni B. Mannuki	Peṭeese b. Nabunathan	Mauziah b. Nathan	missing
VIII. Place	x		x		missing
IX. Dictation	x	x	x	x	missing
X. Witnesses	8	8	4	4	missing
XI. Endorsement	ספר מרחק	missing	ספר מרחק	ספר מרחק	missing

Three of these documents (*TAD* B2.8; B2.9; and B5.2) include a release clause, which is also not constructed uniformly, after the satisfaction clause. Two of them (*TAD* B2.8 and B5.2) use the active Peal construction, 'I withdrew from you from this day and forever', while the remaining one (*TAD* B2.9) uses the adjective Peil construction, 'we are

119 The numbers in the columns refer to the relative order in which the formulae are found in the documents. (x) = the clause is present, (-) = it is absent.

far from you from this day forever'. Regarding the function of the withdrawal formulae within these documents, in the case of Clause V. (Release), it is quite clear that the withdrawal is always from the person and has, therefore, the same meaning as in *TAD* B5.5:4.

A more complex and problematic case is that of the withdrawal formula as a component of Clause VI. B. 4 (Release within Quitclaim), since we are looking at three occurrences with two different legal meanings (nos. 1 and 2–3). In the quitclaim, therefore, the withdrawal formula adopts the following expressions:

1. A declaration of Party 1 that Party 2 is far (released) from any future suit regarding the property, meaning he cannot be sued (*TAD* B2.2). An unusual usage.
2. A declaration of Party 1 that he is the one who is released from suit, meaning that he cannot sue regarding the property (*TAD* B2.8).
3. A declaration of Party 1 that the one who initiates a suit against Party 2 will have to pay a penalty, without any right to claim the property (*TAD* B2.9).

5.1.3. *The Use of* רחק *in North West Semitic*

As we mentioned in the introduction, most of the studies dealing with the origins of the legal terminology of the Aramaic documents from Elephantine attribute a Mesopotamian origin to the legal formulae displayed in them; the Aramaic legal tradition is considered as the historical bridge between the Mesopotamian and the Egyptian legal formulae.

A survey of the West Semitic use of רחק therefore, is very pertinent to the discussion of the origin of the withdrawal clause. The basic questions are: (1) is there any attestation of the legal use of רחק in the west Semitic realm? and (2) how do they relate to the Aramaic use in Elephantine?[120]

5.1.3.1. *The use of* רחק *in the Marzeaḥ Papyrus*

The papyrus published by P. Bordreuil and D. Pardee[121] (dated mid- to late seventh century BCE) is quite significant for the legal history of Canaan as it documents the only attestation of the practice of divine verdict in the West Semitic realm and the only West Semitic attestation of a

120 For alleged biblical legal uses of רחק see A. F. Botta 'רחק in the Bible, a Reevaluation', *Bib* 87 (2006): 418–20.

121 P. Bordreuil and D. Pardee, 'Le Papyrus du marzeaḥ', *Semitica* 38, Hommages à Maurice Sznycer (2 vols.; 1990): 1.49-69, pls. VII-X. The authenticity of the papyrus was not widely accepted at first, cf. by Hoftijzer and Jongeling, *DNWSI*, s.v. šlš, but was later supported by Cross, 'Papyrus', by S. Aḥituv, 'A Divine Verdict – A Judicial Papyrus of the Seventh Century BCE', *ErIsr* 26 (Frank Cross volume) (1999): 1–4 (in Hebrew); and by a new examination of the papyrus by P. Bordreuil and D. Pardee, 'Nouvelle présentation du "Papyrus du Marzeaḥ"', *Semitica* 50 (2001): 224–26. I want to thank Prof. Pardee for providing me a copy of the article before publication.

legal use of רחק antedating the Elephantine documents. The papyrus reads:

כה אמרו אלהן לסרא	'Thus said the god(s) to Sara:[122]
לך המרזח והרחין והבית	The marzeaḥ[123] and the millstones
וישעא רחק מהם	and the house are yours.
ומלכא השלש	And Yiš'a', is far from them.
	And Malka' is the depositary.'
	Bulla: Malka' scribe

The divine verdict attempted to resolve a possible dispute between Sara and Yiš'a'. The final decision assigned the ownership of the object in dispute to Sara and declared that Yiš'a' is 'far from them', i.e. has no claim to them. The depositary of the document (i.e. the guarantor of the verdict) was the scribe Malka', whose name and title (scribe) appear on the bulla used to seal the papyrus. This is an example of the withdrawal from object which (although formulated in the third person) provides evidence for use of the legal formula in the West Semitic realm. Neither a court decision registered in an Aramaic docket from the Gozan-Harran area (ca. 704–700 BCE)[124] nor a settlement tablet from Nerab (ca. 614 BCE)[125] used a withdrawal formula. In this case, therefore, it is not possible to assess the extent of the use of the formula in Canaan because additional evidence is unavailable.

5.1.3.2. *The use of* רחק *in Palmyra*

Located in an oasis in the Syrian desert, the city of Palmyra (ancient Tadmor) is already mentioned in the nineteenth century BCE,[126] but its best documented periods are the Seleucid and Roman periods, from which about twelve hundred private and public inscriptions had been found. These inscriptions reflect the cosmopolitan and multicultural character of the city.[127]

122 F. M. Cross reads 'Gara', mentioning that Sara (*sr*ʾ) is a unique name, but the name is attested in Palmyra and in Syriac, *PAT* C4042. See Hillers and Cussini, *Palmyrene Aramaic Texts*, 84; J. K. Stark, *Personal Names in Palmyrene Inscriptions* (Oxford: Clarendon Press, 1971), 102. In their new study, P. Bordreuil and D. Pardee, 'Nouvelle Présentation', confirmed that the reading Sara is correct (although misspelled *Srh* in the article).

123 See, P. J. King, 'The Marzeah: The Textual and Archaeological Evidence', *ErIsr* 20 (1989): 98–106.

124 E. Lipiński, 'Aramaic Clay Tablets from the Gozan-Harran Area', *Jaarbericht van het vooraziatisch-egyptisch genootschap Ex Oriente Lux* 33 (1993–94): 144–47.

125 M. F. Fales, *Aramaic Epigraphs on Clay Tablets of the Neo Assyrian Period* (Rome: Università degli studi 'La Sapienza', 1986), 253–58.

126 Tadmor is mentioned in texts from Kültepe (nineteenth century BCE) and Mari.

127 See I. Browning, *Palmyra* (Park Ridge, N.J.: Noyes Press, 1979); and J. Starcky and M. Gawlikowski, *Palmyre* (Paris: Librairie d'Amérique et d'Orient, 1985).

The verb רחק is attested 33 times in Palmyrene inscriptions, termed 'cession texts', dated between 160 CE and 279 CE.[128] The occurrences of the רחק formulae can be classified in ten types:[129]

(1) Seller + רחק + ל + buyer + מן + portion sold.[130]
(2) Seller + רחק + ל + buyer + portion sold.[131]
(3) Seller + רחק + מן + portion sold + ל + buyer.[132]
(4) Seller + רחק + portion sold + ל + buyer.[133]
(5) Portion sold + רחק + seller + ל + buyer.[134]
(6) Portion sold + seller + רחק + מן + portion sold + ל + buyer.[135]
(7) Seller + חבר + רחק + ל + buyer + portion sold.[136]
(8) Seller + חבר + buyer + רחק + buyer + מן + portion sold.[137]
(9) Seller + שותף + רחק + ל + buyer + portion sold.[138]
(10) רחק + seller + ל + buyer + portion sold.[139]

The diverse formulaic ways in which רחק was used in Palmyra deserves a study of its own. Regarding its legal meaning, however, it is possible to affirm that,

> the use of a cession term in Palmyra shows that the verb underwent a development from the notion of *separation, relinquishment* (from the property) which it expresses in the Elephantine documents, to the idea of *sale* in the Palmyrene inscriptions.[140]

The way in which the formulaic use of רחק in Elephantine/*wy* in Demotic could have evolved has already been explained by Yaron, who had already suggested that the Palmyrene use of רחק should be understood as a translation of the Greek. As he stated:

128 See Cussini, 'Aramaic Law of Sale', 78–79; idem, 'Transfer of Property at Palmyra', *Aram* 7 (1995): 242–43; D. R. Hillers and E. Cussini, *Palmyrene Aramaic Texts* (Baltimore: Johns Hopkins University Press, 1996), Glossary, s.v. rḥq.

129 Cussini, 'Aramaic Law of Sale', 78, classified the formulae in five types, including the location of the portion sold as one of the variables. Except when noted, the formulae are written in objective style.

130 *PAT* 1153.2-3; 0523.1; 0524.1; 0075.3-4; 0525.1; 0526.1-2; 0048.1; 0041.4-6; 0051.3-4; 0052.2-3; 0043.3-4 (Aphel); 4206.1-2 (subjective); 0527.3; 2725.3.

131 *PAT* 0042.3; 0042.9; 0047.2, 9 (subjective); 2729.4.

132 *PAT* 0050.1-2; 0049.1-2 (both from the same tomb); 0058.2-3, 7.

133 *PAT* 0071.1-2; 2761.1.

134 *PAT* 0118.6 (bilingual); 0560.1-2; 0039.1-2; 0040.1-2; 0042.13-14; 2786.3-4 (bilingual); 0057.1-2; 0053.6; 0054.5-6; 0555.12; 0055.4.

135 *PAT* 0565.1-3 (bilingual, restored).

136 *PAT* 0029.1.

137 *PAT* 0067.4-6.

138 *PAT* 0045.1.

139 *PAT* 0095.3-6.

140 Cussini, 'Transfer of Property', 242.

> The notion of 'removal,' – be it of demotic or Aramaic origin – was taken up by the Greek papyri and from there in turn transferred elsewhere, e.g. to the Palmyrene inscriptions (...) *Rḥq l ... mn* becomes intelligible as the translation of the Greek παραχωρέω τινί ἀπὸ τινός (or τινός alone without ἀπὸ), the construction usual in the Greco-Egyptian deeds of cession.[141]

Yaron's position on the matter was supported recently by H. J. W. Drijvers.[142] Comparing the translation techniques from two bilingual Aramaic-Greek inscriptions he concluded that,

> the Aramaic of the bilingual Palmyrene inscriptions often shows certain characteristics and peculiarities in its choice of words, and its idioms and even its syntax, that make clear that the Aramaic is translated from the Greek and only understandable in the light of the Greek version. In other words, the Aramaic of Palmyra is to a certain extent hellenized and displays expressions that are fundamentally alien to the Aramaic language.[143]

Cussini's argument to prove it otherwise is solely based on the Palmyrene use of traditional Aramaic legal terminology. It is true, the Aramaic translation uses Aramaic words. But at the level of the legal formulae, her classification of the Palmyrene transfer formulae in the cession texts[144] proves precisely that the legal formulae used in Palmyra transfer clauses were mostly alien to the Aramaic formulaic tradition. Only two[145] out of thirteen transfer formulae correspond to previously known Aramaic transfer formulae.[146] The peculiar use of רחק in Palmyra, we must conclude, is the result of Greek influence and bears no consequence for the discussion on the ultimate origin of the withdrawal formula.

141 Yaron, 'Aramaic Deeds of Conveyance', 384. Yaron cites as examples of this use P. Grenf. 1.27 (= Mitteis, *Chrestomathie*, no. 156), lines 8ff.; BGU 1129 (= Mitteis, *Chrestomathie*, no. 254), lines 8ff. Yaron, 'Aramaic Deeds of Conveyance', 384 n. 7.

142 H. J. W. Drijvers, 'Greek and Aramaic in Palmyrene Inscriptions', in M. J. Geller, J. C. Greenfield, and M. P. Weitzman, eds., *Studia Aramaica* (Oxford: Oxford University Press, 1995), 31–42.

143 Drijvers, 'Greek and Aramaic in Palmyrene Inscriptions', 33.

144 Cussini, 'Transfer of Property', 249.

145 *yhb* 'to give', and *zbn* 'to sell'.

146 The remaining eleven are: *bʿd* "to alienate," *ʾḥbr* "to make a partnership," *lwy* "to make an association," *rḥq*, *ʾrḥq* "to withdraw," *šwtp*, "to make an association," *ʾḥbr wyhb* "to take a partnership and give," *ḥbr wrḥq*, "to take a partnership and cede," *yhb wʾḥbr*, "to give and to take in partnership," *yhb wbʿd*, "to give and to alienate," *šwtp wrḥq*, "to make an association and to withdraw." Cussini, "Transfer of Property," 249.

6

THE USE OF *w3y* IN THE EGYPTIAN LEGAL TRADITION

In the following sections, we proceed to list the evidence for the use of the *wy*-based formula from the earliest attestations to the most recent. We begin with the period before the Assyrian conquest, continue through the Saite and Persian periods and conclude with the Ptolemaic periods.

6.1. *The Untold Story: Legal Uses of w3y before the Assyrian Conquest*

The generally accepted scholarly opinion is that the Aramaic legal formulary originated in Mesopotamia and was brought into Egypt during the Assyrian conquest (671–664 BCE).[1] In order to prove otherwise, i.e. that the withdrawal formula has Egyptian roots, it is necessary to provide examples of its use in Egypt before the seventh century BCE. We may ask if this is in fact possible. As is widely known, the limited quantity of Egyptian legal documents that has survived to the present day is in no way comparable to the thousands of cuneiform legal tablets from the Mesopotamian realm.

The scarcity of legal documents from the earliest periods of Egyptian legal history makes it necessary, therefore, to turn to other sources. In the near absence of documentary papyri, other types of legal and also literary texts can nonetheless provide evidence of legal practices and legal formulae.[2] The literary texts usually refer to customary laws and help us to understand the age and diffusion of legal formulae.[3]

1 Muffs, *Studies*, 14; Fales, 'La tradition assyrienne'; Cussini, 'Aramaic Law of Sale'; Levine, 'On the Origins', 46; and Gropp, 'The *šalliṭ* Clause', 31–36.

2 In his review of Muffs, *Studies*, Levine suggests this direction. See Levine, 'On the Origins', 45.

3 See for example, S. Allam, 'Legal Aspects in the "Contendings" of Horus and Seth', in A. B. Lloyd, ed., *Studies in Pharaonic Religion and Society in Honour of J. Gwyn Griffiths* (London: Egypt Exploration Society, 1992), 137–45; M. Campagno, *La contienda entre Horus y Seth* (Buenos Aires: Del Signo, 2004), esp. 'Prácticas judiciales en el Reino Nuevo', pp. 115–18, and 'Prácticas judiciales en La contienda entre Horus y Seth', pp. 118–35. Shupak, 'A New Source', 1–18; R. de Spens, 'Droit International et Commerce au début de la XXIe Dynastie. Analyse Juridique du Rapport D'Ounamon', in N. Grimal and B. Menu,

In what follows, we present several attestations of the use of legal formulae constructed with the verb *wꜣy* 'to be far' that precede the Assyrian conquest by hundreds of years. The first example (1. Withdrawal Formula in the Coffin Texts) comes from the Middle Kingdom and is the earliest attestation of the withdrawal clause in Egypt, predating the Aramaic papyri by more than a thousand years. The second two cases (2. Removal from Office and Name) illustrate uses of the formula in the removal of name and from office. The third (3. Demand for Release: The Tomb Robberies Papyri of the XXth Dynasty) is a demand for release, and the fourth example (4. Transfer: The Endowment Stela of Ioureot) shows the use of *wy* in the context of transfer of property.

6.1.1. *Withdrawal Formula in the Coffin Texts*

Inscribed in ink on the walls of wooden coffins during the first Intermediate Period (ca. 2198–1938 BCE) and Middle Kingdom (ca. 1938–1759 BCE), the Coffin Texts repeat themes and spells of the Old Kingdom pyramid texts. In the Middle Kingdom coffin of *Dꜣg.y* from Deir el Bahari we read:[4]

ḥwg pw [m] tp ʾInpw
n sẖm smꜣy.t Ḥr Stẖ im=f
wꜣy ḥr nn
didi n=k ir nn t nn ḥnḳt

This funerary meal is before Anubis,
The confederacy of Horus and Seth has no authority over it,[5]
they being far[6] from this,
which is given to you, from[7] this bread and this beer.

In this spell, we are presented with legal formulae found in the Demotic and Aramaic documents: 'being far from' the funerary meal (the bread and beer), means that Horus and Seth do not have a right to them because the funerary meal is 'given to' the dead.

eds., *Le commerce en Égypte ancienne*, BdE 21 (Cairo: Institut Français d'Archéologie Orientale, 1998), 105–26. H. Limet, 'Traditions juridiques en contact dans le Proche-Orient achéménide', *Transeuphratène* 12 (1996): 163–79, for a legal analysis of the Greek novel *Chaireas and Callirhoe*.

4 *Coffin Texts* VII, 48 g, Spell 843.

5 Or 'over him', referring to Anubis (so Faulkner).

6 Old perfective 3rd Plural.

7 We correct Faulkner's translation 'for this bread and this beer'. Here *ḥr* is meant as synonym of *ir*: 'from' as in the Demotic formula. See Gardiner, *Egyptian Grammar*, §165.2 and §163.8. They are removed from the bread and the beer, which belong to the dead.

6.1.2. *Removal from Office and Name*

The Lisht tablets, mud tablets with grotesque human faces and Hieratic inscriptions from the Middle Kingdom, contain two to four short lines written in Hieratic.[8] Most of them read only 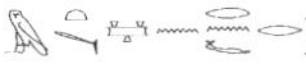PN: i.e. *mt wꜣ.n rn=f r* PN or the feminine *mtt wꜣ.n rn=s r* PN. In one case (kept in Cairo), the text reads *mt wꜣ r mr ḫtmṯw wꜣ.n rn=f r* PN.

G. Posener translated *wꜣ* as 'deprived of', i.e. 'The deceased (who was) deprived of the name PN', and 'the deceased (who was) removed from (the post of) overseer of sealers and deprived of the name PN'. J. P. Allen[9] explains *wꜣ.n rn=f r* NN as the relative *sḏm.n=f*: literally, 'whose name has become away from (the name) NN', and *wꜣ r ḫ* as the perfective active participle: literally, 'who has become away from (the post of) X'. Posener's explanation of these phrases is as follows:[10]

> Le cas soulevait une difficulté pour les scribes. Voila un homme qui avait perdu son emploi et son identité. On pouvait néanmoins avoir besoin du designer de façon précise sans qu'il y ait eu aucun risque d'erreur. Comment le faire s'il n'a plus ni titre ni nom? C'est à cela que servent les constructions avec *w3*
>
> Elles permettent de le nommer sans lui attribuer une fonction et un nom. En simplifiant, nous dirions 'ex-patron de bateau ex-NN.'

Fifteen tablets do not have the formula, rather only a name and title. Posener considers the individuals named here as lesser criminals, whose condemnation did not deprive them of their identity.[11]

The earliest example of this formula occurs in the Theban Papyrus Brooklyn 35.1446, l. 58d (ca. 1800 BCE).[12] The text reads *wꜣ r nfꜣw n pr-ḥḏ wꜣ.n rn=f r* PN: 'the one removed from (the post of) sailor of the treasury and deprived of the name PN'. Besides this example, the phrase also occurs in the second Intermediate Period stela of the Theban king Neb-

8 Notice of the discovery in the *Bulletin of the Metropolitan Museum of Art (New York)* Nov. 1933, sect. ii, 23–24, fig. 32. Mentioned by Hayes, *Papyrus*, 57, and P. Vernus, 'Sur une formule des documents judiciaires de l'Epoque Ramesside', *RdE* 26 (1974): 122. Prof. G. Posener was in charge of the publication before his death. Dr James P. Allen, former curator of the Metropolitan Museum of Art, will publish Posener's manuscript along with his transcriptions of the texts, in a forthcoming article in the *Metropolitan Museum Journal*, entitled 'Execration Figures from Lisht'. I thank Dr Allen for his kindness in sharing with me his comments and some of Prof. Posener's observations.

9 J. P. Allen, personal communication, 25 February 1997.

10 J. P. Allen, 'Execration Figures from Lisht', forthcoming.

11 For the religious and legal implications of these practices see G. Posener, 'Les Criminels Débaptisés et les Morts sans Noms', *RdE* 5 (1946): 51–56.

12 Hayes, *Papyrus*, 53–4.

Kheperu-Re Inyotef (ca. 1630 BCE),[13] which illustrates the consequences for the person of the removal of the name:

> Let him be expelled from the temple (...) and let him be removed from his office of the temple (...) while his income (...) is taken away (...) that his name is not recalled as is done to the likes of him, a criminal and an enemy of his god. Remove his documents from the temple of Min and from the treasury, and any other papyrus likewise.[14]

All of these occurrences of the verb *wꜣy* clearly denote a legal-administrative meaning in complete harmony with the use of *wy* in the Demotic documents. The act of being-far clearly implies a cessation of the person's rights to the name and office.

We have, therefore, another documented use of the withdrawal formula in a different context but with the same general meaning. The continuous attestation in different contexts of a legal formula with the same core meaning but with different nuances points to the widely accepted legal use in ancient Egypt of the metaphor of physical withdrawal to denote a termination and renunciation of rights.

6.1.3. *Demand for Release: The Tomb Robberies Papyri of the 20th Dynasty*

We also find a different nuance in the use of the withdrawal formula in another context: during an interrogation in a judicial procedure. Hieratic papyri attest to certain judicial inquiries and trials, conducted at Thebes during the late 20th Dynasty (1125–1069 BCE), which were related to tomb robberies in the Theban necropolis. P. BM. 10052, dated in year 1 of the Renaissance Era of Ramesses XI (ca. 1097 BCE), documents the trial of two groups of thieves by a panel of judges. At the beginning of the judicial process against a suspect, he claims:

> *wꜣ r=y wꜣ r ẖꜥt=y*
>
> Be far from me. Be far from me (lit. my body).[15]

Since the reports of these processes are strictly of a legal nature, the declaration of the suspects cannot be interpreted as having other than a legal meaning. It should be interpreted as a claim of innocence and/or as a

13 W. Helck, *Historisch-biographische Texte der 2. Zwischenzeit und neue Texte der 18. Dynastie*, 2nd edn. (Wiesbaden: Harrassowitz, 1983), 73–74.

14 The most recent translation of the text is found in Lorton, 'Treatments of Criminals', 18–22.

15 P. BM 10052, page 4, line 8; page 8, line 4; page 11, lines 2, 11, and 15–16. T. E. Peet, *The Great Tomb-Robberies of the Twentieth Egyptian Dynasty* (Oxford: Oxford University Press, 1930), 146, 150, 152–53.

demand for release as attested by a similar use of the verb *wy* 'to be far' in the cases registered in the Rosetta Stone.[16]

6.1.4. *Transfer: The Endowment Stela of Ioureot*[17]

The last example of the early attestation of the withdrawal formula in Egypt that we wish to discuss comes from the context of the transfer of real property, which is the most documented context for the use of the withdrawal formula in the Ptolemaic period. It is found in the endowment stela of Ioureot. Discovered in the Temple of Amon at Karnak, the stela, dated 914 BCE, records an endowment of land by Ioureot to his son Khaenwase. In lines 5 and 6, the pedigree clause explains how Ioureot purchased the land:[18]

> *ỉw di=f wiꜣ.w nꜣ ꜣḥ r-di=f ḥḏ r-ḏbꜣ=w*
> *(...) di.w grḥ n=f tꜣy 556 n sꜣ(t) ꜣḥ nmḥw nʿ*
>
> He has caused that the fields be relinquished, (the fields) for which he had paid a price
> (...)
>
> they put at his disposal these 556 arouras of released private land.

In these two sentences, we have a very nice example of the use of the legal expression *di wiꜣ* (to cause to relinquish, to remove, to be far)[19] in close relation with the word *nʿ* ('to be clear, to release').[20] The fields which were

16 See below, 6.3.12, p. 174.

17 A. Moret, 'Un procès de familie sous la XIXe dynastie', *ZÄS* 39 (1901): 30–31; J. Pirenne and B. Van de Walle, 'Documents Juridiques Égyptiens', *Archives d'Histoire du Droit Oriental* 1 (1937): 41–65. B. Menu, 'La stèle dite de L'Apanage', in M. M. Mactoux and E. Gens, eds., *Mélanges Pierre Lévêque* (Paris: Les Belles Lettres, 1989), 337–58.

18 For the pedigree clause, see Porten, *Elephantine Papyri*, 185 n. 6.

19 B. Gunn has established that 'it is *a priori* extremely likely that in the late New Kingdom the verbs *wiꜣ* "to separate", *wꜣy* "to be far" (...) are by no means accurately distinguished', B. Gunn, 'The Word ', *ZÄS* 62 (1927): 85. Cf. the discussion by A. H. Gardiner, 'A Late-Egyptian Idiom', *ZÄS* 47 (1910): 134–36; and K. Sethe, 'Zu *ÄZ* 62, 83ff', *ZÄS* 63 (1928): 99–101, and Ritner, 'Third Intermediate Period Antecedents', 345–47.

20 *nʿ* 'frei sein', Erichsen, *Glossar*, 207. Cf. *snʿʿ*, *Wb* IV, 56. In Aramaic this formula is expressed by אנקה (*TAD* B1.1:10) and אפצל (*TAD* B3.2:9; 3.4:20). See Porten, 'Aramaic-Demotic Equivalents', no. 7, p. 261. For a comparison between Aramaic and Demotic clauses see Porten and Szubin, 'Abandoned Property', 126–29; see also Yaron, *Introduction*, 105; J. Greenfield, 'The "Defension Clause" in some Documents from Naḥal Ḥever and Naḥal Ṣe'elim', *Revue de Qumran* 15 (1991–92): 467–71. None of the aforementioned studies, however, dealt properly with the Egyptian evidence. Cf. Ritner, 'Third Intermediate Period Antecedents', 351, who provides evidence of the use of the Egyptian legal term since the Old Kingdom onwards where tombs are built in a 'pure place' (*s.t wʿb.t*), i.e. 'unencumbered by older tombs or competing claims of ownership' (Urk. I, 50/13 (Hetepherakhti); 260/11 (Nenki)). In the Mesopotamiam realm, the formula based on the verbs *elēlu* (*CAD* vol. 4 E, 80–83 esp. 1.b.) and ebēbu (*CAD* vol. 4 E, pp. 4–8 esp. c and d) is attested since the Old

'set apart, removed' are also 'clear, released'.[21] The legal meaning of these two words will become apparent when we compare the following parallel passages coming from the Late Period:

> P. Rylands 8, line 5 (562 BCE, El Hibeh): *pꜣ nt iw=f iy r-r=k r-ḏbꜣ.ṱ=s r ṯ.ṱ mtw=k r ḏd bn tꜣy=k iḥ(.t) in tꜣy ink iir ti nꜥ=s n=k*
>
> (As for) the one who shall come to you in regard of her in order to take her from you saying 'she is not your cow', I am the one who will cause her to be *clear* for you.
>
> P. Berlin 13571, lines 6–7 (588 BCE, Edfu):[22] *pꜣ nt iw=f iy r-r=k r-ḏbꜣ.ṱ=s r ṯ.ṱ=s mtw=k ḏ bn mtw=k s in n rn(=y) n rn rmt nb n pꜣ tꜣ iw=y r ti wy=f r-r=k n-im=s*
>
> (As for) the one who shall come to you in regard of her in order to take her from you saying 'she does not belong to you' in my name or in the name of any man in the land, I will cause him to be *far* from you concerning her.

These examples display a clear continuity in the legal use of the withdrawal formula between the stela of Ioureot in the tenth century BCE and the use in these Demotic documents of the sixth century BCE.

6.2. *The Uses of wy in the Saite and Persian Periods (664–332 BCE)*

As we get close to the time of production of the Aramaic documents from Elephantine, the amount of Egyptian documents that have been preserved increases notably. We have evidence of the writing of notarized acts that registered legal transactions in previous periods of Egyptian legal history, but it is only from after the 25th Dynasty that a multitude of legal papyri have survived to the present day.[23] Suddenly, we have a continuous series of documents in Demotic interrupted only rarely, perhaps due to abrupt

Assyrian period (ca. 2000–1800 BCE) Cf. P. Steinkeller, *Sale Documents of the Ur-III-Period* (Stuttgart: F. Steiner, 1989), 64; Kienast *Das Altassyrische Kaufvertragsrecht* (Wiesbaden: Harrassowitz, 1984), 58–61, 133, 144–45.

21 See Menu, 'Stèle', 194. Cf. Ritner, 'Third Intermediate Period', 346.

22 W. Erichsen, 'Zwei frühdemotische Urkunden aus Elephantine', in *Coptic Studies in Honor of Walter Ewing Crum* (Boston: Byzantine Institute, 1950), 272, suggested that these documents came from Elephantine. K.-Th. Zauzich, on the other hand, taking into consideration the similar formulary with the Edfu documents, suggests that P. Berlin 13571 could have been produced in Edfu. K.-Th. Zauzich, 'Ein Kaufvertrag aus der Zeit des Nektanebos', *MDAIK* 25 (1969): 228.

23 The lack of similar amounts of legal documents from previous periods has always intrigued Egyptologists. Cf. W. F. Edgerton, 'Demotica Papyri und Altertumswissenschaft', *Münchener Beiträge zur Papyrusforschung and antiken Rechtsgeschichte* (Munich: C. H. Beck, 1934), 286ff.; Seidl, *Einführung*, 21ff. F. L. Griffith is probably right when he attributes this

changes in the political and social situation. Several causes might have contributed to this development: increasing trade, political stability,[24] etc. Diodorus tells us that Bocchoris (24th Dynasty: 720–715 BCE) 'drew up the regulations that governed the kings and gave precision to the laws of contracts',[25] and that 'their laws governing contracts (περὶ τῶν συμβλαίων) they attribute to Bocchoris'.[26] Probably, the essential constitutive elements of the Egyptian customary law regarding sale transactions continued unaltered for centuries and although the elements of a sale transaction remained, the legal procedures and legal instruments became more complex.

The period between the beginning of the 26th Dynasty and the conquest of Egypt by Alexander the Great exhibits several points of interest for the legal historian. We can still observe the local development of different legal traditions and the consolidation of some types of legal documents that during Ptolemaic times became standard for the whole country. Such are the *sẖ n wy* and the *sẖ ḏbꜣ ḥḏ* which appear already in the Saite and Persian periods.

In this period, the development of legal instruments is documented through deeds written in Hieroglyphs, Hieratic, Cursive Hieratic, Abnormal Hieratic, Early Demotic, and Demotic. The system of writing is very significant for tracing the development of the legal formularies. However, the writing is neither the definitive nor the only criterion for establishing a pattern of development of the legal traditions.[27] Therefore, both the place of origin and internal formulae of the documents should also be considered. As expected, the transition between the different writing systems in which the legal instruments are written is not abrupt and varies geographically.[28]

After the triumph of Psammetichus I, the political programme of the Saite rulers was to move the centre of activities from Upper Egypt to the

situation to the 'increase in the number of the transactions and greater necessity of written records', F. L. Griffith, *Catalogue of the Demotic Papyri in the John Rylands Library Manchester* (Manchester: Manchester University Press, 1909), vol. 3, 11.

24 Cf. A. B. Lloyd, 'The Late Period', in B. G. Trigger, B. J. Kemp, D. O'Connor, and A. B. Lloyd, eds., *Ancient Egypt: A Social History* (Cambridge: Cambridge University Press, 1983), 325–31.

25 Diodorus Siculus I, 94.5.

26 Diodorus Siculus I, 79.1. E. Seidl suggests an earlier date (21st Dynasty) for the account given by Diodorus. See Seidl, *Ägyptische Rechtsgeschichte*, 53ff.

27 *S. Florence* 1659, a sale of tombs from the year 4 of Psammetichus I (Memphis, 661 BCE), for example, is a hieroglyphic transcription of an early Demotic deed. See M. Malinine, 'Ventes de Tombes à L'Epoque Saïte', *RdE* 27 (1975): 164–68.

28 K. Donker van Heel has provided a detailed study of the transition from Abnormal Hieratic to Demotic in a family of Theban scribes of the sixth century BCE. See K. Donker van Heel, 'The Lost Battle of Peteamonip son of Petehorresne', in *Acta Demotica* (1994), 115–24.

Delta, and for this purpose, they had to counteract the power of the priests of Amon Ra in Thebes. Psammetichus appointed his daughter, Nitocris, as the High Priestess and established a special administrative unit from the Memphite Nome to Assuan.[29] There was also a reform regarding the administration of justice. The *ḳnbt*, a very well known institution during the New Kingdom, would give up its place to the *ḏ3ḏ3t* council and to the *ʿwi n wpy.t* 'house of the judges',[30] where one could initiate legal proceedings.

S. Allam postulates that there was a real reorganization of the administrative and judicial activities during the 26th Dynasty: 'whereas the *ḳnbt* had had administrative, as well as judicial responsibilities, the later "judges" show no sign of administrative activity ... this separation might have culminated in a kind of separation of administrative and judicial powers'.[31] In this process, the officials appointed to implement the reforms came from the northern scribal-law tradition and, therefore, would follow northern practices. They thus began to use legal formulae belonging to the Delta area, thereby putting an end to the Abnormal Hieratic southern school.[32]

The decline of Abnormal Hieratic, therefore, should be understood in terms of the political defeat of Thebes by the Saite kings and the consequent appointment of northern scribes to positions of influence, which in turn led to a progressive retraining of the new generations of scribes in the Demotic tradition.[33] A. B. Lloyd concludes that 'by the year 22 of Amasis, at the latest, Saite administrative control of the entire country was no longer a matter of dispute'.[34] and this is precisely the year in which we have the last document written in Abnormal Hieratic, P. Louvre E 7846 (Thebes, 549 BCE) after which, the Demotic tradition became dominant in the whole country.[35]

The corpus of Demotic private legal documents can be classified in the

29 Cf. R. A. Caminos, 'The Nitocris Adoption Stele', *JEA* 50 (1964): 71–101; and J. Vandier, 'L'Intronisation de Nitocris', *ZÄS* 99 (1972): 29–33.

30 See M. Lurje, *Studien zum altägyptischen Recht (des 16. Bis 10. Jh. V.u.Z.)* (Weimar: H. Böhlaus Nachfolger, 1971), 63ff., and also the discussion in S. Allam, 'Egyptian Law Courts in Pharaonic and Hellenistic Times', *JEA* 77 (1991): 109–27.

31 Allam, 'Egyptian Law Courts', 119.

32 For a discussion of the relationships between legal tradition and system of writing in the Abnormal Hieratic and Early Demotic documents, see Vleeming, 'La phase initiale du Demotique Ancien', *Chronique d'Egypte* 56 (1981): 31–48.

33 See Donker van Heel,'Lost Battle'.

34 Lloyd, 'Late Period', 336.

35 The largest number of documents preserved from the Saite and Persian periods come from the south of the country, more specifically, from the Theban area. This situation led scholars to think that almost half of the corpus of Demotic documents originated in a single archive (E. Cruz-Uribe, 'A Saite Request for Payment', *JEA* 71 (1985): 129–33; but see K. Donker van Heel, 'A Small Note on Early Demotic Texts and Archives', *JEA* 78 (1992), 287.

following categories:[36] marriage settlements, which include the 'woman's document' (*sẖ n ḥm.t*); the 'document of maintenance' (*sẖ n sʿnḫ*);[37] documents of divorce, documents concerning money (*sẖ ḏb3 ḥḏ*); documents of withdrawal (*sẖ n wy*); exchanges; donations and property transfers; divisions and wills (*sẖ dni.t pš*); partnerships; leases; loans; deposits; public protests; deeds of obligation; and private receipts. In this chapter we shall be concerned only with documents where the withdrawal formula is attested.

In what follows, we present a list of the uses of the Demotic *wy*-based formulae in different transactions: (1) Transfer, (2) Litigation, (3) Release from obligation, (4) Marriage and divorce settlements, and (5) Vacancy of property. Afterwards, we shall analyse the use of *ḫ3ʿ* in the Hieratic tradition as a functional equivalent of *wy* and, finally, briefly explore the posterior development of the use of *wy*-based formulae during the Ptolemaic period. Our attempt in this chapter on the Egyptian material is to bring to the forefront the Egyptian formulae based on the verb *wy* in order to help us to understand the uses of רחק in the Aramaic documents and, at the same time, look for further clarification as to the question of the original legal tradition in which the withdrawal formula might have emerged. [38]

6.2.1. *The Use of wy in Transfers*

In this section we deal with documents related to transfers of property in which we find the *wy*-based formula. Our purpose is to study the Demotic equivalent of the Aramaic ספר מרחק, the *sẖ n wy*. It is precisely in the *sẖ n wy* that we have the earliest surviving examples that document the *wy*-type withdrawal clause: P. Rylands 4 (El-Hibeh, 568 BCE);[39] P. BM 10792 (Asyut , 522 BCE); P. Cairo 50059 (Asyut, 522 BCE)[40] and P. Loeb 43 (Gebelein, 485 BCE), where the withdrawal clause appears as the initial clause in the document. In P. Louvre AF 9761 (Thebes, 494 BCE) this

36 See Zauzich, 'Die demotischen Dokumente', 93–110; M. Depauw, *A Companion to Demotic Studies* (Brussels: Fondation égyptologique reine Élisabeth, 1997), 139–48. We follow the order of Depauw.

37 For further clarification and bibliography see H. S. Smith, 'Marriage and the Family', 48–54.

38 For formulary considerations on this period see B. Menu, 'Un Document Juridique "Kouchite." Le P. Vienne D 12002', in *Hommages à Jean Leclant* (Cairo: Institut Français d'Archéologie Orientale, 1994), vol. 2, 301–02; idem, 'Les Actes de Vente', 173–81.

39 Restored with certainty by Griffith, *Catalogue*, transliteration vol. 2, 208, translation vol. 1, 52–53.

40 As suggested by A. F. Shore, 'Swapping Property at Asyut in the Persian Period', in J. Baines *et al.*, eds., *Pyramid Studies and Other Essays Presented to I. E. S. Edwards* (London: Egypt Exploration Society, 1988), 202.

formula appears as the second clause. Later we have it again in P. Louvre *N* 2430 (Thebes, 335 BCE).

The verb *wy* displays three forms for the qualitative in these documents: *wy.k*[41] *wy.ṯ*[42] and *wy(.w)*.[43] Five of the eight *sẖ n wy* that have been preserved are related to transfer of property/services (nos. 1, 3, 4, 8, and 9), two are most likely the result of litigation (nos. 6 and 7), and one is a discharge of obligation (no. 6). See Table XI.[44]

Table XI: *Sẖ n wy* Saite and Persian Period

No.	Museum	Date	Kind of document	Objects	Place
1	P. Rylands 4	568	Withdrawal	Document of Servitude	El-Hibeh
2	Ref. in. P. Cairo 50058	543	Withdrawal	Inheritance of Priestly Offices	Asyut
3	P. BM 10792	522	Withdrawal in Division	Priestly Office	Asyut
4	P. Cairo 50059	522	Withdrawal *sẖ n wy* in Division	Priestly Office	Asyut
5	P. Louvre A F 9761	494	Discharge Obligation	*hp* Donkey	Thebes
6	P. Loeb 43	485	Litigation	Female Donkey	Gebelein
7	P. Cairo 50150 + 155	375	Withdrawal after Judgment	*hp* House	Edfu
8	P. Inv. Sorbonne 1277	343	Withdrawal in Sale	Slave	Unknown
9	P. Louvre 2430	334	Division	House	Thebes

In what follows, we analyse the various types of transfers attested in the documents: (a) transfer of services, (b) donations and divisions, and (c) sales.[45]

41 P. Cairo 50058.7 (Asyut, 543 BCE); P. Berlin 3076.5 (Thebes, 513 BCE ?); P. Loeb 43.2 (Gebelen, 485 BCE); P. Cairo 50150 + 155.1 (Edfu, 375 BCE); P. Libbey 2 (Thebes, 337 BCE).

42 P. Louvre E 7839.10 (Thebes, 534 BCE); P. Cairo 50059.5 (Asyut, 522 BCE); P. BM 10792.6 (Asyut, 522 BCE); P. Berlin 3078.5 (Thebes, 492 BCE); P. BM 10449.4 (Thebes, 492 BCE); P. Berlin 3079.6 (Thebes, 489 BCE); P. Berlin 3077.4 (Thebes, 488 BCE); P. Cairo 50144.2 (Edfu, 368 BCE); P. Libbey 2 (Thebes, 337 BCE); P. Louvre N 2430.1 (Thebes, 335 BCE).

43 P. Louvre E 7850.6 (Thebes, 533 BCE); P. Louvre AF 9761.6 (Thebes, 494 BCE).

44 In Table XI we include the reference to a *sẖ n wy* in P. Cairo 50058.

45 The documents involving litigation are dealt with in the next section.

6.2.1.1. *Transfer of Services*

P. Rylands 4 is the oldest *sẖ n wy* to have reached us. Although the first part of the formula has to be restored, there should be no doubt as to the restoration proposed by Griffith in the *editio princeps*.[46] The formulary of P. Rylands 4 reads as follows:

P. Rylands 4: Document of Withdrawal (El-Hibe, 569 BCE)

I. Date: Year 2 of Pharaoh Amasis
II. Parties: Zeubestefʿnkh son of Hor speaks to Essemteu son of Peteesi.
III. Withdrawal
- **A. Withdrawal:** I am far from you (*[tw(=y) wy.k] r-ḥr=k)*
- **B. Object:** document of services (*n p3 ḏmʿ bk*) which Peftuakhonz zon of Ìeriubazti made for me [in year 2...?]

IV. Investiture
- **A. Personal:** [He is your servant]. (*bn iw(=y) rḫ ir sḫy n-im=f*) I shall not be able to exercise authority over him.

V. Quitclaim
- **A. Personal:** I shall not be able to produce an old papyrus or a new papyrus [...] in the name of this document of services that I have given to you
- **B. General:** The man that shall produce a papyrus saying 'he is not your slave' shall give you 20 artabas of wheat. I [*sic* = He] still being your slave forever

VI. Scribe Zeubestefʿnkh son of Hor himself
VII. Witnesses: 8

In order to understand the legal purpose of P. Rylands 4, it is necessary to analyse P. Rylands 3 and 5. P. Rylands 3–7 are related to Peftuʿkhons son of Heriubʿsti. Peftuʿkhons son of Heriubʿsti declares himself a servant (*b3k*)[47] of Zeubestefʿnkh son of Hor in P. Rylands 3. In P. Rylands 5, however, he declares himself a servant of Essemteu son of Peteesi in exchange for what seems to be maintenance and medical assistance he received while he was still under the mastership of Zeubestefʿnkh son of Hor, his former master.[48]

46 Griffith, *Catalogue*, 53 n. 1. Although Pestman affirms, 'Dans P. Ryl. 4, 2 (569 av. J.-C.), le verbe est en lacune et sa restitution est donc incertaine' (Pestman and Vleeming, *Papyrus démotiques*, 87 n. 2), there is no other initial formula in Demotic that will continue with *r-ḥr=k* than the withdrawal clause. Vleeming tacitly supports Griffith's restoration when commenting on P. Loeb 43, and affirms that the withdrawal formula 'first occurs in the much older Pap. Ryl. 4 (569 B.C.)', Vleeming, *Pap Hou*, 129, dd. See also Seidl, *Ägyptische Rechtsgeschichte*, 20.

47 Menu has demonstrated that these documents deal with cession of services and not with slavery. The contract could be renewed on an annual basis. Idem, 'Cession', 83–86.

48 The reading of these words is regarded by Griffith as 'extremely doubtful', Griffith, *Catalogue*, 53 n. 7.

This should be regarded as the necessary consideration that motivates the transfer of mastership from Zeubestefꜥnkh son of Hor to Essemteu son of Peṭeesi. However, in order to be assured that Zeubestefꜥnkh son of Hor will not complain in the future, it is natural that Essemteu son of Peṯeesi demanded a renunciation by Zeubestefꜥnkh son of Hor of the rights conferred upon him by Peftuꜥkhons son of Heriubꜥsti in P. Rylands 3 and the transfer of the document. This is the reason for the production of P. Rylands 4, whose second line *[tw=y wy.k] r-ḥr=k n pꜣ ḏmꜥ bk* is best translated: 'I am far from you regarding the document of services.' The specific legal function of this document of withdrawal is, therefore, that of a renunciation of the mastership rights held by Zeubestefꜥnkh son of Hor in favour of Essemteu son of Peṭeesi.

The formulary of P. Rylands 4 follows the standard general structure of the *sẖ n wy*.[49] The withdrawal formula reflects the transfer of the document of slavery, the possession of which, as in the case of the possession of sale documents of realty, gives to Essemteu son of Peṭeesi proof of ownership. This use of the withdrawal formula will continue through Ptolemaic times.[50] In the following section, we analyse the uses of *sẖ n wy* in donations and divisions.

6.2.1.2. *Donations and Divisions*

The legal transaction in the context of which the withdrawal formula is most frequently attested in this period is that of division of inheritance. Documents from this period related to the transfer of property in the context of donations and divisions are P. Cairo 50058 (Donation, 543 BCE, Asyut); P. BM 10792 (*sẖ n wy*, 522 BCE, Asyut); P. Cairo 50059 (*sẖ n wy*, 522 BCE, Asyut);[51] P. Louvre N 2430 (*sẖ n wy*, 334 BCE, Thebes), and the *sẖ n wy* mentioned in P. Cairo 50058. The legal function of the *sẖ n wy* in donations and divisions is to state the renunciation of claims by one of the parties to the share transferred to the other party and vice versa. This function of the *sẖ n wy* and the withdrawal formula is also attested in the Ptolemaic period. P. Mallawi 602/10 records a litigation in Middle Egypt dated 117/116 BCE. In line 5, one of the parties declares, 'we apportioned (*iw=n pš*) from (out of) our stipendiary foundations the northern side together with our fellows with a deed of cession (*sẖ wy*) to each'.[52]

The initial formula of donation documents, 'Schenkungsurkunden', is

49 See below 6.2.1.3.2.

50 Cf. below 6.3.1, 'Initial Withdrawal Clause in *sẖ n wy* in Transfers of Property', p. 169.

51 We follow the suggestion by Shore regarding P. Cairo 50059 that 'the obliterated passage in l.s should read *tw=y wy r-r=k* as in P. BM 10972'. Shore, 'Swapping', 202.

52 O. El-Aguizy, 'A Ptolemaic Judicial Document from ḤWT-NSW', *BIFAO* 88 (1988): 55.

ti=y n=k X Property 'I gave you X property',[53] while in division contracts, 'Teilungsurkunden',[54] the initial formula is *pš=y irm=k pš=k irm=y n n3 nkt.w n* PN 'I have made a division with you (and) you have made a division with me of the possessions of PN.'[55]

The formulary of a typical donation document reads as follows:

P. Cairo 50058 (Donation, Asyut, 543 BCE)

I. **Date:** Year 28, month Paophi, Pharaoh Amais
II. **Parties:** Oupwethope speaks to Espame
III. **Transference**
  A. **Transfer:** I gave you (priestly and scribal offices)
  B. **Investiture:** they are yours
  C. **Withdrawal:** I am far from you regarding the priestly offices etc.
IV. **Investiture II:** it is yours all what is written above as your part of the revenues that belonged to our father
V. **Quitclaim**
  A. **Covenant of Non-claim:** I do not have any claim at all
VI. **General Warranty**
  A. **Defension:** the one who shall come in my name or in the name of our father regarding it, I will cause him to be far from you
VII. **Withdrawal of Espametcheps:** you are far from me regarding the priestly offices ... concerning which you have written for me a withdrawal (*sẖ n=y r-r=w n wy*)
VIII. **Scribe:** Kanofre son of Horkhebi

53 For this formula in Saite-Persian period sale documents see Menu, 'Les Actes de vente', 174–75. Some examples of documents with the *ti=y n=k X Property* formula from the Ptolemaic period are: P. Strassburg 1 (Thebes, 223 BCE); P. Philadelphia 1 (Thebes, 307 BCE); P. Philadelphia 5 (Thebes, 302 BCE); P. BM 10827 (Thebes, 270 BCE); P. Philadelphia 18 (241 BCE); P. Louvre 2425; P. Louvre 3263; P. BM 10829 (Thebes, 209 BCE).

54 The division documents from the Ptolemaic period are not very numerous, P. Heidelberg 740 (Gebelein, 180–170 BCE); P. Turin 6104 (Thebes, 106 BCE); DP CG 30602 and 30603 (Memphis, 116/115 BCE); DP Berlin 3089 (Thebes, 230 BCE); DP Berlin 3099, 3100, 5508 (Thebes, 124 BCE); DP CG 30649 (Gebelein). See Zauzich, 'Die demotischen Dokumente', 101; Depauw, *Companion*, 144 and the bibliography cited there. E. Seidl, 'Die Teilunschrift', *MDAIK* 8 (1939): 198–200; U. Kaplony-Heckel, *Die demotischen Gebelen-Urkunden der Heidelberger Papyrus-Sammlung* (Heidelberg: C. Winter, 1964), 20–21. Seidl, *Ptolemäische Rechtgeschichte*, 51, 178, and 180. Examples of *sẖ n wy* in divisions of inheritance are P. Brooklyn 37.181 (Memphis, 181 BCE); P. Brooklyn 37.1839 A; and P. Brooklyn 37.1839 B (both produced at the same time in Memphis, 201 BCE). (Pestman *et al.*, *Recueil*, docs. 1–3). The three documents belong to the private archive of Horos son of Petosiris and relate to the division of family property between November/December 201 and November 181 BCE among the cousins Horus and Teebes. The purpose of the *sẖ n wy* in this case is to recognize the rights of the parties to the assigned share (see Pestman *et al.*, *Recueil*, 3–7).

55 Documents with this initial clause are: P. BM 10227 (Thebes, 230 BCE); P. Berlin 3089 + P. BM 10426 (Thebes, 230 BCE).

Although both donation and division documents represent two different legal transactions, their function is similar in cases where both deal with inherited property.[56] The difference is that documents of division beginning with the formula *pš=y ỉrm=k pš=k ỉrm=y n nꜣ nkt.w n* PN are drawn up between siblings as owners with equal rights whereas divisions of inheritance constructed as donations are drawn up by the owner of the property, or by the firstborn of the deceased, for another member of the family.[57] In both cases, we have mention of *sẖ n wy* being exchanged that are related to the transaction.[58]

6.2.1.3. *Sales: The sẖ ḏbꜣ ḥḏ and the sẖ n wy*

In the Saite and Persian periods, conveyances of real property tended to be registered in a single document. In the Ptolemaic period, however, two documents became necessary for the transaction:[59] the *sẖ ḏbꜣ ḥḏ* (συγγραφὴ πράσεως)[60] and the *sẖ n wy* (συγγραφὴ ἀποστασίου).[61] The practice of producing two documents also began to be attested, though infrequently, in the last years of the earlier period.

The first pair of such documents in the context of a sale[62] that have reached us are the fragmentary P. Inv. Sorbonne 1277 (Place unknown, 343 BCE), which seems to be related to the *sẖ ḏbꜣ ḥḏ* P.Inv. Sorbonne 1276

56 Zauzich, 'Die demotischen Dokumente', 102. See for example the Theban archive of Timounis daughter of Thabis (270–175 BCE): P. BM 10827 (270 BCE); P. BM 10227 (230 BCE); P. BM 10377 (214 BCE); and P. BM 10829 (209 BCE) where is recorded the division and cession of the property within the family. Andrews, *Catalogue*, 47–59.

57 See P. W. Pestman, 'The Law of Succession in Ancient Egypt', in J. Brugman *et al.*, eds., *Essays on Oriental Laws of Succession* (Leiden: Brill, 1969), 58–77; idem, 'Inheriting in the Archive of the Theban Choachytes (2nd cent. B.C.)', in S. P. Vleeming, ed., *Aspects of Demotic Lexicography* (Leuven: Peeters, 1987), 57–73.

58 In the donations from the Ptolemaic period P. BM 10827.5 (Thebes, 270 BCE), the alienor states that he has drawn up a *sẖ n wy* for the alienee (this *sẖ n wy* must have fulfilled the same function as *TAD* B2.10. P. BM 10829.5 (Thebes, 209 BCE) is a division of tombs as a share of the inheritance. The alienor states that the alienee (his sister) has received a *sẖ n wy* from him regarding the share of the inheritance that he received.

59 P. BM 10027.2 (Thebes, 311 BCE) *r mḥ sẖ 2* 'to fulfil the two documents'. The same expression occurs in the Theban documents P. BM 10464.3 (210 BCE); P. BM 10392.7 (208 BCE); P. BM 10390.8 (136 BCE); P. BM 10407.11 (224 BCE); P. BM 10386.6 (210 BCE).

60 Cf. P. Giss. 39 (Thebes, 205–151 BCE), Lond I 3 (p. 44) = Mitteis, Chrestomathie, 129 (146 BCE); P. Leid. (136 BCE), cf. U. Wilcken in *APF* II, 142ff., and F.LL. Griffith and U. Wilcken, in *ZAS* 45.103ff.; P. Giss. 38 and P. Giss. Inv. 187 (time of Phil. and Evergetes II); P. Tebt. I 164 (end of second century BCE); BGU 1002 (55 BCE); C. Wessely, *Papyrorum Scriptural graecae specimina isagogica* (Leipzig: Avenarium, 1900), tab. 5,5 0 SB 5275; 6,6 = SB 5231; 9, 10; 12, 24; 14,30 0 SB 5247; 15, 16 (time of August).

61 Wessely, *Papyrorum*, tab. 13, 129 = SB I 5246 (Augustus).

62 We have previous examples of donations/division of property where the *sẖ n wy* was drawn up as complement of the donation document. This seems to be the case of the aforementioned P. Cairo 50059 and P. BM 10792. See A. F. Shore, 'Swapping', 202.

(Place unknown, 343 BCE). According to F. de Cenival, 'Il pourrait s'agir soit d'une copie, soit de l'«écrit de renonciation» relatif à la même vente. La formule spécifique: «je suis éloigné de toi ... » devrait, dans cette dernière hypothèse, être restituée dans la lacune, au début de la l. 2.'[63]

6.2.1.3.1. *The Document in Exchange for Silver, the sẖ ḏbꜣ ḥḏ*

The *sẖ ḏbꜣ ḥḏ*, 'Geldbezahlungschriften', is translated as a 'document in exchange for silver'.[64] The word  *ḏbꜣ* is found as far back as the Old Kingdom, with the meaning 'Erzats, Bezahlung'.[65] In Late Egyptian, *r-ḏbꜣ* is used with the meaning 'in exchange'.[66] It is found in Demotic in the compounds *in (r) ḏbꜣ ḥḏ* 'to buy', and *di r ḏbꜣ ḥḏ* 'to sell'.[67] The *sẖ ḏbꜣ ḥḏ* is characterized by its use of the formula *ti=k mty ḥꜣty=y n pꜣ ḥḏ n* X,[68] which has been commonly translated 'you have caused my heart to be satisfied with X'.[69] There is no agreement among scholars as to whether the satisfaction clause conveys the meaning of receipt-quittance (Sethe-Partsch, Muffs)[70] or volitional concurrence with the oral contract (Griffith, Seidl, Pierce, Cruz-Uribe).[71]

It has been noted the root *mtj* does not convey the idea of satisfaction.[72] In Ptolemaic times the Demotic formula was translated into Greek using

63 F. de Cenival, 'Une Vente d'Esclaves de L'Époque d'Artaxerxès III', *RdE* 24 (1972): 32.

64 See Zauzich, 'Die demotischen Dokumente', 51, 118, 171, and 173. Depauw, *Companion*, 140–42 and the bibliography cited there.

65 *Wb* V, 558.

66 Gardiner, *Egyptian Grammar*, §180; A. Erman, *Neuägyptische Grammatik*, 2nd edn. (Hildesheim and New York: Olms, 1979), §662.

67 Erichsen, *Glossar*, 619.

68 Zauzich, states that 'Die erste Klauses einer demotischen Urkunden sollte man m.E. entsprechend der Urkundenart benennen.' *Schreibertradition*, Klause 1 'Geldbezahlungsklausel', 134. See also Seidl, *Ägyptische Rechtsgeschichte*, 19–20.

69 'Du hast mein Herz zufriedengestellt mit diesem Geld für X', Zauzich, *Schreibertradition*, 11 *et passim*. 'Tu m'as contenté le coeur avec l'argent pour X', Malinine, *Choix*, 51 *et passim*.

70 Sethe and Partsch, *Demotische Urkunden*, 262; Muffs, *Studies*, 158; assumes that Pestman, *Marriage*, 19, follows the same opinion but the context of the citation does not support such assumption.

71 Griffith, *Catalogue*; Seidl, *Ägyptische Rechtsgeschichte*, 49; Cruz-Uribe, *Cattle Documents*, 44–45; A final conclusion could only be reached through an extensive study of the formula in its active and passive formulation in the various legal contexts and geographical distribution.

72 Already proposed by Muffs, *Studies*, 150 n. 5. See Erichsen, *Glossar*, 190; *Wb* II, 173; R. Hannig, *Grosses Handwörtesbuch ägyptisch-deutsch (2800–950 v. chr.): die Sprache der Pharaonen* (Mainz: ven Zabern, 2006), 373; W. E. Crum, *A Coptic Dictionary* (Oxford and New York: Clarendon, 1962), 189a; J. Osing provided evidence that the Egyptian satisfaction formula derives from *mty* 'be exact, straightforward', J. Osing, *Die Nominalbildung des Ägyptischen* (Mainz: von Zabern, 1976), 643 ff. For additional discussion see Cruz-Uribe, *Cattle Documents*, 44–45.

the verb πείθω 'to persuade',[73] e.g., 'you have persuaded me by the price of my property'[74] and as εὐδοκέω 'to approve or content',[75] e.g., 'you make me approve the price of the (property)'.[76] In the Demotic documents, therefore, *ti=k mty ḥ3ty=y n p3 ḥḏ n property* could perhaps be understood as a volition clause based on the consensual type of sale reflecting the agreement of the vendor to the price offered by the buyer, but this use would go against the traditional use of the legal metaphor of 'satisfaction' within the Egyptian legal tradition.[77]

As expected, the formulae used by the scribe in the *sẖ ḏb3 ḥḏ* would vary according to the particular school of scribes to which he belonged, the system of writing he was using, and any changes in the local legal tradition he was following.[78] Table XII displays the *sẖ ḏb3 ḥḏ* from this period.

Table XII: *Sẖ ḏb3 ḥḏ*

No.	Museum	Date	Kind of Document	Place
1	S. Florence 1659 (2507)	-661	Sale	Memphis
2	Stele Louvre C 101	-657	Sale	Memphis
3	P. Rylands 1	-645	Sale	El-Hibeh
4	Coupe Louvre E 706	-592	Servitude	Thebes ?
5	P. Berlin P 13571	-591	Sale	Edfu
6	P. Rylands 6	-567	Servitude	El-Hibeh
7	P. Rylands 8	-563	Sale	El-Hibeh
8	P. Louvre E 7832	-539	Sonship	Thebes
9	P. BM 10117	-529	Sale	Coptos
10	P. Bibl. Nat. 223	-516	Sale	Thebes

73 Liddell-Scott, 1353.

74 BGU 1002.3 Hemopolis Ushmun 55 BCE.

75 Liddell-Scott, 710, citing P. Rylands 120.24 etc.

76 The Grey Papyrus (146 BCE) is a Greek translation of a Demotic contract, cited by Griffith, P. Rylands Dem. P. 118, and also Pestman, *Marriage*, 96 n. 8. The Greek parallels are cited in Muffs, *Studies*, 157, following Sethe and Partsch (*Demotische Urkunden*, 262), without mentioning that both variants in the Greek translations of the Demotic documents support the volitional interpretation of the formula. For a comparison with similar Byzantine and Arabic idioms see G. Frantz-Murphy, 'A Comparison of Arabic and Earlier Egyptian Contract Formularies, Part III: The Idiom of Satisfaction', *JNES* 47 (1988): 105–12.

77 In a recent publication of six settlement documents from Hermopolis Magna, A. Farid seems to reflect this ambiguity by translating the Demotic *ti=k mtr ḥ3ty(=y) n Object* in two different ways as 'You have satisfied my heart to the house' (p. 188) and 'You have caused my heart to agree to the house', (p. 192). Farid, 'Unpublished Early Demotic Family Archive'. See also Ritner, 'Third Intermediate Period Antecedents', 347–49.

78 See our methodological discussion above, 2.3, pp. 61ff. The result of these variations is the existence of several formulary traditions; Zauzich lists sixteen different formularies for the *sẖ ḏb3 ḥḏ* and 23 for the *sẖ n wy*. Zauzich, *Schreibertradition*, 114–24.

No.	Museum	Date	Kind of Document	Place
11	P. Louvre E 7128	-510	Sale	Thebes
12	P. Turin 2124 (209)	-507	Exchange	Thebes
13	P. Loeb 68	-501	Sale	Gebelein ?
14	P. Louvre E 9292	-494	Sale	Thebes
15	P. Louvre E 9204	-491	Sale	Thebes
16	P. BM 10450	-491	Sale	Thebes
17	P. Louvre E 9294	-491	Sale	Thebes
18	P. Loeb 44 + P. Loeb 49	-489	Sale	Gebelein
19	P. Lille 26	-393	Sale	Heracleopolis
20	P. Cairo JE 98507	-360	Sale	Elephantine
21	P. Cairo JE 98508	-356	Sale	Elephantine
22	P. Lille 27	-343	Sale	Unknown
23	P. Inv. Sorbonne 1276	-343	Sale	Unknown

The earliest *sẖ ḏbꜣ ḥḏ* including a *wy*-based formula (in the defension clause) that has been preserved is P. Berlin P 13571 (Edfu, 591 BCE) and its formulary reads as follows:

- **I. Date and parties of the document**: After the date, the document began with 'said' (perfective *sḏm=f*) followed by the names of the parties in objective style.
- **II. Satisfaction:**[79] *ti=k mty ḥꜣty=y n ḥḏ*[80] *n* X 'You have caused my heart to agree to the silver for the value of X property …'[81]
- **III. Transference of the property**:[82] 'I have given it to you in exchange for money', *tj=y s n=k r-bnr r-ḏbꜣ ḥḏ*.[83] As we mentioned above, this clause contains the *ḏbꜣ ḥḏ* expression that gives the name to our document and represents *per se* the kind of deed with which we are dealing.

79 Clause 1 in Zauzich, *Schreibertradition*, 134.

80 An earlier attestation of the formula uses *ḏꜣr* 'price' instead of *ḥḏ* (*Stele Louvre* C 101, Memphis, 657 BCE). Cf. Seidl, *Ägyptische Rechtsgeschichte*, 19 and 49.

81 Some documents from Thebes, (P. Philadelphia 19 and 26), Pathyris (P. Rylands 23; P. Adler 7 and 23; P. Strassburg 6 and 8); Tebtynis (P. Cairo 30613, 30615, and 31079), and all of the *sẖ ḏbꜣ ḥḏ* from Edfu (Hauswaldt papyri) include a payment clause *mḥ=k ṯ(=y)* before the satisfaction clause. See Zauzich, *Schreibertradition*, 118, Formular B; Sethe and Partsch, *Demotische Urkunden*, 261–62 §11. Pierce suggests that 'the insertion of the *mḥ=k ṯ(=y)* formula before the paragraph of satisfaction may have taken place under the influence of the Greek conception of sale' (Pierce, *Three Demotic Papyri*, 100). For this formula in Aramaic understood as a term for receipt/payment and quittance see Muffs, *Studies*, 50.

82 Clause 2 in Zauzich, *Schreibertradition*, 135.

83 We only have the addition *r bnr ḏbꜣ ḥḏ* 'in exchange for money' in the Hauswaldt papyri from Edfu. See Zauzich, *Schreibertradition*, 135.

IV. **Receipt**:[84] *di=k n=y p3y=s ḥḏ šp=y s d.t=k ḥ3tj=y mtj=w n.im=f* 'You have given me its money. I have received it from your hand. My heart is satisfied with it.'

V. **Investiture I:**[85] *mtw=k st* 'It belongs to you (namely) this your aforementioned property': A typical *verba solemnia* probably pronounced at the moment of the transfer. This *verba solemnia* was similar to the declarations, 'you are my son', in documents of adoption or, 'she is my wife', in documents of marriage.

VI. **Investiture II**:[86] *bn iw rḫ rmṯ nb n p3 t3 ṯ3j it mw.t sn sn.t šr šr.t ink ḥʿ-j mjt3j ir sḫy n-im=s p3y=k bnr* 'No man at all in the world – father, mother, brother, sister, son daughter – including me, will be able to have authority over it except you.'

VII. **Defension**:[87] *p3 nty iw=f r iy r-r=k r ḏb3.t=s r ṯ3y.t=s mtw=k ḏd bn mtw=k s in rn=y rn rmt nb n p3 t3 iw=y r di.t wy=f r.r=k n.im=s*: 'As for anyone who shall come to you on account of it to take it saying "it is not yours" in my name or in the name of someone else, I will cause him to be far from you.' Here we meet for the first time a withdrawal formula used in a defension clause.[88] This formula is without parallel in the Aramaic documents.[89]

VIII. **Warranty**. *iw=y tm dy.t wy=f r-r=k n.im=s iw=y r dy.t n=k* Object

84 Clause 4 in Zauzich, *Schreibertradition*, 135.

85 Clause 3 in Zauzich, *Schreibertradition*, 135.

86 Clause 6a in Zauzich, *Schreibertradition*, 137.

87 Clause 6b in Zauzich, *Schreibertradition*, 138. Following P. Steinkeller's definition we adopt the term 'Eviction' for this formula; according to *Judicial and Statutory Definitions of Words and Phrases*, Second Series, II (St Paul, 1914), 353b s.v. 'Eviction', 'Civil Codes impose upon the seller the obligation of warranting the buyer against the latter's "eviction" of the thing sold, and defines "eviction" in article 2500, as the loss suffered by the buyer of the totality of the thing sold, or a part thereof, occasioned by the right or claim of a third party.' Steinkeller, *Sale Documents*, 50 n. 126. This clause is recorded in almost every *sḫ ḏb3 ḥḏ*. Zauzich, *Schreibertradition*, 138.

88 Also attested in the business letter P. Berlin P. 13572 (Elephantine, 493 BCE) where it is stated that the sender will 'cause PN to withdraw from you regarding X money' he received. Previous sale documents from this period, such as P. Rylands 1 (El-Hibeh, 645 BCE); Stele de Florence 1659 (2507) (Memphis, 661 BCE); P. Rylands 8 (El-Hibeh, 562 BCE); followed by P. Loeb 68 (Gebelein?, 501 BCE) have instead *ink i.ir nʿ=object n=k* translated by Malinine as 'Je ferai de la sorte qu'il se purifie (?) vis-à-vis de toi' M. Malinine, 'Ventes de Tombes à L'Epoque Saïte', *RdE* 27 (1975): 168. The legal meaning of the clause is best expressed in the translation 'I will cause it to be cleansed (=cleared) for you.' On the other hand *wʿb* is used in P. Louvre 7128 (Thebes, 510 BCE) while P. BM 10117 (Thebes, 529 BCE) has both *wy* and *wʿb*. The *wʿb*-based formula will slowly replace the *nʿ*-based formula. Menu, 'Les actes de vente', 171. The *wy*-based formulae and the *nʿ*-based formula, although intended to provide a similar remedy in case of a claim against the property sold, do not have 'interchangeable meaning', as Cruz-Uribe suggested (*Cattle Documents*, 64). They reflect different scribal traditions and can be considered isogloses.

89 For the defension clause in Ptolemaic documents, cf. above 6.3.9, p. 173.

'In case I don't cause him to be far from you, I will give you Object.'

The rest of the document is missing.

B. Menu classified the defension clauses of the Saite-Persian period as follows:[90]
   a. When used alone: 'As for the one who will come ... I will cause him to be far from you.'[91]
   b. Combined with a clause of restitution: 'As for the one who will come.... I will cause him to be far from you; ... if I do not cause him to be far from you, I will give you (a similar object/amount).'[92]
   c. Combined with a release clause: 'As for the one who will come ... I will cause him to be far from you; ... I will clear it for you from every title.'[93]
   d. Combined with a clause of restitution and a release clause: 'As for the one who will come ... I will cause him to be far from you; ... if I do not cause him to be far from you, I will give you (a similar object/amount) I will clear it for you from every title.'[94]

The transfer of the property is assured by the transfer of the money and by the declaration that no claim regarding the property will arise from the seller, his relatives, or any other person. We thus conclude that the function of the *sẖ db3 ḥd* in the context of sale during this period is the transfer of full rights of ownership from the buyer to the seller.[95]

90 Menu, 'Les actes de vente', 180.

91 For example, P. Loeb 43 (Gebelein, 485 BCE).

92 P. Berlin 13571 (Edfu, 571 BCE); P. BM 10792 (Asyut, 522 BCE); P. Turin 2122 (Thebes, 517 BCE); P. Michigan 3525b (Thebes or Edfu, 498 BCE); P. Turin 2128 (Thebes, 487 BCE); P. Loeb 44 (Gebelein, 489 BCE); P. Berlin P. 13572 (Elephantine, 493 BCE).

93 P. BM 10117 (Coptos, 529 BCE); P. Bibl. Nat. 223 (Thebes, 516 BCE); P. Turin 2123 (Thebes, 512 BCE); P. Louvre E. 7128 (Thebes, 510 BCE).

94 P. Wien 10151 (Elephantine, 338 BCE); P. Loeb 68 (Gebelein?, 501 BCE); P. Louvre E. 9292 (Thebes, 494 BCE).

95 See J. Partsch, 'Die Rechtliche Bedeutung der Vertrage', in W. Spiegelberg, *Die demotischen Papyri Hauswaldt* (Leipzig: J. C. Hinrichs'sche Buchhandlung, 1913), 11–18; and Seidl, *Ptolemäische Rechtsgeschichte*, 118. The shift in the possessive pronoun from 'my lands' (*n3y=y 3h.w*) in the *sẖ db3 ḥd* and 'your lands' in the *sẖ n wy* attests that the transfer of ownership was effective after the production of the *sẖ db3 ḥd*. See, J. G. Manning, 'Demotic Egyptian Instruments of Transfer as Evidence for Private Ownership of Real Property', in *Symposium on Ancient Law, Economics and Society*, ed. J. Lindgren *et al* *Chicago Kent Law Review* (1995): 249–57.

6.2.1.3.2. *The Document of Withdrawal sẖ n wy*

As mentioned previously, it seems that the only pair of *sẖ ḏbꜣ ḥḏ* and *sẖ n wy* from this period is the fragmentary P. Inv. Sorbonne 1277 (343 BCE) *sẖ n wy*, which is related to the *sẖ ḏbꜣ ḥḏ* P. Inv. Sorbonne 1276 (343 BCE). The *sẖ n wy* 'Abstandschriften', or 'document of cession/withdrawal',[96] is an instrument that became widely attested in Ptolemaic times. This document is characterized by the initial formula *dỉ=y wy.k r-r=k n* X: 'I am far from you (person) regarding X (property).' In Ptolemaic times they are mostly, but not exclusively, related to a specific *sẖ ḏbꜣ ḥḏ* or are produced as a result of litigation.

According to Zauzich's analysis for the Ptolemaic period,[97] these are the basic formulae[98] of the *sẖ n wy* documents:

Date: Year, month, season, Pharaoh

Clause I: Renunciation of Rights: *dỉ=y wy.k r-r=k n*: 'I am far from you regarding …'

Clause II: Transfer: *dỉ=y s n=k*: 'I have given it to you.'

Clause III: Declaration of Proprietary rights: *mtw=k st*: 'It is yours.'

Clause V: Declaration of Quitting the Claim: *mn mtw=y mt nb n pꜣ tꜣ ỉw.ỉr-n=k rn=f ṯꜣy pꜣ ḥrw n ḥry*: 'I do not have any claim at all against you on account of it from this day onwards.'

Clause VI a: Declaration of Proprietary rights: *bn ỉw rḫ rmṯ nb n pꜣ tꜣ ỉnk mjtꜣj ỉr sẖy n-ỉm=f bnr=k ṯꜣy pꜣ ḥrw r ḥry*: 'No man on earth including me, will be able to have authority over it except you from this day onwards.'

Clause VI b: Defension: *pꜣ rmt nb n pꜣ tꜣ nty ỉw=f r ỉy r-r=k r ḏbꜣ.t=f r ṯꜣy.t=f rn=y rn rmt nb pꜣ tꜣ ỉw=y r dỉ.t wy=f r.r=k*: 'As for anyone who shall come to you on account of it to take it in my name or in the name of someone else, I will cause him to be far from you.'

Clause VI c: Eviction: *mtw=y dỉ.t wꜥb=f n=k r md nb n pꜣ tꜣ n ssw nb*: 'and I shall clear it for you from anything at all at any time.'

Clause VII: The clause about the possession of the documents: *mtw=k sẖ nb r-ỉr=w r-r=f*… 'Yours are every document which has been drawn regarding it.'

Clause VIII: Oath.[99]

Clause IX: *ỉw=k m-sꜣ=y n pꜣ hp n pꜣ sẖ ḏbꜣ ḥḏ r.ỉr=y n=k r-r=w* Date *ỉr n=k pꜣy=f hp n ssw nb* 'You are behind me regarding the

96 See Zauzich, 'Die demotischen Dokumente', 93. Seidl, *Ptolemäische Rechtsgeschichte*, 4ff., 51, 62, 99, 119ff., and 162. Depauw, *Companion*, 143 and the bibliography cited there.

97 Zauzich, *Schreibertradition*, 152–53. We follow his numeration.

98 We include only the typical phraseology of the formulae. For the variations, see Zauzich, *Schreibertradition*, Tables 3 and 4.

99 This and the preceding clause are not common in the *sẖ n wy*. See Zauzich, *Schreibertradition*, 153.

> right of the *sḫ db3 ḥd* which I made for you on Date to carry out for you its obligations at any time.'[100] This clause is a recognition of the rights that the buyer has to force the seller to make the aformentioned oath to certify the *sḫ db3 ḥd* in court.[101]

Considering that the Aramaic documents have not provided an equivalent of the double document transaction represented in Egyptian documents by the *sḫ db3 ḥd* and the *sḫ n wy* we do not consider it necessary here to delve into the discussion about the legal function of each of these documents in the legal transaction.[102] It is relevant to note, however, that the continuous use of the *sḫ n wy* in transfers of property leads to the conclusion that to enjoy full ownership and right of disposition of the property, a *sḫ n wy* or a withdrawal formula must be produced by the alienor to the alienee.[103]

6.2.2. *The Use of wy in Litigation*

We do not have many examples of withdrawal after litigation in this period. The first example of a document which registers the renunciation of claims related to a lawsuit – but without a *wy* formula – is provided by P. Louvre E 3228c,[104] a document written in cursive Hieratic (Year 6 of Taharqa, Thebes, 685 BCE).

100 C. A. Andrews correctly translates this clause 'you will be able to constrain me by the rights conferred by the document of silver.' *Catalogue*, P. BM 10380.8 (Thebes, 198 BCE) *et passim*.

101 For the use of *iw=y m-s3=k* 'I am behind you', see Zauzich, *Schreibertradition*, Clause IX, p. 153. The obligation to defend the sale is stated in P. Berlin 13621 II, 1, a fragment of a manual of legal procedures. See Seidl, *Ptolemäische Rechtsgeschichte*, 3.

102 For Revillout, 'L'écrit pour argent ou de mancipation intervenait d'abord pour conférer la nue-propriété de la chose à l'acheteur. L'écrit de cession intervenait ensuite pour lui conférer la jouissance.' E. Revillout, *Précis de droit égyptien comparé aux autres droits de l'Antiquité* (Paris: V. Giard & E. Brière, 1899–1903), vol. 2, 678; for L. Mitteis, The *sḥ n ḏb3 ḥd* would reflect the agreement. The *sḫ n wy* would reflect the fulfilment of the obligation that arose with it, as it was the actual instrument that transferred the property rights L. Mitteis and U. Wilcken, *Grundzüge und Chrestomathie der Papyrusurkunde*, vol. 2/1 (Leipzig-Berlin: B. G. Teubner, 1912), 169–70; see also P. M. Meyer, *Juristische Papyri* (Berlin: Weidmann, 1920), 77, 114. Seidl argued against this view, stating that if the *sḫ n db3 ḥd* would not transfer the property in full, the price would have to be mentioned. The price will be worth mentioning in the event that a dispute may arise regarding it. Mentioning the price would no longer be necessary except in the case that the *sḫ n db3 ḥd* indicates a complete transfer of the property. The need for a *sḫ n wy* is not related to the *sḫ db3 ḥd* but to the jurisprudence of the claim, for the *sḫ db3 ḥd* will not completely protect the buyer against future actions of the seller. E. Seidl, *Ptolemäische Rechtsgeschichte*, 118ff.; *Handbuch der Orientalistik* – Orientalisches Recht, 30; Seidl, *Ägyptische Rechtsgeschichte*, 50.

103 Cf. Pestman, *Marriage*, 96.

104 M. Malinine, 'Un jugement rendu à Thèbes sous la XXVe Dynastie', *RdE* 6 (1951): 157–78. See also Seidl, *Ägyptische Rechtsgeschichte*, 19.

P. Louvre E 3228c contains the declaration of a man who litigated over an amount of money and lost the lawsuit. Consequently, he had to renounce his claim and to acknowledge the right of the other party. He stated (line 10–11), 'I do not have anything against PN (*mn-md(i) mdt nbt ỉwd* PN).' The statement is repeated in lines 19–20, adding a warranty against third party claims, 'We do not have son, daughter, brother, sister or any man who will be able to make a claim regarding this matter, and for the man who will make a claim, his claim will not be heard (*bn sḏm=f rꜣ=f*)[105] in any of the archives.' This formula attempts to provide a warranty to the other party that the quitclaim will not be contested in the future. The difference between this clause and the defension clauses (to cause to be far, to clear, etc.) is that in this case, there is no promise of any action by the speaker.

The earliest Demotic example of a document of release after litigation is P. Loeb 43 (Gebelein, 485 BCE), where the withdrawal formula functions as initial clause of the *sẖ n wy*. The other example of release after litigation comes many years later, P. Cairo 50150 + 155 (Edfu, 375 BCE). The structure of P. Loeb 43 reads as follows:

P. Loeb 43 (Gebelein, 485 BCE)[106]

I. **Date:** Year 2, 3rd month of the *ꜣḫ.t* season under Pharaoh Psammetichos
II. **Parties:** Erehteuenhor, son of Oaphre speaks to [... son of] Inarou
III. **Release:** I am far from the right
IV. **Object:** of the black donkey
V. **Record of Litigation:** because of which I came to you saying, 'I have acquired it for money'
VI. **Investiture:** [It is your] donkey this is, [from] today onwards till eternity. Not any man on earth will be able to exercise authority over it [except you]
VII. **Defension:** The one who will come to you because of it, saying, 'your donkey this is not' [I] will make him be far from you. [If I fail to make him be] far, your donkey still be yours, [. . . . .] from today onwards till eternity.
VIII. **Scribe:** Peteharpochrat son of Teho
IX. **Witnesses:** 4

There is no mention of any judgment by any authority, but the litigation is clear from the formula, 'because of which I came to you saying, "I have

105 See M. Černý, 'The Will of Naunakhte', 41 n. e (3). Cf. Aramaic לא ישתמע לה *TAD* B3.8:42.

106 We follow S. Vleeming, *Pap. Hou*, 127–41.

acquired it for money" '[107] which is a typical Demotic expression that refers to a lawsuit.

The need for producing a *sẖ n wy* is described by S. Allam, 'wenn zwei Parteien miteinander vor Gericht Prozess geführt hatten, mußte die unterlegene Partei für die siegreihe eine solche Urkunde über den Streitgegenstand ausstellen und darin deren Recht anerkennen'.[108] This definition fits very well in almost all the cases where the Legal Manual of Hermopolis[109] requires the writing of a *sẖ n wy.*[110] It does not, however, cover all the cases in which a *sẖ n wy* was produced, for a release after litigation can be produced by a claimant also after proper satisfaction (some restitution, an oath, etc.) has been performed by the defendant.[111]

The documents of release after litigation were produced after a dispute was resolved by a court decision, a third party arbitration or private settlement after a public dispute. The party who had initiated the claim and was properly compensated, or the party who had lost it, drew up the necessary document of release for the other party. Although only two examples of release after litigation have survived from this period, the widespread use of *wy* in this context is well attested in the Legal Manual of Hermopolis.

The uses of *wy* formula in the Legal Manual are mostly related to the production of a *sẖ n wy* by the party defeated in a lawsuit:

> Legal Manual VI.3, After an oath is required, *iw]=w (r) di.t ir p3 [i.ḏd] ʿḏ sẖ n wy n p3 i.ḏd m3ʿ*
>
> The one [who told] a falsehood shall be required to produce a document of withdrawal for the one who told the truth.

The following clauses provide instructions in case someone complains that someone else has built on his property.

> 7–8, *⸢ir s⸣ iw=f ḏd iw=j di.t ʿḥʿ-rd mtw=f tm di.t ʿḥʿ-rd iw=w di.t p3 ʿ.wy n p3 nty {iw=w} smj r.r=f iw=f [[tm]] sẖ n=f [n wy]*
>
> If he says (the accused) I will provide proof and he does not provide proof, the house will be granted to the plaintiff and the accused will write a document of withdrawal for him (the plaintiff).

107 For discussion of this formula see Vleeming, *Pap. Hou*, 9 n. 11.

108 E. Seidl, 'Altägyptische Recht', in *Handbuch der Orientalistik*, abt. 1, erg. 3 (Leiden: Brill, 1964), *Orientalische Recht* 10f.; idem, *Ptolemäische Rechtsgeschichte*, 118ff., followed by S. Allam, 'Bemerkungen zur Abstandschrift', *Enchoria* 13 (1985): 1.

109 See the bibliography on the Hermopolis Manual above, Chapter 3 note 18.

110 *Legal Manual* VI, 3, 8, 10, 11; VII, 10, 11, 16; VIII, 13, 22.

111 See P. BM 10380 A.5 *ir=k n=y p3y=y hp p3y=f wpy p3y=f ʿnḫ* 'You have carried out on my behalf its rights, its judgment, its oath.'

In column VII, 10, 11, and 16, the Manual mentions the production of a *sẖ n wy m-sꜣ object of dispute* by the defeated party in litigation. Column VIII, 22 refers to the case in which a man brings a claim against another that his digging the foundation of his house caused the plaintiff's house to fall. In this case, if the accused swears an exculpatory oath saying that it was not his intention to cause any damage, then the plaintiff will be caused to recede from him *iw=w di.t wy=f r-r=f.*

Another hitherto unnoticed text for the discussion of the origins of the withdrawal clause in the context of litigation is the Petition of Peteêsi (P. Rylands 9). Dated 512 BCE, but covering the struggle of a family for their privileges from 664 BCE onward, the Petition of Peteêsi is a well-preserved example of the procedures of the Egyptian judicial system.[112] The papyrus relates how Peteêsi appeals to the Chief of Herakleopolis regarding a long unresolved conflict between his priestly family and the clergy of Amon at El-Hibeh. Peteêsi's purpose is to claim restitution from the priests who usurped his titles and shares, burned his house, and tried to kill him. The Chief mediated between them and persuaded Peteêsi to 'be far from the priests',[113] (*di.t wy=w r nꜣ wꜥb.w*), in exchange for an exculpatory oath and a payment in silver (10 deben) that would cover part of the damages. In his address to the priests, the Chief tells them: 'I have persuaded him to be far from you,'[114] (*di.t wy=w i-ḥr=tn).* After some negotiating, the priests finally agreed to the condition, paid the silver, and swore an exculpatory oath[115] saying, 'we took no property of yours, we caused (it) not to be taken, we did not cause your house and your temple-place to be pulled down'.[116] The story then recounts that after that, 'they demanded that I withdraw from the priests' (*mtw=w di.t wy(=y) r nꜣ wꜥb. w).*[117] It is noteworthy that the priests were actually guilty of the crimes, but after the settlement, they were able to make an oath denying it and get Peteêsi to withdraw from them.

The last document that attests the use of *wy* in litigation that we want to bring to the discussion is P. Louvre 7850.[118] This is a business letter

112 Griffith, *Catalogue*, 9, pp. 60–112 and 218–53 and the re-edition by G. Vittmann, *Der demotische Papyrus Rylands 9*, ÄAT 38 (Wiesbaden: Harrassowitz, 1998), 2 vols. The text was written down sometime in the reign of Darius I (521–486 BCE), but narrates events that happened at different periods beginning with the rule of Psammetichus I (664 BCE).

113 P. Rylands 9, 20.12.

114 P. Rylands 9, 20.12-13.

115 The Oath as a judicial procedure is still valid among bedouins, Kennett, *Bedouin*, 39–48. For Ancient Egypt: Wilson, 'The Oath', 129–56.

116 P. Rylands 9, 20.16-17.

117 P. Rylands 9, 20.19.

118 See Cruz-Uribe, *Cattle Documents*, 10–11; K. Donker van Heel, 'Abnormal Hieratic and Early Demotic Texts Collected by the Theban Choachytes in the Reign of Amasis, Papyri from the Louvre Eisenlohr Lot' (Ph. D. diss, Rijksuniversiteit, Leiden, 1996), 222–25. I want to thank Dr. Donker van Heel for providing me a copy of his unpublished dissertation.

written in Early Demotic in 533 BCE by Peteamon, son of Djeho, overseer of the necropolis, before his superior, the god's father Djechy. The statement records the receipt of a bull from the first god's servant of Horoeris, Pamety son of Petehorpebik, by the declarant. This text is very valuable for our discussion of the Demotic-Aramaic formulary and, therefore, we cite it in full:

P. Louvre 7850 (Thebes, 533 BCE)	
ḫrw-bꜣk PN_1 pꜣ mr-ḫꜣs.t m-bꜣḥ PN_2 *pꜣy=f ḥry i di Pꜣ-Rꜥ ḳj pꜣy=f ꜥḥꜥ*	Declaration of PN_1, the overseer of the necropolis, in the presence of PN_2 his superior, may Pre give that his life be long:
di n=y PN_3 pꜣy ỉḥ tšr ỉw=f šp i pꜣ ḥtp-ntr n ỉmn n rn n PN_4 tꜣ šb(.t) n nꜣ nkt nty ỉw=w di.t s n pꜣ mr-ḫꜣs.t n pꜣ ỉmnṱ n Niw.t	PN_3 gave to me this red bull, it being assigned to the God's Offering of Amon in the name of PN_4 as the replacement of the commodities which are (customarily) given to the overseer of the necropolis in the west (?) of Thebes
šp(=y) pꜣy ỉḥ nty ḥry ṯꜣy(=y) s {t} r-bnr	I have received the aforementioned bull, I have taken it away[119]
ḥꜣ.t(=y) mtr.w n.ỉm=f	My heart is satisfied with it
tw=y wy r.r=f n md nb n rn n pꜣ ḥm-ntr 4-nw n rn n pꜣy=f ḳs n tꜣ ỉmnṱ Wꜣs.t	I am far from him (PN_3)[120] from every suit in the name of the fourth god's servant in the name of his burial in the west (?) of Thebes
sẖ di-ḫnsw-ỉw.t sꜣ ḳn-ḥr	Scribe: Techonsiout son of Qenhôr
ḥꜣ.t-sp 38.t ibd-4 šmw	Date. Year 38 4th month of *šmw*

It seems that the declarant Peteamon (PN_1) had complained to the authorities,[121] perhaps to his superior Djechy, that Pamety (PN_3) did not fulfil his obligations in delivering the 'commodities which are (customarily) given to the overseer of the necropolis in the west (?) of Thebes'. The litigation was resolved when Pamety gave the bull mentioned in the letter

119 This phrase is problematic. For discussion see Donker van Heel, 'Abnormal Hieratic', 22 n. V

120 Vleeming considered that the *=f* in the formula *tw=y wy r-r=f* referred to the bull and, therefore, affirmed that 'In *P. Louvre* E. 7850, the thing concerned shifts to the place of the person concerned, and is accordingly, construed with *r* "from" '; *Pap. Hou*, 130 and see also *Pap. Hou*, 130 n. 10. The *=f*, however, refers to the person who gave the bull to Peteamon and not to the bull itself.

121 The evidence of litigation is provided in this document not by a litigation report but by the complement of the withdrawal formula, 'I am far from him from every suit.'

to Peteamon to fulfil his obligation. P. Louvre 7850 is, therefore, a withdrawal after litigation caused by the cancellation of an obligation as P. Loeb 43 above. After the bull is delivered, Peteamon writes in lines 5–7 of his letter:

> *šp(=y) p3y iḥ ntj ḥry t3j(=y) s ḥ3.t(=y) mtr.w n.im=f tw=y wy r-r=f n md nb n rn n p3 ḥm-ntr 4-nw ˈnˈ rn n p3y=f qs*
>
> I have received the aforementioned bull. I have taken it. My heart is satisfied with it. I am far from him (i.e from Pamety) regarding every suit[122] in the name of the fourth god's servant, regarding his burial.

Here we not only have the Demotic parallel of the Aramaic formula used by the Syenian scribes 'I am far from every suit'[123] but also a very early association of the satisfaction and withdrawal clauses. It is worth noting that one of the arguments on which Y. Muffs based his thesis of a Mesopotamian origin of the satisfaction clause was the lack of evidence of the association of the satisfaction clause and the withdrawal clause in Demotic.[124]

6.2.3. *Wy in Release of Obligations*

Legal historians of Ptolemaic Egypt have made a clear distinction between evidential receipts ('Beweisquittung') i.e. those whose function is just to provide evidence of payment, and dispositive receipts ('dispositive Quittung') i.e. those which cancel the obligation to pay.[125] The corresponding formulae are as follows:

	Evidential Receipts	Dispositive Receipts
Demotic	*dy=k n=y mn* 'you have given me such and such' 'you have paid me in full'	*mḥ=k t̰=y*
Greek	ἔχειν 'to receive'	ἀπέχειν 'to have been paid'

The Demotic term usually translated as 'receipt' is *iw*, and, together with the Greek term ἀποχη, is evidence of payment that cancels the

122 *md* 'dispute, suit', see S. Allam, *Hieratische Ostraka und Papyri aus der Ramessidenzeit* (Tübingen: Allam, 1973), 47 n. 13; idem, *JEA* 53 (1967): 47–50; for non-legal contexts see A. Théodorides, *Annuaire del'Institut de Philologie et d'Histoire Orientales et Slaves* 22 (1978): 77–96. McDowell, *Jurisdiction*, 143–70.

123 Cf. above p. 126.

124 Muffs, *Studies*, 161. P. Louvre 7850 was not available to Muffs.

125 Cf. Pierce, *Three Demotic Papyri*, 94ff.

obligation. Pierce wants to equate the *iw* with the *sẖ n wy*. The following example is cited by Pierce in support of his argument.[126] In P. BM 10528, we find *iw* equated with a *sẖ n wy*. P. BM 10528 is a business letter where party A requests:[127]

mtw=tn ir n=y iw r-r=f ḏd tw=n wy.ṯ r-r=f n pꜣ ḥḏ ...

You will make for me a release for it, saying, 'we are far from him (i.e. the sender) regarding the money ... '

Glanville[128] translated *iw* in P. BM 10528 as 'receipt', as did Pierce.[129] We prefer, however, Hughes and Nims's rendering of *iw* as 'release', 'since the *iw* is here not an acknowledgment of money received, but rather a *sẖ n wy*, a renunciation of all claim to the money named'.[130] Party A is, therefore, claiming acknowledgement 'that he is not to be held responsible for paying a sum of money rather than (...) receipt of a sum of money already paid'.[131] Two more documents are mentioned by Pierce as examples of *sẖ n wy* as release of obligations: P. Adler 20 and P. Turin 2136.

P. Adler 20 (Gebelein, 93 BCE) was understood by Griffith as a release from a mortgage made for a loan of corn.[132] Loan documents[133] often included the formulae of the *sẖ ḏbꜣ ḥḏ*: in case the borrower does not repay the loan, he considers himself satisfied with the amount he already received in exchange for his property. The document reads:

tw=n wy.w r-r=k n pꜣ hp n pꜣy sḥ ḏbꜣ ḥḏ ir-r=k n PN

We are far from you regarding the right of the document for silver (*sẖ ḏbꜣ ḥḏ*) which you made for PN.

In P. Turin 2136 (Thebes, 126 BCE)[134] the declarant has received complete payment of the debt that the second party owed him and thus expresses the release of the obligation as follows:

di=y ⸢wwy⸣ r-r=k n pꜣ ⸢hp⸣ [n pꜣ sẖ] ⸢rʿ⸣-wẖʿ i.ir=k n=y

I am far from you regarding the right of the credit document (*sẖ rʿ-wẖꜣ*).

126 Pierce, *Three Demotic Papyri*, 107.

127 Pierce, *Three Demotic Papyri*, 106–07.

128 S. R. K. Glanville, *Catalogue of Demotic Papyri in the British Museum*, vol. 1: *A Theban Archive of the Reign of Ptolemy I Soter* (London: British Museum, 1939), 16.

129 Pierce, *Three Demotic Papyri*, 107.

130 G. H. Hughes and C. F. Nims, 'Some Observations on the British Museum Demotic Theban Archive', *AJSL* 57 (1940): 255.

131 G. H. Hughes, review of Erichsen, *Glossar*, *JNES* 16 (1957): 58.

132 The loan itself is P. Adler Gr. 15.

133 The 'Kaufpfandverträge', see Zauzich, 'Die demotischen Dokumente', 97–98.

134 = Pestman, *L'Archivio di Amenothes*, 15.

Taking into consideration the previous analysis, we turn to the remaining *sẖ n wy* from Table XI above, P. Louvre AF 9761 (Thebes, 494 BCE): a document of cancellation of obligation. The structure reads as follows:

P. Louvre AF 9761 (25 March-23 April 494 BCE) [135]

I. Date: Year 28, fourth month, *ꜣḫ.t* Pharaoh Darius
II. Parties: *Tꜣ-sn-Ḥr* speaks to *ḏd-Ỉmn-Ỉw=f-ꜥnḫ*
III. Satisfaction: 'you have satisfied my heart'
IV. Performance: '(with the performance of) your obligation (resulting from) the document that you made for *Pꜣ-šn-n-Ỉs.t* son of *Hrjrm*, my husband . . .'
V. Release: 'I am far from you'
VI. Defension: 'As for anyone who shall come to you on account of it (the aforementioned document) in my name or in the name of someone else, I will cause him to be far from you.'
'<If I don't cause him to be far from you> I will give you 5 kite of silver without any suit at all {citing any document in the world}.'
VII. Scribe: *hr-wḏꜣ sꜣ Ns-ḥr-pꜣ-ẖrd*

Because no mention of litigation is recorded in this document, it would be better to consider it a cancellation of an obligation rather than a release after litigation,[136] using the withdrawal formula in a similar way to the Ptolemaic documents cited above.

6.2.4. *Wy in Marriage, Divorce, and Inheritance Settlements*

The *wy* clause is also well documented in divorce settlements. In these documents, the waiver of claims on the divorced party is the natural consequence of the act of repudiation.[137] Typical expressions of the withdrawal formula in marriage and divorce documents are:[138]

ḫꜣꜥ(=y) ṱ=t ḥm.t tw=y wy=k r-ḥr=t

135 We basically follow the translation and analysis by Pestman, *L'Archivio di Amenothes* 15, with the exceptions noted.

136 So think Pestman and Vleeming, *Papyrus démotiques*, 86, I. Vleeming considers that 'apparently the woman had raised unjust objections against the received consideration and withdrew these in P. Tsenhor 15' (*Pap. Hou* 8, 131). The main reason to disregard the argument that any litigation had taken place is that every document of release after litigation includes a clause referring explicitly to the litigation itself (cf. P. Cairo 50150 + 155.1; P. Michigan 3523.3-4; and P. Carlsberg 37b). It is safer, therefore, to assume that the second party in the document fulfilled an obligation contracted with Tsehnor's late husband nine years before and that after the obligation was cancelled, Tsenhor wrote the correspondent withdrawal.

137 See Pestman, *Marriage*, 58–79.

138 Cf. Chapter 6.3.7, below, p. 173.

I have divorced you as wife. I am far from you.

(P. Berlin 3076 [Thebes, 513 BCE])[139]

We also find this formula in some marriage documents in the section dealing with potential divorce, where the declarant assumes the payment of the divorce money, waiving any future claims on the rest of the property, as for example:[140]

iw(=y) wy.ṯ nty nb nkt n p3 t3

I am far (from you) regarding everything.

(P. Berlin 3078 [Thebes, 493/2 BCE])

iw=y wy.ṯ r.r=k p3 1/3 *Property.*

I am far from you (regarding) 1/3 Property.

(P. Libbey [Thebes, 337 BCE])

The function of the withdrawal formula in this clause is similar to its use as complement of the waiver of suit clause.[141]

The withdrawal clause is also used in a series of early Demotic documents dealing with an inheritance settlement between siblings. After the inheritance of the father was distributed by the elder brother, documents are issued where the siblings declare to the elder brother:

tw(=y) wy.k r.r=k Property[142]

I am far from you regarding Property.

The documents also include a *wy*-based defension clause:

p3 nty iw=f iy r.r=k [. . . . . .] . . . [iw=y di w]y=f r.r=k iw(=y) tm di wy=f r.r=k iw(=y) di wy=f . . .[143]

'As for anyone who shall proceed against you . . . [I shall cause] him [to be] far from you. If I do not cause him to be far from you, I shall cause him to be far.'

139 Also in P. Berlin 3079 (Thebes, 489 BCE); P. Berlin 3077 (Thebes, 488 BCE) and possibly in *P. Cairo* 30665 (Gebelein, 542 BCE). The formula includes the addition *hp n ḥm.t* after the withdrawal in P. Philadelphia 2 (Thebes, 281 BCE); P. BM 10074 (Thebes, 230 BCE); P. Heidelberg 779a (Gebelein, 123 BCE); P. Turin 6094 (Thebes, 114 BCE); P. Heidelberg 762 + 770 + 774 (Gebelein, 100 BCE); and P. Heidelberg 754c (Gebelein, 100 BCE).

140 Cf. 6.3.8, below, p. 173.

141 Cf. *TAD* B2.9:15.

142 P. Philadelphia E 16322 Text 1.3 and Text 4.3-4 (Hermopolis Magna, 487 BCE). See Farid, 'Unpublished Early Demotic Family Archive', 185–205.

143 P. Philadelphia E 16322 Text 1.6 and Text 4.6.

6.2.5. *The Use of wy in Withdrawal from Object*

The Legal Manual of Hermopolis records two uses of the withdrawal clause that are distinctive from the cases of the withdrawal formulae seen above. Legal Manual VIII, 13–14, refers to the case of a dispute regarding a wall of a house claimed by two neighbours. It explains that if the house is located in the same city as the judges, they should decide the issue and require the defeated party to draw up a document of withdrawal from the wall: *di.t sẖ n=f p3j=f iry-dd* ⸢*n*⸣ *wy r.r=s*. It is interesting that the preposition *r.r=s* is used instead of the expression *m-s3* used in VII, 10 *iw=f sm r.r=f sẖ n wy m-s3 ʿ.wy* 'The defendant shall be required to make for him a document of withdrawal regarding the house.'[144] While *m-s3* 'regarding' clearly points to the object regarding which the withdrawal is made, the use of *r.r=s* could imply that the withdrawal is from that object.

Legal Manual VII.2 refers to the case in which the buyer of a house still owes the owner half of its price. The owner brings suit against him after the recognition of the debt by the buyer. The Manual offers the possibility to the owner to give the money back to the buyer and cancel the operation or to accept the rest of the payment. In the first case, it is said that if the owner gives the buyer his money back, then he should vacate the house: *iw=w (r) wy p3y=f iry-dd r p3 [ʿ.wy]*.

These are the only two cases in the Manual in which the removal is 'from the property,' implying a peculiar use of the withdrawal formula that might refer to a real physical withdrawal from the property in dispute or to a quitclaim expressed in the form 'withdrawal from object.'[145]

A document that could also be interpreted in this way in its use of the withdrawal formula is P. Louvre 7839 (Thebes, 534 BCE). This document is a land lease, where the tenant receives the land 'to till it from year 37 to year 38' and promises to pay the harvest tax and give the rest of the harvest to the owner. In lines 9–10 the tenant promises:

> *mtw(=y) ʿr ḥr* ⸢*ḫ.t-n*⸣ *p3y=k 3ḥ iw=(y) wy.ṯ i-r=f n t3y* ⸢*ḥ3.t*⸣ *sp 38 ibd-2 šmw r-ḥry dd qnb.t* ⸢*nb*⸣
>
> I (will) depart from (lit. on) your land, I being far from it from year 38 2nd month of the *šmw*-season onwards, without citing any document.[146]

144 The same expression appears in VII, 16, and is accordingly restored in VII, 11. For *m-s3* 'regarding', see C. F. Nims, 'Notes on University of Michigan Demotic Papyri from Philadelphia', *JEA* 24 (1938): 78.

145 Hughes followed this interpretation: 'the idiom probably amounts to "giving up claim to it"'. G. R. Hughes, *Saite Demotic Land Leases*, SAOC 28 (Chicago: Oriental Institute, 1952), 71, §n.

146 See the commentary on P. Louvre E 7839 by Malinine, *Choix*, 101 n. 11. For the use of *ʿr* in this sense see W. Spiegelberg, 'Der gegenwärtige Stand und die nächsten Aufgaben der demotischen Forschung', *ZÄS* 59 (1924): 135. The expression also occurs in P. Louvre E. 7845.9-10.

6.2.6. *Functional Equivalents in the Hieratic Formulary Tradition*

As we mentioned before, the Hieratic and Demotic formulary traditions were two competing traditions originating in different regions of Egypt. Considering that the verb *wy* is not attested in the Hieratic legal documents during the late period, we do not consider it necessary to further investigate into the Hieratic legal formulary. What we would like to demonstrate, however, is that a functional equivalent was present in the Hieratic formulary tradition that closely resembles the uses of *wy* in the Demotic formulary tradition.

The verb *ḫꜣʿ*  is used in both the Hieratic and Demotic legal traditions in the legal sense of 'to divorce'.[147] In Hieratic, however it is also attested in the legal meaning of release as we see in P. Cairo 30657. The situation in P. Cairo 30657 resembles that of *TAD* B2.9 (in P. Cairo 30657 there is no trace of litigation). Both refer to a deposit and the subsequent return of it.[148]

P. Cairo 30657 (Abnormal Hieratic, Gebelein, 547 BCE)

Date:	Year 34 of Amasis
Parties:	Petethowt son of Ienharow speaks to Reri son of Tesmonth
Satisfaction:	*di=k mtj ḥꜣtj(=y) (n) nkt nb.t* You have satisfied my heart with all the things
Release:	*di.t ḫꜣʿ i-r=k n.im=w* I withdrew from you regarding them
Quitclaim:	Son or daughter of mine will not be able to come against you regarding them
Satisfaction:	*ḥꜣtj(=y) mtr n.im=w* my heart is satisfied
Scribe:	Peteamenope son of Peteharresent

The use of *ḫꜣʿ* in this document exactly follows the use of *wy* in the Demotic documents. The verb *ḫꜣʿ* is also used in a document best classified as a document of withdrawal. The initial clause of P. Turin 2118 B (Abnormal Hieratic, 633 BCE)[149] reads:

> *ink m-ḫꜣʿ.t n=k* Property
>
> I cede to you Property.[150]

147 In Coptic, Xω has also the meaning of 'quit, abandon', Crum, *Coptic Dictionary*, 95, i.

148 We follow M. Malinine, 'Deux documents égyptiens relatifs au dépôt', *MDAIK* 16 (1958): 225–29.

149 See the discussion by S. Pernigotti, 'Un nuovo testo giuridico in ieratico «anormale»', *BIFAO* 75 (1975): 73ff.

150 Cf. the Palmyrene cessions above 5.1.3.2.

O. Ashmolean Museum 1945.37 + 1945.33 tells about two women accused of taking objects from a royal storehouse without authorization. Two men are placed 'after' *m-s3* them and later we read that *ḥr tw.tw ms3=s m-rʿ bn tw.tw ḥr ḫ3ʿ s* 'one is after her [*sic*] still, one will not release her'.[151]

It seems, therefore, that the Egyptians had more than one legal term to cover the legal meaning of release and cession. The use of *ḫ3ʿ* in the Egyptian legal tradition dates back at least to the 19th–20th Dynasties. In a business letter (Bankes Papyrus I.10) the sender writes, 'I went with you before the Commander of the Tuhir-troops, Iuhapi, your superior, and he said to me *ḫ3ʿ n=k t3 b3k* "release to you (the recipient of the letter) the servant" '. The use of *ḫ3ʿ* in this letter equals the use of *wy* in the releases after litigation.

6.3. *Further Developments of wy-Based Formulae in the Ptolemaic Period*

The conquest of Egypt by Alexander marks the beginning of the best-known period in the history of ancient Egypt. The Ptolemaic period has provided more legal documentary evidence than all the previous periods of Egyptian history combined.[152] The amount of the material involved makes it impossible to provide an extensive list of all the attestations of the *wy*-based formulae, as we have provided for the Aramaic documents in the previous chapter. At this point, we will present a catalogue of the various expressions of the withdrawal formulae to show the extent and continuity of the use of *wy*-based formula in Egypt after the Saite-Persian period. We shall continue, then, with the best-documented period in Egyptian legal history, where the withdrawal formulae appears in legal documents as: initial withdrawal clause in *sẖ n wy* in transfers of property; withdrawal clause in *sẖ n wy* after litigation; initial withdrawal clause in release from obligation; a quitclaim by party B formulated by party A in divisions; a complement of the waiver of suit clause; a complement of a consent-quitclaim clause; release of wife in divorce documents; quitclaim by husband in divorce documents; defension clause; a withdrawal clause at the end of a *sẖ ḏb3 ḥḏ*; withdrawal formula in the transfer clause in *sẖ ḏb3 ḥḏ*; in release of prisoners.

151 See the discussion in A. G. McDowell, *Jurisdiction in the Workmen's Community of Deir El-Medina* (Leiden: Nederlands Instituut voor het Nabije Oosten, 1999), 30.

152 For an analysis of the modifications to Demotic contracts during the Ptolemaic period see J. G. Manning, *Land and Power in Ptolemaic Egypt: The Structure of Land Ternure* (Cambridge: Cambridge University Press, 2003), 211f.

6.3.1. *Initial Withdrawal Clause in sẖ n wy in Transfers of Property*

One of the best-attested expressions of the withdrawal formula in Ptolemaic Egypt is the initial clause of the *sẖ n wy*, a withdrawal clause from the person regarding the property involved in the transaction. The following example is taken from P. Hauswaldt 1b..2:

ty=y wy r-r=k n n3y=k Property

I am far from you regarding your Property.

(P. Hauswaldt 1b..2 [P. Berlin 11331 left side], Edfu, 265 BCE)

Similar, although less frequent, is the withdrawal formula regarding *hp* 'right'.[153] In the following example the withdrawal regarding *hp* is the initial clause of a *sẖ n wy* that fulfils the same function as a consent clause.[154] A son is declaring that he renounces his claims to a house transferred by a *sẖ ḏb3 ḥḏ* by his father to his mother:

tw=y ww r-ḥr=t n p3 hp n p3 pr (...) ir n=t PN sẖ ḏb3 ḥḏ

I am far from you regarding the right of the house (...) PN made for you a *sẖ ḏb3 ḥḏ*.

(P. BM 10522.1 [297 BCE])

6.3.2. *Withdrawal Clause in sẖ n wy after Litigation*[155]

The *sẖ n wy* produced after litigation usually includes an initial clause: *ḏd=y qnbt irm=k i.ir-ḥr n3 wpti.w* 'I have been in dispute against you before the judges',[156] adding a withdrawal clause afterwards;[157] or begins with the clause *dy=y wy.k r.r=k n* Property, 'I am far from you regarding the Property', followed by a mention of the litigation.[158]

6.3.3. *Initial Withdrawal Clause in Release from Obligation*

The withdrawal clause also works as the initial clause of *sẖ n wy* used as release from obligations as in the following example from P. Hawara 13.4:

tw=y ww r.r=k n p3 hp n p3 sẖ n sʿnḫ

153 For additional examples concerning the use of *hp* in renunciations of claims see C. F. Nims, 'He "Law, Right"', 247ff.

154 See below.

155 See Sethe and Partsch, *Demotische Urkunden*, 754ff.; E. Lüddeckens, 'Demotische und koptische Urkundenformeln', *Enchoria* 2 (1974): 25 n. 24; S. Allam, 'The Agreement after Judgment', *Egitto e Vicino Oriente* 17 (1994): 19–28.

156 As in P. Berlin P 3113.4 (Thebes, 141 BCE); P. BM 10446.2 (Thebes, 230 BCE); P. Berlin P 13554.2 (Elephantine, 245 BCE).

157 As in P. BM 10446 (Thebes, 230 BCE) where the withdrawal clause is in the last line of the document (l. 5).

158 As in P. BM 10380 A.3 (Thebes, 225 BCE) where the litigation is mentioned in line 5; P. Carlsberg 37 B (Hawara, 220 BCE).

I am far from you regarding the right of the document of annuity.

(P. Hawara 13.4 [P. Hamburg dem. 7] 99 BCE)

The document includes in line 7 the clause '*mḥ=k ṯ̂=y*' *tw=k mtr ḥ3ṯ̂=y*.

More examples of the use of *wy* as release of obligations are attested in the Rossetta Stone.[159] This priestly decree written in Greek, hieroglyphic, and Demotic registers three occurrences of the *wy* formula that have passed hitherto unnoticed by scholars discussing the origin and meaning of the Demotic *wy* or Aramaic רחק formulae. The withdrawal formula (*wy=f r-r=w)* is attested in the Demotic text, in reference to the benefactions conferred by Ptolemy V Epiphanes (205–180 BCE). This is a very useful text for understanding the withdrawal clause because of the accompanying Greek translation,[160] which helps to establish the meaning and different nuances of our clause. The Demotic text tells us that:

Line 7*: p3 ḥtr p3 škr r-wn-n3w ꜥḥꜥ Kmy wn-n3w qš=f ẖn=w wn-n3w wy=f r-r=w n d̠3d̠3*

The dues and the taxes that were in force in Egypt, he had reduced some (?) or had renounced his right to them (*wn-n3w wy=f r-r=w)* completely (*n d̠3d̠3*).[161]

And similarly in the next line:

Line 8*: [n3 zp].w n Pr-ꜥ3 r-wn-n3w (r-)ꜥwy n3 rmṯ.w n Kmy..*
irm n3 nt n t3y=f i3w(.t) (n) pr-ꜥ3 d̠r=w ir itp ꜥš3y wy=f r-r=w

159 W. Spiegelberg, *Der demotische Text der Priesterdekrete von Kanopus und Memphis (Rosettana): mit den hieroglyphischen und griechischen Fassungen und deutscher Übersetzung nebst demotischem Glossar* (Heidelberg: Carl Winters Universitatsbuchhandlung, 1922); S. Quirke and C. Andrews, *The Rosetta Stone: Facsimile Drawing with an Introduction and Translation* (London: Published for the Trustees of the British Museum by British Museum Publications, 1988); R. S. Simpson, *Demotic Grammar in the Ptolemaic Sacerdotal Decrees* (Oxford: Griffith Institute, Ashmolean Museum, 1996) and the bibliography cited there.

160 There is no agreement whether the text of the Rosetta Stone is an Egyptian translation of an original Greek text or vice versa. For a survey of the problem see Simpson, *Demotic Grammar*, 22–24. Regarding the withdrawal formula, however, the Greek version of the Rosetta Stone is more specific in its formulation.

161 This is the only example in which *n d̠3d̠3* has this meaning, and the *n* is not clearly distinguished from the previous word *r-r=w*. See Erichsen, *Glossar*, 673. The interpretation of the expression is based on the Greek text. Demotic Line 7: *wy=f r-r=w n d̠3d̠3*, Lit. 'He withdrew from them'; Greek line 12: εἰς τέλος ἀφῆκεν: 'He has abolished (them) completely'. ἀφῆκεν (3rd Sing. Aor. Indic. απο + ιημι 'to send') means in legal sense 'to remit someone a charge' (Liddell-Scott, 290a, II 2, c) or 'to acquit of a charge or engagement' (Liddell-Scott, 290a, II 1.b.). These three acts of remission seem to be arranged according to a fixed pattern. Diodorus reports that Sesoösis 'showed kindnesses to everyone ... by remission (ἀπολύσει) of penalties ... for he set free (ἀφῆκε) ... everyone who was held for some crime against the king.... and cancelled (ἀπολυσε) the obligations of those who were in prison for debt'. Diodorus I, 54.3.

> [the arrear]s which were due to the King from the people who were in Egypt, and all those which are subject to his kingship, and (which) amounted to a large total, he withdrew from them (*wy=f r-r=w*).[162]

These two examples from the Rosetta Stone refer to various obligations (*p3 ḥtr* 'tax, obligation',[163] *p3 škr* 'payment, tax';[164] and *p3 sp.w* 'remainder, debt)'[165] which the people owed to the Pharaoh. The Pharaoh was the legal owner of these amounts of money. Now, 'he withdrew from them', that is, he released the people from those obligations.

6.3.4. *A Quitclaim by Party B Formulated by Party A in Divisions*

By means of the withdrawal formula the declarant states that Party B renounces any claim on the declarant's share.[166]

> *wy=k r-ḥr=y n t3y dny.t*
>
> You are far from me regarding my share.
>
> (P. Hauswaldt 5.11-12 [=P. Berlin 14948] Edfu, 219 BCE)

We mentioned this formula in our analysis of *TAD* B2.11.[167]

6.3.5. *A Complement of the Waiver of Suit Clause*

After the waiver of suit and penalty in this *sẖ n wy*, Party A declares:

> *p3 šr t3 šr.t mtw=y nty iw=f r ij r.ḥr=t r.ḏb3.ṯ=w iw=f tj.t n=t Penalty ʿn iw=f wy.ṯ r.ḥr=t n.im=w ʿn*
>
> Moreover, the son (or daughter) of mine, who will come against you because of this, he shall give you Penalty, and moreover he will be far from you regarding this.
>
> (P. Louvre 2433 [Thebes, 252 BCE])[168]

6.3.6. *A Complement of a Consent-Quitclaim Clause*

This clause is an additional provision against claims from members of the family of the alienor.[169] By means of a consent-quitclaim clause a possible

162 Demotic Line 8: *wy=f r-r=w*, Lit. 'he withdrew from them' Greek line 13: αφηκεν: 'he has remitted'.

163 Erichsen, *Glossar*, 343.

164 Erichsen, *Glossar*, 525.

165 Erichsen, *Glossar*, 426–7.

166 See also P. BM 10827.5 a donation of tombs as share of an inheritance (Thebes, 270 BCE).

167 See above, 5.1.1.4.

168 See also: P. Hawara 13.11 (P. Hamburg dem. 7) 99 BCE. Penalty – *iw=y ww.w r.r=k n.im=w* 'Penalty (Moreover) I am far from you regarding them.'

169 This clause has been labelled 'Beitrittserklärung', 'confirmation', 'adhesion', or 'consent' by demotists. The legal meaning, however, includes not only the agreement to the

claimant to the property, usually a family member of the alienator, declares that he/she agrees with the transaction and that he/she renounces any future claim to the property. In the following example, labelled as a division (μεριτείας) in the Greek abstract, a father is transferring property to one of his sons, and his 'oldest son' from a previous marriage declares:

> *sẖ i.iry mt nb nty ḥry ḥ3ṯ=y mtj.w n.im=w ti=y ww [r]* PN *p3y=y sn* Property
>
> Write (and) do what is written above. My heart is satisfied with it. I am far from PN my brother (regarding the) Property.
>
> (P. Hawara 16a.13 [=P. Hamburg dem. 4] 92 BCE).[170]

---

transaction, but also the quitclaim of possible claimants to the property (as clearly explained by Pestman, *Marriage*, 128–33 (also noted by Muffs, *Studies*, 170). See Sethe and Partsch, *Demotische Urkunden*, 683ff., and Lüddeckens, *Eheverträge*, 331–33. In this case the consent-quitclaim clause fulfils the same legal function as a *sẖ n wy*. A formula with the same legal function is also attested in the *Murabbaᶜat* documents (Mur. 30.28 – 134 BCE) and Naḥal Ḥever (XḤev/Se 8a.13 and possibly XḤev/Se 7.5, both 135/4 BCE). In Mur. 30.25 the formula reads: (...) PN דברים אין לי להמכר הזה ואני 'and I PN (...) do not have claims to this sale'. In Naḥal Ḥever the formula reads: 'And I PN (...) have no claims and forever regarding the sale of that house, and forever, בתה דך ולעלם. מלין לאיתי לי ולעלם בזבן Talmudic parallels to this clause were pointed out by Rabinowitz, 'Some Notes', 15–16. For previous discussions see Muffs, *Studies*, 169–72. For this formula in the context of annuity contracts see also J. Johnson, '"Annuity Contracts" and Marriage' in *For His Ka: Essays offered in Memory of Klaus Baer* (Chicago: Oriental Institute of the University of Chicago, 1994), 123–24. The other type of consent clause, the consent-guarantee clause, is used when a third party not only declares his agreement with the transaction, but also assumes the responsibility for the obligations assumed by the declarant in the contract (as in P. BM 10075, Sale, Memphis, 64 BCE; P. BM 10229, Marriage, Memphis, 78 BCE,). See Pestman, *Marriage*, 131.

170 Other examples of consent-quitclaim clauses built up with *wy* are P. Louvre 2412 (Memphis, 305/4 BCE), the son of party A relinquishes claims on the property; P. Leiden 379 (Division, Memphis, 256 BCE), the mother of party A relinquishes claims; P. BM 10392 (Sale, Thebes, 208/7 BCE); P. BM 10525 (Kaufpfandurkunde, Thebes, 284 BCE), where party A's wife is the one who relinquishes claims on the property; Berlin P 3089 (Division, Thebes, 230 BCE), where the person who relinquishes claims on the property is party's A's mother; P. Louvre 2438 (Doc. of Withdrawal, Thebes, 245 BCE) and P. BM 10073 (Sale, Thebes, 219 BCE), where the son and daughter of party A relinquish claims. In P. Louvre 3263 (Division, Thebes, 224/3 BCE) it is the wife who relinquishes her claims. Other documents with consent-quitclaim clauses but without *wy* are P. Strassburg 7 (Sale, Gebelein, 111 BCE); P. Cairo 31254 (Sale, Tebtynis, 106–5 BCE); P. Cairo 30616b (Annuity, Tebtynis, 79/8 BCE); P. Berlin 3099, 3100, 5508 (124 BCE); P. Bologna (209/8 BCE); P. Louvre 2430 (334 BCE); P. Cairo JE 89364 (Phil 7); P. Cairo JE 89372 (Phil 21); P. Cairo JE 89375 (Phil 25); P. BM 10071 (212 BCE); Papyrus Vat (218 BCE). All of them include the satisfaction clause followed by different formulae, i.e.: *iwṯ ḏd qnb nb md nb p3 t3 irm=k* 'without alleging any title or anything at all against you' (P. BM 10071.5-6); *iw.ṯ sẖ nb* 'without (alleging) any document' (P. Louvre 2430.6).

6.3.7. *Release of Wife in Divorce Documents*

In order to renounce any claim arising from the man's right to his wife (*hp n ḥm.t*), the husband states in deeds of divorce:

> *dỉ=y wy.ṱ r-ḥr=t n hp n ḥm.t*
>
> I am far from you regarding the right of wife.[171]
>
> (P. Philadelphia II.1 [Thebes, 281 BCE]).

6.3.8. *Quitclaim by Husband in Divorce Documents*

In P. BM. 10074 (Thebes, 231 BCE) *Pn-nfr* divorces his wife and in the document of divorce includes his renunciation of various properties that will remain in the wife's family. The formulae (lines 12 and 22) follow the standard expression *ty=y wy r-r=k n* Property, 'I am far from you regarding (the) Property.'

6.3.9. *A Defension Clause*

This expression of the withdrawal formula is shared by both the *sẖ ḏbꜣ ḥḏ* and the *sẖ n wy*.[172] The following example is taken from a *sẖ ḏbꜣ ḥḏ*:

> *pꜣ rmt nb n pꜣ tꜣ nt ỉw=f<r> ỉy.t r-ḥr=t ḏbꜣ.ṱ=z n rn=y ỉw=y<r> dy.t wy=f r ḥr=t n-ỉm=s ỉw=y tm dy.t wy=f ỉw=y dy.t wy=f n ḥtr ỉwṱ mn*
>
> Any man on earth who will come against you concerning it in my name, I will cause him to be far from you concerning it (the share). If I do not cause him to be far, I will cause him to be far compulsorily, without delay.
>
> (P. Hauswaldt 5.11-12 [=P. Berlin 14948] Edfu, 219 BCE).

6.3.10. *A Withdrawal Clause at the End of a sẖ ḏbꜣ ḥḏ*

P. Carnavon 1 and 2 (Pois, 202 BCE) refer to transfer of property among family members, and although both documents are built up as *sẖ ḏbꜣ ḥḏ* we might be dealing with a division of inheritance. The inclusion at the end of the documents of a withdrawal clause is uncommon in the formulary of the *sẖ ḏbꜣ ḥḏ*. In both documents, the formula reads:

> *ỉw=y wy r-r=k n pꜣy=k* Object
>
> I am far from you regarding your Object.

171 P. Heidelberg 754c (Gebelein, ca. 100 BCE); P. Heidelberg 762+770+774 (Gebelein, 100 BCE); P. Turin 6094 (Thebes, 114 BCE); P. Heidelberg 779a (Gebelein, 123 BCE); P. BM 10074 (Thebes, 230 BCE); see Pestman, *Marriage*, 17ff.

172 See Zauzich, *Schreibertradition*. In *sẖ n wy* after litigation see P. Berlin 3113 (Thebes, 141 BCE); P. Berlin 13554 (Elephantine, 245 BCE); P. BM 10380 A (Thebes, 231 BCE); P. BM 10446 (Thebes, 230 BCE).

6.3.11. Withdrawal *Formula in the Transfer Clause in the sẖ db3 ḥd*
P. Lille (136 BCE) is a sale (*sẖ db3 ḥd*) of cattle. Its formulary differs from the rest of the *sẖ db3 ḥd* from this period and we quote it in full.[173]

> *P. Lille (Memphis?, 136 BCE)*
>
> **I. Date:** Year 34 Ptolemy VIII
> **II. Parties:** Hor-kheb (?) son of Thotertaïs speaks to Hermogenes son of Hemogenes
> **III. Satisfaction:** 'You satisfied my heart with the money of my cow.'
> **IV. Investiture:** *[mtw=k] t3y=k iḥ.t t3y* 'It is yours, this is your cow.'
> **V. Transference**
> **A. Sale:** *di=y st n=k (r)-db3 ḥd* 'I gave it to you in exchange for silver.'
> **B. Withdrawal:** *tw=y wy.k r-r=k* 'I am far from you.'
> **C. Transfer:** *di(=y) st (n=k)* 'I gave it to you.'
> **VI. Quitclaim**
> **A. Covenant of Non-claim (Personal):** 'I do not have any claim at all against you in her name from this day and forever.'
> **B. General Warranty (Defension):** 'As for anyone who shall come to you on account of it, I will cause him to be far from you and I shall clear it for you from any right, any writing, and any legal document at all.'
> **VII. Investiture:** 'She is yours with her rights.'
> **VIII. Oath Clause:** 'The oath (or) the proof which will be imposed upon you, I will swear it.'
> **IX. Scribe:** (. . .)haty son of Thoteraïs
> **X. Date:** Year 34

This association of the withdrawal clause with the transfer clause reminds us of P. Louvre 7850 (Thebes, 533 BCE),[174] and of *TAD* B3.4:10-11 *et al.* and provides further evidence of the continuity of this Egyptian formula.[175]

6.3.12. *The wy Formula in Release of Prisoners*
In our study of the use of רחק in the Aramaic documents, we noted that a

173 Menu, 'Vente d'une vache', 230, considers this document to follow the formulary of Memphis (Zauzich, *Schreibertradition*, Urk. 94 and 95) but in those documents the withdrawal formula is part of a consent clause and not of the transfer clause as is the case in P. Lille.

174 See above p. 115.

175 Cruz-Uribe, *Cattle Documents*, 46, suggests that this Ptolemaic document was following Saite-Persian practice in including a withdrawal formula in the sale document. See also S. P. Vleeming, 'Notes on Some Early-Demotic Cattle Documents', *BO* 42 (1985): 515.

document of release of slaves was called ספר מרחק.[176] The Rosetta Stone will use *wy* in a similar context, the release of prisoners. The Demotic text reads:

> Line 8: *n3 rmṯ.w r-wn-n3w wn lwḥ (r-) ʿwj=w n sw ʿš3y wy=f r-r=w.*
>
> the people who were in prison and those against whom there had been charges from a long time, he released *(wy=f r-r=w).*[177]

The Demotic *wy=f r-r=w*, therefore, covers two legal acts in the Rosetta Stone: the condonation of debts = the release of obligations, as seen before, and the release of prisoners. In the case of the prisoners, they were also under the Pharaoh's control. By releasing them, he has no such control over them any more.

This list attests to the wide use of the withdrawal formula in Ptolemaic times. The available evidence clearly establishes that the withdrawal formula was not confined to a single type of transaction but manifested its presence in a large variety of documents and contexts. While some of the uses of *wy* listed above parallel the uses of רחק in the Aramaic documents (as for example nos. 1, 2, 5, 11, and 12) other uses of *wy* in the Demotic documents are completely unattested in Aramaic (3, 4, 6, 7, 8, 9, and 10).

The subsequent development and use of the withdrawal formula beyond the Ptolemaic period falls beyond the scope of this volume and is not relevant, as such, to the interrelationship between the Aramaic and Demotic formulae. It is worth noting, however, that the withdrawal formula has continued to be used on Egyptian soil in deeds written in Greek, Coptic,[178] and Arabic[179] until the present day, in an almost unprecedented example of continuity and adaptation of a legal formula through the ages.

6.4. *Summary*

Based on these attestations of *w3y* and according to the levels of analysis proposed in chapter 2.3.3, we are able to conclude that the legal metaphor

176 *TAD* B3.6, see above Table VIII, p. 97.

177 Demotic line 8: *wy=f r-r=w*, Lit. 'he withdrew from them' Greek line 14: ἀπέλευσε τῶν ἐνκεκλημένων: 'he has absolved of the charges'. ἀπέλευσε, (3rd Sing. Aor. Indic. Act. ἀπολύω) means 'set free, release' (Liddell-Scott, 208).

178 Cf A. Schiller, *Ten Coptic Legal Texts* (New York: Metropolitan Museum of Art, 1932), 17.

179 The wide acceptance of the withdrawal as a legal figure is supported by the fact that Arabic legal vocabulary can display as many as thirteen synonyms which connote separation: *khls* II, 'to clear'; *bʿd* 'to remove far from'. See G. Frantz-Murphy, 'A Comparison of the Arabic and Earlier Egyptian Contract Formularies, Part II: Terminology in the Arabic Warranty and the Idiom of Clearing/Cleaning', *JNES* 44 (1985): 109 n. 28.

of removal by physical distance, the legal term *wꜣy*, and the withdrawal formula were widely accepted in Egypt from early times. The semantic domain of the word and its derivatives refers to a separation by physical movement and distance regarding persons, actions, and objects. The legal term *wꜣy* is not the only attested realization of the legal metaphor of physical withdrawal before the Saite and Persian periods. The verb *ḥꜣꜥ* is another example of the use of that metaphor. The legal metaphor of physical withdrawal provides a range of legal meanings in different legal contexts.

Although all of the early examples exhibit a common basic legal meaning related to the loss of control or authority by the person regarding the object, each should be translated differently into English. As demonstrated above: *wꜣy ḥr* PN_2 regarding X = PN_1 does not have any authority, i.e. proprietary rights regarding X;[180] PN *wꜣ r* Name or Office = PN_1 is deprived of his name and/or his office;[181] the lands that are *wꜣy* are lands that are clear from any encumbrance.[182]

Thus far, the early examples – hitherto unnoticed – of the withdrawal clause lead us to some preliminary considerations. First, the attestation of this clause in non-legal contexts in a period which has yielded few legal documents suggests that the formula could have been widely accepted. Second, we must judge the single attestation from that early period in Mesopotamia, where we have thousands of legal documents, differently from the case of Egypt, where we have just a few. In Mesopotamia, this attestation would most likely have been an isolated one and would imply that although this formula was known and of valid use, it was not widely accepted.[183] In Egypt, however, we have to keep open the possibility that this formula was not only known and of valid use, but also that its use may have been widely established. The third consideration is that such an early attestation of the withdrawal formula on Egyptian soil already refutes the presently accepted theory that this formula was brought to Egypt by the Aramaean scribes.[184]

The scarcity of the material and its geographic distribution does not allow us to trace the development and diffusion of the *wꜣy*-based formulae in Egyptian soil in early periods. The diverse provenance of the texts presented in our first section can be visualized in Map 1. Three of the texts come from the Theban area of influence (Deir el Bahari; Thebes; Karnak) while the Lisht tablets come from the Memphite area of influence. This

180 Coffin Texts VII, 48 g. Spell 843. See above, 6.1.1.

181 Lisht Tablets, P. Brooklyn 35.1446, and the Second Intermediate Period stela of the Theban king Neb-Kheperu-Re Inyotef. See above, p. 140.

182 As in the Ioureot stela. See above, 6.1.4.

183 This would be the case for an isolated use of *requ* in Nuzi. See above, p. 187.

184 As Muffs *et al.* proposed. See note 1 above.

situation points to the widespread use of the legal term *wꜣy*, and the withdrawal formula in both the Northern and the Southern regions of the country.

When we turn to the Saite-Persian period, the amount of evidence provides more elements for analysis. Table XIII displays a list of the legal documents dated before the Aramaic documents where both the withdrawal formula 'I am far from you . . . .' and/or the removal formula 'I will cause him to be far from you' are constructed with *wy* 'to be far'.

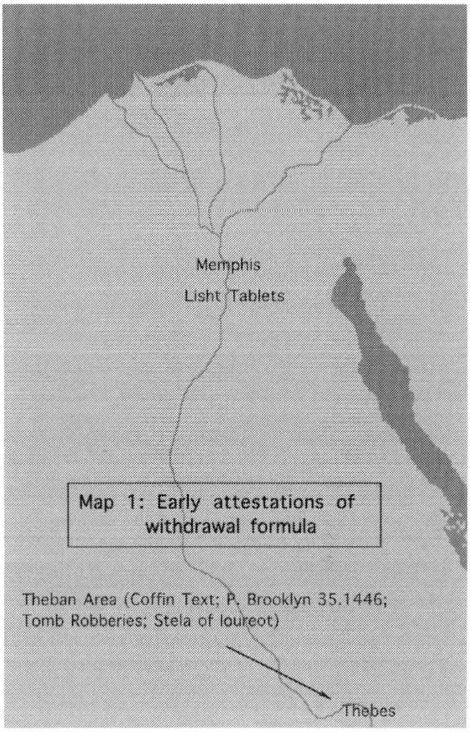

Map 1: Early attestations of withdrawal formula

Table XIII: Documents with Withdrawal Formula

No.	Museum	Date	Kind of document	Place	Formula
1	P. Berlin P 13571	-591	Sale	Elephantine	*iw=y r di.t wy.f r-r=k n-im=s*
2	P. Rylands 4	-568	Document of Withdrawal	El-Hibeh	*tw=y wy.k] r-ḥr=k n pꜣ* Object
3	P. Louvre E 7845 A	-568	Lease	Thebes	*di(.t) wy* Person *r-r=k n* Object
4	P. Cairo 50058	-543	Division	Asyut	*tw=y wy.k r-r=k n* Object *iw=k wy.ty r-r=y n* Object 2
5	P. Louvre E 7833 A	-535	Lease	Thebes	*di.t wy=y nꜣ* PN *r-r=k n* Object
6	P. Louvre E 7837	-535	Lease	Thebes	*di(.t) wy* Person *r-r=k n* Object
7	P. Louvre E 7850	-533	Business Letter	Thebes	*tw = y r-r = f n md [nb] n*
8	P. Louvre E 7839	-533	Lease	Thebes	*iw(= y) wy.t r-r = f*
9	P. BM 10117	-529	Sale	Coptos	*di.t wy=f*

No.	Museum	Date	Kind of document	Place	Formula
10	P. BM 10792	-522	Document of Withdrawal	Asyut	*tw=y [wy.k r-r=k n* Object. . .*]* *di.t wy=f r-r=k*
11	Ref. in. P. Cairo 500-59	-522	Document of Withdrawal	Asyut	not preserved
12	P. Cairo 50059	-522	Exchange	Asyut	*ỉw=y wy=ṱ r-r=k n* Object
13	P. Turin 2122 (228)	-517	Sale	Thebes	*di.t wy=f r-r=k*
14	P. Bibl. Nat. 223	-516	Sale	Thebes	*ỉw(=y) di.t wy=f*
15	P. Turin 2123 (231)	-512	Donation	Thebes	*ỉw(=y) di.t wy=f r-ḥr=t*
16	P. Louvre E 7128	-510	Sale	Thebes	*ỉ[w](=y) di.t wy=f r-r=k*
17	P. Turin 2124 (209)	-507	Exchange	Thebes	*ỉw(=y) di.t wy=f r-r=k*
18	P. Loeb 68	-501	Sale	Gebelein ?	*ỉw=y di,t wy[=f r-r=k]*
19	P. Michigan 3525 a	-501	Sale	Thebes or Edfu	*ỉw(=y) ti wy=f r-ḥr=tn*
20	P. Michigan 3525 c	-498	Sale	Thebes or Edfu	*in [ỉw=y ti] wy=f r-r=k*
21	P. Michigan 3525 b	-498	Sale	Thebes or Edfu	*in ỉw=y ti wy+f r-r=k*
22	P. Turin 2126 (251)	-498	Investiture	Thebes	*ỉw(=y) di.t wy=f r-ḥr=t*
23	P. Louvre E 9292	-494	Sale	Thebes	*di.t wy=f*
24	P. Louvre A F 9761	-494	Document of Withdrawal	Thebes	*tw(=y) wy(.ṱ) r-r=k*
25	P. Berlin P 3078	-493	Document of wifehood	Thebes	*ỉw(=y) wy.ṱ nty nb nkt nb . . .*
26	P. Berlin 13572	-493	Business letter	Elephantine	*ỉw(=y) r di.t wy PN r-r=k n-ỉmw*
27	P. Louvre E 9294	-491	Sale	Thebes	*ỉw(=y) r di.t wy=f r-r=k*
28	P. BM 10449	-490	Divorce	Thebes	*tw=y wy=k r-[ḥr=t]*
29	P. Loeb 44 + P. Loeb 49	-489	Sale	Gebelein	*[ỉw di.t wy=f r-r=k n-ỉm=f*
30	P. Turin 2128 (230)	-487	Exchange	Thebes	*ỉw(=y) di.t wy=f r-r=k*
31	P. Loeb 43	-485	Document of Withdrawal	Gebelein	*tw=y wy.k pꜣ hp*

As we see in Table XIII, the withdrawal clause and the removal formula appear in different kinds of documents – sale, division, lease, exchange, and divorce – the earliest case predating the Aramaic documents almost by a hundred years.

The survey of the various uses of the *wy* formula in the Saite and Persian, and Ptolemaic periods displays the widespread use of the *wy*-based formulae among different types of documents and legal transactions. Generally speaking, we find the withdrawal formula to be used in reference to persons without any further specification (*wy* + *r-r* + personal suffix); in reference to persons regarding property or rights to property (*wy* + *r-r* + personal suffix + *n* + property or right to property); and in reference to obligations (as in the Rosetta Stone). The common factor in all the uses of the *wy*-based formulae in the different legal instruments and contexts is that of release.

Taking into account all the evidence, there is no reason to assume an Aramaic origin of *wy* as a legal term, of the withdrawal formula, or of the withdrawal clause. Reversing Muffs' conclusion, we maintain that the Egyptian use, attested several centuries before the Demotic, is the original and that the later Aramaic usage was patterned after it. There are far too many cases where the Egyptian use anticipates the later Aramaic use; the facts cannot be interpreted any other way.[185] This conclusion, however, does not imply that the withdrawal clause is Egyptian in its ultimate origin. We merely claim, based on the new evidence presented in this chapter, that it is the Aramaic which borrowed from the local Egyptian use and not vice versa. In the following chapter we shall examine the Aramaic use of the withdrawal formula and compare it with its Egyptian counterpart.

185 Cf. Muffs, *Studies*, 165.

7

A Comparison of the Aramaic and Egyptian Uses of Withdrawal Formulae

In the previous chapters we listed the different uses of withdrawal formulae in the Egyptian and Aramaic legal traditions with occasional references to corresponding formulae attested in both legal traditions. In this chapter, we present a comparative description of the various uses and expressions of the withdrawal formula, pointing to the similarities and the divergences that we find in its use in Aramaic and in Egyptian. We present the comparison according to the levels of analysis proposed in Chapter 2.3.3, and will concentrate on the first three levels of comparison, namely, the legal concept and the legal term; the legal formula; and the legal clause. Although the purpose of this volume is to examine the interrelationships between the Aramaic and Demotic formulae, it is not possible to ignore the wider context in which these traditions developed. The remarkable continuity in the legal and formulaic tradition that are attested in Elephantine through the millennia[1] is also a well-established characteristic in the rest of the ancient Near East. However, these striking similarities between some of the legal terms and formulae used in documents, separated by centuries and thousands of miles, should not obscure the differences among the different legal and formulaic traditions in which those legal terms and formulae are attested.

In the Mesopotamian realm, for example, the existence of two principal mainstreams of legal and formulaic traditions has been established: the Assyrian and the Babylonian traditions,[2] and also a marked contrast between the central tradition of central and southern Mesopotamia[3] and the peripheral tradition of the fringe areas, such as Susa, Nuzi, and

1 Cf. the continuity of some of the legal formulae and formulary in Porten, *Elephantine Papyri*.

2 M. San Nicolò, *Beiträge zur Rechtsgeschichte im Bereich der keilschriftlichen Rechtsquellen* (Oslo: H. Aschehoug; Cambridge, Mass.: Harvard University Press, 1931), 1.

3 The documents included in this category are those stemming from the Early Dynastic Period (ca. 2800–2500 BCE) through the Ur III Period (ca. 2050–1950 BCE) written mainly in Sumerian.

Kültepe.[4] Such differences between regions in close proximity and constant interaction might be explained by the legal comparatist as the result of political opposition between those regions. Although Muffs's study provides a valuable analysis of the development of some of the legal formulae in Mesopotamia, a thorough study of the inner development of the various legal traditions within the Mesopotamian realm is still pending.

Considering that we are approaching the study of the Aramaic and Demotic formulae from an Egyptological perspective, we do not intend to present a complete survey of the several uses of withdrawal formulae throughout the ancient Near East or even within the Mesopotamian legal tradition. Such a task, although necessary to determine the antiquity and geographical distribution of the several terms and formulae used in withdrawal clauses, would need a study of its own.

Consequently, in the following sections we shall concentrate mainly on the Aramaic and Demotic use of the withdrawal formulae. We shall provide examples of the Mesopotamian legal traditions when available with the sole purpose of setting the Aramaic and Demotic formulae in the wider stream of ancient Near Eastern formulaic traditions.

7.1. *The Legal Metaphor and the Legal Term*

The withdrawal formula in Aramaic and Demotic is an expression of the metaphor of removal by physical distance. As we saw, it is expressed in Egyptian by the legal term *wy* (Demotic) and by *ḥ3ʿ* (Abnormal Hieratic), and in Aramaic by רחק. Both legal traditions, the Egyptian and the Aramaic, therefore, made use of this metaphor in their legal vocabulary. In the Mesopotamian legal realm, Muffs recorded three terms related to the metaphor of removal by physical distance.[5] First, the use of *duppur*[6] in Susa dating from the Old Babylonian period,[7] second, *rêqu*[8] (the equivalent of Aramaic רחק), which the lexical tablets equate with *duppur* and which conveys a similar meaning when 'an owner of property removes (*irêq*) himself from his property',[9] or an indentured hand 'removes (*irêq*) himself' from his owner's service.[10] Third, late Neo-Babylonian *eṭir*

4 Noted already by L. Oppenheim, 'Der Eid in den Rechtsurkunden aus Susa', *WZKM* 43 (1936): 242–62.

5 Muffs also offers a list of legal terms related to the metaphor of satisfaction and purity which are not the object of this study. Muffs, *Studies*, 116–28.

6 Cf. *CAD* D, 186–8, s.v. *duppuru*; *AHW* I, 177.

7 Muffs, *Studies*, 117–20.

8 Cf. *CAD* R, 265–68.

9 Cf. *JEN* 221.18, cited by Muffs, *Studies*, 118 n. 5.

10 Cf. *HSS* V 105.18, cited by Muffs, *Studies*, 118 n. 6.

'removed',[11] which becomes a term for quittance during the late Neo-Babylonian period.[12] In addition to *duppuru*, *rêqu*, and *eṭir*, the verb *nesû* also conveys the meaning of 'to withdraw, to depart, to remove'.[13] In the next section, we discuss Muffs's interpretation of the formula in more detail. Here, we are only concerned with the terms themselves.

Taking into account that the legal metaphor of physical withdrawal is also present in the Mesopotamian realm,[14] it is clear that we are dealing with an ancient and widespread legal technical term.[15] Its use is traceable in Mesopotamia and Egypt to almost the very beginning of written records. We must conclude that, based on the available evidence, the problem of where and when this metaphor began to be used cannot be resolved at the level of the legal term. Regarding the question of which legal tradition, the Aramaic or the Demotic, would be the borrower or lender, it would be risky to point to either the Egyptian or the Mesopotamian legal traditions considering that the use of this metaphor was so widespread in the ancient Near East. It must be noted, however, that the absence of רחק in the Wadi Daliyeh documents[16] suggests that the Aramaic scribes might have included the term in their documents because of the normative use of the term in Egypt at that time. The way in which they assimilated the legal term into their legal formulae and legal formulary will be discussed in the following section.

7.2. *Legal Formulae*

When we turn to the development of legal formulae based on the legal terms *wy*, *ḫ3ʿ*, and רחק we are in a better position to point out different trends in the developments. At this stage, we do not deal with the incorporation of the legal formulae in the various legal clauses, which will be the topic of the next section. The variations in the expression of the withdrawal formula are displayed in Table XIV. Following the same criteria used to describe the scribal traditions in Elephantine-Syene, the various columns highlight the continuity of formulaic traditions even in the case when only one instance was found.

11 Cf. *CAD* E, 401; *AHW* I, 264.

12 Muffs, *Studies*, 125–26.

13 Attested in Old Babylonian, *ARM*, Middle Babylonian and Standard Babylonian. Cf. *CAD* N, 184–89; *AHW* II, 781.

14 See below.

15 For its use in Arabic legal documents see G. Frantz-Murphy, 'A Comparison of Arabic and Earlier Egyptian Contract Formularies, Part IV: Quittance Formulas', *JNES* 47 (1988), where the following expressions are attested: (a) the seller removes the buyer from the price; (b) the seller removes himself from the property; and (c) mutual removal.

16 Cf. Gropp, *Wadi Deliyeh II* (WDSP).

Table XIV: Typology of Legal Formulae based on *wy*, *ḫ3ʿ*, and רחק

Date	Withdrawal from Object	Withdrawal from Name	Withdrawal from Office	Withdrawal from Person	Withdrawal from Person regarding Object	Withdrawal from Suit/Person regarding Suit	Withdrawal from Person regarding Rights	Cause to Release Land	Cause to Release from Person regarding Object
Middle Kingdom	*w3y ḥr object* they being far from this.[17]								
		mt w3.n rn=f r PN the deceased (who was) deprived of the name PN.[18]	*mt w3 r mr ḫtmtyw* the deceased (who was) removed from (the post of) overseer of sealers.[19]						
New Kingdom				*w3 r=y w3 r ẖʿt=y* be far from me. Be far from me.[20]					
Third Intermediate Period								*iw di=f wi3.w n3 3ḥ* he caused the fields to be relinquished.[21]	
Saite and Persian Period	וישעא רחק מהם And Yiš'a', is far from them.[22]			*tw(=y) wy(.t) r-r=k* I am far from you.[23]	*tw=y wy.k r-r=k n* object I am far from you regarding object.[24]	*tw=y r-r=f n md [nb]* I am far from him regarding any suit.[25]	*tw=y wy.k r p3 hp n* object I am far from the right of object.[26]		*iw=y r di.t wy.f r-r=k n-im=s* I will make him withdraw from you regarding it.[27]
	dj.t sẖ n=f p3j=f irj-dd 'n' wy r.r=s He will write for his adversary a			ורחקת מנך and I withdrew from you.[29]	*dj.t ḫ3ʿ i-r=k n.im=w* I withdrew from you regarding them[30]	ורחיקן אנחנה מנך ומן בניך מן דין עלדבר פטוסירי and we are far from you and			

Date	Withdrawal from Object	Withdrawal from Name	Withdrawal from Office	Withdrawal from Person	Withdrawal from Person regarding Object	Withdrawal from Suit/Person regarding Suit	Withdrawal from Person regarding Rights	Cause to Release Land	Cause to Release from Person regarding Object
	withdrawal regarding it.[28]					from your children from (any) suit on account of that *Peṭosiri*[31]			
	wy.ṭ i-r=f I being far from it (land).[32]			ורחקת מנכי מן יומא זנה ועד עלם I withdrew from you from this day and forever.[33]	רחקת מנכם מן בית יזניה בר אוריה I withdrew from you from the house of Jezaniah son of Uriah.[34]	ואנת רחיק מן כל דין and you are far from any suit.[35]			
	ורחקת מנה and withdrew from it.[36]			ועננית רחיקן אנחנה מנך מן יומא זנה עד עלם we are far from you from this day forever.[37]		ואנה רחיק מן כל דין ודבב and I am far from every suit or process.[38]			
	ורחקן מנה מן ימא זנה ועד עלם and withdrew from it from this day and forever.[39] והו אפם רחיק מן אלה נכסיא and he is likewise far from these goods.[40]								

17 Coffin texts, see above, 6.1.1.
18 Lisht tablets and P. Brooklyn 35.1446 (Middle Kingdom) see above 6.1.2.
19 Lisht tablets and P. Brooklyn 35.1446 (Middle Kingdom) see above 6.1.2.
20 P. BM. 10052 (Thebes, 1125–1069 BCE) see above 6.1.3.

21 Stela of Ioureot, see above 6.1.4.
22 The Marzeaḥ papyrus, see above 5.1.3.1.
23 Tsenhor 15 (= P. Louvre AF 9761, Thebes, 494 BCE).
24 P. Cairo 50058 (Asyut, 543 BCE).
25 P. Louvre E 7850 (Thebes, 533 BCE).
26 P. Loeb 43 (Gebelein, 485 BCE).
27 P. Berlin P 13571 (Elephantine, 591 BCE).
28 Legal Manual of Hermopolis.
29 *TAD* B3.2:7.
30 P. Cairo 30657 (Gebelein, 547 BCE).
31 *TAD* B2.11:11.
32 P. Louvre 7839 (Thebes, 533 BCE).
33 *TAD* B2.8:5-7.
34 *TAD* B2.10:4.
35 *TAD* B2.2:15-16 זי יקבלון עליך עלדבר ארעא זך that they shall complain against you on account of that land.
36 *TAD* B2.7.
37 *TAD* B2.9:9.
38 *TAD* B2.8:11.
39 *TAD* B3.4:10-11.
40 *TAD* B2.9:15

7.2.1. *Withdrawal from Object*

The withdrawal from object represents the basic concept of the metaphor of physical withdrawal. The distancing of the holder of rights or occupant of the object/property which is being transferred is at the same time the representation and the consequence of the transfer of rights upon the property to the new owner/occupant. The Aramaic[41] and Egyptian formula are linguistic equivalents and are constructed in the same way, verb + preposition + suffix/object. The problem is that while the Aramaic withdrawal from object/property is widely attested in Elephantine,[42] it is completely absent from the Demotic formulary. And, although the formula is attested in one Middle Kingdom text[43] and possibly in two other Demotic texts,[44] the withdrawal in the Demotic legal documents is from the person *regarding* the object (Demotic = *n* + object) and not *from* the object *itself* (Aramaic = מן + object) as in the Elephantine documents.

Before trying to solve the problem let us turn to the Mesopotamian realm to search for similar formulations. According to Muffs, the use of *duppur* in Susa conveys the aspects of (a) a right-holder who removes himself from his property; (b) a servile person who removes himself (illegally) from his master's service.[45] Muffs's interpretation of *duppur* is partially based on the semantic equivalence of *duppur* with *rêqu*.[46] A closer examination shows, however, that the use of *duppur* in Susa was meant to describe another kind of withdrawal than the withdrawal from object. In Susa, the use of *duppur* does not point to the withdrawal from object, but expresses the mutual departure after the transaction is completed, i.e. the departure after which no claim is possible.[47]

This use certainly has the connotation of a quittance formula, but its formulaic use equals neither the use of *rêqu* in Nuzi nor the use of רחק in Elephantine. An additional difference between the use of *duppur* in Susa and רחק in Elephantine is that in Susa the formula is composed by the stative cluster *zīzū mesû duppurū* 'they have divided, they are finished, they are quit'[48] (i.e. each has gone his separate way),[49] while in Aramaic and

41 Cf. *TAD* B2.7:7, 16; B3.4:10-11; B2.9:15.

42 *TAD* B2.10:4; B2.7:7, 16; B3.4:10-11, 13.

43 Coffin texts, see above 6.1.1.

44 Legal Manual of Hermopolis and P. Louvre 7839 (Thebes, 533 BCE).

45 Muffs, *Studies*, 118.

46 Cf. *CAD* R, 265–68.

47 Cf. the use of *bari'a* in Arabic deeds. G. Frantz-Murphy, 'A Comparison of Arabic and Earlier Egyptian Contract Formularies, Part IV: Quittance Formulas', *JNES* 47 (1988): 272.

48 Muffs, *Studies*, 117.

49 This is the precise legal antonym of *qerēbu*, 'to approach, come near', in the sense of beginning a legal action. *CAD* Q s.v. 5. *qerēbu*, p. 234.

Demotic there is no such stative chain. Withdrawal in Susa is neither from property, nor from person as in Aramaic and Demotic.[50]

The withdrawal from property is, however, attested in just one case in Nuzi.[51] Located in present day Kirkur, the ancient city of Nuzi has yielded some 4,500 clay tablets written in a dialect of Akkadian with Hurrian influence. The relevance of the Nuzi material for the legal history of the ancient Near East cannot be overestimated. The tablets, dated to the second half of the fifteenth century BCE,[52] include lists of rations, inventories, records of expenditures, letters, lists of people, and private family records, which provide different kinds of information about transactions over several generations and represent an enormous contribution to the social history of the region.

The most relevant legal document for our discussion is *JEN* 221, a tablet of division of property between the brothers *Mušuya* and *Šukriya* sons of *Puitae*, and *Mušeya* son of *Ḫašiga*. Following the record of both *Mušuya* and *Šukriya* receiving an amount of barley, the document reads, 'from this day *Mušuya* and *Šukriya* shall not draw near to these fields; on the contrary, they shall distance themselves from the fields'.[53] Should we consider the use of *rêqu* in *JEN* 221 a standard Nuzi formula? A. H. Friedmann's dissertation[54] provides useful tables from whence it is possible to draw more precise statistical conclusions regarding the corpus. The name of the scribe is usually provided in the legal documents (about 1100 scribes according to Friedmann). Based on this information, Friedmann produced a list of some 300 names of scribes.[55] The scribe of *JEN* 221, *Adad-Naṣir*, was responsible for only two other documents in

50 The mutual withdrawal from persons and the withdrawal from object is attested in literary works, not in legal contexts. Cf. *YOS* 10 47.81; cited on *CAD* D, p. 87.

51 There are not several attestations of the withdrawal formula in Nuzi (*contra* Cussini, 'Transfer of Property', 243 n. 32). It is true, however, as Cussini states, that 'an attempt to find the verb *rêqu* in Neo-Assyrian documents chronologically closer to the Elephantine ones give negative results', 'Transfer of Property', 243 n. 32.

52 Cf. B. L. Eichler, '*Indenture at Nuzi*': *The personal* Tidennūtu Contract and Its Mesopotamian Analogues (New Haven: Yale University Press, 1973), 2 n. 7; *CAH* fasc. 44, pp. 30 and 59ff.

53 Translation by J. S. Paradise, 'Nuzi Inheritance Practices' (Ph.D. diss., University of Pennsylvania, 1972), 349.

54 A. H. Friedmann, 'Economic Geography and Administration at Nuzi' (Ph.D., diss., Hebrew Union College – Jewish Institute of Religion, Ohio, 1982).

55 Friedmann, 'Economic Geography', Index VIII, and ch. 5, 'Notes on Scribal Activity at Nuzi', 199–211. This figure comes from counting a different PN from the same PN with patronymic. If we count as being the same person the PN alone and the PN with patronymic, it will result in about 197 scribe names. See also P. Negri-Scafa, 'Scribes locaux et scribes itinérants dans le royaume d'Arrapḫa', in D. Charpin and F. Joannès, eds., *La circulation des biens, des personnes et des idées dans le Proche-Orient ancien. Actes de la XXXVIIIe Rencontre Assyriologique Internationale (Paris, 8–10 juillet 1991)* (Paris: Editions Recherche sur les civilisations, 1992), 235–40.

the corpus: *JEN* 47 and 89, and in neither of them did he use the withdrawal formula.[56]

The phraseology used by the scribe equates 'shall not draw near' with 'shall distance themselves', and involves the use of a stylistic feature widely used in legal material for emphatic purposes, the negated antonym.[57] Although the negative use of *qarābu* is well attested in the legal material from Nuzi,[58] this is the only occasion in which *qarābu* is followed by *rêqu*. Actually, this is the only instance of *rêqu* within a withdrawal formula throughout the whole Nuzi corpus of legal documents.[59] This suggests that in *JEN* 221, we have an isolated case involving a stylistic use with emphatic purpose rather than use of a legal formula with independent meaning and substance.

The lack of any other attestation of withdrawal formula in Nuzi leads to the conclusion that the absence of evidence of use of a withdrawal clause signifies evidence of absence. Therefore, the use of *rêqu* in *JEN* 221 points to a scribal idiosyncrasy rather than the presence or widespread use of the withdrawal formula in the Nuzi formulary traditions.

Regarding the use of *eṭir*, another term mentioned by Muffs,[60] in Neo-Babylonian formulae it covers the meaning of a payment formula and does not reflect the metaphor of physical withdrawal any more.[61]

A more compelling piece of evidence for the existence of the withdrawal from object in the Semitic realm is the *Marzeaḥ* papyrus.[62] There we find an early (mid- or late seventh-century BCE) attestation of the formula outside of Egypt, which may aid in understanding the peculiar Aramaic formulation of the withdrawal from object formula.[63] It seems that the Aramaean scribes persisted in using the withdrawal from object formula while the Demotic scribes used the withdrawal from person *regarding* the object ('withdrawal from person from property', instead of following *verbatim* the Demotic 'withdrawal from person regarding property'). This

56 Because of no additional use of the withdrawal formula in Nuzi, it is not possible to determine whether its use was desiderated in these two texts or not.

57 See R. Yaron, 'Stylistic Conceits: The Negated Antonym', *JNES* 22 (1993): 141–48; = *Comparative Studies in Honor of Yochanan Muffs*.

58 See Paradise, 'Nuzi Inheritance Practices', 32 n. 9. Cf. *HSS* V 71, 14.

59 For the use of *rêqu* as synonymous of *wāṣu* 'go out' regarding servants leaving their obligations in Nuzi, see B. L. Eichler, 'Nuzi Personal "DITENNUTU" Transactions' (Ph.D. diss., University of Pennsylvania, 1967), PS 25, p. 104, n. 12 and N 312, p. 44, n. 20.

60 Muffs, *Studies*, 117.

61 Cf. *CAD* E, 404ff.

62 See above, 5.1.3.1.

63 Cf. above, 5.1.3.1.

variation seems to be due to the North West Semitic usage of the formula (withdrawal from object) as attested in the Marzeaḥ papyrus.

We must keep in mind that the process of adaptation and assimilation of legal formulae by the Aramaic scribes was not mechanical. Another Aramaic modification of the Demotic withdrawal from property formula is the addition of the temporal complement 'from this day and forever',[64] found already at Ugarit.[65]

The Egyptian equivalent of this expression is attested in Abnormal Hieratic documents,[66] and in Demotic.[67] In Demotic we find it as a complement of the Investiture Clause 1 'it is yours from today onwards till eternity',[68] in the Investiture Clause 2 *bn iw rḫ rmṯ nb n p3 t3 ink mjt3j ir sḫy n-im=f bnr=k ṯ3y p3 ḥrw r ḥry*: 'No man at all including me, will be able to have authority over it except you from this day onwards'.[69] Quitclaim *mn mtw=y mt nb n p3 t3 iw.ir-n=k rn=f ṯ3y p3 ḥrw n ḥry*: 'I do not have any claim at all against you on account of it from this day onwards'[70] The only example that I have found of a Demotic withdrawal clause which includes a temporal complement is P. Louvre 7839 (Thebes 534 BCE):

> *mtw(=y) ʿr ḥr 'ẖ.t-n' p3y=k 3ḥ iw=(y) wy.ṯ i-r=f n ṯ3y 'ḥ3.t' sp 38 ibd-2 šmw r-ḥry iwty ḏd qnb.t 'nb'*
>
> I (will) depart from (lit. 'on') your land, I being far from it from year 38 2nd month of the *šmw*-season onwards, without citing any document.

In any case, the Demotic formula *r-ḥry*, although a functional equivalent, is not the exact translation of the Aramaic מן יומא זנה ועד עלם for which the closest Demotic expression is *n ṯ3y p3 ḥrw r ḥry šʿ ḏt*.

Considering the available evidence regarding the use of the withdrawal formula in the expression of withdrawal from object, we can neither conclude that the Aramaic use of the 'withdrawal from object' formula has been modelled after Demotic usage (the Marzeaḥ papyrus attests a West Semitic use of the formula similar to the Aramaic documents), nor

64 *TAD* B2.8:6; B3.4:11; B2.9:9; B5.2:8; B5.5:4; B5.5:8; a featured shared by Elephantine and Syenian scribes.

65 1. ish-tu UD-mu an-ni-i-im (...) 17. (...) a-na da-ri du-[ri]. *PRU* III (Paris 1955) Text 16.295, transliterated and translated pp. 70–71, and also in I. Mendelsohn, 'A Ugaritic Parallel to the Adoption of Ephraim and Manasseh', *IEJ* 9 (1959): 180–83.

66 *n ṯ3y p3 ḥrw r ḥry* P. Louvre E 3228c (Thebes, 685 BCE); P. Turin no. 266 = 2118 (Thebes, 634 BCE); P. Turin no. 248 = 2121 (Thebes, 617 BCE).

67 *r ḥry šʿ ḏt P. BM* 10117 (Thebes, 553–526 BCE); and *n ṯ3y p3 ḥrw r ḥry šʿ ḏt* P. Louvre E 10935 (Thebes, 553 BCE); P. Louvre E 7128 (Thebes, 511 BCE); P. Louvre E 9204 (Thebes, 502 BCE); P. Loeb 43 (Gebelein, 485 BCE). Later Demotic legal formulary sees the alternative of these two forms (*n ṯ3y p3 ḥrw r ḥry* and *n ṯ3y p3 ḥrw r ḥry šʿ ḏt*).

68 As in P. Loeb 43 (Gebelein, 485 BCE).

69 The standard Clause VI.a in the *sh n wy*. See above 6.2.1.3.2, p. 156.

70 The standard Clause V in the *sẖ n wy*. See above 6.2.1.3.2, p. 156.

that the Demotic was modelled after the Aramaic, as Muffs suggested.[71] The use of the formula in Egypt from early times,[72] antedating the use within the Marzeaḥ papyrus for more than a thousand years, and the precedence in time of the Egyptian use *vis-à-vis* the Aramaic usage by more than a hundred years[73] preclude that possibility.

In conclusion, the expression of the withdrawal formula as withdrawal from object in the Elephantine documents responds to a West Semitic use of the withdrawal formula. The absence of this formula in the Mesopotamian realm and in any other Aramaic documents outside Egypt[74] suggests that the inclusion of the formula in the Aramaic documents from Egypt responds to Egyptian influence on the Aramaic formulary.

7.2.2. *Withdrawal from Name*

The deprivation of name[75] as attested in Egyptian usage during the Middle Kingdom is a good example of the diverse application of the withdrawal formula within the Egyptian legal tradition. The fact that no other instance of withdrawal from name is documented so far outside Egypt reinforces the idea that the withdrawal clause is well at home in the Egyptian legal tradition.

7.2.3. *Withdrawal from Office*

The removal of a person from office is another case of Egyptian use of the withdrawal formula not found in Aramaic, which is not surprising considering the nature of the Aramaic documents, related not to public affairs, but to private matters. The removal/withdrawal from office is, nevertheless, attested in the Mesopotamian legal tradition, as in the following examples: 'everybody speaks of removing me from the office of mayor (*du-up-pu-ri-ia-ma ina ḫa-<za>-an-nu-tim*)',[76] 'his lordship will be removed from him (*bēlūtašu ud-da-pár*)'.[77] A similar use is attested for *nasāḫu*; 'the king will remove (*i-na-as-sà-aḫ-ma*) and install officials'.[78] These similarities between the Egyptian and the Mesopotamian legal tradition support the hypothesis that the contact between both legal

71 Muffs, *Studies*.

72 Cf. above 6.1.

73 Cf. above 6.2.

74 Cf. Lipiński, *The Aramaeans*, 557–97.

75 Cf. above, 6.1.2.

76 *ARM* 2 137.34; *CAD* D, 187, s.v. *duppuru*.

77 *RA* 17 157.11; *CAD* D, 188, s.v. *duppuru*.

78 *YOS* 10 46 ii 17 (Old Babylonian); *CAD* N, 3, s.v. *nasāḫu*. See also the passive use, 'to be removed from office', *CAD* N, 14, s.v. *nansuḫu*.

traditions took place at a very early stage of their respective development.[79]

7.2.4. *Withdrawal from Person*

The withdrawal from person, in its indicative form (*tw=y wy.k r-r=k* 'I am far from you') and causative form (*iw=y r di.t wy=f r.r=k n.im=s* 'I will cause him to be far from you regarding Object') are the most attested uses of the withdrawal clause in Egypt. As displayed in Table XIV, the withdrawal from person is attested in Egypt from the New Kingdom onwards.[80] In Aramaic, the withdrawal from person is expressed with the verb in perfect tense (רחקת מנך 'I withdrew from you')[81] or with a verbal adjective (אנחנה מנך ורחיקן 'and we are far from you').[82] Again, the Aramaic scribes added the temporal complement מן יומא זנה ועד עלם 'from this day and forever' in four of the seven cases.[83] As we mentioned above, the mutual withdrawal from person is attested in the Mesopotamian use of *duppur* in Susa. Its formulaic expression, however, is in no way similar to the Aramaic or Demotic use. In the following sections we compare the use of the withdrawal formula as: (a) Withdrawal from Person regarding Object; (b) To Cause to Release from Person Regarding Object; (c) Withdrawal from Person regarding Suit; and (d) Withdrawal from Person regarding Rights.

7.2.4.1. *Withdrawal from Person Regarding Object*

The withdrawal from person regarding object formula (*tw=y wy.k r-r=k n object* 'I am far from you regarding Object') is documented in Egypt, from the Saite and Persian Periods onwards.[84] The formula can be used also in regard to offices,[85] documents,[86] and rights.[87] The Aramaic expression of this formula,[88] as we noted above, diverges from the Demotic in its repetitive use of the preposition מן while Demotic uses the preposition *n*.[89] In Aramaic, the withdrawal is 'from the person from the object', while in Demotic, the withdrawal is 'from the person regarding the object'. The Aramaic formula is modelled after the Demotic and its

79 This was suggested by Muffs in his 'corrigenda' but his statement found no echo among scholars. Muffs, *Studies*, 205, note to p. 142.

80 See above, p. 183.

81 Cf. *TAD* B3.2:7; B2.8:5-6; B5.2:8; B5.5:4; D2.21:6.

82 Cf. *TAD* B2.2:15; B2.9:9.

83 Cf. *TAD* B2.8:5-6; B2.9:9; B5.2:8; B5.5:4.

84 Mostly in *sẖ n wy* after judgment.

85 Cf. P. Cairo 50058 (Asyut, 543 BCE).

86 Cf. P. Rylands 4 (El-Hibe, 569 BCE).

87 See below.

88 Cf. *TAD* B2.10:4; B5.5:7-8.

89 As mentioned above, the exact translation of Demotic *n* would have been עלדבר.

variation from the Demotic is to be understood in terms of 'formulaic interference' by the usual West Semitic withdrawal formula, i.e. the withdrawal from object.

7.2.4.2. *To Cause to Withdraw from Person Regarding Object*
The causative form of the withdrawal formula is found only in Demotic. Its earliest documented case is P. Berlin P. 13571 (Elephantine, 591 BCE) *ỉw=y r di.t wy.f r-r=k n-ỉm=s*. There is no similar formula either in Aramaic or in the Mesopotamian legal tradition.

7.2.4.3. *Withdrawal from Person Regarding Suit*
As we noted in our analysis of the uses of רחק in the Aramaic documents, the withdrawal from person/suit is attested in only three documents produced by the Aramaean scribes.[90] In two of them the withdrawal is from suit,[91] a formula not found in Demotic; the third[92] follows the Demotic pattern, withdrawal from person regarding suit, as in the example *wy r-r=f n md nb n* ... 'I am far from him regarding every suit.' Outside of Egypt there is no similar use of this withdrawal formula.

The adaptation by the Aramaean scribes of the Demotic formula seems to follow in this case a pattern similar to the withdrawal from person regarding object/withdrawal from object discussed above. In one case (*TAD* B2.11:11 = withdrawal from person from suit) the Aramaic formula uses the preposition מן for Demotic *n*. In two cases (*TAD* B2.2:15 and B2.8:11) the Aramaean scribe simplified the Demotic formula according to what was best known to him, as evidenced in the *Marzeaḥ* text, namely, the withdrawal from X (object, suit), instead of the withdrawal from person regarding X.

7.2.4.4. *Withdrawal from Person Regarding Rights*
The withdrawal from person regarding rights fulfils a legal function equivalent to the withdrawal from person regarding object, i.e. cession of the right of ownership of the object.[93] In this case, the mention of the object is replaced by the rights, as in the following examples: *tw=y wy.k r pꜣ hp n* object, 'I am far from the right of the black donkey';[94] *tw=y ww r-ḥr=t n pꜣ hp n pꜣ pr (...) ỉr n=t* PN *sẖ ḏbꜣ ḥḏ* 'I am far from you regarding the right of the house (...) PN made for you a *sẖ ḏbꜣ ḥḏ*';[95] *di=y wy.ṯ r-ḥr=t n*

90 Cf. *TAD* B2.11:11; B2.8:11; B2.2:15.
91 *TAD* B2.2:15 and B2.8:11.
92 *TAD* B2.11:11.
93 Cf. Nims, 'Hp, Law, Right', 251a; Seidl, *Ägyptische Rechtsgeschichte*, 2 n.1.
94 P. Loeb 43 (Gebelein, 485 BCE).
95 P. BM 10522.1 (Thebes, 297 BCE).

hp n ḥm.t 'I am far from you regarding the right of wife'.[96] This specific use of the withdrawal formula is not documented outside of the Egyptian legal tradition.

7.2.5. *To Cause to Release Land*

Although it is restricted to only one example from the Third Intermediate Period, the use of the withdrawal formula in the Ioureot stela[97] illustrates its use in Egypt from early times. Nothing similar is found in Aramaic or in the Mesopotamian legal tradition.

7.2.6. *Summary*

It is possible to affirm, based on the collected instances of the withdrawal formula in Aramaic and Egyptian, that each basic Aramaic withdrawal formula finds its counterpart in the Egyptian tradition (the withdrawal from object, the withdrawal from object regarding person, and the withdrawal from person regarding suit), the only exception being the withdrawal from suit. The Egyptian attestations always precede the Aramaic cases in time, not in a decisively long period, as Yaron pointed out,[98] but still relevant for our argument. On the other hand, not every expression of the Egyptian withdrawal formula finds its counterparts in the Aramaic formula; absent there are, withdrawal from name, withdrawal from office, and 'released fields' in the Ioureot stela. Therefore, considering that no other cases of the withdrawal formula are found in Aramaic documents outside of Egypt, it is not imprudent to conclude that the Aramaic tradition is dependent on the Egyptian legal tradition in its inclusion of the withdrawal formula in its formulary.

This dependence, however, does not imply that the Aramaean-Jewish scribes just reproduced the Egyptian formula. A complex process of assimilation/adaptation certainly took place. Such creative use of the Egyptian legal formula by the Elephantine-Syene scribes is apparent in the different variations of the withdrawal formula attested in the Aramaic documents. The most common deviation from the Demotic is the use of the preposition מן + object in the expression רחקת מנכם מן בית יזניה בר אוריה 'I withdrew from you from the house of Jezaniah son of Uriah'

96 P. Philadelphia II.1 (Thebes, 281 BCE); P. Heidelberg 754c (Gebelein, ca. 100 BCE); P. Heidelberg 762+770+774 (Gebelein, 100 BCE); P. Turin 6094 (Thebes, 114 BCE); P. Heidelberg 779a (Gebelein, 123 BCE); P. BM 10074 (Thebes, 230 BCE); see Pestman, *Marriage*, 17 ff.

97 See above, 6.1.4.

98 Yaron, 'Aramaic Deeds of Conveyance', 386.

(*TAD* B2.10:4) instead of the preposition עלדבר 'regarding', which would have rendered the Demotic *n* + object.[99]

Another variation found in the Elephantine corpus is the addition of the temporal complement מן יומא זנה ועד עלם 'from this day and forever'. The ways in which the withdrawal formula was incorporated into the Aramaic legal clause is the topic of the next section.

7.3. *Legal Clause*

The Aramaean scribes manage to incorporate the withdrawal formula in the legal clauses that build up their legal documents in different ways. The analysis of the Aramaic and Egyptian legal clauses in which withdrawal formulae are found leads to the conclusion that the Aramaic dependence on the Egyptian legal tradition is less great at the level of the legal formula than at the level of the legal clause, but the coincidences are still striking. Let us follow our previous classification of the uses of the withdrawal clause in Aramaic and then compare them with their Egyptian counterparts.

7.3.1. *Withdrawal Formula in the Initial Release Clause*

The legal function of the initial withdrawal clause is that of a release. It is expressed in Aramaic by PN + רחק + מן + Person + מן + Property: 'I withdrew from you from the X property' רחקת מנכם מן בית יזניה בר אוריה (*TAD* B2.10:4). As noted, the Aramaic withdrawal clause is a modification of the Demotic *tw=y wy.k r-r=k n* Object 'I am far from you regarding Object',[100] which also fulfils the same function in the *sẖ n wy*. The Demotic use is attested as early as the Sixth century (P. Rylands 4, El-Hibe, 569 BCE)[101] and through Ptolemaic times.[102] It is in this use that the Aramaic legal clause follows most closely the Demotic use without any point of comparison with the Mesopotamian realm.

7.3.2. *Withdrawal Formula within the Release Clause after Performance*

All of the Aramaic instances of this clause are in documents of release after judgment following a receipt or satisfaction formula: (a) 'You gave me X and I withdrew from you' (*TAD* B3.2:7); (b) 'My heart was satisfied ... and I withdrew from you' (*TAD* B2.8:5-6 and B5.2:8); (c) 'You

99 As mentioned before, the Demotic preposition *n* is an expression of the preposition *m* (*n-im*) of predication, as is demonstrated by the use of *m* + personal suffix.

100 The standard initial clause of the *sẖ n wy*. Cf. above, 6.1.3.2.

101 See above, p. 146.

102 Cf. above, 6.3.1.

satisfied our heart, our heart was satisfied, we are far from you' (*TAD* B2.9:9).[103]

For this use of the Aramaic withdrawal formula within the release clause, we find antecedents in both the Abnormal Hieratic and Demotic traditions. Let us examine first the Hieratic document P. Cairo 30657:

P. Cairo 30657 (Abnormal Hieratic, Gebelein, 547 BCE)

Date:	Year 34 of Amasis
Parties:	Petethowt son of Ienharow speaks to Reri son of Tesmonth
Satisfaction:	*dỉ=k mtj ḥꜣtj(=y) (n) nkt nb.t* You have satisfied my heart with all the things
Release:	*dỉ.t ḫꜣꜥ ỉ-r=k n.ỉm=w* I withdrew from you regarding them
Quitclaim:	Son or daughter of mine will not be able to come against you regarding them
Satisfaction:	*ḥꜣtj(=y) mtj n.ỉm=w* my heart is satisfied
Scribe:	Peteamenope son of Peteharresent

The similarities are quite apparent. P. Cairo 30657 antedates the earliest Aramaic use of this formula (*TAD* B3.2:7, 451 BCE) by 96 years displaying an exact parallel to the Aramaic usage at the level of the legal clause.

Within the Demotic tradition another parallel is found in P. Louvre 7850 (Thebes, 533 BCE):

P. Louvre 7850 (Thebes, 533 BCE)

ḫrw-bꜣk PN_1 *pꜣ mr-ḫꜣs.t m-bꜣḥ* PN_2 *pꜣy=f ḥry ỉ dỉ Pꜣ-Rꜥ k̤j pꜣy=f ꜥḥꜥ*	Declaration of PN_1, the overseer of the necropolis, in the presence of PN_2 his superior, may Pre give that his life be long:
dỉ n=y PN_3 *pꜣy ỉḥ tšr ỉw=f šp ỉ pꜣ ḥtp-ntr n Ỉmn n rn n PN4 tꜣ šb(.t) n nꜣ nkt nty ỉw=w dỉ.t s n pꜣ mr-ḫꜣs.t n pꜣ ỉmnṱ n Nỉw.t*	PN_3 gave to me this red bull, it being assigned to the God's Offering of Amon in the name of PN_4 as the replacement of the commodities which are (customarily) given to the overseer of the necropolis in the west (?) of Thebes

103 See above, 5.1.2.4.

šp(=y) p3y iḥ nty ḥry t3y(=y) s{t} r-bnr	I have received the aforementioned bull, I have taken it away[104]
ḥ3.t(=y) mtr.w n.im=f	My heart is satisfied with it
tw=y wy r.r=f n md nb n rn n p3 ḥm-ntr 4-nw n rn n p3y=f ḳs n t3 imnṯ W3s.t	I am far from him (PN_3)[105] regarding every suit in the name of the fourth god's servant in the name of his burial in the west (?) of Thebes
sẖ di-ḫnsw-iw.t s3 ḳn-ḥr	Scribe: Techonsiout son of Qenhôr
ḥ3.t-sp 38.t ibd-4 šmw	Date. Year 38 4th month of *šmw*

In both cases, the Abnormal Hieratic and the Demotic, the withdrawal clause is used in the same way as it is in the Aramaic documents. And, again, no similar use is found in legal documents outside of Egypt.

7.3.3. *Withdrawal Formula within the Transfer Clause*

The use of a withdrawal formula within the transfer clause is found in Aramaic in the expressions: (a) 'I gave it to you and withdrew from it' (*TAD* B2.7:7 and 16); (b) 'We sold and gave it to you and withdrew from it' (*TAD* B3.4:10-11 and 13); and (c) 'I gave it to you/You gave it to me, and I withdrew from you' (*TAD* B5.5:4 and 7–8).

In the case of (a) and (b), there are no exact parallels in Demotic legal documents where the withdrawal is usually from the person and not from the object conveyed. Regarding (c), there are close examples in Demotic as we have illustrated with the release letter P. Louvre 7850 (Thebes, 533 BCE) cited in the previous section,[106] where a transfer clause is found in the context of a release (a similar case as the mutual quitclaim *TAD* B5.5), and in the typical formula of donation documents as P. Cairo 50058 (543 BCE),[107] where the first withdrawal formula is also associated with the transfer clause.

104 This phrase is problematic. For discussion see Donker van Heel, 'Abnormal Hieratic', 22 n. V.

105 S. Vleeming considered that the =*f* in the formula *tw=y wy r-r=f* referred to the bull and, therefore, affirmed that 'In *P. Louvre* E. 7850, the thing concerned shifts to the place of the person concerned, and is accordingly, construed with *r* "from."' *Pap. Hou*, 130 and see also n. 10 there. The =*f*, however, refers to the person who gave the bull to Peteamon and not to the bull itself.

106 See above, p. 195.

107 See above, p. 149.

P. Cairo 50058 (Donation, Asyut 543 BCE)[108]

I. Date: Year 28, month Paophi, Pharaoh Amais
II. Parties: Oupwethope speaks to Espame
III. Transference
  A. Transfer: I gave you (priestly and scribal offices)
  B. Investiture: they are yours
  C. Withdrawal: I am far from you regarding the priestly offices etc.
IV. Investiture II: it is yours all what is written above as your part of the revenues that belonged to our father
V. Quitclaim
  A. Covenant of Non-claim: I do not have any claim at all
VI. General Warranty
  A. Defension: the one who shall come in my name or in the name of our father regarding it, I will cause him to be far from you
VII. Withdrawal of Espametcheps: you are far from me regarding the priestly offices . . . concerning which you have written for me a withdrawal (*sẖ n=y r-r=w n wy)*
VIII. Scribe: Kanofre son of Horkhebi

7.3.4. *Withdrawal Formula within the Waiver of Suit Clause*

The use of the withdrawal formula within the waiver of suit clause is found in two forms within the Aramaic documents. The first is expressed in the withdrawal from suit or from persons regarding suit, a particularity of the Syene-Aramaean scribes: (a) 'You are far from any suit that they shall complain' (*TAD* B2.2:15); (b) 'I am far from any suit or process' (*TAD* B2.8:11); (c) 'We are far from you and from your children from any suit' (*TAD* B2.11:11). For this Aramaic use of the withdrawal formula within the waiver of suit clause, there is an exact parallel in Demotic: P. Louvre 7850.[109]

The second use of the withdrawal formula within the waiver of suit clause is expressed in the withdrawal from object or from person regarding object as in the following examples: (d) 'And he is likewise far from these goods' (*TAD* B2.9:15); (e) '[And withdrew] from you and from [your] c[hildren . . .] ' (*TAD* D2.21:6).

108 Cf. the related documents P. BM 10792 (Asyut, 522 BCE) and P. Cairo 50059 (Asyut, 522 BCE), A. F. Shore, 'Swapping Property at Asyut in the Persian Period,' in J. Baines *et al.*, eds., *Pyramid Studies and Other Essays presented to I. E. S. Edwards* (London: Egypt Exploration Society, 1988), 201–03; and E. Jelínková-Reymond, 'Gestion des rentes d'Office', *CdE* 28.56 (1953): 228–37.

109 Cf. above, p. 195.

In this case, there is a close parallel in the use of the withdrawal formula by the scribe of P. Louvre 2433:

> *pꜣ šr tꜣ šr.t mtw=y nty iw=f r ij r.ḥr=t r.ḏbꜣ.ṯ̂=w iw=f tj.t n=t Penalty ꜥn iw=f wy.ṯ̂ r.ḥr=t n.im=w ꜥn*
>
> Moreover, the son (or daughter) of mine, who will come against you because of this, he shall give you Penalty, and moreover he will be far from you regarding this.
>
> (P. Louvre 2433 [Thebes, 252 BCE])[110]

After comparing the four uses of the withdrawal formula within legal clauses in Aramaic with the Demotic use, the result is that we have a Demotic parallel for every generic legal clause in Aramaic: (1) withdrawal formula in the initial release clause; (2) withdrawal formula within the release clause after performance; (3.a–c) withdrawal formula within the transfer clause; (4.a–d) withdrawal formula within the waiver of suit clause). Some of the particular expressions, however, seem to be unparalleled in the available Demotic documents (3.a and b; 4.a, b, and d).

110 See also: P. Hawara 13.11 (P. Hamburg dem. 7) 99 BCE. Penalty *iw=y ww.w r.r=k n.im=w* 'Penalty (Moreover) I am far from you regarding them.'

8

Reconsidering the Origins of Aramaic and Demotic Legal Formulae

Ancient Near Eastern historians are very aware that every synthesis, every conclusion that we reach in our field is based on a meagre amount of data when compared with the sources a modern historian has at his disposal when studying more recent periods of human history. A new family archive or even a few cuneiform tablets or hieroglyphic inscriptions can sometimes radically challenge our historical reconstructions. The study of the origins and transmission of Ancient Near Eastern legal formulae is, therefore, an ongoing scholarly attempt to understand processes for which we have many more questions than answers. A giant puzzle with more lost pieces than those available to us. Although our Egyptological approach to the two legal formulae treated in this monograph, the שליט and withdrawal clauses, has uncovered new possibilities for the study of ancient Near Eastern legal formulae, new findings could challenge the conclusions of our study.

Based on the evidence presented in Chapter 6, the *wy*-based withdrawal formulae can be understood as originating either in the transfer of property where the alienor removes himself far from the object, renouncing any right to it, or in the claims process, where the defeated party in the suit recognizes the rights of the other party to the property. The legal meaning of the metaphor, which represents quittance by physical movement and distance, is the loss or renunciation of rights.

The comparison of the legal terms, based on the metaphor of physical withdrawal, the legal formulae which employed those terms, and the legal clauses in which withdrawal formula were used, can provide firm ground for further elaboration of the origin of the Aramaic and Demotic legal formulae.

As we stated in our methodological discussion,[1] the degree of interaction between two legal or formulaic traditions is directly related to the level in which the coincidences are found. Coincidences in the legal clauses (level 4) amount to a greater degree of interaction than coincidences at the level of the legal concept or legal term (levels 1 and 2).

1 See above, 2.3.3.

The similarities and coincidences between the Aramaic and Demotic legal traditions found at all three levels of legal terms, namely, legal formulae, legal clauses, and legal formulary indicate a very high degree of interaction between them. The interaction between either the Aramaic or the Demotic legal traditions and the Mesopotamian legal tradition is well attested at the level of legal terms, but is less convincing at the level of legal formulae and legal clauses, and minimal at the level of the legal formulary.

The lack of coincidences at the higher levels of complexity (legal formula, legal clause, and legal formulary) between the Aramaic and the Mesopotamian legal traditions is a strong argument against the affirmation that it was the Aramaic scribes who brought the use of the withdrawal clause to Egypt from Mesopotamia.[2] This theory was adopted by Muffs in his first 'edition' (before the 'corrigenda') and followed by Fales, Levine, Gropp, and Cussini.[3] It is based mainly on the absence of evidence of any use of the withdrawal formula before the Assyrian conquest of Egypt and a lack of differentiation between the proper levels of analysis. This study has provided ample evidence of several uses of withdrawal formulae in Egypt before the seventh century BCE and challenged such conclusions. Aramaic can not any longer be considered the only bridge between the Mesopotamian and the Egyptian legal traditions.

It is possible that early contacts between Egypt, Canaan, and Mesopotamia account for the similarities. However, the case to prove Mesopotamian influence should be looked for much earlier than the sixth century BCE, and Aramaic, as we stated, should be discarded as the only channel by which Mesopotamia would have influenced the Egyptian legal formulae. As Y. Muffs stated,

> West-Semitic legal loan-words are found in Egypt before the Saitic period. (…) [Early New Kingdom a. 1200 BCE]. This information forces us to revise our ideas concerning the process by which Western cuneiform legal elements were transmitted to Egypt: it was much earlier than previously assumed, and not necessarily through an Aramaic medium alone. Further study of the problem is in order.[4]

Muffs didn't consider the possibility that many of the legal terms used in the Aramaic papyri could be traced back to native Egyptian legal

2 As already stated by Seidl, *Ägyptische Rechtsgeschichte*, 87.

3 See Fales, 'La tradition assyrienne', E. Cussini, 'Aramaic Law of Sale'; Levine, 'On the Origins', 46; D. M. Gropp, 'The Wadi Daliyeh Documents Compared to the Elephantine Documents', in L. H. Schiffman, E. Tov, and J. C. Vanderkam, eds., *The Dead Sea Scrolls, Fifty Years after their Discovery: Major Issues and New Approaches, Jerusalem 20–25 July 1997* (Jerusalem: Israel Exploration Society, 2000), 826–35.

4 Y. Muffs, 'Addenda et Corrigenda', in *Studies*, 205, corrigenda to n. 1, p. 142.

terminology. As Seidl suggested, the Aramaic papyri would exhibit neither a complete assimilation of Egyptian law and formulary, nor a fully independent development, but a middle way between these extremes.[5] Seidl also denied the possibility that Near Eastern legal practices could have come to Egypt through the Aramaic documents and even suggested a possible Egyptian influence on the Aramaic formulary before the Aramaic papyri were produced in Egypt.[6]

Our study on the *šallīṭ* clause has demonstrated that the Egyptian legal tradition influenced the Mesopotamian use of legal formulae through the Aramaic legal tradition. In his prologue to the new edition of Y. Muffs's work, B. Levine pointed out that the origins of Aramaic legal terms should be traced to:

> 1. Terms and formulae that most likely entered Aramaic from Akkadian in the Neo-Assyrian period; [883–609 BCE] (...) 2. Terms and formulae that entered Elephantine Aramaic from Akkadian in the Neo-Babylonian period [625–539 BCE]; (...) and 3. Terms and formulae native to West Semitic/Aramaic and not taken from Akkadian.[7]

We have provided enough evidence to add a fourth possibility: native Egyptian legal terms being incorporated by Aramaean scribes and native Egyptian legal terms being exported to Mesopotamia. Recent studies have pointed to a considerable amount of Egyptian cultural influence in Mesopotamia.[8] Assyriologists dealing with the Aramaic legal formulae have always ignored that possibility. Also, the Egyptian influence on the West Semitic legal realm – which might have had an impact on the Aramaic legal tradition – was never seriously taken into consideration.

This is not the place to produce a survey of the Egyptian influence on Syro-Palestinian scribes, but the amount of Egyptian influence on biblical wisdom literature should suffice to prove the strong impact that the Egyptian civilization had on the literary production of the region.[9] Egyptian political and cultural influence on Syro-Palestine can be discerned since the first and second Egyptian dynasties (ca. 3150–2700

5 Seidl, *Ägyptische Rechtsgeschichte*, 86.

6 Seidl, *Ägyptische Rechtsgeschichte*, 87.

7 B. Levine, 'Prolegomenon', to Muffs, *Studies*, xxxviii–xxxix.

8 See the evidence for early Egyptian influence on Mesopotamia presented by O. Kaelin, *Modell Aegypten. Adoption von Innovationen im Mesopotamien des 3. Jahrtausends v. Chr.* (Fribourg: Academic Press Fribourg, 2006); also L. D. Morenz, *Herrscherpräsentation und Kulturkontakte, Ägypten, Levante, Mesopotamien: Acht Fallstudien* (Münster: Ugarit-Verlag, 2003); and O. Kaelin, *Ein assyrisches Bildexperiment nach ägyptischem Vorbild: Zu Planung und Ausführung der 'Schlacht am Ulai'* (Münster: Ugarit-Verlag, 1999).

9 See for example the extensive study by N. Shupak, *Where Can Wisdom be Found? The Sage's Language in the Bible and in Ancient Egyptian Literature* (Fribourg: University Press; Göttingen: Vandenhoeck & Ruprecht, 1993), who concludes that Hebrew was influenced by Egyptian and not *vice versa*. *Where Can Wisdom be Found?*, 348.

BCE)[10] and through Hellenistic times. The zenith of Egyptian domination was reached during the 18th and 19th Dynasties (ca. 1552–1188 BCE), but Egyptian cultural influence did not vanish after that period. In her study of the relationships between Egyptian and Israelite wisdom literature, N. Shupak concluded that the most plausible historical background for their contact was the Solomonic period.[11] As Higginbotham states, 'local Palestinian princes emulated Egyptian culture because Egypt was the core civilization in whose periphery those princes defined themselves'.[12]

A balanced appraisal of the degree of interaction between the Mesopotamian and the Egyptian legal traditions requires a similar study dedicated to the rest of the legal formulae found in the Egyptian and Mesopotamian legal documents. Based on the study of the withdrawal clause and on our previous study of the *šallīṭ* clause, we can advance the following hypothesis.

Legal terms and metaphors emerged in the ancient Near East at a very early stage, even prior to the invention of writing. In a similar way, as we have a common stock of Afro-Asiatic vocabulary, we postulate a common stock of Afro-Asiatic legal concepts, legal metaphors, and legal terms. The metaphor of withdrawal by physical distance would be one of these common legal terms. Its attestation in Mesopotamia and Egypt from the third millennium and onwards is witness to this fact. The metaphors of satisfaction and cleaning could also fit in this category of common terms.

However, in the same way that the various regions developed in different ways regarding language, art, etc., their legal traditions began to define their own ways of expression. Legal formulae began to emerge, and later became widely established, or became obsolete and were replaced by new formulae conveying a similar meaning.[13] The Egyptian scribes began to use different expressions of the withdrawal formula from the very beginning of Egyptian legal history; it found its place in inscriptions

10 See W. Helck, *Die Bezienhungen Ägyptens zu Vorderasien im 3. und 2. Jahrtausend v. Chr.* (Wiesbaden: Harrassowitz, 1971), 4–37; M. Wright, 'Contacts between Egypt and Syro-Palestine during the Protodynastic Period', *BA* 48 (1985): 240–53; D. B. Redford, 'Egypt and Western Asia in the Old Kingdom', *JARCE* 23 (1986): 125–32; idem, *Egypt, Canaan, and Israel in Ancient Times* (Princeton: Princeton University Press, 1992), 29–55; and D. Warburton, *Egypt and the Near East: Politics in the Bronze Age* (Paris: Recherches et Publications, 2001).

11 Shupak, *Where Can Wisdom be Found?* 353. See also R. J. Williams, 'A People Come out of Egypt', *Supplements to VT* 28 (1975): 231–52, who demonstrates how several aspects of the Israelite monarchy display a strong Egyptian influence. But see N. S. Fox, *In the Service of the King: Officialdom in Ancient Israel and Judah* (Cincinnati: Hebrew Union College Press, 2000), who challenges this view.

12 C. R. Higginbotham, *Egyptianization and Elite Emulation in Ramesside Palestine: Governance and Accommodation on the Imperial Periphery* (Leiden: Brill, 2000), 141.

13 Political and economic factors also account for such development.

reflecting legal transactions and literary texts, and later in legal documents from the Demotic and Abnormal Hieratic formulaic traditions.

The Jewish/Aramaic scribes arrived in Egypt with a solid background of legal terminology and legal formulae. They certainly had knowledge of some expressions of the withdrawal formula (especially the withdrawal from object formula as attested in the *Marzeaḥ* papyrus)[14] and their own formulary tradition. But the need to produce legal documents that would be valid within the Egyptian context compelled them to modify/adapt their own formulae/formulary to the Egyptian tradition. The legislation recorded in the Demotic Chronicle serves as evidence for translation of Demotic formulae into Aramaic.[15] In this way the Aramaic tradition benefited from the richness of the Egyptian legal tradition and its legal terminology.

14 See above, 5.1.3.1.

15 *Die Sogenannte demotische Chronik des Pap. 215 der Bibliothèque Nationale zu Paris*, ed. W. Spiegelberg (Leipzig: Hinrichs, 1914), 215, vo. 3/6–16. S. Lippert also suggested that previous Egyptian codes were written in Demotic and translated into Aramaic under Darius I. Lippert, *Ein demotisches juristiches Lehrbuch*, 177. See also Ritner's Postcript in 'Third Intermediate Period Antecedents', 358.

WORKS CITED

Aḥituv, S., 'A Divine Verdict – A Judicial Papyrus of the Seventh Century BCE', *Eretz-Israel* 26 (1999), pp. 1–4.

Aimé-Giron, N., *Textes araméens d'Égypte* (Cairo: Institut Français d'Archéologie Orientale, 1931).

Aistleitner, J., *Wörterbuch der Ugaritischen Sprache* (ed. Otto Eissfeldt; Berlin: Akademie-Verlag, 1965).

Albertz, R., *Persönliche Frömmigkeit und offizielle Religion: Religionsinterner Pluralismus in Israel und Babylon* (Stuttgart: Calwer, 1978).

—*A History of Israelite Religion in the Old Testament Period* (trans. John Bowden; Louisville: Westminster John Knox Press, 1994).

Alexander, A. and McCay, B., 'The Concept of Adaptation in Biological and Cultural Evolution'. in John J. Honigmann (ed.), *Handbook of Social and Cultural Anthropology* (Chicago: Rand McNally, 1973), pp. 143–78.

Allam, S., *Hieratische Ostraka und Papyri aus der Ramessidenzeit* (Tübingen: Allam, 1973).

—'La problématique des quarante rouleaux de lois', in *Studien zu Sprache und Religion Aegyptens* (Festschrift W. Westendorf; Göttingen: F. Junge, 1984).

—'Bemerkungen zur Abstandschrift', *Enchoria* 13 (1985), pp. 1–5.

—'Egyptian Law Courts in Ptolemaic and Hellenistic Times', *Journal of Egyptian Archaeology* 77 (1991), pp. 109–27.

—'Legal Aspects in the "Contendings" of Horus and Seth', in A. B. Lloyd (ed.), *Studies in Pharaonic Religion and Society in Honour of J. Gwyn Griffiths* (London: Egypt Exploration Society, 1992), pp. 137–45.

—'The Agreement after Judgment', *Egitto e Vicino Oriente* 17 (1994), pp. 19–28.

Amin, S. H., *Middle East Legal Systems* (Glasgow: Royston, 1985).

Andrews, C., *Catalogue of Demotic Papyri in the British Museum, vol. 4: Ptolemaic Legal Texts from the Theban Area* (London: British Museum Press, 1990).

Arangio-Ruiz, V., 'La codification dans l'Égypte ancienne', *Journal of Juristic Papyrology* 11–12 (1957–58), pp. 25–46.

Ash, P. S., *David, Solomon and Egypt: A Reassessment* (Sheffield: Sheffield Academic Press, 1999).

Austin, M. M., *Greece and Egypt in the Archaic Age* (Cambridge: Cambridge Philosophical Society, 1970).

Avishur, Y. and M. Heltzer, 'The Scribe and Priest Ezra: A Leader under Achaemenian Rule', *Transeuphratène* 29 (2005), pp. 17–36.

Ayad, B. A., *The Jewish Aramean Civilization* (Colorado: Greely, 1982).

Bakir, A. M., *Slavery in Pharaonic Egypt* (Cairo: Institut Français d'Archéologie Orientale, 1952).

Barth, F. (ed.), 'Introduction', in *Ethnic Groups and Boundaries: The Social Organization of Culture Differences* (London: Allen & Unwin, 1969).

Benoit, P., *et al.*, *Les grottes de Murabba'at* (Oxford: Clarendon Press, 1961).

Black, H. C., *et al.*, *Black's Law Dictionary* (St Paul, Minn.: West Publishing Co., 1990).

Blau, L., 'Zur demotischen und griechischen Papyrusurkunde', in *Judaica, Festschrift zu H. Cohens Siebzigsten Geburstage* (Berlin: B. Cassirer, 1912).

Bolla, S. v., 'Zur Rechtskontinuität der Volksrechte in Ägypten', *Journal of Juristic Papyrology* 7–8 (1953–54), pp. 149–56.

Bontty, M., 'Conflict Management in Ancient Egypt: Law as a Social Phenomenon' (Unpublished Ph.D. dissertation, University of California, Los Angeles, 1997).

Bordreuil, P. and D. Pardee, 'Le Papyrus du marzeaḥ', *Semitica* 38, Hommages à Maurice Sznycer (2 vols.; 1990), pp. 1.49–69, pls. VII–X.

—'Nouvelle examen du "Papyrus du Marzeaḥ"', *Semitica* 50 (2001), pp. 224–25.

Botta, A. F., 'Matrimonio y Divorcio en los Papiros Arameos de Elefantina', *Revista de Estudios de Egiptología* 4 (1993), 113–33.

—'Las Cartas Arameas de Hermópolis y el Formulario Epistolar del Cercano Oriente antiguo', *Revista de Estudios de Egiptología* 6–7 (1996–99), pp. 57–80.

—'רחק in the Bible, a Reevaluation', *Biblica* 87 (2006), pp. 418–20.

—'Scribal Traditions and the Transmission of Legal Formulae in the Aramaic Papyri from Elephantine', *Revista del Institute de Historia Antigna Oriental* n.s. 1 (2006), pp. 153–68.

—'The Legal Function and Egyptian Background of the שליט Clause: A Reevaluation', *Maarav* 13.2 (2006), 193–209.

—'A Reevaluation of the use of זבן and יהב in Elephantine', *Antiguo Oriente 6* (2008), 99–108.

Bovati, P., *Re-Establishing Justice: Legal Terms, Concepts and Procedures*

in the Hebrew Bible (trans. Michael J. Smith; Sheffield: JSOT Press, 1994).
Braun, T. F. R. G., 'The Greeks in Egypt', in J. Boardman and N. G. L. Hammond (eds.), *The Cambridge Ancient History* (Cambridge: Cambridge University Press, 1982).
Breasted, J. H., *Ancient Records of Egypt* (5 vols.; Chicago: University of Chicago Press, 1906).
Bresciani, E., 'Frammenti de un "prontuario legale" demotico da Tebtuni nell'Instituto Papirologico "G. Vitelli" di Firenze', *Egitto e Vicino Oriente* 4 (1981), pp. 201–15.
—'Egypt, Persian Satrapy', in W. D. Davies and L. Finkelstein (eds.), *Cambridge History of Judaism, vol. 1: Introduction; The Persian Period* (Cambridge: Cambridge University Press, 1984), pp. 358–72.
Bresciani, E. and M. Kamil, *Le lettere aramaiche de Hermopoli* (Rome: Accademia nazionale dei Lincei, 1966).
Browning, I., *Palmyra* (Park Ridge, N. J.: Noyes Press, 1979).
Broze, M., *Les Aventures d'Horus et Seth dans le papyrus Chester Beatty I* (Leuven: Peeters, 1996).
Brunner, H., 'Menes als Schöpfer', *Zeitschrift der Deutschen Morgenländischen Gesellschaft* 103 (1953), pp. 22–26.
Buhl, F., 'Remarques sur les papyrus juifs d'Elephantine', *Oversigt over det Kongelige Danske Videnskabernes Selskabs* 2 (1908), pp. 37–64.
Burdick, W. L., *Principles of Roman Law and their Relation to Modern Law* (Rochester, NY: Lawyers Cooperative, 1938).
Burton, A., *Diodorus Siculus Book I, A Commentary* (Leiden: Brill, 1972).
Byrne, R., 'The Refuge of Scribalism in Iron Age I Palestine', *Bulletin of the American Schools of Oriental Research* 345 (2007), pp. 1–31.
Caminos, R., *Late Egyptian Miscellanies* (London: Oxford University Press, 1954).
—*A Tale of Woe from a Hieratic Papyrus in the A. S. Pushkin Museum of Fine Arts* (Oxford: Griffith Institute, 1977).
Campagno, M., *La contienda entre Horus y Seth* (Buenos Aires: Del Signo, 2004).
Cardellini, I., *Die biblischen 'Sklaven'-Gesetze im Lichte des keilschriften Sklaven rechts: Ein Beitrag zur Tradition, Überlieferung und Redaktion der alttestamentlichen Rechtstexte* (Bonn: Peter Hanstein, 1981).
Cassin, E., 'Symboles de Cession Immobilière dans l'ancient Droit Mésopotamien', *L'Année Sociologique 3rd series* (1952–55), pp. 107–61.
Cenival, F. de., 'Nouvelles sources démotiques concernant le recensement et la taxe sur le sel à l'époque Ptolémaïque', in E. Van't Dack, P. Van Dessel and W. Van Gucht (eds.), *Egypt and the Hellenistic World:*

Proceedings of the International Colloquium, Leuven, 24–26 May 1982 (Louvain: Lovanii, 1983), pp. 31–41.

Černý, J., 'The Will of Naunakhte and the Related Documents', *Journal of Egyptian Archaeology* 31 (1945), pp. 29–53.

Chauveau, M., 'P. Carlsberg 301: Le manuel juridique de Tebtunis', in P. J. Frandsen (ed.), *The Carlsberg Papyri I: Demotic Texts from the Collection* (Copenhagen: Carsten Niebuhr Institute of Ancient Near Eastern Studies, University of Copenhagen, 1991), pp. 103–29.

Clarysse, W., 'Ethnic Diversity and Dialect among the Greeks of Hellenistic Egypt', in A. M. F. W. Verhoogt and S. P. Vleeming (eds.), *The Two Faces of Graeco-Roman Egypt: Greek and Demotic and Greek-Demotic Texts and Studies resented to P. W. Pestman* (Leiden: Brill, 1998), pp. 1–14.

Cotton, H. M. and A. Yardeni, *Aramaic, Hebrew and Greek Documentary Texts from Nahal Hever and Other Sites* (Oxford: Clarendon Press, 1997).

Couroyer, B., 'Termes egyptiens dans les papyri araméen du Musée de Brooklyn', *Revue Biblique* 61 (1954), pp. 554–59.

Cowley, A. E., 'Some Egyptian Aramaic Documents', *Proceedings of the Society of Biblical Archaeology* 25 (1903), pp. 202–08.

—*Aramaic Papyri of the Fifth Century B.C.* (Oxford: Clarendon Press, 1923).

Cross, F. M., 'Samaria Papyrus I: An Aramaic Slave Conveyance of 335 BCE found in Wadi ed Daliyeh', *Eretz-Israel* 18 (1985), pp. 7–17.

—'A Papyrus Recording a Divine Legal Decision and the Root rḥq in Biblical and Near Eastern Legal Use', in M. V. Fox, V. A. Hurowitz, and A. Hurvitz (eds.), *Texts, Temples and Traditions: A Tribute to Menahem Haran* (Winona Lake, Ind.: Eisenbrauns, 1996), pp. 311–20.

Crum, W., *Coptic Dictionary* (Oxford: Clarendon Press, 1939).

Cruz-Uribe, E., *Saite and Persian Demotic Cattle Documents: A Study in Legal Forms and Principles in Ancient Egypt* (Chico, Calif.: Scholars Press, 1985).

—'A Saite Request for payment', *Journal of Egyptian Archaeology* 71 (1985), pp. 29–133.

Currid, J. D., *Ancient Egypt and the Old Testament* (Grand Rapids, Mich.: Baker Books, 1997).

Cussini, E., 'The Aramaic Law of Sale and the Cuneiform Legal Tradition' (Unpublished Ph.D. dissertation, Johns Hopkins University, Baltimore, 1993).

—'Transfer of Property at Palmyra', *Aram* 7 (1995), pp. 233–50.

Dandamaev, M., 'The Neo-Babylonian Citizens', *Klio* 63 (1981), pp. 45–49.

—'The Composition of the Citizens in First Millenium Babylonia', *Altorientalische Forschungen* 24 (1997), 135–47.

David, A., *Syntactic and Lexico-Semantic Aspects of the Legal Register in Ramesside Decrees,* Göttinger Orientforschungen IV. Reihe Ägypten 38 (Wiesbaden: Harrassowitz, 2006).

De Buck, A., *The Egyptian Coffin Texts* (Chicago: University of Chicago Press, 1935–61).

Den Brinker, A. A., B. P. Muhs, and S. P. Vleeming, *A Berichtigungsliste of Demotic Documents* (Leuven; Dudley, Mass.: Peeters, 2005).

Depauw, M., *A Companion to Demotic Studies* (Brussels: Fondation egyptologique Reine Elisabeth, 1997).

Depuydt, L., 'Egyptian Regional Dating under Cambyses and the Date of the Persian Conquest', in P. Der Manuelian (ed.), *Studies in Honor of William Kelly Simpson* (Boston: Dept. of Ancient Egyptian, Nubian, and Near Eastern Art, Museum of Fine Arts, 1990), pp. 179–90.

Devauchelle, D., 'Un problème de chronologie sous Cambyse', *Transeuphratène* 15 (1998), pp. 9–17.

Dion, P., *Les Araméens à l'âge du fer: histoire politique et structures sociales* (Paris: J. Gabalda, 1997).

Donbaz, V. and S. Parpola, *Neo-Assyrian Legal Texts in Istanbul* (Saarbrücken: In Kommission bei DSV Saarbrücker Druckerei und Verlag, 2001).

Donker van Heel, K., *The Legal Manual of Hermopolis [P. Mattha]* (Leiden: Papyrologisch Institut, 1990).

—'A Small Note on Early Demotic Texts and Archives', *Journal of Egyptian Archaeology* 78 (1992), p. 287.

—'The Lost Battle of Peteamonip son of Petehorresne', in *Acta Demotica* (1994), pp. 115–124.

—'Abnormal Hieratic and Early Demotic Texts collected by the Theban Choachytes in the Reign of Amasis, Papyri from the Louvre Eisenlohr Lot' (Unpublished Ph.D. dissertation, Rijksuniversiteit, Leiden, 1996).

Drijvers, H. J. W., 'Greek and Aramaic in Palmyrene Inscriptions', in M. J. Geller, J. C. Greenfield, and M. P. Weitzman, eds., *Studio Aramaica* (Oxford: Oxford University Press, 1995), pp. 31–42.

Driver, G. R., *Aramaic Documents of the Fifth Century B.C.* (Oxford: Clarendon Press, 1954).

Dušek, J., *Les manuscrits araméens du Wadi Daliyeh et la Samarie vers 450–332 av. J.-C.* (Leiden: Brill, 2007).

Earle, T. K. and J. E. Ericson (eds.), *Contexts for Prehistoric Exchange* (New York: Academic Press, 1982).

Ebeling, E., *Keilschrifttexte aus Assur juristischen Inhalts* (Leipzig: Wissenschaftliche Veröffentlichung der Deutschen Orient-Gesellschaft, 1927).

—*Urkunden des Archivs von Assur aus mittelassyrischer Zeit* (Leipzig: Harrassowitz, 1933).

Edgerton, W., 'Demotica Papyri und Altertumswissenschaft', *Münchener Beiträge zur Papyrusforschung und antiken Rechtsgeschichte* 19 (1934), pp. 280–301.

Edwards, I. E. S., 'Kenhikhopshef's Prophylactic Charm', *Journal of Egyptian Archaeology* 54 (1968), pp. 155–60.

Edzard, D. O., *Sumerische Rechtsurkunden des III Jahrtausends aus der Zeit vor der III Dynastie von Ur*. Abhandlungender Philosophisch-historischen Klasse der Bayerischen Akademie der Wissenschaften 67 (Munich: Verlag der Bayerischen Akademie der Wissenschaften, 1968).

El Aguizy, O., 'A Ptolemaic Judicial Document from ḤWT-NZW', *Bulletin de l'Institut Français d'Archéologie Orientale* 88 (1988), pp. 54–63.

El-Amir, M., *A Family Archive From Thebes: Papyri in the Philadelphia and Cairo Museums from the Ptolemaic Period* (Cairo: Antiquities Department of Egypt, 1959).

Eph'al, I., 'The Western Minorities in Babylon in the 6th–5th Centuries BC: Maintenance and Cohesion', *Orientalia* 47 (1978), pp. 74–90.

Erichsen, E., 'Zwei früdemotische Urkunden aus Elephantine', in *Coptic Studies in Honor of Walter Ewing Crum* (Boston: Byzantine Institute of America, 1950).

Erichsen, W., *Demotisches Glossar* (Copenhagen: E. Munksgaard, 1954).

Euting, J., 'Notice sur un papyrus égypto-araméen', *Memoires présentés par Divers Savants à l'Académie des Inscriptions et Belles Lettres* (1903), pp. 297–311.

Fales, M. F., 'La tradition assyrienne à Élephantine d'Égypte: nouvelles donnés et perspectives', *Transeuphratène* 9 (1995), pp. 119–30.

Farid, A., 'An unpublished Early Demotic Family Archive', in K. Ryholt, ed., *Acts of the Seventh International Conference of Demotic Studies. Copenhagen, 23–27 August 1999* (Copenhagen: Museum Tusculanum Press, 2002), pp. 185–205.

Faulkner, R. O., *The Papyrus Bremner-Rhind* (Brussels: Fondation égyptologique Reine Élisabeth, 1933).

—'The Bremner-Rhind Papyrus IV', *Journal of Egyptian Archaeology* 24 (1938), pp. 41–53.

—*A Concise Dictionary of Middle Egyptian* (Oxford: Oxford University Press, 1962).

—*The Ancient Egyptian Coffin Texts* (Warminster: Aris & Phillips, 1973–78).

Fitzmyer, J. A., 'The Syntax of Imperial Aramaic based on the Documents found in Egypt' (Unpublished Ph.D. dissertation, Johns Hopkins University, Baltimore, 1956).

—'A Re-study of an Elephantine Aramaic Marriage Contract (AP 15)', in H. Goedicke (ed.), *Near Eastern Studies in Honor of William Foxwell Albright* (Baltimore: Johns Hopkins University Press, 1971), pp. 137–68.

Folmer, M., *The Aramaic Language in the Achaemenid Period: A Study in Linguistic Variation* (Leuven: Peeters, 1995).

Frankfort, H., *The Birth of Civilization in the Near East* (New York: Doubleday, 1956).

Frantz-Murphy, G., 'A Comparison of the Arabic and Earlier Egyptian Contract Formularies, part II: Terminology in the Arabic Warranty and the Idiom of Clearing/Cleaning', *Journal of Near Eastern Studies* 44 (1985), pp. 99–114.

—'A Comparison of the Arabic and Earlier Egyptian Contract Formularies, part III: The Idiom of Satisfaction', *Journal of Near Eastern Studies* 47 (1988), pp. 105–12.

Freund, L., 'Bemerkungen zu Papyrus G des Fundes von Assuan', Wiener Zeitschrift für die Kunde des Morganlandes 21 (1907), pp. 169–77.

Friedmann, A. H., 'Economic Geography and Administration at Nuzi' (Unpublished Ph.D. dissertation, Hebrew Union College – Jewish Institute of Religion, Ohio, 982).

Gagarin, M., *Early Greek Law* (Berkeley: University of California Press, 1989).

Gagos, T. and P. van Minnen, *Settling a Dispute: Toward a Legal Anthropology of Late Antique Egypt* (Ann Arbor: University of Michigan Press, 1994).

Gardiner, A. H., 'A Late-Egyptian Idiom', *Zeitschrift für Ägyptische Sprache und Altertumskunde* 47 (1910), pp. 134–36.

—*The Chester Beatty Gift,* Hieratic Papyri in the British Museum, 3rd Series (London: British Museum, 1935).

—*Late-Egyptian Miscellanies* (Brussels: Fondation égyptologique Reine Élisabeth, 1937).

—'The Gods of Thebes as Guarantors of Personal Property', *Journal of Egyptian Archaeology* 48 (1962), pp. 57–69.

Garis Davies, N. de., *The Tomb of Rekh-mi-Re at Thebes* (New York: Metropolitan Museum of Art, 1943).

Garner, B. A., *A Dictionary of Modern Legal Use* (Oxford: Oxford University Press, 1995).

Gelb, I. J., 'Definition and Discussion of Slavery and Serfdom', *Ugarit – Forschungen* 11 (1980), pp. 283–98.

Gelb, I. J., P. Steinkeller, *et al.*, *Earliest Land Tenure Systems in the Near East: Ancient Kudurrus* (Chicago: Oriental Institute of the University of Chicago, 1991).

Geller, M. J., 'Elephantine Papyri and Hosea 2, 3', *Journal for the Study of*

Judaism in the Persian, Hellenistic and Roman Period 8 (1977), pp. 139–48.

—'New Sources for the Origin of the Rabbinic Ketubah', *Hebrew Union College Annual* 49 (1978), pp. 227–45.

Genin-Meric, R., *La maxime 'locus regit actum,' nature et fondement* (Paris: Librairie générale de droit et de jurisprudence, 1976).

Ginsberg, H. L., 'Aramaic Dialect Problems', *American Journal of Semitic Languages* 50 (1933), pp. 1–9.

—'Aramaic Dialect Problems', *American Journal of Semitic Languages* 52 (1936), pp. 90–101.

Gödecken, K. B., *Eine Betrachtung der Inschtriften des Meten im Rahmen der sozialen und rechtliche Stellung von Privatleuten im ägyptischen Alten Reich* (Wiesbaden: Harrassowitz, 1976).

Goedicke, H., 'Juridical Expressions of the Old Kingdom', *Journal of Near Eastern Studies* 15 (1956), pp. 27–32.

—*Die privaten Rechtsinschriften aus dem Alten Reich* (Vienna: Verlag Norting, 1970).

—'Bilateral Business in the Old Kingdom', *Discussions in Egyptology* 5 (1986), pp. 74–78.

—'The expression *ini r isw*', *Discussions in Egyptology* 6 (1986), pp. 67–78.

Goldstein, J. A., 'The Syriac Bill of Sale from Dura-Europos', *Journal of Near Eastern Studies* 25 (1966), pp. 1–16.

Golésnicheff, W., *Papyrus Hierátiques* (Cairo: Institut Français d'Archéologie Orientale, 1927).

Goodman, M. D., *State and Society in Roman Galilee, A.D. 132–212* (Totawa, N. J.: Rowman & Allanheld, 1983).

—'Texts, Scribes and Power in Roman Judaea', in A. K. Bowman and G. Woolf (eds.), *Literacy and Power in the Ancient World* (Cambridge: Cambridge University Press, 1994), pp. 99–108.

Görg, M., *Die Beziehungen zwischen dem alten Israel und Ägypten. Von den Anfängen bis zum Exil* (Darmstadt: Wissenschaftliche Buchgesellschaft, 1997).

Goudriaan, K., *Ethnicity in Ptolemaic Egypt* (Amsterdam: J. C. Gieben, 1988).

Graham, A. J., 'The Colonial Expansion of Greece', in J. Boardman and N. G. L. Hammond (eds.), *The Cambridge Ancient History,* part III (Cambridge: Cambridge University Press, 1982), pp. 83–162.

—'The Western Greeks', in J. Boardman and N. G. L. Hammond (eds.), *The Cambridge Ancient History,* part III (Cambridge: Cambridge University Press, 1982), pp. 163–95.

Green, M., 'A Means of Discouraging Perjury', *Göttinger Miszellen* 39 (1980), pp. 33–40.

Greenberg, M., *Ezekiel 1–20: A New Translation with Introduction and Commentary* (Garden City, NY: Doubleday, 1983).

Greenfield, J. C., 'Studies in the Terminology of the Nabatean Funerary Inscriptions (Hebrew)', in E. Y. Kutscher, S. Lieberman, and M. Z. Kaddari (eds.), *Henoch Yalon Memorial Volume* (Ramat Gan: Bar Ilan University, 1974), pp. 79–82.

—'Studies in the Aramaic Legal Papyri from Elephantine', *Israel Exploration Journal* 26 (1976), pp. 214–15.

—'The Dialects of Early Aramaic', *Journal of Near Eastern Studies* 37 (1978), pp. 93–99.

—'The Genesis Apocryphon: Observations on Some Words and Phrases', in G. B. Sarfatti, P. Artzl, J. C. Greenfield, and M. Kaddari (eds.), *Studies in Hebrew and Semitic Languages Dedicated to the Memory of Prof. Eduard Yechezkel Kutscher* (Ramat Gan: Bar Ilan University, 1980), pp. 32–39.

—'The Aramaic Legal Texts of the Achaemenian Period', *Transeuphratène* 3 (1990), pp. 85–92.

—'The "Defension Clause" in some Documents from NaḫalḤever and Naḫal Se'elim', *Revue de Qumran* 15 (1991–92), pp. 467–71.

Greengus, S., 'The Aramaic Marriage Contracts in the Light of the Ancient Near East and Later Jewish Materials' (MA thesis, University of Chicago, 1959).

—'Some Issues relating to the Comparability of Laws and the Coherence of the Legal Tradition', in B. M. Levinson (ed.), *Theory and Method in Biblical and Cuneiform Law. Revision, Interpolation and Development* (Sheffield: Sheffield Academic Press, 1994), pp. 60–87.

Grelot, P., *Documents araméens d'Égypte* (Paris: Éditions du Cerf, 1972).

Griffith, F. L., *Catalogue of the Demotic Papyri in the John Rylands Library Manchester Vols 1–3* (Manchester: Manchester University Press, 1909).

Grimal, N. *A History of Ancient Egypt* (Oxford; Cambridge, Mass.: Blackwell, 1992).

Gropp, D. M., 'The Samaria Papyri from Wadi ed-Daliyeh. The Slave Sales', (Unpublished Ph.D. dissertation, Harvard University, Cambridge, Mass., 1986).

—'The Origin and Development of the *šallîṭ* Clause', *Journal of Near Eastern Studies* 52 (1993), pp. 31–36.

—'The Wadi Daliyeh Documents Compared to the Elephantine Documents', in L. H. Schiffman, E. Tov, and J. C. VanderKam (eds.), *The Dead Sea Scrolls, Fifty Years after their Discovery: Major Issues and New Approaches, Jerusalem 20–25 July 1997* (Jerusalem: Israel Exploration Society, 2000), pp. 826–35.

—*Wadi Daliyeh II: The Samaria Papyri from Wadi Daliyeh,* DJD 28; and Qumran Miscellanea, Part 2 (D. M. Gropp, J. VanderKam, and M. Brady (eds.); Oxford: Clarendon Press, 2001).

Gross, A. D., *Continuity and Innovation in the Aramaic Legal Tradition,*

Supplements to the Journal for the Study of Judaism, 128 (Leiden: Brill, 2008).

Grunert, S., *Der Kodex Hermopolis und ausgewählte private Rechtsurkunden aus dem ptolemäischen Ägypten* (Leipzig: Reclam, 1982).

Gulliver, P. H., 'Dispute Settlement Without Courts: The Ndendeuli of Southern Tanzania', in L. Nader (ed.), *Law in Culture and Society* (Chicago: Aldine, 1969), pp. 24–68

Gunn, B., ' "The Word" ', *Zeitschrift für Ägyptische Sprache und Altertumskunde* 62 (1927), p. 85.

—'The Decree of Amonrasonther for Neskhons', *Journal of Egyptian Archaeology* 41 (1955), pp. 85–91.

Hall, H. R. *Ancient History of the Near East from the Earliest Times to the Battle of Salamis* (New York: Methuen, 1913).

Hall, J. M., *Ethnic Identity in Greek Antiquity* (Cambridge: Cambridge University Press, 1997).

Hallo, W. W., 'New Viewpoints on Cuneiform Literature', *Israel Exploration Journal* 12 (1962), pp. 13–26.

—'Biblical History in its Near Eastern Setting: The Contextual Approach', in C. D. Evans, W. W. Hallo, and J. B. White (eds.), *Scripture in Context I: Essays in the Comparative Method* (Pittsburgh, Penn.: Pickwick, 1980), pp. 1–26.

Halpern, B., 'The Centralization Formula in Deuteronomy', *Vetus Testamentum* 31 (1981), pp. 20–38.

Hammel, E. A., 'The Comparative Method in Anthropological Perspective', *Comparative Studies in Society and History* 22 (1980), pp. 145–55.

Harrison, A. R. W., *The Law of Athens* (Oxford: Clarendon Press, 1971).

Hartnung, U., 'Zur Entwicklung des Handels und zum Beginn wirtschaftlicher Administration im prädynastischen Ägypten', *Studien zur altägyptischen Kultur* 26 (1998), pp. 35–50.

Hayes, W. C., *A Papyrus of the Late Middle Kingdom in the Brooklyn Museum (Papyrus Brooklyn 35.1446)* (Brooklyn, NY: Brooklyn Museum, 1955).

Helck, W., *Die Beziehungen Ägyptens zu Vorderasien im 3. un 2. Jahrtausend v. Chr.* (Wiesbaden: Harrassowitz, 1971).

—*Historisch-biographische Texte der 2. Zwischenzeit und neue Texte der 18. Dynastie* (Wiesbaden: Harrassowitz, 1983).

Held, M., 'The Action-Result (Factitive-Passive) Sequence of Identical Verbs in Biblical Hebrew and Ugaritic', *Journal of Biblical Literature* 84 (1965), pp. 272–82. Hezser, C., *Jewish Slavery in Antiquity* (Oxford: Oxford University Press, 2005).

Higginbotham, C. R. *Egyptianization and Elite Emulation in Ramesside*

Palestine: Governance and Accommodation on the Imperial Periphery (Leiden: Brill, 2000).

Hillers, D. R. and E. Cussini, *Palmyrene Aramaic Texts* (Baltimore: Johns Hopkins University Press, 1995).

Hoch, J., *Semitic Words in Egyptian Texts of the New Kingdom and Third Intermediate Period* (Princeton: Princeton University Press, 1994).

Hoffmeier, J. K., *Israel in Egypt: The Evidence for the Authenticity of the Exodus Tradition* (Oxford: Oxford University Press, 1997).

Holladay, W. L., *Jeremiah 2: A Commentary on the Book of the Prophet Jeremiah, Chapters 26–52* (Minneapolis: Augsburg Fortress, 1989).

Hughes, G. H. and C. F. Nims, 'Some Observations on the British Museum Demotic Theban Archive', *American Journal of Semitic Languages* 57 (1940), p. 255.

Isajiw, W. W., 'Definitions of ethnicity', *Ethnicity* 1 (1974), pp. 2–16.

Ishikida, M. Y., 'The Structure and Function of Dispute Management in the Public Administration of Larsa under Hammurapi', *Orient* 23 (1998), pp. 66–78.

Jackson, B. S., *Essays in Jewish and Comparative Legal History* (Leiden: Brill, 1975).

Jamieson-Drake, D. W., *Scribes and Schools in Monarchic Judah: A Socio-Archaeological Approach* (Sheffield: Almond Press, 1991).

Jasnow, R. 'Old Kingdom and First Intermediate Period', in R. Westbrook (ed.), *A History of Ancient Near Eastern Law*, Handbuch der Orientalistik 72 (Leiden and Boston: Brill, 2003), pp. 93–140.

—'Middle Kingdom and Second Intermediate Period', in R. Westbrook (ed.), *A History of Ancient Near Eastern Law*, Handbuch der Orientalistik 72 (Leiden and Boston: Brill, 2003), pp. 255–88.

—'New Kingdom', in R. Westbrook, (ed.), *A History of Ancient Near Eastern Law,* Handbuch der Orientalistik 72 (Leiden and Boston: Brill, 2003), pp. 289–359.

—'Third Intermediate Period', in R. Westbrook (ed.), *A History of Ancient Near Eastern Law*, Handbuch der Orientalistik 72 (Leiden and Boston: Brill, 2003), pp. 777–818.

Jelínková-Reymond, E., 'Gestion des rentes d'Office', *Chronique d'Égypte* 28 (1953), pp. 228–37.

Jenni, E., *Die hebräischen Präpositionen, vol. 1: Die Präposition Beth* (Stuttgart, Berlin, and Cologne: W. Kohlhammer, 1992).

Johns, C. H. W. and A. S. G. Johns, *Assyrian deeds and documents recording the transfer of property, including the so-called private contracts, legal decisions and proclamations preserved in the Kouyunjik collections of the British museum, chiefly of the 7th century B.C., copied, collated, arranged, abstracted, annotated and indexed by the late Rev. C. H. W. Johns* (Cambridge: Deighton Bell & Co, 1898).

Johnson, J. H., 'The Demotic Chronicle as an Historical Source', *Enchoria* 4 (1974), pp. 1–17.

—'The Demotic Chronicle as a Statement of a "Theory of Kinship" ', *Journal of the Society for the Study of Egyptian Antiquities* 13 (1983), pp. 61–72.

—'Is the Demotic Chronicle an Anti-Greek Tract', in *Grammata Demotika. Festschrift für Erich Lüddeckens zum 15. Juni 1983* (Würzburg: Gisela Zauzich Verlag, 1984).

—'The Persians and Continuity of Egyptian Culture', in H. Sancisi-Weerdenburg, A. Kuhrt, and M. Cool Root (eds.), *Continuity and Change* (Leiden: Brill, 1994).

—' "Annuity Contracts" and Marriage', in D. P. Silverman (ed.), *For His Ka: Essays Offered in Memory of Klaus Baer* (Chicago: Oriental Institute of the University of Chicago, 1994).

—'The Legal Status of Women in Ancient Egypt', in A. K. Capel and G. E. Markoe (eds.), *Mistress of the House, Mistress of Heaven: Women in Ancient Egypt* (New York: Hudson Hills Press, 1997), pp. 175–86.

Jones, S., *The Archaeology of Ethnicity: Constructing Identities in the Past and Present* (London and New York: Routledge, 1997).

Joüon, P., 'Notes grammaticales, lexicographiques et philologiques sur les papyrus araméens d'Égypte', *Mélanges de l'Université Saint Joseph* 18 (1934), pp. 1–89.

Kaelin, O., *Ein assyrisches Bildexperiment nach ägyptischem Vorbild: Zu Planung und Ausführung der* 'Schlacht am Ulai' (Münster: Ugarit-Verlag, 1999).

—*'Modell Ägypten': Adoption von Innovationen im Mesopotamien des 3. Jahrtausends v. Chr.* (Fribourg: Academic Press; Göttingen: Vandenhoeck & Ruprecht, 2006).

Kaplony, P., 'Eid', in *Lexicon der Ägyptologie*, pp. 1188–1200.

Kaplony-Heckel, U., *Die Demotischen Gebelen-Urkunden der Heidelberger Papyrus-Sammlung Heidelberg* (Heidelberg: Carl Winter, 1964).

Kaser, M., *Das romische Privatrecht*, 2nd rev. edn., (Munich: Beck, 1971–75).

Kasher, A., *Jews in Hellenistic and Roman Egypt: The Struggle for Equal Rights* (Tübingen: J. C. B. Mohr, 1985).

Kataja, L. and R. M. Whiting, *Grants, Decrees and Gifts of the Neo-Assyrian Period* (Helsinki: Helsinki University Press, 1995).

Kaufman, S. A., *The Akkadian Influences on Aramaic* (Chicago: University of Chicago Press, 1974).

Kemp, B. J., 'Old Kingdom, Middle Kingdom and Second Intermediate Period c. 2686–1552', in B. G. Trigger, B. J. Kemp, D. O'Connor, and A. B. Lloyd (eds.), *Ancient Egypt: A Social History* (Cambridge: Cambridge University Press, 1983), pp. 71–182.

Kennett, A., *Bedouin Justice: Laws and Customs among the Egyptian Bedouin* (Cambridge: Cambridge University Press, 1925).
Kienast, B., *Das altassyrische Kaufvertragsrecht* (Wiesbaden: Harrassowitz, 1984).
Kienitz, F. K., *Die politische Geschichte Ägyptens vom 7. bis zum 4. Jahrhundert vor der Zeitwende* (Berlin: Akademie-Verlag, 1953).
King, P. J., 'The Marzeah: The Textual and Archaeological Evidence', *Eretz Israel* 20 (1989), pp. 98–106.
Kitchen, K. A., *The Third Intermediate Period in Egypt (1100–650 BC)* (Warminster: Aris & Phillips, 1995).
Koehler, L. and W. Baumgarten, *Hebräisches und Aramäisches Lexicon zum Alten Testament* (Leiden: Brill, 1995).
Koschaker, P., *Babylonisch-assyrisches Bürgschafsrecht: Beitrag zur Lehre von Schuld und Haftung* (Leipzig: B. G. Teubner, 1911).
—'Neue Keilschriftliche Rechtsurkunden aus der el-Amarna Zeit', in *Abhandlungen der Philologisch-Historischen Klasse der sächsischen Akademie der Wissenschaften* XXXIX, V (Leipzig: S. Hirzel, 1928).
—'Eheschließung und Kauf nach alten Rechten, mit besonderer Berücksichtigung der älteren Keilschriftrechte', *Archiv Orientální* 18 (1950), pp. 210–96.
Kottsieper, I., *Die Sprache der Ahiqarsprüche* (Berlin: De Gruyter, 1990).
Kraeling, E. G. H., *The Brooklyn Museum Aramaic Papyri: New Documents of the Fifth Century B.C. from the Jewish Colony at Elephantine* (New Haven: Yale University Press, 1953).
Kruchten, J. M., *Le décret d'Horemheb. Traduction et commentaire épigraphique, philologique et institutionnel* (Brussels: Editions de l'Université de Bruxelles, 1981).
Krückmann, O., *Babylonische Rechts- und Verwaltungsurkunden aus der Zeit Alexanders und der Diadochen* (Weimar: Hof-Buchdruckerei, 1931).
Kutscher, E. Y., 'New Aramaic texts', *Journal of the American Oriental Society* 74 (1954), pp. 233–48.
—'Aramaic', in T. Seebok (ed.), *Current Trends in Linguistics, vol. 4: Linguistics in South West Asia and North Africa* (The Hague: Mouton, 1970), pp. 347–412.
Kwasman, T. S., *Neo-Assyrian Legal Documents in the Kouyunjik Collection of the British Museum* (Rome: Pontificio Istituto Biblico, 1988).
Kwasman, T., S. Parpola, *et al.*, *Legal Transactions of the Royal Court of Nineveh* (Helsinki: Helsinki University Press, 1991).
Landsberger, B., 'Scribal Concepts of Education', in C. H. Kraeling and R. M. Adams (eds.), *City Invincible: A Symposium on Urbanization and Cultural Development in the Ancient Near East held at the Oriental*

Institute of the University of Chicago, December 4–7, 1958 (Chicago: University of Chicago Press, 1960), pp. 94–123.
Leach, E. R., 'The Comparative Method in Anthropology', in D. L. Sillis (ed.), *International Encyclopedia of the Social Sciences* (New York: Macmillan, 1968), pp. 339–45.
Leclant, J., 'Les Phéniciens et l'Egypte', in *Atti del II Congresso internazionale di studi fenici e punici: Roma, 9–14 novembre 1987* (Rome: Consiglio nazionale delle ricerche, Istituto per la Civiltà Fenicia e Punica, 1991), pp. 7–17.
Leemans, W. F., 'The Importance of Trade', *Iraq* (1977), pp. 1–10.
Legrin, G., *Statues et statuettes des rois et de particuliers*, vol. 3 (CGC) (Cairo: Institut Français d'Archéologie Orientale, 1914).
Lemaire, A., 'Les Formules de Datation en Palestine au premier Millénaire avant J.-C.', in F. Beiquel-Chatonet and H. Lozachmeur (eds.), *Proche-Orient ancien: temps vécu, temps pensé: actes de la table-ronde du 15 novembre 1997 organisée par l'URA 1062* (Paris: Jean Maisonneuve, 1998), pp. 53–82.
Lemaire, A. and H. Lozachmeur, 'Remarques sur le Plurilinguism en Asia Mineur à L'Époque Perse', *in Antiquités Semitiques I. Mosaïques de langues, mosaïque culturelle. Le bilinguisme dans le Proche Orient ancien. Actes de la table ronde du 18 novembre 1995 organisée par l'URA 1062, 'Etudes Sémitiques'*, F. Briquel-Chatonnet (ed.) (Paris: Adrien Maisonneuve, 1996), pp. 91–123.
Levine, B. A., 'On the Origins of the Aramaic Legal Formulary at Elephantine', in *Christianity, Judaism and Other Greco-Roman Cults* (Leiden: Brill, 1975).
Levinson, B. M., *Deuteronomy and the Hermeneutics of Legal Innovation* (Oxford: Oxford University Press, 1997).
Levinson, J. H., 'The Nabatean Aramaic Inscriptions' (Unpublished Ph. D. dissertation, New York University, New York City, New York, 1974).
Lichtheim, M., *Ancient Egyptian Literature*, vol. 1: *The Old and Middle Kingdom* (Berkeley: University of California Press, 1973).
Lidzbarski, M., *Ephemeris für semitische Epigraphik* (Giessen: J. Ricker, 1908–15).
Limet, H., 'Traditions juridiques en contact dans le Proche-Orient achéménide', *Transeuphratène* 12 (1996), pp. 163–79.
Lipiński, E., 'Aramaic Clay Tablets from the Gozan-Harran Area', *Jaarbericht van het vooraziatisch-egyptisch genootschap Ex Oriente Lux* 33 (1993–94), pp. 144–47.
—*The Aramaeans: Their Ancient History, Culture, Religion* (Leuven: Peeters, 2000).
Lippert, S. L., *Ein demotisches juristisches Lehrbuch. Untersuchungen zu Papyrus Berlin P 23757 rto* (Wiesbaden: Harrassowitz, 2004).

Lloyd, A. B., 'The Late Period', in B. G. Trigger, B. J. Kemp, D. O'Connor, and A. B. Lloyd, *Ancient Egypt: A Social History* (Cambridge, London, New York, New Rochelle, Melbourne, Sydney: Cambridge University Press, 1983), 279–348.

Logan, T., 'The *Jmyt-pr* Document: Form, Function, and Significance', *Journal of the American Research Centre in Egypt* 37 (2000): pp. 49–73.

Lorton, D., 'The Treatments of Criminals in Ancient Egypt', *Journal of the Economic and Social History of the Orient* 20 (1977), pp. 53–64.

Lovejoy, A. O. and G. Boas, *Primitivism and Related Ideas in Antiquity* (Baltimore: Johns Hopkins University Press, 1935).

Lozachmeur, L. A. a. H., 'Remarques sur le Plurilinguisme en Asia Mineur à L'Époque Perse', in *Antiquités Sémitiques I. Mosaïque de Langues, Mosaïque Culturelle. Le Bilinguisme dans le proche-Orient Ancien* (Paris: J. Maisonneuve, 1996), pp. 91–123.

Lüddeckens, E., *Ägyptische Eheverträge* (Wiesbaden: Harrassowitz, 1960).

—'Demotische und koptische Urkundenformeln', *Enchoria* 2 (1974), pp. 21–32.

—*Demotische Urkunde aus Hawara* (Stuttgart: F. Steiner, 1998).

Lurje, M., *Studien zum altägyptischen Recht (des 16. Bis 10. Jh. V.u.Z)*, Forschungen zum Romischen Recht 30 (Weimar: Hermann Bohlaus Nachfolger, 1971).

Maezawa, N. 'Slave Societies in the Greco-Roman Antiquity', in T. Yuge and M. Doir (eds.), *Forms of Control and Subordination in Antiquity* (Leiden: Brill, 1988), pp. 16–18.

Maidman, M., 'A Socio-Economic Analysis of a Nuzi Family Archive' (Unpublished Ph.D. dissertation, University of Pennsylvania, Philadelphia, Penn., 1976).

Malinine, M., 'Notes juridiques (propos de l'ouvrage de E Seidl)', *Bulletin de l'Institut Français d'Archéologie Orientale* 46 (1947), pp. 93–123.

—'Un jugement rendu à Thèbes sous la XXVe Dynastie (Pap Louvre E3228c)', *Revue d'Égyptologie* 6 (1951), pp. 157–78.

—*Choix de textes juridiques en Hieratique Anormal et en Demotique: Première Partie* (Paris: Librairie Ancienne Honore Champion, 1953).

—'Deux documents Egyptiens relatifs au dépôt (P Louvre E 7861 et P. Caire 30657)', *Mitteilungen des Deutschen Archäologischen Instituts Abteilung Kairo* 16 (1958), pp. 225–29.

—'Ventes de Tombes à L'Epoque Saïte', *Revue d'Égyptologie* 27 (1975), pp. 164–68.

Malinine, M. and J. Pirenne, 'Documents Juridiques Egyptiens', *Revue Internationale des Droits de l'Antiquite*, Third Series, 5 (1937), pp. 11–91.

Malul, M., *Studies in Mesopotamian Legal Symbolism* (Kevelaer: Butzon & Bercker; Neukirchen-Vluyn: Neukirchener, 1988).

—*The Comparative Method in Ancient Near Eastern and Biblical Legal Studies* (Kevelaer: Butzon & Bercker; Neukirchen-Vluyn: Neukirchener, 1990).

Mann, A. M., 'The Jewish Marriage Contracts from Elephantine: A Study of Text and Marriage' (Unpublished Ph.D. dissertation, New York University, New York City, New York, 1985).

Manning, J. 'Demotic Law', in R. Westbrook (ed.), *A History of Ancient Near Eastern Law* Handbuch der Orientalistik 72 (Leiden and Boston: Brill, 2003), pp. 819–62.

Márquez Rowe, I. *The Royal Deeds of Ugarit: A Study of Ancient Near Eastern Diplomatics* (Münster: Ugarit-Verlag, 2006).

Martin, A., 'Der Rechtskodex von Hermupolis (P. Kairo JE 89.127-30 +89.137-43)', in *Dokumente zur Rechts- und Wirtschaftsgeschichte. Texte aus der Umwelt des Alten Testaments*, new edn. (Gütersloh: Verlag Mohn, 2004), pp. 196–218.

Martin, C. J., 'Marriages, Wills and Leases of Land', in M. J. Geller *et al.*, eds., *Legal Documents of the Hellenistic World* (London: Warburg Institute, 1995).

Mathieson, L., 'A Stela of the Persian Period from Saqqara', *Journal of Egyptian Archaeology* 81 (1995), pp. 23–41.

Mattha, G. and G. R. Hughes, *The Demotic Legal Code of Hermopolis West* (Cairo: Institut Français d'Archéologie Orientale, 1975).

McDowell, A. G., *Jurisdiction in the Workmen's Community of Deir el-Medina* (Leiden: Nederlands Instituut voor het Nabije Oosten, 1990).

Meissner, B., *Beiträge zum altbabylonischen Privatsrecht* (Leipzig: J. C. Hinrichs, 1893).

Mélèze-Modrzejewsky, J., 'Law and Justice in Ptolemaic Egypt', in M. J. Geller and H. Maehler (eds.), *Legal Documents of the Hellenistic World* (London: Warburg Institute, University of London, 1995).

—'Jewish Law and Hellenistic Legal Practice in Egypt', in N. S. Hecht, B. S. Jackson, S. M. Passamaneck, D. Piatelli, and A. M. Rabello (eds.), *An Introduction to the History and Sources of Jewish Law* (Oxford: Oxford University Press, 1996), pp. 75–100.

Menu, B., 'Vente d'une vache de labour sous Ptolémée VIII Evergète II', *Cahiers de Recherches de l'Institute de Papyrologie et d'Égyptologie de Lille* 6 (1981), pp. 229–42.

—'Cession de Services et Engagements pour dette sous les Rois Kouchites et Saïtes', *Revue d'Égyptologie* 36 (1985), pp. 73–87.

—'Ventes de maisons sous L'Ancien Empire Egyptien', in *Melanges offerts à Jean Vercoutter* (Paris: Editions Recherche sur les Civilisations, 1985), pp. 249–62.

—'Les Actes de Vente en Égypte Ancienne, particulièrerment sous les Rois Kouchites et Saïtes', *Journal of Egyptian Archaeology* 74 (1988), pp. 165–81.

—'La stèle dite de L'Apanage', in M. M. Mactoux and E. Geny (eds.), *Mélanges Pierre Lévêque* (Paris: Les Belles Lettres, 1989), pp. 338–57.
—'Women and Business Life in the First Millennium B.C.', in *Women's Earliest Records from Ancient Egypt and Western Asia*, ed. B. Lesko (Atlanta, Ga.: Scholars Press, 1989).
—'Le serment dans les actes juridiques de L'Ancienne Égypte', in R. Verdier (ed.), *Le serment I, Signes et Fonction* (Paris: Editions du Centre National de la recherche scientifique, 1991), pp. 329–44.
—'Un Document Juridique "Kouchite" Le PVienne D 12002', *Bibliothèque d'Études* 106 (1993), pp. 293–304.
Mettinger, T. N. D., *Solomonic State Officials: A Study of the Civil Government Officials of the Israelite Monarchy* (Lund: Gleerup, 1971).
Meyer, P. M., *Juristische Papyri: Erklärung von Urkunden zur Einführung in die juristische Papyruskunde* (Berlin: Weidmann, 1920).
Mitteis, L. and U. Wilcken, *Grundzuge und Chrestomathie der Papyrusurkunde* (Leipzig and Berlin: B. G. Teubner, 1912).
Morenz, L. D., *Herrscherpräsentation und Kulturkontakte, Ägypten, Levante, Mesopotamien: Acht Fallstudien* (Münster: Ugarit-Verlag, 2003).
Morenz, S., 'Traditionen um Menes', *Zeitschrift für ägyptische Sprache und Altertumskunde* 99 (1972), pp. 10–16.
Mrsich, T., *Untersuchungen zur Hausurkunde des Alten Reiches*, Münchner Ägyptologische Studien 13 (Berlin: B. Hessling, 1968).
Muffs, Y., *Studies in the Aramaic Legal Papyri from Elephantine* (Leiden: Brill, 1969).
Muraoka, T. and B. Porten, *A Grammar of Egyptian Aramaic* (Leiden: Brill, 1998).
Na'aman, N., 'Population Changes in Palestine following Assyrian Deportations', *Tel Aviv* 20 (1993), pp. 104–12.
Nader, L. and H. F. J. Todd (eds.), *The Disputing Process: Law in Ten Societies* (New York: Columbia University Press, 1978).
Naveh, J., *The Development of the Aramaic Script* (Jerusalem: Israel Academy of Sciences and Humanities, 1970).
—'The Aramaic Ostraca', in Y. Aharoni (ed.) *Beer-Sheba I: Excavations at Tel Beer-Sheba 1969–1971* (Tel Aviv: Tel Aviv University, Institute of Archaeology, 1973), pp. 79–82.
Negri-Scafa, P., 'Scribes locaux et scribes itinérants dans le royaume d'Arrapxa', in D. Charpin and F. Joannès (eds.), *La circulation des biens, des personnes et des idées dans le Proche-Orient ancien. Actes de la XXXVIIIe Rencontre Assyriologique Internationale (Paris, 8–10 juillet 1991)* (Paris: Editions Recherches sur les Civilisations, 1992), pp. 235–40.

Niemeyer, H. G., 'Expansion et colonisation', in V. Krings (ed.), *La Civilisation Phénicienne et Punique* (Leiden: Brill, 1995).

Nims, C., 'Notes on University of Michigan Demotic Papyri from Philadelphia', *Journal of Egyptian Archaeology* 24 (1938), pp. 73–82.

—'Hp "Law, Right," in Demotic', *Journal of Near Eastern Studies* 7 (1948), pp. 243–60.

Nutkowicz, H., 'Note sur une institution juridique à Eléphantine, 'dh, «la cour»', *Transeuphratène* 27 (2004), 181–85.

—'Concerning the Verb śnʾ in Judaeo-Aramaic Contracts from Elephantine', *Journal of Semitic Studies* 52 (2007), 211–25.

Oded, B., *Mass Deportations and Deportees in the Neo-Assyrian Empire* (Wiesbaden: Reichert, 1979).

Oelsner, J., B. Wells, and C. Wunsch, 'Neo-Babylonian Period', in R. Westbrook (ed.), *A History of Ancient Near Eastern Law*, Handbuch der Orientalistik 72 (Leiden and Boston: Brill, 2003), pp. 911–74.

Oldfather, C. H., *Diodorus of Sicily I* (New York: G. P. Putnam's Sons, 1933).

Olmo Lete, G. del and J. Sanmartín, *Diccionario de la lengua ugarítica* (Sabadell: AUNSA, 1996–2000).

Oppenheim, L., 'Der Eid in den Rechtsurkunden aus Susa', *Wiener Zeitschrift für die Kunde des Morgenlandes* 43 (1936), pp. 242–62.

Osing, J., *Die Nominalbildung des Ägyptischen,* Sonderschriften des Deutschen Archäologischen Instituts Kairo 3 (Mainz: Philipp von Zabern, 1976).

Otto, E., *Die biographischen Inschriften der ägyptische Spätzeit* (Leiden: Brill, 1954).

Paradise, J. S., 'Nuzi Inheritance Practices' (Ph.D. dissertation, University of Pennsylvania, 1972).

Parker, R. A., 'Some Considerations on the Nature of the Fifth-Century Jewish Calendar at Elephantine', *Journal of Near Eastern Studies* 14 (1955), pp. 271–74.

—*A Saite Oracle Papyrus from Thebes in the Brooklyn Museum [Papyrus Brooklyn 47.218.3],* Brown Egyptological Studies 4 (Providence, R. I.: Brown University Press, 1962).

—'A Demotic Settlement from Deir el Ballas (MFA 38.2063b)', *Journal of the American Research Center in Egypt* 3 (1964), pp. 113–16.

Partsch, K. J., 'Die Rechtliche Bedeutung der Vertrage', in W. Spiegelberg (ed.), *Die demotischen Papyri Hauswaldt* (Leipzig: Hinrichs, 1913), pp. 11–24.

Pedersén, O., *Archives and Libraries in the City of Assur: A Survey of the Material from the German Excavations* (Uppsala: Uppsala University; Stockholm: Almqvist & Wiksell, 1985–86)

Peet, T. E., *The Great Tomb Robberies of the Twentieth Egyptian Dynasty* (Oxford: Clarendon Press, 1930).

Peiser, F. E., 'Review of *Die jüdisch-aramäischen Papyri von Assuan sprachlich und sachlich erklärt* by W. Staerk (Bonn, 1907)', *Orientalische Literaturzeitung* 10 (1907), pp. 622–27.

Pestman, P. W., *Marriage and Matrimonial Property in Ancient Egypt* (Leiden: Brill, 1961).

—'The Law of Succession in Ancient Egypt', in M. D. J. Brugman, F. R. Kraus, P. W. Pestman, and M. H. Van der Valk (eds.), *Essays on Oriental Laws of Succession,* Studia et Documenta ad Iura Orientis Antiqui Pertinentia 9 (Leiden: Brill, 1969), pp. 58–77.

—'Een juridisch "Hanboek" uit het oude Egypte in twe talen', *Phoenix* 25 (1979), pp. 25–31.

—*L'Archivio di Amenothes, figlio di Horos (P. Tor. Amenothes: testi demotici e greci relativi ad una famiglia di imbalsamatori del secondo sec. a.C.* (Milan: Istituto Editoriale Cisalpino-La Goliardica, 1981).

—'Le manuel de droit d'Hermoupolis. Les passages transmits en démotique et en grec', in *Textes et études de papyrologie grecque, démotique et copte* (Leiden: Brill, 1985), pp. 116–43.

—'Inheriting in the Archive of the Theban Choachytes (2nd cent. B.C.)', in S. P. Vleeming (ed.), *Aspects of Demotic Lexicography* (Leuven: Peeters, 1987), pp. 57–73.

Pestman, P. W., J. Quaegebeur, *et al.*, *Recueil des textes démotiques et bilingues* (Leiden: Brill, 1977).

Pestman, P. W. and S. P. Vleeming, *Les papyrus démotiques de Tsenhor (P. Tsehnor): les archives privées d'une femme égyptienne du temps de Darius 1er* (Leuven: Peeters, 1994).

Petschow, H., *Die neubabylonischen Kaufformulare* (Leipzig: T. Weicher, 1939).

Pierce, R. H., *Three Demotic Papyri in the Brooklyn Museum* (Oslo: Universitetsforlaget, 1972).

Pirenne, J. and B. Van de Walle, 'Documents Juridiques Égyptiens', *Archives d'Histoire du droit oriental* 1 (1937), pp. 11–91.

Porten, B., *Archives from Elephantine: The Life of an Ancient Jewish Military Colony* (Berkeley: University of California Press, 1968).

—'Structure and Chiasm in Aramaic Contracts and Letters', in *Chiasmus in Antiquity* (Hildesheim: Gerstenberg, 1981), pp. 169–82.

—'An Aramaic Oath Contract: A New Interpretation (Cowley 45)', *Revue Biblique* 90 (1983), pp. 563–75.

—'The Jews in Egypt', in W. D. Davies and L. Finkelstein (eds.), *Cambridge History of Judaism*, vol. 1: *Introduction; The Persian Period* (Cambridge: Cambridge University Press, 1984), pp. 372–400.

—'Cowley 7 Reconsidered', *Orientalia* 56 (1987), pp. 89–92.

—'Fragmentary Aramaic Deeds of Obligation and Conveyance: New Collations and Restorations', *Journal of Near Eastern Studies* 48 (1989), pp. 161–83.

—'The Calendar of the Aramaic Texts from Achaemenid and Ptolemaic Egypt', *Irano-Judaica* 2, S. Shaked and A. Netzer, eds. (1990), pp. 13–32.

—'Aramaic-Demotic Equivalents: Who is the Borrower and Who the Lender', in J. H. Johnson (ed.), *Life in a Multi-Cultural Society: Egypt from Cambyses to Constantine and Beyond* (Chicago: Oriental Institute of the University of Chicago, 1992), pp. 259–64.

—*The Elephantine Papyri in English: Three Millennia of Cross-Cultural Continuity and Change* (Leiden: Brill, 1996).

—'Egyptian Aramaic Texts', in E. M. Meyers (ed.), *The Oxford Encyclopedia of Archaeology in the Near East* (Oxford: Oxford University Press, 1997), pp. 393–410.

—'Egyptian Names in Aramaic Texts', in K. Ryholt ed., *Acts of the Seventh International Conference of Demotic Studies. Copenhagen, 23–27 August 1999* (Copenhagen: Carsten Niebuhr Institute of Near Eastern Studies, Museum Tusculanum Press, 2002), 283–328.

—'Elephantine', in R. Westbrook (ed.), *A History of Ancient Near Eastern Law,* Handbuch der Orientalistik 72 (Leiden: Brill, 2003), vol. 2, pp. 863–81.

Porten, B. 'Settlement of the Jews at Elephantine and the Arameans at Syene', in *Judah and Judeans in the neo-Babylonian Period,* O. Lipschits and J. Blenkinsopp, eds. (Winona Lake: Eisenbrauns, 2003), 458.

Porten, B. and Greenfield J. C., *Jews of Elephantine and Arameans of Syene* (Jerusalem: Hebrew University, 1974).

Porten, B. and H. Z. Szubin, '"Abandoned Property" in Elephantine: A New Interpretation of Kraeling 3', *Journal of Near Eastern Studies* 41 (1982), pp. 123–31.

—'"Ancestral Estates" in Aramaic Contracts: The Legal Significance of the Term MHHSN', *Journal of the Royal Asiatic Society* 1 (1982), pp. 3–9.

—'Exchange of Inherited Property at Elephantine (Cowley 1)', *Journal of the American Oriental Society* 102 (1982), pp. 651–54.

—'Testamentary Succession at Elephantine', *Bulletin of the American Schools of Oriental Research* 252 (1983), pp. 35–46.

—'Litigation Concerning Abandoned Property at Elephantine (Kraeling 2)', *Journal of Near Eastern Studies* 42 (1983), pp. 279–84.

—'Hereditary Leases in Aramaic Letters', *Bibliotheca Orientalis* 42 (1985), pp. 283–88.

—'An Aramaic Deed of Bequest (Kraeling 9)', in N. Waldmam (ed.), *Community and Culture: Essays in Jewish Studies in Honor of the Ninetieth Anniversary of the Founding of Gratz College* (Philadelphia: Seth, 1987), pp. 179–92.

—'A Dowry Addendum (Kraeling 10)', *Journal of the American Oriental Society* 107 (1987), pp. 231–38.

—'Litigants in the Elephantine Contracts: The Development of Legal Terminology', *Maarav* 4 (1987), pp. 45–67.

—'Royal Grants in Egypt: A New Interpretation of Driver 2', *Journal of Near Eastern Studies* 46 (1987), pp. 39–48.

—'Life Estate of Usufruct: A New Interpretation of Kraeling 6', *Bulletin of the American Schools of Oriental Research* 269 (1988), pp. 29–45.

—'An Aramaic Joint Venture Agreement: A New Interpretation of the Bauer-Meissner Papyrus', *Bulletin of the American Schools of Oriental Research* 288 (1992), pp. 67–84.

—'The Status of the Handmaiden Tamet: A New Interpretation of Kraeling 2 (*TAD* B3.3)', *Israel Law Review* 29 (1995), pp. 43–64.

Porten, B. and A. Yardeni, *Textbook of Aramaic Documents from Ancient Egypt*, 4 vols. (Jerusalem: Hebrew University, 1986–99).

Posener, G., 'Les Criminels Débaptisés et les Morts sans Noms', *Revue d'Égyptologie* 5 (1946), pp. 51–56.

—'Les quarante rouleaux de lois', *Göttinger Miszellen* 25 (1977), pp. 63–66.

Postgate, J. N., *The Governor's Palace Archive Cuneiform Texts from Nimrud II* (London: British School of Archaeology in Iraq, 1973).

—*Fifty Neo-Assyrian Legal Documents* (Warminster; Aris & Phillips, 1976).

—*Early Mesopotamia: Society and Economy at the Dawn of History* (New York: Routledge, 1994).

—'Middle Assyrian to Neo-Assyrian: The Nature of the Shift', in H. Waetzoldt and H. Hauptmann (eds.), *Assyrien im Wandel der Zeiten. XXXIX Reencontre Assyriologique International, Heidelberg 6–10 Juli 1992* (Heidelberg: Heidelberg Orientverlag, 1997), 159–68.

Pritsch, E., 'Jüdische Rechtsurkunden aus Aegypten', *Zeitschrift für vergleichende Rechtswissenschaft* 27 (1912), pp. 7–70.

Quaegebeur, J., 'Sur la "Loi Sacrée" dans l'Égypte Gréco-Romaine', *Ancient Society* 11–12 (1980–81), pp. 236–38.

Quirke, S. and C. Andrews, *The Rosetta Stone: Facsimile Drawing with an Introduction and Translation* (New York: British Museum Press, 1988).

Rabinowitz, J. J., 'Some Notes on an Aramaic Contract from the Dead Sea Region', *Bulletin of the American Schools of Oriental Research* 135 (1954), pp. 15–16.

—'A Legal Formula in the Susa Tablets in an Egyptian Document of the Twelfth Dynasty, in the Aramaic Papyri, and in the Book of Daniel', *Biblica* 36 (1955), pp. 74–77.

—*Jewish Law: Its Influence on the Development of Legal Institutions* (New York: Bloch, 1956).

—'Brooklyn 12 and the Kyreia Clause of the Graeco Egyptian Papyri', *Jewish Law: Its Influence on the Development of Legal Institutions* (New York : Block, 1956), 124–40.

—'A Legal Formula in Egyptian, Egyptian-Aramaic and Murabba'at Documents', *Bulletin of the American Schools of Oriental Research* 145 (1957), pp. 33–34.

—'Demotic Papyri of the Ptolemaic Period and Jewish Sources', *Vetus Testamentum* 7 (1957), pp. 398–400.

—*Studies in Legal History* (Jerusalem: s.n., 1958).

—'Neo-Babylonian Legal Documents and Jewish Law', *Journal of Juristic Papyrology* 13 (1961), pp. 131–75.

Radner, K., *Die Neuassyrischen Privatrechtsurkunden als Quellen für Mensch und Umwelt*, State Archives of Assyria Studies 6 (Helsinki: Helsinki University Press, 1997).

—'Neo Assyrian Period', in R. Westbrook (ed.) *A History of Ancient Near Eastern Law*, Handbuch der Orientalistik 72 (Leiden, Boston: Brill, 2003), pp. 883–911.

Ratzel, F., *Anthropogeographie* (Stuttgart: J. Engelhorns, 1882–91).

Ray, J. D., 'Literacy and Language in Egypt in the Late and Persian Periods', in A. K. Bowman and G. Woolf (eds.), *Literacy and Power in the Ancient World* (Cambridge: Cambridge University Press, 1994), pp. 51–66.

Redford, D. B., *Egypt, Canaan and Israel in Ancient Times* (Princeton, N. J.: Princeton University Press, 1992).

Revillout, E., *Précis du droit égyptien comparé aux autres droits de l'antiquité* (Paris: V. Giard & E. Brière, 1903).

—*Les origines égyptiennes du droit civil romain; nouvelle étude faite d'après les textes juridiques hiéroglyphiques, hiératiques et démotiques, rapprochés de ceux des Assyro-Chaldéens et des Hébreux, avec un premier supplément sur les contrats égypto-araméens d'Eléphantine, un index alphabétique des questions juridiques, économiques et historiques, un index alphabétique des noms propres et des addenda* (Paris: P. Geuthner, 1912).

Ribera, J., 'El doble significado de la partícula aramea ḥlf', *Aula Orientalis* 8 (1990): pp. 136–38.

Ritner, R., 'Third Intermediate Period Antecedents of Demotic Legal Terminology', in K. Ryholt (ed.), *Acts of the Seventh International Conference of Demotic Studies, Copenhagen 23–27 August 1999* (Copenhagen: Museum Tusculanum Press, 2002), pp. 343–59.

Rollston, C. A., 'Scribal Education in Ancient Israel: The Old Hebrew Epigraphic Evidence', *Bulletin of the American Schools of Oriental Research* 344 (2006), 47–74.

Rosenberg, S. G., 'The Jewish Temple at Elephantine', *Near Eastern Archaeology* 67 (2004), pp. 4–13.

Roth, M. 'A Case of Contested Status', in H. Behrens *et al.* (eds.), *DUMU-E2-DUB-BA-A: Studies in Honor of Åke W. Sjöberg*, (Philadelphia: University Museum, 1989), 486–87.

Sabloff, J. A. and C. C. Lamberg-Karlovsky, *Ancient Civilization and Trade* (Albuquerque: University of New Mexico Press, 1975).

Sachau, E., *Drei aramäische Papyrusurkunden aus Elephantine* (Berlin: 1908).

San Nicolò, M., *Die Schlußklauseln der altbabylonischen Kauf- und Tauschverträge, Ein Beitrag zur Geschichte des Barkaufes* (Munich: C. H. Beck, 1922).

—'Zur Entwicklung der babylonischen Urkundenformen', in *Festschrift für Gustav Hanausek* (Graz: U. Mosers Buchhandlung, 1925), pp. 1–13.

—'Vorderasiatisches Rechtsgut in den ägyptischen Eheverträgen der Perserzeit', *Orientalische Literaturzeitung* 30 (1927), pp. 217–21.

—'Die Stellung der Keilschrifturkunden in der vorderasiatischen Rechstentwicklung', *Zeitschrift der Savigny-Stiftung, romanistische Abteilung* 48 (1928), pp. 21–50.

—*Beiträge zur Rechtsgeschichte im Bereich der keilschriflichen Rechtsquellen* (Oslo: H. Aschehoug & Co, 1931).

Saretta, P., 'Egyptian Perceptions of West Semites in Art and Literature During the Middle Kingdom (An Archaeological, Art Historical and Textual Survey)' (Unpublished Ph.D. dissertation, New York University, New York City, New York, 1997).

Sarna, N., *Understanding Genesis* (New York: Jewish Theological Seminary of America, 1970).

Sayce, A. H., A. E. Cowley, *et al.*, *Aramaic Papyri Discovered at Assuan* (London: A. Moring, 1906).

Schaeder, H. H., *Esra der Schreiber* (Tübingen: Mohr, 1930).

Schams, C., *Jewish Scribes in the Second-Temple Period* (Sheffield: Sheffield Academic Press, 1998).

Scharff, A., 'Neues zur Frage der ältesten ägyptisch-babylonischen Kulturbeziehungen', *Zeitschrift für ägyptische Sprache und Altertumskunde* 71 (1935), pp. 89–106.

Schenkel, W., 'Schreiber; in *Lexicon der Ägyptologie* (Wiesbaden: Harrassowitz, 1984), pp. 698–700.

Schulman, A. R., *Military Rank, Title, and Organization in the Egyptian New Kingdom* (Berlin: B. Hessling, 1964).

Segal, J. B., *Aramaic Texts from North Saqqâra, with some Fragments in Phoenician* (London: Egypt Exploration Society, 1983).

Seidl, E., 'Rechtgeschichte. Sammelbericht, Übersetzungen und Abhandlungen zum vorptolomäischen Rechte Ägyptens (1903–1929)', *Kritische Vierteljahre Schrift* 2 (1931), pp. 53–54.

—*Der Eid in römish-ägyptischen Provinzialrecht* Münchener Beiträge zur

Papyrusforschung und antiken Rechtsgeschichte 17 (Munich: C. H. Beck, 1935).
—'Die Teilunschrift', *Mitteilungen des Deutschen Archäologischen Instituts Abteilung Kairo* 8 (1939), pp. 198–200.
—'Law', in S. R. K. Glanville (ed.), *The Legacy of Egypt* (Oxford: Clarendon Press, 1942).
—*Einführung in die ägyptische rechtsgeschichte bis zum Ende des Neuen Reiches* (Glückstadt: J. J. Agustin, 1957).
—*Ptolemäische Rechtsgeschichte* (Glückstadt: J. J. Agustin, 1962).
—*Ägyptische Rechtsgeschichte der Saiten- und Perserzeit* (Glückstadt: J. J. Agustin, 1968).
—'Eine demotische Juristenarbeit', *Zeitschrift der Savigny-Stiftung, romanistische Abteilung* 96 (1969), pp. 17–30.
Semeka, G., *Ptolemäische Prozessrecht: Studien zum Ptolemäische Gerichsverfassung und zum Greichtsverfahren* (Munich: C. H. Beck, 1913).
Service, E. R., *Primitive Social Organization: An Evolutionary Perspective* (New York: Random House, 1962).
—*Origins of the State and Civilization* (New York: Norton, 1975).
Sethe, K., 'Zur ältesten Geschichte des ägyptischen Seeverkehrs mit Byblos und dem Libanongebiet', *ZÄS* 45 (1909), pp. 7–14.
—'Ein Prozessurteil aus dem alten Reich', *Zeitschrift für Ägyptische Sprache und Altertumskunde* 61 (1926), pp. 67–79.
Sethe, K., and J. Partsch, eds., *Demotische Urkunden zum ägyptischen Bürgschaftsrechte vorzüglich der Ptolemäerzeit* (Leipzig: Teubner, 1920).
Shore, A. F., 'Swapping Property at Asyut in the Persian Period', in J. Baines, T. G. H. James, A. Leahy and A. F. Shore (eds.), *Pyramid Studies and Other Essays presented to I.E.S. Edwards* (London: Egypt Exploration Society, 1988), pp. 200–06.
Shore, A. F. a. H. S. S., 'Two Unpublished Demotic Documents from the Asyut Archive', *Journal of Egyptian Archaeology* 45 (1959), pp. 52–60.
Shupak, N., 'A New Source for the Study of the Judiciary and Law of Ancient Egypt: "The Tale of the Eloquent Peasant" ', *Journal of Near Eastern Studies* 51 (1992), pp. 6–18.
—*Where Can Wisdom be Found? The Sage's Language in the Bible and in Ancient Egyptian Literature* (Freibourg, Switzerland: University Press, 1993).
Sikes, E. E., *The Anthropology of the Greeks* (London: D. Nutt, 1914).
Silverman, H. *Religious Values in the Jewish Proper Names at Elephantine* (Kevelaer: Verlag Butzon & Bercker; Neukirchen-Vluyn: Neukirchener Verlag, 1985).

Simpson, R. S., *Demotic Grammar in the Ptolemaic Sacerdotal Decrees* (Oxford: Griffith Institute – Ashmolean Museum, 1996).

Skaist, A., 'The Clasula [*sic!*] Salvatoria in the Elephantine and Neo-Assyrian Conveyance Document', in *Arameans, Aramaic and the Aramaic Literary Tradition* (Ramat-Gan, 1983), pp. 31–41.

Smith, H. S., 'Marriage and the Family in Ancient Egypt', in H. M. M. J. Geller and A. D. E. Lewis (eds.), *Legal Documents of the Hellenistic World* (London: Warburg Institute – University of London, 1995), pp. 46–57.

Smith, M., *Catalogue of Demotic Papyri in the British Museum*, vol. 3: *The Mortuary Texts of Papyrus BM 10507* (London: British Museum, 1987).

Sokoloff, M., *A Dictionary of Jewish Palestinian Aramaic of the Byzantine Period* (Ramat-Gan: Bar Ilan University Press, 1990).

Soldt, W. H. v., *Altbabylonische Briefe XIII. Letters in the British Museum* (Leiden: Brill, 1994).

—'Babylonian Lexical, Religious and Literary Texts and Scribal Education at Ugarit and its Implications for the Alphabetic Literary Texts', in Manfried Dietrich and Oswald Loretz (eds.), *Ugarit: ein ostmediterranes Kulturzentrum im Alten Orient: Ergebnisse und Perspektiven der Forschung* (Münster: Ugarit-Verlag, 1995), pp. 171–212.

Spiegelberg, W., 'Ägyptisches Sprachgut in den aus Ägypten stammenden aramäischen Urkunden der Perserzeit', in *Orientalischen Studien Theodor Nöldeke zum 70 Geburstag gewindet* (Giessen: Alfred Töpelmann, 1906), vol. 2, pp. 1093–1115.

—*Die sogenannte demotische chronik des pap. 215 der Bibliothèque nationale zu Paris nebst den auf der rückseite des papyrus stehenden texten* (Leipzig: J. C. Hinrichs, 1914).

—*Der demotische Text der Priesterdekrete von Kanopus und Memphis (Rosettana): mit den hieroglyphischen und griechischen Fassungen und deutscher Übersetzung nebst demotischem Glossar* (Heidelberg: C. Winter, 1922).

—'Agyptologische Mitteilungen', *Sitzungsberichte der Bayerischen Akademie der Wissenschaften Philosophisch-philologische und historische Klasse,* 2. Abhandlung (1925), pp. 3–35.

Sprengling, M., 'The Aramaic Papyri of Elephantine in English', *American Journal of Theology* 21 (1917), pp. 411–52.

—'The Aramaic Papyri of Elephantine in English', *American Journal of Theology* 22 (1918), pp. 349–75.

Starcky, J. and M. Gawlikowski, *Palmyre* (Paris: A. Maisonneuve, 1985).

Steiner, G., 'Kaufmanns- und Handelsprachen im Alten Orient', *Iraq* 39 (1977), pp. 11–18.

Steinkeller, P., *Sales Documents of the Ur-III Period* (Stuttgart: Franz Steiner, 1989).

Steinmetzer, F., *Die babylonischen Kudurru (Grenzsteine) als Urkundenform* (Paderborn: F. Schöningh, 1922).

Steinwerter, A., *Die Streitbeendigung durch Urteil, Schiedsspruch und Vergleich nach griechischem Rechte* (Munich: C. H. Beck, 1925).

Strassmaier, J. N., *Inschriften von Cambyses, König von Babylon* (Leipzig: Eduard Pfeiffer, 1890).

Szubin, H. Z. and B. Porten, 'Litigation concerning Abandoned Property at Elephantine (Kraeling 1)', *Journal of Near Eastern Studies* 42. 4 (1983), pp. 279–84.

Tadmor, H., 'The Aramaization of Assyria: Aspects of Western Imact', in H. –J. Nissen and J. Renger (eds.), *Mesopotamien und seine Nachbarn: politische und kulturelle Wechselbeziehungen im alten Vorderasien vom 4. bis 1. Jahrtausend v. Chr. XXV. Rencontre assyriologique internationale Berlin, 3. bis 7. Juli 1978* (Berlin: D. Reimer, 1982), vol. 2, pp. 449–69.

Tait, W. J., 'P. Carlsberg 236: Another Fragment of a Demotic Legal Manual', in P. J. Frandsen (ed.), *The Carlsberg Papyri I. Demotic Texts from the Collection* (Copenhagen: Museum Tusculanum Press, 1991), pp. 93–101.

Taubenschlag, R., *The Law of Greco-Roman Egypt in the Light of the Papyri* (New York: Herald Square Press, 1944).

—'Customary Law and Custom in the Papyri', *Journal of Juristic Papyrology* 1 (1946), pp. 41–54.

—'The Provisional Legal Protection in the Papyri', *Journal of Juristic Papyrology* 5 (1951), pp. 143–54.

—'Das babylonische Recht in den griechischen Papyri', *Journal of Juristic Papyrology* 7–8 (1953–54), pp. 169–85.

Temerev, A., 'Social Organization in Egyptian Military Settlements of the Sixth–Fourth Centuries B.C.E', in C. L. Meyers and M. V. O'Connor (eds.), *The Word of the Lord Shall Go Forth* (Winona Lake: Eisenbrauns, 1983), pp. 523–24.

Tepstad, G. K., 'Contributions to the Study of the Aramaic Legal Papyri of Elephantine' (Unpublished Ph.D. dissertation, University of California, Los Angeles, 1989).

Theodorides, A., 'The Concept of Law in Ancient Egypt', in J. Harris (ed.), *The Legacy of Egypt* (Oxford: Clarendon Press, 1971), pp. 291–322.

Thissen, H. J., 'Zwei demotische Prozeßprotokolle', in E. Bresciani (ed.), *Acta Demotica. Acts of the Fifth International Conference for Demotists = Egitto e Vicino Oriente* 18 (1994), pp. 283–88.

Thompson, H., *A Family Archive From Siut, From Papyri in the British*

Museum, Including an Account of a Trial before the Laocritae in the Year B.C. 170 (Oxford: Oxford University Press, 1934).
Trever, J. C., *The Dead Sea Scrolls from St. Mark's Monastery* (New Haven: American Schools of Oriental Research, 1950).
Trigger, B. S., 'Egypt and the Comparative Study of Early Civilizations', in K. Weeks (ed.), *Egyptology and the Social Sciences* (Cairo: American University in Cairo Press, 1979), pp. 23–56.
Unger, E., *Babylon. Die heilige Stadt nach der Beschreibung der Babylonier*, 2nd edn. (Berlin:De Gruyte, 1970).
Ungnad, A., *Aramäische Papyrus aus Elephantine. Kleine Ausgabe unter Zugrundlegung von Eduard Sachau's Erstausgabe Aramäische Papyrus aus Elephantine* (Leipzig: J. C. Hinrichs, 1911).
van den Boorn, G. P. F., *The Duties of the Vizier: Civil Administration in the Early New Kingdom* (London: Kegan Paul, 1988).
van der Molen, R., *A Hieroglyphic Dictionary of Egyptian Coffin Texts* (Leiden: Brill, 2000).
Vandier, J., 'L'Intronisation de Nitocris', *Zeitschrift für Ägyptische Sprache und Altertumskunde* 99 (1972), pp. 29–33.
Venhof, K. R., 'Some Social Effects of Old Assyrian Trade', *Iraq* 39 (1977), pp. 109–18.
Verger, A., 'Note sul diritto dei papiri aramaici di Elefantina', *Oriens Antiqus* 3 (1964), pp. 47–59.
—'L'amministrazione della giustizia nei papiri aramaici di Elefantina', *Rendiconti della Academia Nazionale dei Lince,* 8th series, 19 (1964), pp. 75–94.
—'Intorno a P. Brooklyn 8', in *Rendiconti della Academia Nazionale dei Lincei,* 8th series, 19 (1964), pp. 294–315.
—*Ricerche giuridiche sui papiri aramaici di Elefantina* (Rome: Centro di studi semitici, Istituto di studi del Vicino Oriente, Università, 1965).
VerSteeg, R., *Law in Ancient Egypt* (Durham, N.C.: Carolina Academic Press, 2002).
Vitta, E., 'The Conflicts of Personal Laws', Part I, *Israel Law Review* 5 (1970), pp. 171–202.
—'The Conflicts of Personal Laws', Part II, *Israel Law Review* 5 (1970), pp. 337–51. Vittmann, G., *Der demotische Papyrus Rylands 9* (Wiesbaden: Harrassowitz, 1998).
—*Agypten und die Fremden im ersten vorchristlichen Jahrtausend* (Mainz am Rhein: Philip von Zabern, 2003).
Vleeming, S. P., 'La phase initiale du Demotique Ancien', *Chronique d'Egypte* 56 (1981), pp. 31–48.
—*The Gooseherds of Hou: (Pap. Hou): A Dossier Relating to Various Agricultural Affairs from Provincial Egypt of the Early Fifth Century B.C.* (Leuven: Peeters, 1991).
—'Some notes on Demotic Scribal Training in the Ptolemaic Period', in

Proceedings of the 20th International Congress of Papyrologists, Copenhagen, 23–29 August, 1992 (Copenhagen: Museum Tusculanum Press, University of Copenhagen, 1994), pp. 185–87.

Vogelsang, F. a. and A. H. Gardiner, *Die Klagen des Bauern*, Hieratische papyrus aus den Königlichen Museen zu Berlin 4–5 (Leipzig: J. C. Hinrichs, 1908).

Volterra, E., 'Review of *The Brooklyn Museum Aramaic Papyri* by E. Kraeling', *Iura* 6 (1955), pp. 349–60.

—'Osservazione sul divorzio nei documenti aramaici', in *Studi orientalistici in onore di Giorgio Levi della Vida*, vol. 2 (Rome: Istituto per l'Oriente, 1956), pp. 586–600.

—'Le affrancazioni di schiavi nei documenti aramaici del V secolo a.C.', *Rivista degli Studi Orientali* 32 (1957), pp. 675–96.

—''YHDW e 'RMY nei Papiri Aramaici del V Secolo Provenienti dall'Egitto', *Rendiconti dell'Accademia Nazionale dei Lincei, Classe di Scienze morali, storiche e filologiche*, 8th series (1963), pp. 131–73.

—'Osservazioni alla Nota del Prof. R. Yaron', *Iura* 15 (1964), pp. 173–80.

von Pilgrim, C., 'Der Temple des Jawveh', in W. Kaise *et al.* (eds.), *Stadt und Tempel von Elephantine,* Mitteilungen des Deutschen Archäologischen Instituts 55 (Cairo: German Archaeological Institute, 1999), pp. 142–45.

—'Das Aramaische Quartier im Stadtgebiet der 27. Dynastie; in G.von Dreyer *et al.* (eds.), *Stadt und Tempel von Elephantine,* Mitteilungen des Deutschen Archäologischen Instituts 58 (Cairo: German Archaeological Institute, 2002), pp. 192–97.

von Recklinghausen, D., 'Ägyptische Quellen zum Judentum', *Zeitschrift für Ägyptische Sprache und Altertumskunde* 132 (2005), 147–60.

Watson, A., *Legal Transplants: An Approach to Comparative Law* (Charlottesville: University Press of Virginia, 1974).

—*Society and Legal Change* (Edinburgh: Scottish Academic Press, 1977).

Watson, W. G. E., 'Non-Semitic Words in the Ugaritic Lexicon', *Ugaritic-Forschungen* 27 (1995), pp. 533–58.

—'Non-Semitic Words in the Ugaritic Lexicon (2)', *Ugaritic-Forschungen* 28 (1996), pp. 705–08.

Weinfeld, I. H., *Labor Legislation in the Bible and the Talmud* (New York: Yeshiva University Press, 1974).

Weinfeld, M., 'Judge and Officer in Ancient Israel and in the Ancient Near East', *Israel Oriental Studies* 7 (1977), pp. 65–88.

Welch, A. C., *The Code of Deuteronomy: A New Theory of Its Origin* (London: J. Clarke & Co., 1924).

—'When was the Worship of Israel Centralized at the Temple?', *Zeitschrift für die alttestamentliche Wissenschaft* 43 (1925), pp. 250–55.

Wenham, G. J., 'Deuteronomy and the Central Sanctuary', *Tyndale Bulletin* 22 (1971), pp. 103–18.

Wessely, C., *Papyrorum scripturae graecae specimina isagogica* (Leipzig: Avenarium, 1900).

Westbrook, R., 'Biblical and Cuneiform Law Codes', *Revue Biblique* 92 (1985), pp. 247–64.

—*Studies in Biblical and Cuneiform Law* (Paris: J. Gabalda, 1988).

—'The Phrase 'His Heart is Satisfied' on Ancient Near Eastern Legal Sources', *Journal of the American Oriental Society* 111 (1991), pp. 219–24.

—'The Female Slave', in V. Matthews *et al.* (eds.), *Gender and Law in the Hebrew Bible and the Ancient Near East* (Sheffield: Sheffield Academic Press, 1998), pp. 214–38.

—*A History of Ancient Near Eastern Law*, Handbuch der Orientalistik 72 (Leiden and Boston: Brill, 2003).

Wijngaards, J. N. M., *The Dramatization of Salvific History in the Deuteronomic School* (Leiden: Brill, 1969).

Wilhelm, G., *Untersuchungen zum Ḫurro Akkadischen von Nuzi, Alter Orient and Altes Testament* 9 (Kevelaer, Neukirchen-Vluyn: Butzon & Bercker, 1970).

Williams, R. J., 'Scribal Training in Ancient Egypt', *Journal of the American Oriental Society* 92 (1972), pp. 214–21.

Wilson, J. A., 'The Oath in Ancient Egypt', *Journal of Near Eastern Studies* 7 (1948), pp. 129–56.

Wiseman, D. J., *The Alalakh Tablets* (London: British Institute of Archaeology at Ankara, 1953).

—'Some Egyptians in Babylon', *Iraq* 28 (1966), pp. 154–68.

Xella, S. G. a. P., 'Égypte', in V. Krings (ed.), *La Civilisation Phénicienne et Punique* (Leiden: Brill, 1995).

Yaron, R., *Gifts in Contemplation of Death in Jewish and Roman Law* (Oxford: Clarendon Press, 1960).

—'The Schema of the Aramaic Legal Documents', *Journal of Semitic Studies* 2 (1957), pp. 33–61.

—'Aramaic Marriage Contracts from Elephantine', *Journal of Semitic Studies* 3 (1958), pp. 1–39.

—'Identities in the Brooklyn Museum Aramaic Papyri', *Biblica* 39 (1958), pp. 344–54.

—'On Defension Clauses of Some Oriental Deeds of Sale and Lease, from Mesopotamia and Egypt', *Bibliotheca Orientalis* 15 (1958), pp. 15–22.

—'Jewish Law and Other Legal Systems of Antiquity', *Journal of Semitic Studies* 4 (1959), pp. 308–31.

—'Aramaic Deeds of Conveyance', *Biblica* 41 (1960), pp. 247–74, 379–94.

—'Aramaic Marriage Contracts: Corrigenda and Addenda', *Journal of Semitic Studies* 5 (1960), pp. 66–70.

—'Minutiae on Roman Divorce', *Tijdschrift voor Rechtsgeschiedenis* 28 (1960), pp. 1–12.

—*Introduction to the Law of the Aramaic Papyri* (Oxford: Clarendon Press, 1961).

—'Vitae Necisque Potestas', *Tijdschrift voor Rechtsgeschiedenis* 30 (1962), pp. 243–51.

—'Who is Who in Elephantine?', *Iura* 15 (1964), pp. 167–72.

—'Si adorat Furto', *Tijdschrift voor Rechtsgeschiedenis* 34 (1966), pp. 510–24.

—'Review of *Ricerche Giuridiche sui Papiri Aramaici di Elefantina* by A. Verger', *Journal of Semitic Studies* (1967), pp. 311–22.

—'Si Pater Filium ter venum duit', *Tijdschrift voor Rechtsgeschiedenis* 36 (1968), pp. 57–72.

—'Review of *Studies in the Aramaic Legal Papyri from Elephantine*, by Y. Muffs', *Revue Biblique* 77 (1970), pp. 408–16.

—'Semitic Elements in Early Rome', in A. Watson (ed.), *Daube Noster: Essays in Legal History for David Daube* (Edinburgh: Scottish Academic Press, 1974), pp. 345–57.

Yuhong, W., 'High-ranking 'Scribes' and Intellectual Governors during the Akkadian and UR III Periods', *Journal of Ancient Civilizations* 10 (1995), pp. 127–45.

Zacagnini, C. 'Nuzi', in R. Westbrook (ed.), *A History of Ancient Near Eastern Law,* Handbuch der Orientalistik 72 (Leiden and Boston: Brill, 2003), pp. 565–617.

Zadok, R., 'On Some Egyptians in First-Millennium Mesopotamia', *Göttinger Miszellen* 26 (1977), pp. 63–68.

—'On Some Egyptians in Babylonian Documents', *Göttinger Miszellen* 64 (1983), pp. 73–75.

Zauzich, K. T., *Die Ägyptische Schreibertradition in Aufbau, Sprache und Scrift der demotischen Kaufverträge aus ptolemäischer Zeit* (Wiesbaden: Harrassowitz, 1968).

—'Ein Kaufvertrag aus des Zeit des Nektanebos', *Mitteilungen des Deutschen Archaeologischen Instituts* 25 (1969), pp. 223–29.

—'Die demotischen Dokumente', in *Textes et langages de l'Egypte pharaonique; cent cinquante années de recherches, 1822–1972. Hommage à Jean-François Champollion* (Cairo: Institut Français d'Archéologie Orientale du Caire, 1972).

—'Ägyptologische Bemerkungen zu den neuen aramäischen papyri aus Saqqara', *Enchoria* 13 (1985), pp. 115–18.

Zweigert, K. and H. Kötz, *An Introduction to Comparative Law* (Oxford: Clarendon Press, 1992).

Index

17905370R00136

Made in the USA
Lexington, KY
03 October 2012